To John —

A fun book

Hulk fan! ... Enjoy!!

Laurie Orange

YOU WOULDN'T LIKE ME WHEN I'M ANGRY!

Also By Pat Jankiewicz

Just When You Thought It Was Safe: A JAWS Companion
(BearManor Media)

As contributor

Stan Lee: Conversations
(University Press of Mississippi, edited by the very Canadian Jeff McLaughlin)

Starlog Presents Star Trek's Greatest Guest Stars
(HarperPrism)

Published in the USA by:
BearManor Media
PO Box 1129
Duncan, Oklahoma 73534-1129
www.bearmanormedia.com

ISBN 978-1-62933-055-6

Printed in the United States of America.
Book design by Brian Pearce | Red Jacket Press.

YOU WOULDN'T LIKE ME WHEN I'M ANGRY!

A **HULK** COMPANION PATRICK A. JANKIEWICZ

TABLE OF CONTENTS

COMICS

TELEVISION

FILM

It's only fair that a book about a hero should be dedicated to several of my heroes. This one's for my dad, Anthony Jankiewicz (the only guy who can outroar The Hulk), my sister Diane Marie (who plays the weirdest version of "Lonely Man" ever heard on piano) and the incredible Allie & Troy Nelson!

Lou Ferrigno *is* The Hulk.

FOREWORD BY LOU FERRIGNO

The first day I played The Incredible Hulk, Bill Bixby and (producer/director) Kenny Johnson were impressed with how natural I was as The Hulk. It was easy for me because I *was* The Hulk my whole life. I knew how The Hulk thought, what he felt, and really identified with him.

I came from nothing. As a kid, I was skinny, always getting picked on while growing up in Brooklyn. Because of my hearing problem, kids would call me names like "Deaf Louie" and beat me up. I would run home crying because they would throw me up against the wall and smack me around. I was scared — and I never forgot that. My childhood made me who I am now. That's why it was easy to play The Hulk

I had an abusive father growing up. As a kid, I was not allowed to have friends. I was isolated and hidden, picked on and made fun of. My father rejected me when I was born because I was not a perfect son. I had a love/hate relationship with my father because of that. He gave me a tremendous work ethic, but at the same time, he was tough. Very tough. Reading comic books while growing up was a way for me to survive it. I gravitated to stories of power. I loved the character of Hulk and how he felt rejected by the world. I really empathized with that.

I was twenty-five when I became The Incredible Hulk. I got a phone call from a casting director named Mark Malis, who said they were casting Hulk. I said, "Wow," because I read *Hulk* comics as a kid and I was training for the Mr. Olympia competition, so I was in the best shape of my life. When I went to the audition, he said, "They wanted Peter Lupus [the strongman from the TV series *Mission: Impossible*] for Hulk, but Lupus wanted $20,000 an episode, so we can't afford him."

They were shooting the pilot with Richard Kiel, who was apparently not fit for the part. They panicked because they had already shot half the pilot and now either had to shelve the project or find somebody who resembled The Hulk. Before he died, my best friend since childhood, Ira Benkofsky, told me, "I'll kill ya if you don't play The Hulk!" He urged me to do it, but it was a big gamble.

I came in for the audition, and they thought I looked good, so they brought me back. The next day, they put me in front of the camera and introduced me to Bill Bixby and Kenny Johnson. I shook Bill Bixby's hand. They were shooting a scene for the pilot when they had me come back. They had me stand in front of the camera and do the Hulk growl. I felt awkward, but I was also excited. I said, "No one else can play The Hulk — I want the part." At that moment, Kenny and Bill looked at each other like *This guy's perfect!* I went home and got a phone call. It was Kenny Johnson. He said, "Come back to the set and meet me at a motor home on the Universal backlot."

Kenny said, "I don't know if you have ever acted before," but he asked me to show emotions of crying and sadness. I improvised to show what I showed, and Kenny said, "Okay, we're going to hire you." I was sent to a makeup man named Werner Keppler. He went way back, to the 1940s. I had never been on the Universal Studios backlot before, so I was like, "Wow, I am going to be part of a TV series!" This is where they created the great monsters like Frankenstein and The Wolf Man. I had never worn a forehead before, or been painted up. Werner did all my makeup. Kenny came down and they figured out how they wanted The Hulk to look.

The next day was my first day of filming. They put me in the makeup chair and it must have taken four hours, because it was the first time they turned me into The Hulk. The first scene I had to shoot was where I was bursting out of the chamber, with water shooting out and steam everywhere. Bill Bixby came up to me and said, "Every person who ever played a monster is beloved, and now you're one of them!" I was so touched, so motivated and so excited after that. On that first day, I ended up working over twenty-two hours straight, because they were behind schedule.

We spent all day in the chamber, and that night, we went up into the hills for the scene where I flip over the car. I kept telling myself, *The show is going to be a hit. I have to do this!* I had arrived on the set at 8:00 in the morning and got home at 5:00 a.m. the next day. We shot a ton of film in twenty-four hours. I was tired when I washed the makeup off, but I felt great. Once I was in the makeup and my speech wasn't perfect, I wouldn't talk to people because I was self-conscious about my speech. Some of the crew would look at me like I was a gorilla that might jump out of a cage at them. That was hard, to try talking to people.

When the series began, I never told anyone working on it that I had a hearing problem. A lot of them thought I was dumb because of my speech impediment. That's why I came out and started openly talking about it, doing commercials about speech problems and hearing loss. I was afraid to say anything to the crew about it, because I was afraid of being rejected again. I really wanted to give back and support deaf children who were going through what I went through as a kid.

My favorite part was meeting Bill Bixby. I loved him on *My Favorite Martian* and *The Courtship Of Eddie's Father*. He was the first real movie star I ever met. At the time, I didn't have any experience with show-business people or filmmaking. Bill took me under his wing and taught me a lot.

Bill was very genuine, quick, and very witty; he had a fast brain. And if he had to be honest with you, he would be. He told you the truth. One morning, I came late to the set. I was tired, so I came in late. I remember Bill saying, "Louie, glad you showed up. I have to talk to you," and I thought, *Oh Jesus, I'm gonna get my ass chewed out!* And I did. Bill really chewed my ass out! I deserved it and never came late again. Other than that, we got along great. The best advice he gave me that day was, "When you come to the set, *don't* be late. Respect the crew, because they work hard." I have always remembered that. I remember being so proud when Bill Bixby later said to me, "Your character has connected with the public."

After I shot the pilot movie, I went to the gym to work out and ran into Richard Jaeckel from *The Dirty Dozen*. He said to me, "Listen, kid, based on what I have heard about your film, in a few days you won't be able to walk down the street." He was exactly right. Little did I realize that I would not be recognized by my face, which was covered in prosthetics and green paint, but by my body. Even the way I walked would give me away! Somebody would yell, "That's him — that's The Hulk!" I could not go anywhere. I was an overnight sensation. They showed the first *Incredible Hulk* TV movie and it got huge ratings. They showed the second one and the ratings were even bigger! We were gonna be a series. I just hit the floor, ecstatic. I gave up training for the Mr. Olympia competition to play The Hulk.

I had a "bodybuilder mentality" about it, but instead of going to the gym and doing my thing by working out alone everyday, I had to do the show. Being a bodybuilder, I like to be by myself, working out, but you can't do that when you're starring in a TV series. Cary Grant told me he was a fan of the show. My jaw still falls open thinking about that. I think one reason the show is still so popular is that it's sci-fi action, but every episode had a message. At one time or another, we all feel like The Hulk! I have had a lot of inner rage myself.

I am very fond of Patrick Jankiewicz's *You Wouldn't Like Me When I'm Angry: A Hulk Companion* because it talks to people I worked with, people

I respect, and they tell stories about making our show. Some I knew and some stories I had never heard before! This book reminds me of another book I loved, *The Twilight Zone Companion*. *The Twilight Zone* is my favorite TV show of all time, and that book had all of these interesting stories behind the series that no one knew about.

You Wouldn't Like Me When I'm Angry brings back memories about doing the show, about Bill Bixby, and what he went through, all the amazing guests, directors, and behind-the-scenes people, even about the episode where Kim Cattrall played an Indian! *You Wouldn't Like Me When I'm Angry: A Hulk Companion* reveals all of the stories that nobody knew, and you learn what all these wonderful people have to say. Patrick even talks to Eric Kramer about playing Thor!

I am pleased to have this book, to have people I respect telling stories about me. One of my frustrations on the show is because of the green makeup I wore as The Hulk, I had to stay in an air conditioned motor home between shots; otherwise, I would sweat it off. Although I wanted to hang around with the crew, I wasn't allowed to. Patrick Jankiewicz found the cast and crew from all of these episodes so, for the first time, I get to hear their stories. I would just want to stand on the set, but I couldn't. I missed a lot in that trailer but because of this book, I get to hear all the stories now!

I am happy the world knows me as The Hulk. I attend comic-book conventions and the kids are excited to see me — and their parents are so excited for their kids to meet me. Looking at these kids' parents, I can see the same joy and excitement on their faces that they had as children watching the show! One woman came up to me and just started crying and crying. I didn't know what to say. I thought she was going to have a heart attack. It's powerful to have something that people still get so excited about three decades later. That's longevity — and it's really humbling to think about.

It's the same thing with Adam West. When I was a kid, Adam West was Batman. You got excited to see Adam West because he was Batman. As a kid, I loved the *Batman* show and Adam West. When I worked with Adam West, I would look at him and think, *That's Batman!* I don't care how many Batmans there have been, Batman *is* Adam West. That's how people are with me. Now with *The Incredible Hulk*, for another generation, I am their Adam West! It's astounding. Adam is a friend and we have actually talked about this.

Life is good. My family and I just signed a deal with TV Land to do a reality show called *The Incredible Ferrignos*. My wife, three kids, and I are all personal trainers. On the show, we're gonna take another family, a TV-watching couch potato family, and change their lifestyle, motivate them, and help them get control of their lives. I treasure my wife and my kids. I enjoy having people's respect. I like having the public know me from the show, from *King Of Queens* and *I Love You, Man*. Ever since that movie came out, people now want to take photos of me putting them in a chokehold! And I know why kids know me.

I am The Hulk.

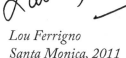

Lou Ferrigno
Santa Monica, 2011

Lou Ferrigno with wife Carla and dogs.

INTRODUCTION

ANGER! DANGER! Who could forget the first two words seen every week in the opening credits of *The Incredible Hulk*? As Joe Harnell's music hits a frenzy, we see an extreme close-up of the DANGER button of a Gamma Ray machine, so close it reads as "ANGER," while the narrator grimly intones, *"Doctor David Banner, physician, scientist, searching for a way to tap into the hidden strengths that all humans have. Then an accidental overdose of Gamma Radiation alters his body chemistry. And now, when David Banner grows angry or outraged, a startling metamorphosis occurs… the creature is driven by rage and pursued by an investigative reporter. The creature is wanted for a murder he did not commit. David Banner is believed to be dead, and he must let the world think that he is dead, until he finds a way to control the raging spirit that dwells within him."*

Forget The Terminator, Darth Vader, and Chuck Norris. Nobody beats The Incredible Hulk!

For five seasons, Dr. David Banner traveled the dusty back roads of America, (which look suspiciously like the Universal Studios backlot in Southern California), on his existential quest to cure himself. David finds that no matter where he goes, The Hulk is there…at least twice per episode!

Dr. David Banner was a man on the run. The "man on the run" show had been a TV staple since *The Fugitive* created the genre in the 1960s. *The Fugitive* featured innocent man Richard Kimble hunted by the police and public who wrongly believe he murdered his wife. Kimble tries to avoid arrest while pursuing the real killer, a one-armed man, and manages to help a number of regular folks along the way.

The Fugitive template had been used many times over the years, for many different shows. The only difference being who the hero is and what he is running from. It's been done with a noble martial artist (*Kung Fu*), a noble undying man (*The Immortal*), a noble dying man (*Run For Your Life*), a noble guy chased by aliens (*The Invaders, V: The Series*), noble mercenaries (*The A-Team*), noble aliens (*Starman, Hard Time On Planet Earth, The Phoenix*), noble ninja (*The Master*), a noble guy who changes into a werewolf (Fox TV's imaginatively titled *Werewolf*), and even a noble dog (*Run, Joe, Run*).

The Incredible Hulk put a unique spin on the concept: Dr. David Banner isn't just running from external forces; he's running from *himself*. After the death of his wife, he tampers with Gamma Radiation in an obsessive quest to tap into that hidden strength that all humans have. Whenever he is upset, afraid, or angry, his heart starts racing and he transforms into a monstrous seven-foot powerhouse known as The Incredible Hulk.

As with *The Fugitive*, every week Dr. David Banner works odd jobs far below his scientist intellect, using his innate skills to help the people he stays with. Even though he labors thanklessly as a janitor, a gardener or handyman, he and his inner demon save the day. At the end of every episode, his rage spent, the problem solved for the strangers he befriended that week, Banner quietly hitchhikes his way out of town.

"Getting angry doesn't solve anything." You heard it from your mom in early childhood, from your fifth-grade teacher, from your girlfriend, co-workers and everyone else whenever a problem leaves you frustrated after being wronged, cheated, or just plain screwed. This is an occasional part of everyday life that you reluctantly learn to accept, and the essential point of *The Incredible Hulk* television series was that a problem would not truly get solved until Doctor David Banner lost his temper.

In the late 1970s when the show made its debut, America had been frog-marched into a massive post-Vietnam sensitivity training class. Society reeled from the recent war, high gas prices, crushing inflation, a stagnant economy and a general malaise. Traditional values like manhood and masculinity were being re-assessed and questioned with derisive suspicion. There was a call for men to express their feelings in a new "touchy feely" way. This brave new world of "I'm okay, you're okay" semantics was led in the media and politics by bland icons like Phil Donahue, Alan Alda, and Jimmy Carter.

The Incredible Hulk was a subversive blast of fresh air. While the gentleness of David Banner paid lip service to these newly adopted social values, The Hulk lurked just below the surface. Banner would explore the problem, make innocent inquiries and try to empower the victims into changing their own plight. Invariably, Banner would be punished for his innocent efforts and suffer terrible indignities.

As they roughed him up, saintly David Banner would warn antagonists that they "wouldn't like him when he was angry." When that didn't work, The Hulk emerged. His power would bring resolution to the problem.

The Hulk is Banner's raging Id, an inarticulate force of nature that, even though unable to express himself, is not stupid. He instinctively knows who provoked Banner and who the innocent are in any situation. Perversely, the show recognizes that Banner and The Hulk make a great team — good cop and the ultimate "bad cop." Sensitivity mixed with decisive brute force can overcome any problem. This brilliant duality elevates the show into something lasting, a pop-culture icon worth celebrating. While The Hulk saves the day by throwing a couch, trashing a car, or hurling guys through the air, it's David Banner, whose wise counsel backed by The Hulk's strength helps repair families and save innocents by the end of the show. The irony is that he can help everyone but himself.

Being the ultimate activist, David Banner can only help others by being personally threatened by whatever issue he is trying to go up against. That is always the highlight: when likable, rational Bill Bixby as David Banner realizes that his "let's talk this out" approach is being met with a beating or some other situation that would put him in harm's way.

When nice guy Banner *gets mad,* the show truly kicks into high gear! You wait for it — that moment when Gamma-irradiated scientist David Banner has taken all he can and can't take it anymore! Usually harassed by goons with mullets and down jackets who resemble stuntmen, or confronted with vexing annoyances like a bee sting or flat tire, the moment arrives when affable David's temper hits the point of no return. His pupils go white, the music speeds up, and his shirt tears to shreds across his back, while his feet literally explode out of his shoes as The Hulk takes over. The Incredible Hulk is the living embodiment of primal rage, a howling beast that celebrates the simple pleasures of "losing it."

The Hulk goes right to the source of his pain and deals with it quickly. Lacking verbal skills to express annoyance, The Hulk lets his temper do the talking. The appeal of that is universal — who hasn't wanted to Hulk Out at the DMV, during rush hour on the 405 freeway, or go see your boss without using the door? The Hulk embraces the aggression that is usually scolded out of every school boy by age ten.

But once his rage is spent, Hulk shrinks back to the polite Banner. There is something really cool about a show where the lead character transforms into a bombastic monster, but still leaves town like a thief in the night, thankless and alone, heading off to his next adventure.

Will there be mail delivery on Lou Ferrigno Day?

AUTHOR'S NOTE

Sci-fi shows come and go. Most of them are not very good. You'll notice that you are not holding a book about *Manimal, Lucan, Fantastic Journey, Automan, Man from Atlantis, Dark Skies, Mutant X*, or any of the hundreds of other lousy TV fantasy shows that have darkened the airwaves for a brief time and then went away like a bad dream.

The Incredible Hulk was a smart one-hour adventure series that dealt with grief, anger, mourning, and the consequences of those strong emotions — especially anger. Made long before cutting-edge FX and computer-generated wonders, *The Incredible Hulk* turned mild scientist David Banner into a seven-foot monster with great difficulty.

The makeup effects on display are very much "of their time" and some of the clothes are dated, but none of that matters because you believe in David Banner and his green alter ego, so you accept the entire premise. Due to the strong writing, directing, and acting, you find yourself rooting for the world-weary scientist on the run. You know that Lou Ferrigno's Hulk, despite his animal rage, great strength, and inability to speak, will stop the bad guys but *not* kill them because he shares David Banner's compassion. You long for Banner to help whoever has the good fortune of putting him up for the night and hope that some day he can come to grips with that "raging spirit that dwells within him."

You Wouldn't Like Me When I'm Angry: A Hulk Companion reveals the inside story behind the classic show. You will meet Stan Lee, creator of The Hulk, Spider-Man, and other pop-culture icons, Kenneth Johnson, the man who brought Hulk to TV, and Lou Ferrigno, the only man to play The Hulk in live action.

You Wouldn't Like Me When I'm Angry tells the true story of Bill Bixby, whose real-life misfortunes left him resembling his famous character; how Lou Ferrigno also overcame great challenges, and an episode guide that reveals the intriguing, weird, and sometimes hilarious stories behind each segment of the show. Cast and crew also share their memories of the series, with surprising and funny anecdotes.

The Incredible Hulk has never stopped running somewhere in the world. It runs as *Le Incroyable Hulk* in France, *The Green Beast* in the Middle East and has all-day marathons on The SyFy Channel. The best genre shows always stand out and build cult followings, like the original *Twilight Zone, Star Trek, Kolchak: The Night Stalker, Buffy The Vampire Slayer, The X-Files, Lost,* and *The Incredible Hulk*. Regardless of the times they were made in, they are embraced by new generations of viewers.

My nephew, Troy, is just like any other eleven-year-old kid who takes for granted CG-dinosaurs, state-of-the-art video games like *HALO, Left 4 Dead* and ipods. When TV went digital, many new channels were made available. Troy discovered the Retro Channel, and began eagerly watching iconic 1980s shows like *The Greatest American Hero, Buck Rogers In The 25th Century, The A-Team,* and *The Incredible Hulk. Hulk* quickly became his favorite, and a kid born long after Bixby and Ferrigno did their reunion TV movies in the 1990s now finds himself engrossed in David Banner's plight. The old-school FX don't deter his enjoyment because the hero — and his monstrous alter ego — are sympathetic and his situation is interesting.

Meeting Lou Ferrigno at this year's Emerald City Comic Con, young Troy casually greeted his hero with a heartfelt "Hey, Hulk!" The gregarious Ferrigno noted how young Troy demonstrated *Hulk*'s popularity among younger viewers, who are discovering the show for the first time. Troy added, "Stay angry, Mr. Ferrigno," which actually sounds like pretty good advice.

Stay angry, Mr. Ferrigno!

Patrick Jankiewicz
Claremont, California 2011

COMICS

BIRTH OF **THE INCREDIBLE HULK**

Long before his television show, The Incredible Hulk actually began life in comic books. The cover to *The Incredible Hulk* #1 says it all: the center image is a meek man in glasses transforming into a sullen gray monster. Surrounded by soldiers, the gray monster stands in the middle of a cover that includes a general, a beautiful girl, and a rocket shooting up into the air. We're informed that this is "THE STRANGEST MAN OF ALL TIME," as the cover blurb asks "IS HE MAN OR MONSTER OR…IS HE BOTH (?)" No doubt about it, readers definitely got their full 12¢ worth in May 1962.

The first appearence of The Incredible Hulk.

The Hulk's story actually began a year earlier in the summer of 1961. Thirty-nine-year-old writer Stan Lee was having a midlife crisis — he was souring on a lifetime of working in comics. He started in the comic-book industry in his late teens, and was finally burning out after years of churning out horror, romance, western, and funny animal stories for various comic titles. When his publisher requested he do a superhero team book to knock off rival publisher DC Comics' *Justice League of America*, Lee thought about quitting instead.

"I kept thinking, 'I'm an adult and a married man; how can I still write comic books?'" Stan Lee states. "I wanted to write the Great American Novel! I thought about changing careers, many, many times, so I would tell my wife Joan, 'Next year, I'll quit!' Then I would get a raise or work on a book that interested me and I would say, 'Next year, I'll quit.' This time, I was really going to quit. When I told Joan that, she said to me,

'Then why don't you write them the way you want to write them? For years, you wanted to do stories the way you wanted to tell them. Go for it — if it's not gonna be the way you want it, do it the way you want to do them. You're gonna be leaving anyway, so what have you got to lose? Do it your way and if they fire you, just remember: you're leaving anyway.' When I wrote the first comic that way, I tried to break all the rules: these

Hulk's creator, Stan (The Man) Lee. PHOTO BY PATRICK JANKIEWICZ

superheroes would be different; they would act the way I would act if I got super powers."

For this new superhero book, Stan Lee teamed up with artist Jack Kirby, the illustrator who co-created Captain America. This title would be the first issue of the brand-new Marvel Comics. The result was *Fantastic Four*, a family of adventurers, led by daring young scientist Reed Richards (with just a dash of gray in his hair), his best friend, grumpy test pilot Ben Grimm, Reed's fiancée Sue Storm, and her pesky younger brother, Johnny, a whiny teenager. "I did that because when I had Reed and Sue get married, Johnny would be the brother-in-law. I wanted *Fantastic Four* to be different from other books and I didn't know of any comic that actually had a brother-in-law!"

Exploring Outer Space in an experimental craft, the team's ship is penetrated by mysterious Cosmic Rays. Crashing back to Earth, they realize they have all been transformed. Reed can stretch, Sue can turn invisible, and Johnny can burst into flame, becoming a literal human torch. He does this by jumping into the air and flying, as he joyfully exclaims, "Flame on!" Poor Ben has mutated permanently into The Thing, a morose monster that looks like a lumpy pile of rocks with eyes. Despite his grotesque exterior appearance, Ben retains his mind and personality. His heart breaks at the way people react to him. On the street and subway, New Yorkers scream when they see him, move to the other side of whatever train or plane he's sharing with them, and Ben has to deal with being seen as a freak and monster by the general public he frequently saves. He also became readers' favorite character.

Unlike other superhero teams, the Fantastic Four bicker constantly. For all his genius, team leader Reed Richards "is a bit of a bore and he's bad with money," Stan Lee adds. The team is even evicted from their headquarters in The Baxter Building for late rent payment. Lee did this because "I wanted The Fantastic Four to be realistic. They would behave the way that real people would. Their identities would be publicly known, because if I had powers, I wouldn't hide it — I would be a bit of a show-off! I always liked Ben Grimm…Ben is a diamond in the rough, a gruff, good-hearted guy despite looking like a monster."

Sales immediately shot up, and Lee began thinking about what he could do for an encore. Because of the surprising popularity of The Thing, the misunderstood monster of The Fantastic Four, Lee started thinking about doing another "superhero monster" and cobbled an origin from the classics.

Creating The Incredible Hulk with artist Jack Kirby "was very simple. I was looking to do something different — I'm always looking to do something different. I remembered *Frankenstein* with Boris Karloff, which I love. I thought to myself, *Why not make a hero who is a monster?* Because in *Frankenstein*, I always thought The Monster was actually the good guy, the film's real hero. I cheered for him because he really didn't want to hurt anybody, The Frankenstein Monster just wanted to hang out with the blind hermit and that little kid. He's good on the inside, but everybody sees him as a monster. He couldn't help the fact that they put him together out of dead people.

"In all his movies, Frankenstein's Monster was just innocently shambling along, and those idiots with torches would chase him up and down the mountains. The villagers would not leave the poor guy alone! I felt sorry for him and I thought, *Why can't I create a monster who is a really nice guy, but nobody knows it?*

"I felt that it would get dull to just have a monster running around in story after story," Lee confesses, "so I thought, *I'll give him a secret identity!* That would also make it possible for him to have a love interest and other stuff that you could not do if he were just a monster. Suddenly, I remembered *Dr. Jekyll and Mr. Hyde*, and said, 'Hey, I'll do it like that!' This guy turns into the monster and then he turns back into the good guy...Lo, a legend is born! By adding that *Dr. Jekyll and Mr. Hyde* angle where this poor guy, through no fault of his own, transforms into a monster gave it a nice twist. I thought, *This made Bruce Banner tragic; he's done nothing wrong, but he turns into this rampaging monster.* Bruce Banner does not want to be The Hulk, and he's always worried about what he did as The Hulk, because he can't remember it."

Having The Hulk's alter ego be a weak, civilized scientist made the book interesting. It highlighted the differences between him and the monster he became. Nice Bruce Banner finds himself confused after changing back from The Hulk in different towns, states, or even countries and planets he's never been to before, wearing nothing but torn purple pants. Because he has no memory of what he's done as The Hulk, he has no idea how he got there or how to get home. Banner eventually started pinning Traveler's Checks inside his pants pockets to have currency after his Hulk Outs.

Stan Lee came up with "The Incredible Hulk" when "I was looking for a name for the monster. I wanted him to be this hulking brute, but I just could not find the right name for him. It suddenly occurred to me that 'Hulking' itself was perfect — he was The Hulk!"

Two years before he made his first appearance, The Hulk's name was first used by Stan Lee in *Journey Into Mystery* #62, when he had a fifteen-foot alien invader in the story drawn by Jack Kirby and Dick Ayers, "I Was A Slave Of The Living Hulk!" This Hulk is a big furry alien with glowing eyes, who bears no resemblance to the Bruce Banner Hulk. Artist Jack Kirby told *Starlog* magazine that Hulk "was simply *Dr. Jekyll and Mr. Hyde*. I was borrowing from the classics. They are the most powerful literature there is. As long as we're experimenting with radioactivity, there's no telling what may happen, or how much our advancements in science may cost us."

With his prominent brow and angry, staring eyes, it is clear that Boris Karloff's Frankenstein Monster was also a clear influence on The Hulk's look. "The Hulk was Frankenstein," Jack Kirby confirmed. "Frankenstein can rip up the place and [like Dr. Jekyll]; The Hulk could never remember who he formerly was."

In the comic book's origin story, "The Coming of the Hulk," Bruce Banner is a frail, pipe-smoking scientist in a lab coat and big glasses. He's bullied by his military handler, General Thaddeus "Thunderbolt" Ross. A blustering military man, Ross shows nothing but contempt for Banner, calling him a "weakling." Despite Banner being the brains behind the whole project, General Ross tells the scientist, "The trouble with you is you're a milksop! You've got no guts!"

The bombastic Ross is also the father of Banner's love interest, the chaste, beautiful Betty Ross. Banner is even picked on by his lab assistant, Igor, a Cold War Russian, who resembles a bushy-browed Commie brute in a lab coat. Minutes before the countdown, Bruce Banner is triple-checking everything because, as he direly informs his fellow scientists and military brass, "We are tampering with powerful forces!"

Jack Kirby's
Hulk has a strong
Frankenstein look.

Despite his bookish, meek exterior and cautiousness, Banner seems a tad overconfident, at one point boasting, "I don't make mistakes." He tells Igor, "You know how I detest men who think with their fists." When Bruce Banner sees teenager Rick Jones parked in the test area playing a harmonica — Rick went out to the Ground Zero missile site on a dare — he's so shocked that he races to personally save the boy. Untrustworthy

Igor agrees to delay the countdown, but Igor's actually an enemy spy out to steal Banner's Gamma Bomb secrets. His name alone should have red-flagged Igor on the security clearance! Igor lets the countdown continue as soon as Bruce is out of the bunker.

When Banner reaches Rick, he drags him across the test area, telling him, "Come on, you fool! We've got to reach the protective trench before the bomb goes off!" Pushing Rick into the trench, Bruce Banner adds, "There! You're safe! And now I'll — AHHHH." Banner is hit by the full force of Gamma Rays, which blasts him for three full comic-book panels. Expecting Banner and the Jones boy to die from Gamma exposure, General Ross has them placed in isolation.

The Moon rises and a Geiger counter goes crazy as Banner transforms into a hulking creature with gray skin. His massive expansion rips his shirt to rags. He swats Rick Jones aside, snarling, "Get out of my way, insect!" He balls up his fists, smashes through the concrete wall, and then wanders off into the desert.

After encountering soldiers and smashing a military vehicle, The Hulk races away with troops in hot pursuit. They are not aware that he's really Bruce Banner and the monster takes his name from an anonymous soldier, who yells, "Fan out, men! We've got to find that — that hulk!"

Returning to Banner's home on the base, The Hulk reacts violently when he sees a photo of Bruce Banner. "That face! I — I know that face!! But it is weak. Soft!! I hate it! Take it away! I'd rather be me, than that puny weakling in the picture!" Puzzled, Rick Jones tells The Hulk, "You *can't* hate it! Don't you understand? This guy in the picture — before you changed, he was — *you!*"

Caught in a Gamma Bomb blast, Bruce Banner's troubles are only beginning!

This scene sets up the mutual antipathy that Bruce Banner and The Hulk feel for each other for the run of the series. Bruce wants to be rid of The Hulk so he can embrace happiness with Betty, while The Hulk hates everything about Banner and the weakness he represents. Ironically, he shares his alter ego's feelings for Betty.

When he comes upon the traitorous spy Igor, rifling through Banner's things, The Hulk stares at him as poor Igor sputters, "You aren't human!" The Hulk snaps, "Human? Why should I want to be human?" The Hulk views humanity as weak and ineffectual as he sees Banner. The first issue also establishes The Hulk's rapidly healing metabolism. Shot in the shoulder, The Hulk doesn't feel it until he morphs back into Banner. The injury heals within minutes. In a brisk 24-page story, we meet Bruce Banner, The Hulk, and their entire supporting cast, see his origin and then join him on a quick trip behind the Iron Curtain, where The Hulk easily brings down a Communist overlord.

Clearly, young Bruce Banner is a comic-book stand-in for the father of the atomic bomb, Dr. Robert J. Oppenheimer. The story even refers to Bruce's Gamma Bomb as "The G-Bomb." When he's altered by the Gamma Rays, Banner literally becomes the living embodiment of

Oppenheimer's most famous quote: "I have become Death, the destroyer of worlds."

Stan Lee chose Gamma Rays for the creation of The Hulk "because it sounded good. I wouldn't know Gamma Rays if they lived next door! I used Gamma Rays to create The Hulk because I had already used Cosmic Rays to create The Fantastic Four and I was gonna have a radioactive spider bite Peter Parker (turning him into The Amazing Spider-Man), so poor Bruce Banner was subjected to Gamma Rays."

Banner has literally seen his life destroyed by his own creation, the Gamma Bomb. "The Coming of the Hulk" reads a lot like the horror stories that Lee and Kirby churned out for comics like *Tales of Suspense*, *Fear* and *Amazing Adult Fantasy* — except Hulk is not destroyed at the end of the story.

While The Hulk's origin of a man being caught in a nuclear blast and becoming a monster is Marvel Comics' reaction to the nuclear age, the story also bears a strong similarity to Bert I. Gordon's 1957 B-movie, *The Amazing Colossal Man*. In *Colossal Man*, Lt. Colonel Glen Manning is caught in a Plutonium blast and miraculously survives. Unfortunately, he finds his body chemistry has been irrevocably altered and he is mutating into a muscular, bald, sixty-foot giant. Because his heart is unable to pump enough blood to his brain, Manning is becoming crazed, unstable and angry. In the end, he attacks Las Vegas, and the Army that unwittingly created him must now try to destroy him. *The Amazing Colossal Man* was a clear influence on The Hulk.

"I had not noticed that resemblance to The Hulk before, but now I can see it," says *The Amazing Colossal Man* director Bert I. Gordon. "With *Colossal Man*, I was just trying to capture how I would feel as a little kid — you wanted to be big so people would pay attention to you. Perhaps they were trying to do the same thing with The Incredible Hulk."

Lee created The Hulk and Spider-Man in the same year. Bruce Banner, like fellow Marvel heroes Reed Richards, Sue Storm, Peter Parker, Scott Summers, Matt Murdock, Pepper Potts, and Dr. Stephen Strange, "has an alliterative name to make it easier for me to remember," Stan Lee confides. "I knew it would be easy to remember if both names started with the same letter!"

Betty Ross, Banner's girlfriend, starts out as your typical early 1960s comic-book female character, prim, proper, and frail. She's so delicate, she faints at the mere sight of The Hulk. Doctor Banner's relationship with Betty is clearly symbolic for the joint science/military merger Banner is in with her father, General Ross.

The highlight of the early *Hulk* stories are Banner's painful changes into The Hulk. Artist Jack Kirby excels in these transformation scenes, as Bruce Banner's slim, delicate fingers morph into the thick, blunt, brutish hands of The Hulk. Lee and Kirby's Hulk is a massive, angry-looking brute with a rogues gallery to match that anger.

In the issues to come, The Hulk matches wits with more evil Russians. In these early stories, Hulk makes a point of showing disdain for "Commies" as he "sends 'em back to Vodka land!"

"I don't know why I have Communists in so many early Hulk and Iron Man stories," Stan Lee winces. "It was just the tenor of the times, I guess." It's important to remember that 1962, the year of The Hulk's birth, is also the time when the Cold War was at its hottest with the Cuban Missile Crisis and nuclear war was a very real possibility.

Because The Incredible Hulk was so powerful, his opponents transcended mere human perpetrators. He duked it out with alien invaders like The Terrible Toad Men and The Metal Master. His former employer, the armed forces of the United States government, hunts The Hulk relentlessly, attacking him with bombs, jets, jeeps and tanks. This is ironic, as the United States accidentally helped create him in the first place, just like *The Amazing Colossal Man*.

Bert I. Gordon's B-Movie *The Amazing Colossal Man* was a big influence on The Hulk.

The Hulk's bright green skin was the result of a printing error. While the color of the monster was originally undetermined, all Lee and Kirby knew was that they didn't want him to be orange, like The Thing from The Fantastic Four. "I finally settled on the color gray, because it seemed like a good scary color," Lee says.

In his book, *Origins Of Marvel Comics*, Stan Lee explains. "I thought it would be interesting to have The Hulk's skin change color when he reverted to his monstrous self. Thinking it would be intensely dramatic looking and somber, I arranged to have his body take on a gray hue in the first issue of his new magazine. But, as soon as the advance copies reached us, I realized the effect was entirely different from what I had intended. In some of the scenes, his gray skin color gave him a chameleon-like quality.

"The printer didn't seem able to give him a consistent shade of gray from page to page, or even from panel to panel. In fact, his skin was light gray in some places and almost black in others. There were a few panels where he seemed red, and for some reason which nobody could explain, in one close-up toward the end of our little epic, he was bright emerald green. As you may have already surmised, it became painfully apparent to me that gray was not the happiest color choice I might have made.

"Shortly thereafter, a seemingly rational comic-book writer spent several long, anguished minutes pacing his office trying to determine the proper skin color for a fictional monster…The color I opted for was a bravely bedazzling basic green."

In his second issue, when The Hulk took on The Toad Men, he did it as a very green giant. Marvel illustrators found that when the green Hulk was placed in purple pants, he was so colorful, he seemed to jump off the page. Because of this, he's worn purple pants ever since.

Smart, suit wearing Hulk is not a big fan of bikers.

Ironically, in the 1980s, *The Incredible Hulk* comic-book writers would revert him to gray again, where he was a less-powerful but smarter monster. So much smarter that in his green form, the gray Hulk worked as a leg breaker for a Las Vegas casino who called himself "Joe Fixit." Humorously, in this incarnation, The Hulk prefers wearing three-piece suits. Seeing the brute in a suit and tie is amusing. Because he was "born" in a desert during a nuclear blast, the comic-book character has kept a fondness for the barren desert.

In green, The Hulk talks in a gruff, primitive speech pattern, usually referring to himself in third person. He defiantly proclaims that "Nobody can stop The Hulk!" and his battle cry is "Hulk Smash!" He sees most people and soldiers as "Puny humans," but General Ross is "Ross" and his daughter is always respectfully referred to as "Betty."

Part of The Hulk's universal appeal is that anger sets him off, something that everyone can relate to. For him, anger is energy. The madder The Hulk gets, the stronger The Hulk gets!

"In the beginning, Bruce Banner changes at nightfall, like a werewolf," Stan Lee shrugs. "I don't know why I switched his transformation to anger setting him off, I just had to have some reason why he changed into a monster and that seemed the easiest way to do it. What would make him change from a human to a monster? The easy thing was to have him get angry or upset. He gets mad, the adrenaline pumps and he becomes The Hulk. It seemed obvious to me!"

Today, Spider-Man and The Hulk rank as Marvel's most recognizable characters, known worldwide to kids and adults. Hulk is also a major part of Marvel tee-shirts, posters, and toys. As hard as it is to believe, *The Incredible Hulk* comic book was cancelled after only six bi-monthly issues. Marvel was limited in how many titles it could publish a month. *The Incredible Hulk* didn't sell as well as *The Fantastic Four* or *The Amazing Spider-Man*, so he took the fall.

The Avengers were first brought together to *stop* The Hulk.

"I knew Hulk was a great character, and I resolved to bring him back so that he would catch on with readers," Stan Lee grins. "He just needed a chance."

To keep him in readers' minds, Lee made The Hulk a popular guest star. When Hulk creates havoc, a group of solo superheroes, including Thor, Ant Man and The Wasp, are thrown together, united by Iron Man to help him stop The Hulk. They end his rampage on a Detroit auto assembly line. It works out so well, at the end of the story, they decide to become a super team permanently in the title, *The Avengers* #1.

The Hulk became a popular sparring partner in other books as well. In *Fantastic Four* #12, he took on Marvel's first family and fought them all to a standstill. It was firmly established in the story that Hulk could even beat the powerful Thing in one-on-one combat. At that point, The Thing was one of the strongest heroes in The Marvel Universe. Readers craved more of the Hulk. Because he wasn't really evil, just misunderstood, Hulk made an interesting guest star. He was feral and nearly unstoppable, so the most popular fights were between Hulk and Marvel's resident Norse god, The Mighty Thor, who he would later meet in a live-action TV movie.

It became a constant debate for readers over which Marvel hero was stronger. "I figure Thor's a god, so maybe he would probably win, because

The Fantastic Four met The Hulk in this epic two-part story.

Hulk is only human and could eventually get tired — but the angrier Hulk gets, the stronger he gets," Stan Lee says slyly. "So they usually just fight to a standstill. That seems to work." Hulk also tangled with the Greek hero Hercules, Spider-Man, Captain America, Silver Surfer, Giant Man, The Inhumans and undersea mutant Prince Namor the Sub-Mariner.

When Hulk had a two-part storyline in *Fantastic Four* #25 and #26, it was considered one of the greatest Marvel stories ever told. Ol' Greenskin (as Lee nicknamed him) takes on the combined forces of good in the Marvel Universe — the Fantastic Four and The Avengers. After these two issues, his reputation was cemented as a Marvel superstar and heavyweight. Readers demanded a regular return for The Hulk. They soon got it — Hulk was revived on a regular basis in the pages of *Tales to Astonish*, where he shared a book with other not-quite-popular-enough-for-their-own-title heroes like Ant Man (who could enlarge into Giant Man) and

Namor. Hulk was clearly seen as the lesser character, with Namor appearing on most covers and if The Hulk made the cover at all, he was usually the size of a postage stamp in the corner.

This half-book served Hulk well, adding to his popular enemies list with his first Gamma-powered foes. When janitor Samuel Sterns is exposed to Gamma Rays, he's turned into green, super-smart maniac, The Leader. Russian spy Emil Blonsky deliberately exposes himself to Gamma Radiation and becomes The Abomination, another green, grotesque monster. Lee also had the world discover that Bruce Banner is The Hulk, making him recognized by the public in either form. By doing this, he set up the storyline of Bruce Banner as a fugitive on the run from the police, public and armed forces, unable to trust anyone. This is where Stan Lee hit his stride with the direction of the character and comic. All *Hulk* movies and animated series' have stayed close to this incarnation.

FRIENDS AND FOES

After his own comic was cancelled, Hulk was crowded out by B-listers like Namor on the cover of *Tales To Astonish*.

As Stan predicted, The Incredible Hulk would not stay down — *Tales to Astonish* booted Giant Man and Namor and became *The Incredible Hulk* with its 102nd issue. A 1965 *Esquire* poll had college students ranking Hulk and Spider-Man alongside Bob Dylan and Che as their "favorite revolutionary icons." Hulk was even on the cover of *Rolling Stone*, drawn by the great Herb Trimpe. Writers and artists flocked to the title after Stan Lee gave it up to run the company, attracted to the book because of The Hulk's primal nature.

"Oh God, I loved writing the Hulk," confesses Len Wein, a longtime *Incredible Hulk* scribe. "I just had a wonderful time writing for him; it was my longest run on any book, about four years. The Hulk is such a primal character, whose response to everything is emotional. He's full of great rage tempered with great humanity. I enjoyed doing Hulk because you could do such great human stories."

Hulk proved so popular, he even triggered spin-off characters, including the most popular member of *The Uncanny X-Men*, "Canada's first and greatest superhero," Wolverine. The short, hairy mutant with the adamantium claws was introduced as an enemy of the green giant in *The Incredible Hulk* #180 and #181. Wolverine creator Wein came up with the character "because Hulk was running amok in Canada, so their government sends

Left: Canadian mutant Wolverine made his debut trying to kill Hulk!
Right: Iron Man in his utterly ineffectual Hulkbuster armor.

in their agent, Wolverine, to stop Hulk! When I wrote the book, I would have The Hulk go around the world to places like Scotland and meet people with different accents. I would write the accents into the characters' dialogue.

"The name 'Wolverine' was given to me by Roy Thomas, the editor in chief of Marvel Comics at that time. Roy said, 'I would like you to do a character called 'Wolverine.' I said, 'Tell me about him.' Roy said, 'Nothing — I just want to see what you do with a Canadian accent.' I did a little bit of research on what a wolverine is and found they were small, nasty animals with sharp claws," Wein recalls.

"I made Wolverine a mutant because there were rumors that Marvel might revive *The Uncanny X-Men* comic which had been cancelled because of low sales. Supposedly, they were going to be revived as an international team of superhero mutants. I figured it couldn't hurt to have a Canadian mutant waiting in the wings. He's called Wolverine because wolverines live up there and have sharp claws…"

"I had no idea that Wolverine would catch on," admits Marvel artist Herb Trimpe, who drew the mutant's first appearance. "To be honest, I thought he was just Hulk's enemy of the month!"

After creating the new X-Men characters like Storm and Colossus, Len Wein decided *not* to pen their monthly adventures, choosing "to write Hulk instead of X-Men. I just loved his strong emotions."

Hulk has battled literally every major hero and villain in the Marvel universe at one time or another, from Doctor Doom to Fin Fang Foom. Iron Man even has a special "Hulkbuster" armor he wears to fight him. That armor is pretty ineffectual at "busting," stopping or even slowing Hulk — but it made a neat action figure for Marvel subsidiary Toy Biz.

Banner's psychiatrist friend, Dr. Leonard Samson, also became a popular supporting character. A respected academic and author, he exposes himself to Gamma Radiation siphoned off from The Hulk. This transforms him into a smart, muscular powerhouse with long green hair who calls himself "Doc Samson." Humorously, he keeps his psychiatric practice.

THE SAVAGE SHE-HULK

The biggest addition to the supporting cast came when The Hulk gained a relative and a spin-off character: The Savage She-Hulk. Inspired by the popularity of the live-action *Incredible Hulk* TV show, She-Hulk came from the fertile mind of Hulk's creator Stan Lee. Lee had been tasked with finding a way to protect Marvel's copyright on a female Hulk. There was a fear that the live-action *Hulk* TV series would introduce a female spin-off like they did on *Six Million Dollar Man* with *The Bionic Woman*, so Lee created a female Hulk in *The Savage She-Hulk* #1 to establish that Marvel owned a female Hulk character, not Universal Studios. "Some business

The Hulk gains a cousin…
And a spin-off!

people really felt we needed a female Hulk to protect our rights to the
name," explains Stan Lee. "I was told that we needed a feminine Hulk
for this reason, so I made her a direct relative of Bruce Banner. Besides,
Hulk was doing well and we're greedy!"

Co-created by artist John Buscema, best known for his work on
Marvel's popular *Conan the Barbarian* title, the cover is a playful female

Family ties (and a life-saving blood transfusion) will cause Bruce
Banner's cousin Jennifer to become The Savage She-Hulk.

variation of Jack Kirby's artwork for *The Incredible Hulk* #1, with a petite
girl transforming into The Savage She-Hulk as a crowd flees behind her.
Marvel made sure that every single reader knew of Stan Lee's involvement
in her creation. At that point, Stan Lee had not written a title in almost
a decade. The cover copy screams "STAN LEE proudly presents THE
SHE-HULK LIVES!" In a cynical attempt to make sure fans realized
the potential worth of the book, it also reads "#1 COLLECTORS ITEM
ISSUE!" Clearly, Marvel felt readers should see their forty cents as not
simply going to entertainment, but as a worthy future investment with the
book. When she was introduced in February 1980, She-Hulk is established
as Bruce Banner's never-mentioned-before "kid cousin," Jennifer Walters.

In keeping with the TV show's lack of mutants and monsters, Stan Lee's
first She-Hulk story made her less tormented than her larger-than-life
cousin. At the beginning of the story, Jennifer is a fun, goodhearted young
lawyer who has successfully prosecuted a crime boss. In retribution, she is
gunned down by gangsters in front of her horrified cousin, Bruce Banner.
As traumatic as all this is, Bruce fights back the urge to transform, knowing
his cousin needs a doctor, not a monster. Because she's a beloved relative,
that gives Banner the impetus to save her life, no matter what. Before she

bleeds to death, poor Jennifer's life is saved only by a timely blood transfusion from Bruce Banner, which turns her into The Savage She-Hulk.

As beautiful and smart as The Hulk is ugly and primal, She-Hulk is tall and Amazonian, a snarling beauty with green skin and dark green hair. Unfortunately for the teenage boys reading the book, her shirt does not come off like The Hulk's, and the tattered remains of her clothes

somehow always manage to cover all of her unmentionables. This was a Comics Code-approved book, after all!

Like Hulk, she obtains her name from a minor character. Seeing her change, one of the hit men who tried to kill her exclaims, "It's a GIRL! But — look at the SIZE of her! Her skin! It — It's GREEN! It's like — she's some kind'a SHE-HULK!" Chasing down her would-be assassins, the green giantess rips through an elevator door and roars, "You called me a She-Hulk and a She-Hulk I'll be! Now let's see how tough you are — against ME!" She thrashes the men within an inch of their lives.

As with her cousin Hulk, She-Hulk's first comic-book series was short-lived and *The Savage She-Hulk* was soon cancelled. She-Hulk was popular enough in her own right to briefly replace The Thing in *Fantastic Four* — where artist John Byrne drew her like a big green Brooke Shields. She-Hulk, or "Shulkie" as she was nicknamed, also served in *The Avengers*, a group her cousin co-founded. Captain America and Iron Man later kicked her out of Avengers Mansion for abusing privileges, bringing strangers in for one-night stands and misusing her Avengers Priority Card to beat parking tickets.

Although she started out as an angry but beautiful monster, Jennifer eventually retained her normal personality in She-Hulk form and maintained her law practice. Many issues would have her addressing juries as a green She-Hulk. In the comics, Jennifer is a lawyer who has worked for Manhattan's District Attorney, handling superhero law and has also been a bounty hunter. Hollywood later noticed She-Hulk, but wasn't as successful in bringing her to life as they were with The Hulk — that will be covered later in the book.

BETTY ROSS

Betty Ross, tired of waiting for Bruce Banner, married Major Glenn Talbot, General Ross' right-hand man. Talbot was a romantic rival that Stan Lee created. A handsome, by-the-book military man, Glenn Talbot died in obsessive pursuit of The Hulk. Betty ran off on Banner with another man and at one point, was so fed up with The Hulk in her life, she joined a convent and became a nun! Bruce Banner eventually married Betty. Her father General Ross not only showed up at the church to object to the wedding, he also shot Best Man Rick Jones in the stomach! Betty went into a coma after being poisoned with Gamma Radiation by The Abomination. The book went through cycles, even General Ross was killed off at one point. He was later resurrected by The Leader when writers realized he was the only human character in the Marvel universe who could credibly threaten The Hulk.

While Bruce and Betty are still technically married, Hulk has romanced Earth-bound and alien women. This is understandable, as he sees himself as a separate entity from Banner. Betty returned from her coma as a red-skinned female Hulk and declared their marriage over because she was legally and clinically dead for three years.

RICK JONES

After debuting in *The Incredible Hulk* #1, Rick Jones went through a lot of changes. He was always the anti-Jimmy Olsen. The cub reporter for the Daily Planet, Jimmy Olsen was supposed to be an audience surrogate to show kid readers how great it would be to hang out with Superman. Rick Jones found hanging out with The Hulk to be a thankless task. An orphan and dropout, Rick Jones knows Bruce Banner's life has been irrevocably shattered by saving him, so he sticks around to help Bruce and The Hulk as they are hunted by the United States. Later, Rick became a sidekick to Captain America and then a cosmic hero in Marvel's revamp of Captain Marvel. He works best as Hulk's one true friend, who frequently suffers for that friendship.

"Happy" Herb Trimpe, one of Marvel's greatest Hulk artists. PHOTO BY PATRICK JANKIEWICZ

Rick Jones mutated into a green teenage version of The Hulk and later morphed into an armor-plated armadillo monster who called himself "A-Bomb." It's his clever way of calling himself an "abomination." Poor Rick was once paralyzed when The Hulk fell on him, but got better. This is a comic-book world, after all. Rick has been kidnapped by The Skrulls,

Kree and Toad Men, all alien races with a beef against Hulk. He's been held by the Army and arrested for vagrancy in small towns that he went into to save Banner or help Hulk.

Jones later married Marlo, a Las Vegas dancer/soft-core film star, but he found even this relationship was tainted by The Hulk. Marlo was the 6'6" Vegas showgirl/ex-girlfriend of the Hulk in his "Joe Fixit" days (!). Despite his messy romantic entanglement with the bride, Bruce Banner generously agreed to be Best Man at their wedding. Happily, no one was shot in the stomach this time!

STRONGEST ONE THERE IS

As the decades rolled on, The Hulk's strength only expanded. He was bulletproof, but only when he was The Hulk and not the puny, frail Banner. Hulk can trash tanks, trucks, spaceships and jets. By the late '80s, Hulk was capable of holding up an entire mountain range single-handedly and could survive a direct nuclear strike. Hulk had become so strong that many of his opponents were robots, as few living beings could realistically go toe to toe with him. He was even (briefly) a member of The New Fantastic Four, an alternate FF composed of Spider-Man and the antisocial trio of Hulk, Wolverine and Ghost Rider, all of whose books were not so coincidentally selling well at the time.

In the 1960s, Hulk quit *The Avengers* by the second issue. He was offended at the way the rest of the group mistrusted him. By the 1970s, Hulk was a member of the dysfunctional superteam The Defenders, written by the late Steve Gerber, who saw The Defenders as "an encounter group." As such, there was no group leader and a lot of squabbling. The biggest names on the team were Hulk and Dr. Strange, Master of The Mystic Arts. The rest were interesting B-listers like former supervillain Nighthawk, Norse goddess The Valkyrie and former-model-turned-super-heroine The Cat. Stories usually ended with The Hulk and others bitterly slamming doors and storming off into the night, after saving the world. They could rescue Mankind, but not get past their petty differences.

Comic-book writers alternately explored Hulk's savage and sensitive sides. Len Wein remembers, "I once did a story where The Hulk was petting a deer like Bambi. When Steve Gerber took over *The Incredible Hulk* comic, he opened a story with The Hulk breaking a deer's neck–That was the end of my run…My Hulk *wouldn't* have done that!"

Because of Hulk's great strength, his villains had to be worthy antagonists. This led to increasingly bizarre enemies like Bi-Beast (no, he's not gay, just a two-faced/one-headed monster android), The Harpy (Betty Ross turned into a flying green bird woman), hairy and hypnotic alien Xemnu the Living Titan (this is the white, furry original Hulk, re-named from Stan Lee's "I Was A Slave of the Living Hulk!"), The U-Foes (a homicidal foursome who tried to replicate The Fantastic Four, with tragic results), Tyrannus (the handsome but cruel leader of sub-humanoid creatures at the center of the Earth), Mercy (a beautiful floating alien who thinks that killing you is the ultimate "Mercy"), The Maestro (an older, balding evil Hulk from a future timeline) and Zzzax, a being of living electricity.

General Ross, Hulk's oldest foe, had to keep up with all of these unusual, downright freakish opponents. He formed a military adjunct, The Hulkbusters, whose only job is to destroy The Hulk. While Ross personally dislikes Hulk, he also sees him as a threat to the United States, with his great strength and unpredictable behavior.

"That's the thing — General Ross is attacking Hulk for the good of the country," says longtime *Incredible Hulk* illustrator/Vietnam veteran Herb Trimpe. "Trying to stop The Hulk doesn't make you a bad guy! After all, Hulk does cause a lot of property damage and wrecks a lot of cars…"

Besides Ross, Hulk also battles General John Ryker, the dark side of the military industrial complex. Unlike Ross, he's warped and evil, wanting The Hulk's power for his own. He even sics the Gamma Hounds on him — mutated dogs enlarged to Hulk proportions. They were later used in the Ang Lee *Hulk* movie.

MARVEL ZOMBIE

Marvel even established an "Undead Hulk" as part of their popular *Marvel Zombies* line. Marvel heroes from a parallel universe are infected by a George Romero-like zombie outbreak that even transforms Bruce Banner and The Hulk into a cannibalistic, undead creature. When these zombies eat every living human on their Earth, as well as The Silver Surfer and omnipotent alien being Galactus, they go off looking for more sustenance in a cheerfully revolting scenario. Zombie Hulk keeps eating people and then complains he's hungry — as he has a large hole in his stomach that the "food" immediately falls out of.

When Marvel established their *Ultimates* line, they created an out-of-continuity Hulk. In this universe, Bruce Banner is an angry, bitter nerd who becomes The Hulk while trying to recreate the Super Soldier Formula that turned sickly Steve Rogers into Captain America. Instead of turning into a superman, he becomes a raging, murderous brute with phallic issues. This Hulk worries about his manhood, wanting to prove to Betty "what a man he is" and occasionally runs around naked. He's also a gray-skinned cannibal who murders thousands of people during his first ten-minute rampage. Ultimate Hulk also killed Peter Parker's parents.

You wouldn't like him when he's dead: Marvel Zombie Hulk.

The normal Hulk briefly headed his own alliance of Greek Myth-inspired heroes and misfits, The Pantheon. Later, Hulk was banished beyond the stars only to become an Outer Space Spartacus in *Planet Hulk*. He returned with an alien army to punish his former friends Reed Richards, Dr, Strange, Iron Man and Professor Xavier, leader of The X-Men, who formed a Think Tank that decided to send him into Space for the good of Mankind. Hulk also attacks the Planet Earth itself in *World War Hulk*.

FAMILY HULK

Hulk also became a dysfunctional father in the comics. He has a hulk-ing green barbarian son, Skaar. Named after Sakaar, the cruel alien planet he was born on, Hulk fathered Skaar with Caiera, a female gladiator in *Planet Hulk*. With the mother dead, Banner and Hulk were oblivious to their son's existence, until he came to Earth with a sword and a strong desire to commit patricide. Ironically, Skaar and Bruce Banner bond over their mutual dislike of Hulk.

The Hulk also had a daughter whose origin is even more convoluted than Skaar's. His daughter Lyra is conceived when Thundra, an Amazon warrior from the future, swabs Hulk's cheek and combines their DNA. Writer Fred Van Lente wanted Hulk and Thundra to create Lyra in a more traditional way, but Marvel editors nixed that! Green like her father, Lyra is tall and sexy like her mother and She-Hulk. Unlike The Hulk, his daughter Lyra loses her great strength whenever she becomes angry. The character was dubbed "She-Hulk," even though they already have one.

Over the years in the comics, Hulk has been portrayed as primal, simple-minded and raging, as well as gray-skinned, calculating, smart and scary. To the character's credit, he works in all of these incarnations.

Hulk's dysfunctional Family: From top left, Hulk, his son Skaar, his daughter Lyra, his cousin She-Hulk

CARTOON CREATURE

The Hulk's first foray into television actually came with a 1966 cartoon. While bigger cartoon companies snatched up The Fantastic Four and Spider-Man, Captain America, Thor, Iron Man, Namor and The Hulk were all sold to a company that adapted them all in a cheap "Marvel Superheroes" cartoon package.

Limited Canadian animation took actual Hulk comic panels, crudely animated them and dubbed in voices with minimal on-screen movement. What they lacked in budget was made up for by enthusiastic Canadian actors performing Stan Lee's scripts. One reason the performances were so good was that a lot of the cartoon's cast had already voiced Rankin-Bass' classic Christmas show, *Rudolph the Red Nosed Reindeer*.

Paul Soles, who plays Bruce Banner and Rick Jones, was Hermey the Elf and had an extended cameo in Edward Norton's *The Incredible Hulk* movie. Paul Kligman, who was the blustering General "Thunderbolt"

Ross on *Hulk*, was reindeer Donner, Clarice's father, and Comet the coach in *Rudolph* — as well as the first person to play J. Jonah Jameson in a *Spider-Man* cartoon. Peg Dixon, who voiced Betty Ross, played reindeer Mrs. Donner, while Banner's romantic rival for Betty, Major Glenn Talbot, was played by John Vernon. The popular character actor Vernon appeared in numerous films, Clint Eastwood westerns and later played vile Dean

Promotional material for the *Marvel Super-Heroes* cartoons.

Wormer in *National Lampoon's Animal House*. Vernon also voiced Namor the Submariner and Tony Stark/The Invincible Iron Man in cartoons from the same producers. Befitting the Canadian cartoon's tiny budget, the voice of Iron Man came from John Vernon talking into a Styrofoam cup!

Although done on the cheap, these are the most faithful comics-to-screen adaptations of *The Incredible Hulk* that have ever been produced. Because they had no money, they could not afford to change anything. They follow the Stan Lee stories and dialogue to the letter, even using the actual comic-book art. Sometimes they would mix and match the art from several comics. A Jack Kirby Hulk would suddenly become a Steve Ditko one and back again in the same episode.

The cartoons are amazingly static; they would usually move one character's arm in a frame or have a character blink to give the slightest hint of movement. As the voice of The Hulk, Max Ferguson sounds angry, suspicious and constipated at the same time! The show is best remembered for its goofy, catchy theme song ("Doc Bruce Banner/belted by Gamma Rays/ Turns into THE HULK! Ain't he unglamorous?"). This show would not be his last time on television.

TELEVISION

Kenneth Johnson and Lindsay Wagner comfort an overheated Bigfoot on the set of *The Bionic Woman*.

THE COMING OF THE TV **HULK**

In 1977, Kenneth Johnson was riding a wave of success. The busy writer/director/ producer was working on *The Six Million Dollar Man* TV series. The adventures of astronaut Steve Austin (Lee Majors) mangled in a crash and re-built with modern technology to become a government agent had already been a hit. When Johnson came onto the show, he successfully brought the popular series' ratings up even higher.

While *The Six Million Dollar Man* usually had the Cyborg spy battling Cold War villains, terrorists and James Bond-style megalomaniacs, Johnson injected hardcore sci-fi and fantasy ideas into the show, even adding Bigfoot in two of the series' most iconic episodes. Bigfoot was played by legendary wrestler Andre the Giant.

"The Sasquatch was an intriguing character because I was always looking for worthy adversaries for Steve Austin to go up against. Then it was fun to turn the tables and discover that Bigfoot was also robotic," Johnson admits. While writing another episode of *The Six Million Dollar Man*, he created Jamie Sommers, *The Bionic Woman*, who became a popular spin-off series that eventually eclipsed the original show in popularity. As *Bionic Woman* started stomping *The Six Million Dollar Man* in the ratings, Johnson became the studio's go-to guy for TV fantasy. This made him Universal's first choice when they decided to adapt the Marvel superheroes.

When he first met Hulk, Johnson wasn't interested. "That's putting it mildly," he jokes. "I came upon *The Incredible Hulk* when I was told that Universal Studios had just bought the rights to several Marvel Comics superheroes, including Captain America, The Human Torch, Ms. Marvel and The Hulk.

"[Then-Universal head] Frank Price asked me which one I wanted to do and I thought, 'Gee, thanks, Frank, NONE of them!' I don't deal that well with spandex or primary colors and frankly, I couldn't relate to The Human Torch…"

AN APPROACH FOR THE HULK

His opinion changed when he came up with an approach for The Hulk. "I was reading *Les Miserables* at the time, a gift from my wife Susie. I had Jean Valjean and *The Fugitive* in my head. In the shower that morning, I was thinking of how I was going to turn Frank down on the Marvel superheroes,

Hulk has a rich supporting cast including Rick Jones, Doc Samson, Betty and her father, General Ross. *None* would be used for television.

when I suddenly thought, 'Maybe there's a way to take this ludicrous thing called *The Incredible Hulk* and turn it into something with Victor Hugo and Robert Louis Stevenson's *Doctor Jekyll & Mr. Hyde.*'"

Johnson decided to "turn it into a psychological drama about a man who is cursed and the whole point of Banner is that he is struggling to make the entire TV series come to an end! I started writing it on Easter Sunday. I called it *The Hulk* because I just couldn't bring myself to type the words '*The Incredible Hulk*' — it sounded too ludicrous!"

Instead of being pursued by a relentless policeman, Banner is doggedly trailed by tabloid reporter Jack McGee (Jack Colvin). "McGee is the Inspector Javert character from *Les Miserables*," Johnson confesses. "Literally, that's exactly who he is! I didn't want to make McGee a cop like Inspector Javert, because *The Fugitive* did that exactly with Inspector Gerard, so I made him a

yellow journalist from a tabloid rag. I didn't want to do *The Incredible Hulk* at all originally, but now I was actually getting excited about it."

He jettisoned Banner's entire supporting cast — there is no General "Thunderbolt" Ross, nor daughter Betty or even loyal teenage sidekick Rick Jones. We never meet Doc Samson, or Major Glen Talbot. No villains like The Leader, Abomination or The Terrible Toad Men show up — especially not the Toad Men. "No, no, no — My Hulk would NEVER meet The Toad Men," Johnson chuckles. "We really didn't want him fighting mole monsters or creatures from Space!"

Johnson also weakened The Hulk. No longer a bulletproof behemoth leaping from state to state and country to country, stopping only to smash tanks and jets, the TV Hulk is a nimble, raging creature incapable of speech. If Hulk smashes a wall or car, that pretty much completes his violence for the episode. He runs away at the end of a conflict, to avoid being shot. In the comics, Hulk usually uses his fists to protect himself from the military and monsters. For the show, this would not do.

"It was important to me that The Hulk never hit anybody," Johnson says.

Mocked by the show's producers, The Terrible Toad Men still caused a lot of trouble for Hulk's Family.

"It seemed kind of unfair, because his fists were so big, nobody would have a chance and it would be too easy to just have him hit people."

On the TV series, The Hulk is treated like the elusive Sasquatch: a creature that is covered by the tabloids who print blurry pictures of him but considered an urban legend by the public at large. Bigfoot was the popular subject of documentaries and TV shows when *Hulk* was on the air. Like Sasquatch, The Hulk is pursued by a few devoted hunters and cryptozoology types, all of whom hope to finally prove Hulk's existence by killing him.

NAME GAME

To complete the comic-to-TV makeover, even Bruce Banner's name was changed. "I did that to avoid comic-book alliteration. 'Bruce Banner' just sounded too comic-booky to me," Johnson explains. "Re-naming him,

I used my son's name. I think my son David was very amused by that. I named Banner 'David' because it's a very solid, substantial name. I wanted a name for him that would take it away from comic-book alliteration, like Clark Kent, Lois Lane and Peter Parker."

At the time, Stan Lee used one of his *Stan Lee's Soapbox* columns to good-naturedly protest the name change. "Universal Studios just com-

David Bruce Banner's empty grave.

pleted a live-action, 2-hour special TV movie of everybody's favorite jolly green giant," he wrote in 1977."What do you think they called ol' Doc Banner? Bruce? Uh uh! Bob? Forget it! They decided to name him Dave. What there is about our recalcitrant little rampager that makes it so tough for people to get his name right, I'll never know!"

"Stan was not too happy with me changing Banner's name," Kenneth Johnson says with a smile. "But I told him, 'Okay, Bruce is his middle name — so it will say 'David Bruce Banner' on his tombstone every week in the opening credits when you see the grave!' When I looked for a new name for Banner, the first name that popped into my head was David! I always thought of it as a good, worthy name. My sons grew up on the set of The *Incredible Hulk*. My younger son Michael was seven at the time, and has fond memories of being chased around the Universal backlot by a big green Lou Ferrigno."

Bruce is actually Banner's middle name in the comics as well. When Stan Lee slipped in an early issue by referring to him as "Bob Banner," a reader called him on it. Marvel awarded "No Prizes" — gaudy envelopes with nothing inside — if readers caught a flaw in the story. Stan quickly explained that his full name was "Robert Bruce Banner," so calling him "Bob Banner" was entirely appropriate. Another reason Kenneth Johnson may have used the name "David" is even more intriguing. Because his *Hulk* borrowed the framework of *The Fugitive*, calling Banner "David" may have been a subconscious tip of the hat to *Fugitive* star David Janssen

PAGING DOCTOR BANNER

Bill Bixby became TV's Dr. Banner.

Before Johnson could begin the series, he needed a star for David Banner. Ironically, he chose a man whose name was perfect for comic-book alliteration: Bill Bixby! A versatile actor, Bixby was adept at comedy and drama. He started out on the popular sitcom *My Favorite Martian*, where he played a likable, befuddled reporter hiding the title alien played by Ray Walston.

After appearing in a couple Elvis Presley movies and starring in the well-received TV series *The Courtship of Eddie's Father*, Bixby gave an acclaimed performance in the PBS movie, *Steambath*, as a guy who refuses to accept that he's dead. He followed that by co-starring in and co-directing the blockbuster *Rich Man, Poor Man*, whose spectacular ratings gave birth to the television miniseries.

There was surprise in the industry when Bill Bixby followed this great success by agreeing to star as a scientist who transforms into a big comic-book monster. Lynda Carter, Adam West, Christopher Reeve, Van Williams and Bruce Lee were all unknowns when they agreed to play Wonder Woman, Batman, Superman, Green Hornet and Kato respectively. Bixby was a trusted "name" in television, so for him to take a gamble on doing a big dramatic fantasy series could have been an embarrassing misstep.

During interviews promoting *The Incredible Hulk*, Bill Bixby addressed this head on, telling the press, "I have my agent to thank for it," because his agent insisted that he read Kenneth Johnson's pilot script. Ironically, Bixby himself had to be talked into doing the show. Bixby admitted to *The Kansas City Star* that "I had just gotten off an airplane and my agent handed me two scripts. One was *The Incredible Hulk*. I laughed. The other was a serious title that rang of American history, something meaningful [that] we actors aspire to and say 'Gosh, we would like to be associated with this.'

"I told him, 'Honest to God, did we go through *The Courtship of Eddie's Father, Steambath* and *Rich Man, Poor Man* just to do *The Incredible Hulk?*' He told me, 'Bill, Read it.'" After reading it, the actor was hooked. Bixby immediately realized the show's wide appeal. "We've all been with our ladies and [been] put down by someone and unable to do anything about it. We've all been in circumstances when we would say, 'God, I wish I had the Hulk in me just once!'"

Paul Brandon, Bill Bixby's agent, was the man who made him read that script. Brandon notes "that Bill was right about that. We were given the script and had a firm deadline [from Universal]. We had to give them an answer the next day, no later than ten a.m. Bill and I met at a little Bistro on Sunset Boulevard. We talked and Bill finally said, 'Okay, I'm leaving. Tell me what we're doing tomorrow about *The Incredible Hulk*.'

"When I thought about it more and more, I felt *The Incredible Hulk* was the right move. I said, 'Yeah, let's do it, let's do *The Incredible Hulk...*' That was it. I knew it would work, because comic-book characters were catching on; they were getting a big-budget *Superman* movie ready and that had quality people in it like (Marlon) Brando and [Gene] Hackman. I liked Kenneth Johnson and his *Hulk* script was really good — it was very serious and interesting. You really wanted to see what happened next while you were reading it," Paul Brandon states. "I knew that by doing *The Incredible Hulk*, it was a good way of changing his cache to give Bill a patina of interest [in fantasy]."

Brandon felt that "because of Kenneth Johnson, I knew the execution of the screenplay would be first class. I also thought the trend towards fantasy was going to be a big one — *Star Wars* actually came out the year we did the *Hulk* pilot, which proved that we were right to do it."

Once he had Bixby on board as Banner, producer/director/writer Johnson knew his Hulk was ready to go. "The network liked my idea for *The*

Incredible Hulk and they were very happy that I convinced Bill Bixby to come aboard. Bill Bixby, who I called 'Bix,' was a great guy, very smart. "Bix was my first and only choice for David Banner. I loved the performance I had seen him give in *Steambath*. He's amazing in that and he was just terrific as David Banner. Bill was as reluctant to do *Hulk* as I was," Kenneth Johnson opines. "If you're a serious actor and somebody

Any pain or stress to David Banner brings out his primal side, The Incredible Hulk!

hands you a script called '*The Incredible Hulk*,' you say, 'I'm not gonna do this childish crap!' But Bill read it and saw what I had done, which was leave the comic-book origins behind and take the core: a man struggling with this psychological problem."

Bixby "and I were great friends from the get-go," Johnson adds happily. "We also had many knock-down, drag-out arguments, but never about bullshit. It was always about character, storylines, etc. Our rule was whoever was right got to win."

At the time, Bill Bixby was mocked for doing *The Incredible Hulk*. Bixby told *The Chicago Tribune*, "At first, everyone was on my case, saying, 'You're doing What?!? Come on, Bill, after *Steambath*, *Rich Man, Poor Man* and [*The Courtship of*] *Eddie's Father*, you're going to do *that?*' They really got me mad and I said, 'Just watch the show.' There is something I knew up front: You hear the title *The Incredible Hulk* and it brings out the intellectual snobbery in the viewing audience, but most of all [in] the critics before they even saw it. We have overcome not only our title, but the negativism. What I love most about the show is that children are not afraid of The Hulk. They know."

Bixby told *Comics Scene* Magazine that by doing the series, "I definitely learned what working long, hard hours was about. Yet I also found playing David Banner was a major acting challenge. Here I was," Bixby explained, "playing somebody who was trying to suppress a primitive alter ego. At one point during the show's run, I became frightened because I thought I would run out of the capacity to keep dealing with Banner's problem. But I didn't, because Banner was a multi-faceted personality and exploring those facets always gave me the opportunity to stretch as an actor."

THE INCREDIBLE HULK

"Within each of us, oft-times there dwells a mighty and raging fury."

Airdate: November 4, 1977
Produced By Kenneth Johnson, Richard Milton and Craig Schiller
Directed By Kenneth Johnson
Written By Kenneth Johnson
Based on the character by Marvel Comics
Director of Photography: Howard Schwartz
120 minutes

Cast

Dr. David Banner . . . . Bill Bixby
Dr. Elaina Marks. . . . . .Susan Sullivan
Jack McGee. . . . . Jack Colvin
The Hulk . . . . .Lou Ferrigno
Mrs. Maier. . . . . .Susan Batson
Martin Bram . . . . Mario Gallo
Policeman . . . . Eric Server
Ben . . . . Charles Siebert
Young Man . . . . .Terence Locke
Mrs. Epstein . . . . Whitley Taylor
Man at Lake . . . . George Brenlin
Jerry. . . . . .Jake Mitchell
Minister. . . . . .William Larsen
Girl at Lake. . . . . .Olivia Barash
BJ Maier . . . . Eric Devon
Laura Banner. . . . . Lara Parker *(Uncredited)*

Out for a drive with his beloved wife Laura, the tire on David Banner's car blows out. The vehicle flips off the road. David is thrown clear, but poor Laura is trapped inside the burning car. Scrambling to her aid,

David cannot free her. As Banner unsuccessfully tries to open her door and pull her from the car, it explodes. Laura dies and David is plagued by nightmares of the accident.

Dr. David Banner tries to find a way to tap into that hidden strength some people get in their moment of need for a scientific study at The Culver Institute. Aided by Dr. Elaina Marks, a platonic friend he's known

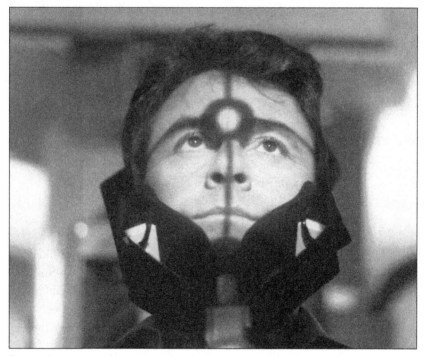

David Banner is about to make a terrible mistake.

since college, he interviews people who have gone through similar situations. Unlike him, however, they found the strength to save their loved ones. Tormented by this, Banner storms out. He and Elaina discover that Gamma Radiation may have played a part in triggering the power when it was needed.

Not content to wait for an answer, Banner uses himself as a guinea pig and gives himself a "Gamma injection." It's a much stronger dosage than he intended. Thinking he's subjecting himself to 300,000 units of Gamma radiation, he's actually been exposed to two million units, a sure-to-be-fatal overdose. He tries lifting a gurney to see if his strength has increased. It hasn't. Going home for the night, Banner sees that it's raining. "Terrific," he groans.

Driving home, his car suffers a flat tire after hitting debris in the road. Trying to change the tire in the downpour is nearly impossible. When Banner cuts his hand on the tire iron, he undergoes an amazing and bizarre transformation. His pupils turn white and dilate, his features become green, brutish and primal, his shirt and shoes rip apart as his rapidly expanding mass tear out of them. He is The Hulk, a large man-beast.

The Hulk gets shot.

Growling, he turns to the object of his ire, the flat, and flings the tire away. Turning to his car, he begins to beat on it, destroying the vehicle and hurling it off the road, before racing off into the night.

Wandering the countryside early the next morning, The Hulk approaches an idyllic lake. He startles a little girl fishing. She panics, and frantically takes her canoe into the middle of the lake to escape him. It flips and she's drowning, frantically calling for her father. To save her, the creature pushes a large tree into the lake for her to climb on. Misreading his intentions, her father shoots Hulk in the shoulder. In pain and fury, Hulk smashes the gun and hurls the father into the lake as well. Staring into the placid water, The Hulk is transfixed as his features soften back into those of David Banner. The scientist confides the incident to Elaina and requests her help in becoming human again.

"I want to be Dr. Banner, not Dr, Jekyll," David tells her. Unable to recall what he has done as the Hulk, Banner is terrified that he may have killed someone during his rampage. Elaina disagrees. She explains that "The creature is not a killer because David Banner is NOT a killer... The creature is an outgrowth of David Banner." Because Hulk comes from the nonviolent David, he wouldn't have murderous impulses either. David Banner is The Hulk, so The Hulk will not do anything that David Banner would not do. While The Hulk explodes into animalistic fury when provoked, he usually just throws his attacker a great distance away and destroys their weapon.

David is sealed in a thick pressure chamber in the lab, but does not change. Elaina decides to replicate the rainy conditions that were present during David's transformation. Sprinklers are set off to cover Banner like the night before to induce his change. Still, nothing. Once asleep, his REM readings jump off the charts during a nightmare over Laura's death. Banner Hulks Out, and the creature punches the chamber to pieces. As steam hisses, The Hulk confronts an astonished Elaina, before stomping off.

The next day, Police question Banner on the wreck of his car. Banner denies any knowledge and claims he gave the keys to a friend. Tabloid reporter Jack McGee also shows up, smelling a story about The Hulk. McGee confronts Banner and Elaina with a plaster cast of The Hulk's footprint. When they sarcastically ask if it's from Bigfoot, the unflappable McGee retorts that it's from a "Big Hulk, about seven feet tall. Greenish tinge to the skin. Pretty mean looking."

Later, McGee hides in a storage closet, suspecting Banner and Elaina know more about The Hulk than they let on. He accidentally knocks over a container that begins leaking a corrosive, volatile substance, but he doesn't notice it. Caught trespassing by David and Elaina, Jack McGee tells Banner, "Admit it, Doctor—you know something about that big Hulking creature that's been attacking people." David Banner says, "Mr. McGee, don't make me angry — you wouldn't like me when I'm angry."

Just as Banner throws McGee out, the lab explodes — due to the substance Jack spilled. "Elaina," Banner screams, as his pupils dilate white and the change begins again. McGee injures his leg in the blast which prevents him from seeing David Banner Hulk Out. The monster races into the blazing, crumbling building. McGee sees The Hulk carry Elaina from the burning lab, which explodes a final time.

"Banner," McGee gasps, as the lab goes up in an apocalyptic fireball. The Hulk takes Elaina into the woods.

Dying from her injuries, she looks up at The Hulk looming over her. "Oh God, my poor David...who will take care of you now?" She lovingly places her small hand on top of the creature's massive one. Elaina confesses to the creature, "I don't know if you can understand me, but I have loved you for such a very long time and I always will." She dies and her hand goes limp. The uncomprehending Hulk tries to lift her hand back up onto his, before realizing that he's lost her. He howls in mourning.

At the end, there's a double funeral for David Banner and Elaina Marks. As the service concludes, McGee, on crutches, tells a scientist friend of the deceased couple that he will find the creature who killed them. Jack McGee has done a cover story on The Hulk for his tabloid, *The National Register*. After they leave, Banner arrives, carrying a knapsack and ready to begin his life as a man on the run. He looks at both graves, then slowly touches Elaina Marks' headstone.

"I love you, Elaina, and although you never said it, I think you loved me, too," says Banner sadly. We realize he has no recollection of what she

Banner starts his life on the road.

told him when he was The Hulk. He slowly walks away from her grave toward a well-deserved series.

The Incredible Hulk pilot stood out from other genre shows and TV dramas in general by taking itself and its premise seriously. The pilot is smart, funny and touching. It's also unique in that there is no villain. While Banner changes into The Hulk three times during the TV movie, it's all from anger, stress and fear from the situations he's in, not an outside threat or violent attack. It's also admirable that Kenneth Johnson holds back The Hulk until he's firmly established David Banner as a character. He's unwilling to sacrifice storytelling for action set pieces. You like and sympathize with David long before Johnson exposes him to Gamma Rays. In contrast, the Edward Norton *Hulk* movie had Banner blasted by Gamma Rays before the end of the credits!

Jack McGee chases The Hulk to prove the creature's existence and catch it for causing the deaths of David Banner and Elaina Marks, a tragedy that he himself unwittingly committed. Because McGee accidentally spilled the chemical that caused the explosion, he's hunting Hulk for a disaster he created.

"McGee *causes* the death of Susan Sullivan's Elaina Marks," Kenneth

Bill Bixby and Lou Ferrigno in full makeup.

Johnson asserts. "My wife Susie was always intrigued by that. She said, 'It makes me crazy — he's chasing this guy because he doesn't know he's actually the one who caused it all!' I said, 'Yeah, Susie, that's called irony!' " Banner's relationship with Elaina is moving and, like his search for a cure, ultimately doomed.

"I am terribly proud of that first movie, the origin of The Hulk," Bill Bixby told Marvel's *Hulk Magazine*. "I believe that in the long run, the original movie itself will become a classic — a television classic. I really do believe that. One of the most moving moments that has been done so far, I feel, is when [Hulk] carries Susan Sullivan into the forest and away from the fire to help save her life, but she's already dying.

"She knows that Banner is inside the creature, but she also knows that he cannot hear her," Bixby mused. "Still, she tells the creature how she has always loved him, meaning Dr. Banner. The creature looks at her

and cannot respond, but he lays her down on the ground as she fin-
ishes her soliloquy, closes her eyes and dies. Then The Hulk, for some
unknown reason in his psyche, raises his head to heaven and bellows
out in anguished pain. The sensitivity of The Hulk is as important as his
strength. In fact, a great deal of his strength may be the fact that he is
sensitive as well as strong."

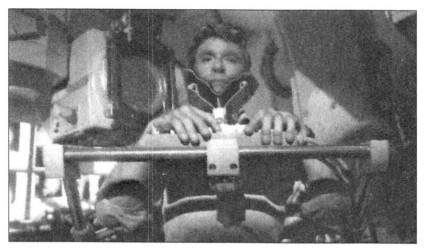

With the press of a button, Banner irrevocably alters his body
chemistry...and his life!

Kenneth Johnson believes one reason the show caught on is because
Bixby's Banner is a flawed hero. "He truly has problems; Banner's problem
before it became one of anger, was obsession. With the death of his wife
in the pilot, I wanted to draw the audience into his obsession. He could
not save his wife, so that fed his obsession to find out why he couldn't
and why other people could under similar circumstances.

"It makes your leading man immediately sympathetic and sets up a
romantic/sexual tension with our leading lady, Susan Sullivan, who played
his friend Dr. Elaina Marks," Johnson continues. "If you look at the pilot
carefully, you will see that he and Elaina never touch each other! There's a
couple times where she almost does, but then pulls her hand back, because
she knows it's not appropriate. He's still mourning his wife. As much as
she loves him, she cannot let it happen. The only time she touches him is
when he comes in wounded, after his first night out as The Hulk. He got
shot and she tends to him as a physician. Every time they try to touch,
something prevents them. When he's inside the hyperbaric chamber, he
puts his hand on the glass and she does, too, on the other side.

"They're touching, but not," Johnson points out. "The only time they ever touch is at the ending, when he's metamorphosized into the creature and carries her out of the burning lab as she dies in his arms. It's very poignant, sweet and human. I was trying to humanize The Hulk and get him away from his comic-book sensibilities and into the real world."

Jack Colvin as Jack McGee — the man who named "The Hulk."

In the telefilm, Banner intentionally exposes himself to Gamma Radiation, "to tap into the hidden strength that all humans have." Instead of the nuclear blast from the comics that accidentally turns him into The Hulk, Banner uses a Gamma Chair and literally bombards himself with Gamma Rays. This alters the character's whole outlook: Instead of being a victim of fate, Banner unwittingly turns himself into a monster, just like Dr. Jekyll did.

Kenneth Johnson is proud that "I changed it from the comic book where he's accidentally caught in a Gamma Ray blast. The only things I took from the comic book is that when he got angry, he turned into the creature, his name was Banner and Gamma Rays had something to do with it. That was it. I wanted to make it as personal a story as I could."

Despite this purported disdain for The Hulk's comic-book origins, Johnson's pilot is surprisingly faithful to Stan Lee and Jack Kirby's first issue of The *Incredible Hulk*. Both TV and comic-book Banners are scientists whose body chemistry is irrevocably altered by Gamma Rays, both have their first transformation at night and spend it wandering the countryside, both the TV and comic Hulks are wounded in the shoulder by a bullet on their first outing. Both Hulks also wear the tattered remnants of their shirts and both obtain their monstrous alter ego's name from a side character; McGee on TV, instead of a random soldier in the comic. McGee accidentally names his nemesis, when he tells Banner the owner of that footprint is a "Big Hulk."

"Yes," Johnson confirms, "as a matter of fact, Jack Colvin's character McGee is the one who names him 'The Incredible Hulk' in the pilot! If you read my original script, you would notice that the word 'Hulk' never appears outside of the title — only in Jack's mouth. In our scripts for the show, we always called The Hulk 'the creature.'"

The scenes in the Gamma Chair were shot in St. Joseph's Hospital in Burbank, the same hospital where Walt Disney and John Ritter died. An impressive POV shot of Banner going upside down in the Gamma Chair was obtained by Johnson attaching the camera to Bill Bixby's feet. There is also a cool shot in the lab, just before Banner transforms himself, where we see the Danger Button on the Gamma Machine in extreme close-up as ANGER. It became the first shot in the TV series' opening credits. "That's something I actually discovered at the Moviola when we were trying to put together the main title," Johnson says happily. "I saw the word DANGER and said, 'Wait a minute — the French word 'Dange' means 'Of Anger'; that's where 'danger' comes from! I discovered that shot in the editing room."

The pilot has several allusions to Boris Karloff's *Frankenstein*, the most obvious one being when Hulk meets the little girl by the lake. Unlike Karloff's creature, Ferrigno's Hulk actually helps the child.

HUNTING A HULK

Finding the perfect Hulk was also a challenge. When *The Incredible Hulk* started filming, Johnson had not yet hired Lou Ferrigno as his green juggernaut. "I actually cast Richard Kiel [best known as hit man "Jaws" from the James Bond movies] as The Hulk for the pilot and we shot a week's worth of film of him," Kenneth Johnson reveals.

"There's a shot of him looking down before he pushes the tree over to save the little girl in the lake and that is the only shot of Dick Kiel as the Hulk that remains in the pilot movie."

While Richard Kiel is tall and lanky, everyone familiar with the comic-book Hulk knows that he's a muscle-bound powerhouse and Kiel truly does not resemble the character. "That's true, but I really wanted an actor for the part of The Hulk," Johnson notes. "Kiel was a massive 7'2", but also an actor. While Dick Kiel is tall, he is *not* a muscleman. We looked at the dailies, and his Hulk wasn't really giving us the visual that we needed for the character. I had to call Dick and say 'Sorry,' because the network and studio both wanted us to re-cast Hulk and go with a muscleman. I was sorry, because I liked Dick and thought he was a wonderful actor."

Julie Orsatti, widow of *Hulk* stunt coordinator Frank Orsatti, remembers, "Frank was there when Richard Kiel was playing The Hulk. He said Frank Price's young son took one look at Kiel and said, 'That guy's not The Hulk! He looks fake.'"

"That's the story I heard as well," says Lou Ferrigno. "Frank Price's son saw Kiel and said 'That's not The Hulk!' His son read the comic book, so they did a nationwide casting call to find The Hulk. I was convinced that I

The first choice for Hulk, actor Richard Kiel. PHOTO BY PATRICK JANKIEWICZ

was born to play The Hulk. The key to The Hulk is his sensitivity *not* his inner rage. Bill and Kenny were nervous; they had to re-shoot half the pilot and they really didn't know if it was gonna work or not."

Dismissed as The Hulk, Kiel was more than happy to go. Richard Kiel recalls that "I was the Hulk, but only in part of the pilot that we shot. I can only see out of one eye; the other one works, although not very well. So, because of that, I had a really difficult time with the contact lenses that you had to wear as The Hulk. They floated the green contact lenses in my eyes with fluid, and the fluid then got absorbed by my cornea. When the first night of shooting was over, after all of the stuff of The Hulk turning green was done, they handed me a towel and a jar of paint remover and said, 'You're on your own, baby.'

"I had a brand-new Chevrolet Caprice convertible, candy-apple red with a white interior," Kiel groans. "The interior of my poor convertible got stained permanently green when I went home that night and every headlight and taillight I saw had multiple rings of rainbow colors around them, since my eyes had absorbed the fluid from those contact lenses.

"When I got home that night, I told my wife, 'We could really use the money from this *Hulk* thing, but I just can't do it.' What you really need after playing The Hulk is a little Japanese woman with a scrub brush. The body makeup covered everything–legs, feet, arms and face! It just wasn't my thing, but it was great for Lou Ferrigno, who is a terrific guy," the actor opines. "It gave him something to get out there with and he was great as The Hulk. It worked out fine all the way around; Lou became the Hulk and I got Jaws in my first James Bond movie that same year, *The Spy Who Loved Me*."

FINDING FERRIGNO

Before he hired Kiel, "I had already met with Arnold Schwarzenegger and Lou Ferrigno when I was looking to cast the role of the Hulk," Kenneth Johnson states. "Arnold Schwarzenegger just wasn't tall enough and I wanted an actor. Arnold's 5'10", but the creature is much bigger.

Lou Ferrigno's first appearance in the TV movie is his most iconic.

Arnold actually suggested that we talk to Lou, who is a 6'4" muscleman, so he really had the 'Hulk look.'"

Returning to his previous "potential Hulk" Ferrigno, Johnson concedes that "I have really got to hand it to Lou. He had never acted before, but he did a really great job. First of all, he's a trooper! Lou is deaf, but he worked really hard. He never gave us any trouble or bullshit, and in addition to getting the acting and makeup on, he also had to work out three hours a day so he would be pumped up as The Hulk when he was on camera. His performance as The Hulk got better and better as it went on. We are still close friends over 30 years later."

Having a deaf star did cause problems. "Yeah, particularly in the beginning," the producer/director agrees. "I remember burning down the lab at Universal's Stage 28, the *Phantom of the Opera* set, for the end of our first *Incredible Hulk* pilot movie. When the lab explodes, Lou had picked up Susan Sullivan and was tiptoeing gingerly through the fire at a snail's pace. I'm shouting at him, 'LOU, GO FASTER! FASTER, LOUIE, FASTER!,' but he has his back to me and it suddenly dawns on me, 'He's deaf!'

"We had to keep someone close to him, so they could just tap him on the shoulder to let him know when he needed to talk to me," Johnson explains. "I realized I didn't need a megaphone when I worked with him, but a magnifying glass so he could read my lips!"

"I didn't have any problems with Lou Ferrigno personally, he's a nice guy, but Lou is quite deaf," adds Alan J. Levi, who directed the second *Hulk* telefilm and several episodes of the series. "Because I grew up with a deaf grandmother, I was a lip reader, so if Lou and I had any problems communicating, he would read my lips and we'd work it out. Lou is a great lip reader—which is good, because when he was green, he couldn't wear his hearing aids at all. This meant you either had to shout at him or he'd have to lip read!"

BEING THE HULK

Considering this was Lou Ferrigno's first real acting role after appearing as himself in the acclaimed documentary *Pumping Iron*, he does an impressive job. When he approaches the father and daughter by the lake, you can see the creature's confusion as they panic at the sight of him.

Director Alan J. Levi feels "the key to the show's success is when David Banner became Hulk; you could still feel him *in* The Hulk. There were times where The Hulk felt terribly connected to whoever he was helping, he would look sad or happy, sometimes he would even cry. The Hulk would run from or toward problems, if it would help people. They made that connection with the audience."

The Hulk's connection to some of the people he saves—or tries to save— is never more apparent than at the end of the pilot film, when Hulk carries Elaina out of the blazing lab. To the monster's sorrow, she dies anyway.

"When I did the dying scene with Susan Sullivan, the entire crew was staring at me — because I had the contact lenses, wig, green paint and everything on," Lou Ferrigno marvels. "I look around, and I am saying to myself, 'Holy mackerel, I have never done this before!' Kenny Johnson said to me, 'Let it out, Lou, because you're in pain over her death.' I let it all out and it was a beautiful scene, like *King Kong* or *Beauty and the Beast*.

"As Susan Sullivan dies in my arms, Kenny said, 'I want you to let out a scream.' I had never howled in pain like that before and Susan Sullivan looked up at me and said, 'Just go for it, Louie.' So I just let everything out and screamed. As I was doing it, Kenny said he was amazed at how powerful it was. I was excited to get the part because I had been a huge Hulk fan," Ferrigno states. "I loved him, Spider-Man and The Fantastic Four. They saved my life when I was a kid, because I used to be into comics to help me overcome things in my life. Comic books provided an escape for me; they helped me fantasize and envision myself being one of their characters in real life, which I have since become."

"I identified with The Hulk because my life was so similar to his. Hulk had so much rejection," Ferrigno says quietly. "I got into weightlifting because I was very introverted as a child. Shortly after birth, I was robbed of 85% of my hearing. This gave me two things to overcome in my life, my hearing and my severe speech impediment. Learning to articulate in speech therapy, I got involved with stage production as a way to use my voice. That's why it was a triumph for me to finally do The Hulk's voice in the last movie."

DESIGNING THE HULK

In the pilot, Hulk has a Neanderthal look. With a giant sloping forehead, thick teeth, green skin, big eyebrows and wild, tangled green hair, The Hulk looks truly feral.

Kenneth Johnson's script describes Hulk in his first appearance as "A HUGE CREATURE. Photographed from a low angle stands where David Banner had been—the lightning silhouettes his enormous stature. The shreds of Banner's clothing hang from his frame. Illuminated by flashes of lightning, we see standing where David Banner had stood a man-beast who is over 7 feet tall. His face is reminiscent of primitive humanity. He emits the angry snarls of a huge animal. His white eyes glint demonically in the dark…"

This look was later softened up for the series. "Werner Keppler did a great job on Hulk's makeup design," Johnson praises. "I loved Werner's work on *Hulk*, *V* and *Alien Nation*. The Hulk may look more like a Neanderthal in the pilot, but I honestly don't remember sitting down and saying, 'Let's re-design the makeup.' It may have been Werner Keppler saying, 'I think we can make it look a little better if we do it this way' or 'I think I can get down to one prosthetic instead of three if we do it that way,' because when you're doing episodic television, you've got to do it as fast as you can!"

Lou Ferrigno stalks the countryside in slippers.

"I thought Hulk looked pretty much the same for the entire series," Johnson continues. "Werner might have altered the prosthetic slightly for ease and speed, but that's all. It was the damn wig we could never get right. Maybe the network thought he looked too scary... I don't ever remember saying, 'Gee, he looks too Neanderthal,' because that would have been okay!"

Lou Ferrigno happily confirms that "In the show's first season, Hulk was much more savage looking, almost primal in appearance. I enjoyed that look, but I didn't like the original forehead piece, because it was so thick, like a caveman. It was actually both Kenny and Bill Bixby's idea to give him a more sensitive appearance [in the later seasons]. They wanted him 'less monster, more creature,' but in the first episode, his forehead was very thick and his teeth were big.

"Hulk was more of a beast, but Kenny and Bill realized that when I was acting, the sensitivity came across. That's what made them change the contours of Hulk's face. They also cut back on the wig. When we first came on, *TV Guide* said 'The Hulk looks like he's wearing a Beatle fright wig and is very monstrous' — that's what convinced them to change his appearance. I think they also wanted me to look more like The Hulk does in the comic book."

"They applied my forehead and nose with speargum glue," Ferrigno adds. "They put grease [paint] makeup on me for the green instead of pancake and when I would perspire, it was really uncomfortable, because you couldn't breathe through the skin."

Makeup man Jim Scribner told *Us* Magazine in 1978 that giving Ferrigno thick wax Hulk teeth, a prosthetic brow and forehead, Hulk hair and green skin "is a miserable, drawn-out ordeal for Lou, but he goes through it with the patience of a saint."

The Incredible Hulk guest Brandon Cruz remembers "watching Lou and Bill go through the Hulk makeup during the episode I was on ("747"). I noticed what a long, painful process it was for both guys. My call time was 9 in the morning and theirs was 4 a.m., because they spent all that time getting into Hulk makeup. All that work for a few minutes of screen time, it was amazing."

Bill Bixby and Lou Ferrigno make *TV Guide*'s cover.

HULKING OUT

The pilot, and the television series that Johnson and Universal hoped to follow it, all depended on one simple thing — would the audience buy Bill Bixby mutating into a raging green Lou Ferrigno? How could he realistically depict the mild-mannered scientist growing into a Gamma-irradiated brute in 1977, when TV FX were still light years behind that year's film sensation, *Star Wars*?

This was decades before the awe-inspiring CG of the movie *Hulk, Jurassic Park, Iron Man, Lord of the Rings* and *Transformers* was available. It was also five long years before physical makeup special FX could even make a plausible werewolf transformation onscreen a reality in films like *An American Werewolf in London*. Still, Johnson figured out a way.

"Because of what we had available at the time, we had to do it like Lon Chaney, Jr., in *The Wolf Man*," Johnson shrugs. For David Banner's change into The Hulk, Johnson started with the eyes. "I wanted there to be some way to show the audience Banner was about to turn into The Hulk. I came up with Banner's eyes going white when he was about to

change. I wanted audiences to get excited and go, 'Here he con
his actual transformation was going to occur off-screen."

"The eye was the key," Johnson declares. "Once you saw the pupi
you knew Hulk was about to appear! That wasn't in the comic book, but
they have used it after me. I did that with his eye because I wanted a triggering mechanism to let the audience know he was changing."

When Bixby tested his Hulk Out lenses, Johnson realized "This show is
a hit!"

Ironically, seeing Bixby in his white pupils triggered a prediction
from the producer. "The day we were filming at the California Institute
of the Arts [which doubles as Banner's Culver Institute in the pilot], I
looked up and saw Bix walking down the hall toward me on the first
day. He had put the white eyes in for the Hulk transformation scene.
I saw him walking toward me wearing those white eye contacts and I
suddenly said, 'This show is a hit!' There's a photo of he and I grinning
like Cheshire Cats that was taken right after I said that! I think it was
that exact moment we both felt it was gonna be a hit. It's my favorite
shot of the two of us.

"My feeling that it would be a hit was also underlined the day we were
filming the scene in the hospital. We were doing the sequence where he

gives himself the Gamma Ray injection. I set up the camera for the close-up of Bix, where the crosshairs of the Gamma Machine line-up on his eyes. As I set up that shot, I said again, 'This show is a hit!'"

Because there was no way he could show Banner's hands elongate and enlarge with 1970s technology as they do in Hulk's comic-book transformation scenes, Johnson had to use old fashioned movie trickery

In the '70s, it was impossible to change Banner into The Hulk on camera like Herb Trimpe does here.

to plausibly depict the change on camera. He would show The Hulk's muscles ripping through Banner's shirt.

"On the pilot, I tried inflating dry scuba suits and lots of other stuff, but that all looked terrible. Just looked like crap. I had to do the best I could with the technology I had at the time. I tried a lot of stuff, before I finally just put a shirt on Louie [Ferrigno] that was much too small for him, weakened the seams and said, 'Swell Up, Louie!' It was low-tech, but effective!"

The transformation was done in a series of stages, adding makeup appliances onto Bixby for each phase of his change.

"First the contact lenses go in and I go before the camera," Bill Bixby told *Hulk Magazine*. "Then they add a forehead piece and change the color of my skin. It takes about an hour and a half in the makeup chair for that. After I have been filmed that way, they peel everything off and start from scratch again. The third sequence of the transformation is where my hair is turning green and my skin is getting even more green. That whole affair takes another two hours to put together. Finally, Lou takes over as The Hulk. His makeup takes two and a half hours a day to put on, and when it's all over, he must get into a shower and scrub it off his entire body. Most people don't think about that, but it's rough."

Bixby told the *Kansas City Star* his favorite fringe benefit of Hulking Out. "I'm pre-Hulk. He's the Hulk...When I turn into the Hulk, I get to go home."

"Banner would only Hulk Out twice per show because it was so expensive," Alan J. Levi points out. "The Bionic Woman could use her powers throughout the show, but on *The Incredible Hulk*, he couldn't, because destroying everything is really expensive!"

Lou Ferrigno says, "When we were shooting the TV show, people didn't think I was real! Some people even walked up and poked me, because they thought I was Bill Bixby in a jumpsuit full of air! They wouldn't believe I was real 'til they walked up and touched me."

They also used an in-between Hulk. Ric Drasin would portray the half-Banner, half-Hulk seen in the middle of thr transformation scenes. This freed up Bixby and Ferrigno to do their acting duties and to credibly show Banner's mass getting larger. "When David Banner would transform, I was the middle Hulk," reveals actor and World Wrestling Federation wrestler Ric Drasin. "They called me The Demi-Hulk, because I was halfway between Bill Bixby and Lou Ferrigno. Bill really hated wearing those contact lenses. They didn't bother me, because they used Opthane, which is liquid Novocaine for your eyes. You put 'em in and the Opthane lasts for about 20 minutes. I did scratch my eye putting in the contacts once..."

GREEN SLEEVES

Despite switching Hulks, three Hulk Outs, special FX, green paint, explosions and complex dialogue scenes, *The Incredible Hulk* TV movie was filmed in a brisk 18 days. Shooting the pilot "was incredibly difficult," Kenneth Johnson admits. "Not just because of the special FX and the

It took hours in the make-up chair to turn Lou Ferrigno into Hulk.
PHOTO COURTESY OF JOHN GOODWIN

fact that we had to replace our Hulk, but even keeping him green was incredibly hard. We tried all sorts of makeups and the only one that really worked had to be imported from Germany."

Hulk's green skin was provided by Kryolin Makeup #512, which the company later dubbed "Incredible Hulk Green."

"The Hulk makeup was waterproof, which was great, because he had scenes in the rain, but that also meant it wouldn't wash out and could only be rubbed off. For the pilot, the greatest difficulty was the makeup, which at the time was greasepaint; it just came off on everything. I still have shirts and jackets with green smudges on them over 30 years later," Johnson laughs.

"We spent around two million dollars on that pilot, which was a lot of money in those days. Most of that went to the makeup and the special FX, which were pretty challenging. We had to build things that Lou could destroy, but also could be re-built so he could destroy them again in the next take!" When The Hulk runs, Johnson films him in slow motion, which makes him seem even more monstrous and powerful.

CRASHING THE CAR

Banner's first transformation comes in the rain, as he's trying to change a flat tire. The sequence is so impressive it became part of the weekly show's opening credits. Bixby told reporters, "The very first time I Hulk Out, it's against an automobile and The Hulk winds up beating [it] to scrap. I can't imagine one driver who has not wanted to kick his car to oblivion." The first appearance of The Hulk in the telefilm is his most iconic appearance in the series. He's seen howling in a raging storm, back-lit by lightning, before smashing Banner's car. This is an appropriate "birth scene" for the monster and is shot like a comic-book panel come to life.

"That's one of my all-time favorite scenes on the show — Bill changing the tire in the rain, the arm ripping, and then me smashing the car," Lou Ferrigno notes. "It took a couple of weeks to film all that, with the car, the rain, the explosion and the shirt tearing, so I was pleased that it wound up in the opening of the show."

"I did that on the Universal backlot at one a.m.," he elaborates. "The explosion from the car went off, I burned my chest and they took me down to The Treatment Center on the backlot. I was lying down there, when Kenny [Johnson] came in and said, 'Hey, Lou, can we do the shot one more time?' So we went back and I did it! The last one was perfect, that's the take you see in the opening."

One of the interesting details is that when David Banner changes into the creature, The Hulk seems incapable of speech, he just growls and snarls like an animal. This works, because he seems genuinely inarticulate with rage. Most Marvel Comics' superheroes like Spider-Man, Iron Man, the X-Men and even Bruce Banner are intelligent, emotional characters whose thoughts are usually laid out for the reader in thought bubbles which provide a running interior monologue. The Hulk is not like them, and in the comics, frequently verbalizes his anger ("HULK Smash!") or confusion.

SOUND OF THE HULK

The Hulk's growling is provided by Ted Cassidy, the tall, 6'9" actor who played Lurch the butler on the popular sitcom *The Addams Family*. Cassidy is also *The Incredible Hulk* show's narrator, doing the iconic opening introduction when it became a weekly series. At the same time he was doing the opening narration and roaring for *The Incredible Hulk*, Ted Cassidy also used his deep baritone voice for the animated Thing on Marvel's *New Fantastic Four* cartoon and the radioactive reptile Godzilla on *The Godzilla Power Hour.*

When Ted Cassidy passed away during the show's second season, Ken-

Hulk's growling was provided by two different actors.

neth Johnson recruited frequent *Hulk* guest Charles Napier to provide the sounds of The Hulk's angry outbursts. Napier, a handsome tough guy, is a popular character actor best known as the leader of The Good Ol' Boys in *The Blues Brothers* and the unfortunate cop who becomes Dr. Lecter's goriest victim in *Silence of the Lambs*. Napier did an impressive job with the Hulk's inarticulate raging.

"Both Ted and Charlie have these great deep voices, so deep they sound like they come straight from the center of the Earth," the producer praises. "You start with those amazing voices and then pitch it lower in post so they just sound inhuman! Ted also did such a great job with that introductory narration, that whole 'Doctor David Banner, physician, scientist, searching for a way to tap into the hidden strengths that all humans have' opening. I saw no reason to change it when we lost him. It seemed a nice tribute to him to keep it on as it was.

"Charlie Napier, who'd been on the show a couple times, also had a great deep voice. Charlie was doing an episode, sounded really good and he came in to do Hulk's growls! Charles was great at doing Hulk's voice and he was always a good guest on the show. Even then, I would pitch his growls down so they didn't sound human. They were both great guys to work with."

Napier was amused to be the Hulk. "It was funny. When people ask, I tell 'em, 'Yep, I was the voice of the Hulk,'" laughs Charles Napier. "Ted Cassidy did it for the first season and when Ted died, Nicholas Corea

Left: Towering Ted Cassidy, seen here behind the stars of *Butch Cassidy And The Sundance Kid,* originally did the voice and narration for The Incredible Hulk. *Right:* Charles Napier took over as the sound of The Hulk with the second season. PHOTO BY PATRICK JANKIEWICZ

brought me in. Nic was a friend of mine and he was producing the show, so Nic calls me up one day and then asks me, 'Can you growl?'

"I said, 'What the hell are you talking about, Nic?' and he explains to me that 'We lost Ted Cassidy the other day and I heard your voice and I thought you might be able to do the voice of The Hulk.' I said, 'Oh hell, I guess I can growl.' I growled for him and got the job! To voice The Hulk, I would look at the screen and follow Ferrigno's expressions — some deep breathing, as well as growls when he got mad like 'Grrrawwwlurgh!' Stuff like that. I did that for four years!"

Eventually, he got screen credit. "Oh yeah, you better believe it," Napier grins. "We argued over that. I said, 'That's acting — it's the way that the Hulk talks.' It was hard to do, because when you growled for The Hulk, you had to do it for fifteen minutes at a stretch! I thought they would have to carry me out on a gurney when I did it the first time; it definitely took a lot out of you."

His secret for The Hulk's guttural howls and growls? "At the time I was a smoker, so that made it easy…I have given smoking up since," Napier adds. "But I can still do The Hulk!" Because of Hulk's voice and other sound FX, it took 14 days to dub *The Incredible Hulk* pilot movie.

Unlike his TV counterpart, the comic book Hulk could talk.

HULK TALK!

Lou Ferrigno "always wanted to do The Hulk's voice on the show. He talks in the comics and it's always very emotional. When you speak as The Hulk, you don't talk in complete sequences. The Hulk doesn't just growl, but what few words he can do, there's genuine emotion behind it."

Ferrigno eventually got his wish in doing the voice of The Hulk in an animated series and the Edward Norton/William Hurt *Hulk* film. One has to wonder: Why didn't The Hulk talk on the live-action TV series?

"Because in the comic book, 'Hulk Talk Dumb,' that's why I didn't want to hear that," Kenneth Johnson professes. "I thought that would have made it stupid. Louie Ferrigno came from Brooklyn. He would always ask me, 'Why doesn't The Incredible Hulk have more dialogue?' and I would say, 'Well, for one thing, Louie, he didn't come from Brooklyn!'"

"I felt The Hulk was better restrained by *not* talking. He just u.. have the skill of language; the most he could do was 'GRRRR!' If I wanted to keep it real, as soon as I had The Hulk start talking like Frankenstein– 'Fire bad, food good'?!?–oh, boy, what a slippery slope that would have been!"

Like Ferrigno, Hulk creator Stan Lee was unhappy about the monster's mute status. "I just wish he could have talked," Lee told *Pizzazz Magazine* in 1978, "One thing I've been saying is that on the TV show they should make The Hulk a bit more intelligent. Or, at least, we should get the feeling that he's trying to understand. In the comics, I used to refer to The Hulk's 'clouded brain.' But so far on the TV show, he's been treated as though he has no brain at all."

"Still," Lee continued, "if he didn't have some kind of brain, how would he know only to attack the bad guys? I'd like to see the TV Hulk try to speak. Ken Johnson, the show's producer, may be leaning in that direction, too. I just think it would be interesting if his IQ were raised a little."

"DON'T MAKE ME ANGRY. YOU WOULDN'T LIKE ME WHEN I'M ANGRY."

The pilot movie also introduced the legendary line where Banner cautions tabloid reporter Jack McGee to back off. Pressing Banner for the truth about The Hulk — who McGee correctly senses is connected to David in some way — Banner gives him a withering look and snaps, "Mr. McGee, don't make me angry. You wouldn't like me when I'm angry." Besides being in the opening credits for the Hulk TV show every week, the line has been quoted in numerous films, TV shows and cartoons.

"I do love that line," Kenneth Johnson confesses. "When I shot the line in the pilot, Bill Bixby has the big confrontation with Jack McGee, and he says it as Banner. For Take One, Bix played it angry, 'DON'T MAKE ME ANGRY — YOU WOULDN'T LIKE ME WHEN I'M ANGRY!' I said 'Cut cut cut,' then went up to Bix and whispered to him: 'Bill…*it's a joke*.'

"Bix said, 'Oh, okay, got it!' and he came back and did it. Take Two is the one that is in the pilot and seen in the main title. Of course, we the audience already know why you wouldn't like him when he's angry!" To Johnson's credit, The Hulk had been around for 15 years before the TV movie, but that line is now indelibly linked to the character, his best-known line next to "Hulk Smash." *TV Guide* named it one of the 100 Greatest Catchphrases of All Time. "I was flattered by that," says a proud Johnson.

You hear everyone quote the "You wouldn't like me when I'm angry" line, from Oscar-winner Jamie Foxx in *The Kingdom* to Homer Simpson and *Family Guy*'s Peter Griffin, as well as being uttered in films like *Click, Dogma, Fanboys* and both *Hulk* movies. On the modern *Battlestar Galactica*, villainous Tricia Helfer sneers, "Don't make me angry, Gaius. You wouldn't like me when I'm angry!" In the video

game *World Of Warcraft*, Male Worgen say "You wouldn't want to see me when I'm angry!"

How does he feel about other movies and TV shows paying tribute to his most iconic line over the years? "It's amusing and very flattering to see it pop up again and again," a pleased Kenneth Johnson observes. "I'm really proud of it; there's been a lot of life to that one line. To see Adam Sandler say, 'Don't make me angry' in *Click* and then he turns green? Wow. In *Dogma*, Matt Damon and Ben Affleck even named a character 'McGee' so they could use the whole line!"

As for the haunting quote seen at the beginning of the pilot, "Within each of us, oft-times there dwells a mighty and raging fury," Johnson smiles, "Oh, I think I might have just made up the quote. I don't know where else it would come from!"

Ironically, the quote predates Johnson's involvement. It first appeared on the back cover of *The Hulk On The Rampage*, a 1975 Marvel Treasury Edition reprinting old Hulk stories. On the back cover is a Herb Trimpe drawing of Banner changing into The Hulk, with the quote, "Within each of us, oft-times, there dwells a mighty raging fury."

SAD PIANO

The pilot also has the series' most iconic image…Bixby walking sadly away. The end of each episode would underscore the ongoing tragedy of Banner's life, with Bixby's unsung hero trudging down the road as a sad piano score plays over the ending credits. That haunting closing theme heard as Banner was hitchhiking out of town was Joe Harnell's "Lonely Man." The late Harnell, who also did the music for Johnson's series' *Bionic Woman, Cliffhangers, V* and *Alien Nation,* is best remembered for this song.

"I can't say enough about that music, because we took great pains to underline the pathos of the story when I sat down with Joe to talk about the music," Kenneth Johnson says. "Normally, at the end of Universal TV shows in those days, there was a big orchestral theme, 'Dum-dum-dum-Dah!,' and Joe started to write a score like that for the closing credits of *The Incredible Hulk.* I said, 'No, Joe, this is about a lonely man, a man alone. How about a solo piano? As long as it has a plaintive kind of feeling that underlines the inherent sadness of his situation.'

"We worked a lot on the piano. As he played different keys, I would say, 'How about this note instead of that one?' What we ended up with was a piece of music that has become as iconic as the show itself has. That music combined with Bix's remarkable performance and our writing made the show a breakout success. *The Incredible Hulk* is still the longest-running television show based on a comic-book and *Hulk* wasn't an iconic comic book; it had even been cancelled once or twice." *Hulk*'s record was broken by *Smallville,* which went 10 years — an amazing feat for a superhero show.

"The *Family Guy* cartoon people have a real jones for *The Incredible Hulk,* they make numerous references to it and frequently use the 'Don't make me angry' line. I loved when they ended an episode with Stewie the baby hitchhiking away to Joe Harnell's *Hulk* theme," Johnson praises. In the *Family Guy* episode "Wasted Talent," Stewie requests his pianist mother "play that sad walking away music from *The Incredible Hulk*!" and then the episode ends with the cartoon baby forlornly hitchhiking on a live-action highway, just as Bixby did every week.

The other great Harnell theme, "Growing Anger," was heard on the series when Banner reached the breaking point and is about to change. With its catchy pounding, Harnell cleverly based it on Russian composer Igor Stravinsky's "Rite of Spring."

HULK FACTS

His tombstone reveals his full name as "David Bruce Banner" — the only time we see Banner's true name from the comics.

Banner and Elaina's graves were shot in the Inglewood Cemetery.

The show's title is referenced in McGee's cover story for the *National Register:* INCREDIBLE "HULK" KILLS 2.

The Culver Institute is taken from Kenneth Culver Johnson's middle name.

Scotty, the gate guard at the Institute, was named after a beloved guard on the Universal backlot.

Olivia Barash (Girl by the Lake) starred in the '80s cult movie classic *Repo Man.*

The comforter on David and Laura Banner's bed is from Kenneth and Susie Johnson's own bed.

Elaina Marks is named after the show's editor, Alan Marks.

When McGee shows Banner and Elaina the Hulk's footprint, they glibly ask if it's Bigfoot. It actually was — that footprint was used in a *Bionic Woman* episode, "Return Of Bigfoot."

Eric Server (Policeman) was the voice of Dr. Theopolis on *Buck Rogers In The 25th Century* and a frequent guest on *The Incredible Hulk* TV series.

Director John Landis claims Universal Studios took his Chapman Crane away after the sixth day of shooting his classic *National Lampoon's Animal House* to use on the *Hulk* TV series. "That showed how important they thought our film was," says Landis.

The Michigan State Police website says the odds of you being "thrown clear" in a car crash like David Banner is by not wearing a seatbelt "is almost impossible. When you're thrown, you may be thrown through the windshield, scraped along the pavement or even crushed by your own vehicle."

HULK (A) SMASH!

The Incredible Hulk pilot garnered huge ratings, but did not immediately go into a television series. A TV movie sequel had already been commissioned. "We did that because Bud Grant, who was running CBS at the time, didn't think Hulk could make a series," Johnson says. "It actually took several meetings before we convinced him that an ongoing series would have any potential. I agreed to two TV movies, one of which would be the genesis of The Hulk and the other would show what an episode of the ongoing series would be like."

1970s television was not a conducive time or place for comic-book superheroes. The biggest genre TV hit of the '70s was *The Six Million Dollar Man*, which emphasized that a superhero did not need a spandex costume, but merely a track suit to thwart evil. This was probably a reaction against the Adam West *Batman* TV show of the 1960s, which embraced the character's costumed culture with a vengeance.

In the '70s, TV producers shied away from a superhero's look in the comics, lest they be accused of camp. Even a premise that should have lent itself to fantastic situations like *The Man from Atlantis* spent most of their episodes with Patrick Duffy as a man-fish from the fabled city, wandering around Los Angeles in a windbreaker.

Ghosts, monsters and robots weren't used until these shows were in dire ratings trouble and about to be cancelled. Then and only then would they give viewers these fantastic elements. Of course, they would desperately go overboard with the fantasy, after spending most of a series only grudgingly giving viewers what they wanted.

The networks even took characters famous for their costumes, like Captain America and Doctor Strange, and stuck them in jeans, muscle shirts or a '70s leisure suit, using whatever costume the characters had in the comics only sparingly. Captain America's mask was reduced to a half-assed motorcycle helmet that showed his face!

Ironically, Wonder Woman, the only comic-book character done faithfully on TV at the time, in her tiara, bulletproof bracelets and full red, white and blue garb, lasso and invisible plane, was an immediate hit. Hulk didn't need a costume, as his green skin and shredded clothes basically functioned as his "uniform."

Taking lively, interesting comic-book characters, stripping them of their quirks and putting them into routine crime shows where their personalities were muted, supervillains were banned and most of the situations were run-of-the-mill terrorists, gangsters or muggers, all but doomed the TV superheroes who showed up in the post-*Star Wars* boom-town of late '70s network TV.

The Amazing Spider-Man, which debuted on CBS the same time as *The Incredible Hulk*, was neither Amazing nor Spider-Man. The character lost his witty, acerbic personality and spent most of his time battling the usual kidnappers and robbers, even getting into car chases that any TV detective could handle. He hardly ever wore the red/blue tights and mask that he is best known for. *The Incredible Hulk* was different from all those loud, stupid shows. A quiet, sensitive and thoughtful series, it still managed to deliver action adventure. What made *Hulk* stand out is the way Kenneth Johnson took the premise seriously.

He tried to inject an earnest realism into the amazing concept. In the pilot and earliest episodes, when he changes back from The Hulk, David Banner is always exhausted, confused, dehydrated and quite thirsty, as you can imagine one would be after gaining and dropping that much body mass. His feelings of guilt and remorse after changing back to human are also realistic. When Banner changes back after his first night out as The Hulk, he mournfully says, "Oh My God, My God…" Little touches like this helped sell the premise to the viewing audience.

In *Pizzazz Magazine*, Stan Lee noted the Hulk's TV success. "In the *Hulk* series, they've been playing up The Hulk's character. They've been focusing on Bill Bixby who plays The Hulk's alter ego, mild-mannered David Banner and they have seriously probed the question: how do you live with the fact that you're the one human being on earth who peri-odically turns into a green-skinned monster? Of course, I'd play this characterization aspect up even more, make Bixby even more anguished."

Lee attributed the TV Hulk's appeal "to the fact that Bill Bixby's such a good, sincere actor, he makes you really care about the character. Also, there's something very exciting about Lou Ferrigno, who plays The Hulk." The pilot was actually released as a movie in Europe, where it became an immediate hit in cinemas.

"That was amazing," Kenneth Johnson chuckles. "My first *Hulk* was actually released in overseas movie theaters and became the top-grossing film for two months in France! Universal made a pot full of money from that, about seven or eight million dollars. A year later, I got a really pecu-liar check from the studio. I asked, 'What's it for?' They said, 'That's your share of the profits from *The Incredible Hulk*'s European theatrical release.' 'My share' of the eight million dollars was six dollars and forty cents!"

THE INCREDIBLE HULK: DEATH IN THE FAMILY

Alternate Title: *Return Of The Incredible Hulk*
Airdate: November 28, 1977
Produced By Kenneth Johnson
Directed By Alan J. Levi
Written By Kenneth Johnson
Based on the character by Marvel Comics.
Director of Photography: Charles W. Short
120 minutes

Cast

Dr. David Banner	Bill Bixby
Jack McGee	Jack Colvin
The Hulk	Lou Ferrigno
Juliet Griffith	Laurie Prange
Margaret Griffith	Dorothy Tristan
Michael	John McLiam
Sheriff	Mills Watson
Dr. John Bonifant	William Daniels
Denny Kayle	Gerald McRaney
Rafe	Victor Mohica
Phil	Robert Phillips
First Nurse	Ann Weldon
Second Nurse	Linda Wiser
Lab Technician	Roger Aaron Brown
Third Nurse	Janet Adams
Receptionist	Socorro Swan
Maid	Rita Gomez
The Cuban	Rick Garcia

David Banner is searching for a possible cure, when he meets Juliet, a crippled girl who is being slowly poisoned by Margaret, her evil, manipulative stepmother. As David gets involved in Juliet's problems, he finds that Margaret's sphere of influence includes local law enforcement and the town doctor. When she realizes that David is trying to help Juliet, Margaret wants him out of the picture.

David Banner gets that sinking feeling when he finds trouble again.

Banner realizes Juliet's only hope of survival is him getting her out of there, carrying her through a treacherous swamp full of quicksand and wild animals — something Margaret and her enforcers have no intention of letting him do. Hulking Out in the swamp, Banner manages to stop Margaret's evil plan, battle her henchmen, help a hermit cope with the loss of his only son, tackle an angry bear and even goad Juliet into walking again.

In the end, he undergoes a procedure that he hopes will rid him of The Hulk forever. Banner has no idea whether it worked or not — the question will only be answered the next time he gets angry. The sad scientist hitchhikes out of town.

Because there had not been a successful fantasy series outside of *The Six Million Dollar Man* and *The Bionic Woman*, CBS did not immediately green-light *Hulk* into a series. *The Incredible Hulk: Death In The Family* sets up the show's *Fugitive* paradigm: David Banner, trying to rid himself of The Hulk, finds himself enmeshed in the problems of others. He's able to solve Juliet's problem, but not his own, which is why the ending is ambiguous over whether David has been cured or not.

"There were two pilots for *The Incredible Hulk* and Kenny wrote both of them," explains the second film's director, Alan J. Levi. "The first pilot was the creation of The Hulk. The second two-hour movie answered the question, 'What is The Hulk gonna do in a TV series every week?' That was the one I did with Laurie Prange. CBS took a look at both of them and said, 'Okay, we now understand what the series is about.' Till then, the network truly did not understand what this *Incredible Hulk* series was gonna be about!

"They actually kept saying to Kenny, 'Tell us what this series is gonna be — This green man can't keep running all over the place!' So Kenny said to them, 'Let me make two movies and I will show you what the series is about.' That was it; they both got huge ratings. The second *Hulk* pilot was action-packed and we shot it everywhere. We shot it at Lake Piru, Indian Dunes...Indian Dunes also had a forest, which is where we shot The Hulk and Laurie Prange being hunted and it looked great, just great."

Female lead Laurie Prange is excellent as the frail, but emotionally strong Juliet. "Laurie was so obvious for that part because she is so immediately sympathetic and we wanted that kind of character for The Hulk to play off of in his first ongoing adventure," Alan J. Levi explains. "Laurie was adorable, but she was more than a little afraid of Lou! Laurie is like a little doll and Lou had to grab her and climb out a window from the second floor! They had stunt doubles, but they had to do the close-up climb themselves!"

"Lou really had to climb out the window with her and she was trembling. I said, 'Would you like a Valium?'" Levi remembers. "She said, 'N-no, I'm f-f-fine!' Laurie was really just scared stiff, the poor thing. Lou Ferrigno first carried her out without any makeup on to show her he could do it, and then she started to worry she would slip out of his grip because the makeup was slippery. Lou was great, he didn't drop her."

The highlight of the second pilot is The Hulk's skirmish with the bear in the swamps. For the first time in the show's history, he has an adversary who can match him pound for pound and they have an impressive fight.

Hulk himself also has a unique memory of his bear battle. "I remember that I had to go into the water with this bear," Lou Ferrigno shrugs. "The bear and I go underwater for a few seconds, then we would come up at the same time. It was a difficult scene, because it was a fully grown bear, seven feet tall. So we would go into the water, go under and come up. When we came up, the whole crew started laughing. I didn't know why, but it turned out to be two things. My wig was floating in the water and the bear's face was all green! The poor bear licked all the green paint off my face!"

Alan J. Levi loved shooting the scene. "The Hulk and this bear are supposed to have a savage fight and then Hulk is gonna throw the bear, but the bear just decided he wasn't gonna fight. All that bear really wanted

Laurie Prange in Lou Ferrigno's arms.

to do was just sit there and lick Lou Ferrigno's face, so that fight took quite a few takes!"

Ironically, Hulk grappling with the bear "was really hard to do," Kenneth Johnson groans, "only because Pooh — that was the bear's name, believe it or not — loved the makeup. He would just lick and lick the makeup off Lou and every time Lou hugged him as The Hulk, green makeup would go all over the bear!

"At that point on *The Incredible Hulk*, we were still using greasepaint for his green skin. Pooh was a very friendly bear. In the same show, Laurie Prange plays a crippled girl being carried by Lou through a swamp. She wears pajamas and we had 24 changes of that outfit for her."

Alan J. Levi found "Some days where we had to stop shooting because we ran out of clean clothes for her! Anytime anybody touched Lou, they came away green. The hardest part about the original pilot and this one was the makeup, which at the time was greasepaint that came off on everything."

After their battle, it was time to hurl the bear. "We had to put a [dummy] bear into a catapult and I remember, the first time we threw him, he only went five feet," Levi laughs. "For the next take, they over-stressed the catapult and that damn bear went flying!"

BIONIC BEAR

The fight with the bear led to a rare conflict between Johnson and Hulk's creator Stan Lee. "I like Stan, although we had some disagreements early on," Johnson concedes. "It came to a head when I did the second *Hulk* screenplay, 'Death in the Family.' I wrote that scene where the Hulk fights with a bear, because I was always looking for worthy adversaries for The Hulk.

"I sent the scripts to Stan as a courtesy. He called me up to say, 'I love the scene with the bear, but it's gotta be a *robot* bear!' I said, 'No, Stan.' He asked, 'Why?' 'Because an audience will only give you so many buys. They will only 'buy' so much. We're asking them to make a really big buy — that Bill Bixby metamorphoses into a big green Lou Ferrigno. That's a huge fucking buy! I have pushed the audience a major step. You add a robot bear to it and you've gone over the top; adults will walk away, saying, 'Sorry, I just don't buy it.'

"Stan said, 'But I don't understand...You had a Bionic Bigfoot on *The Six Million Dollar Man*, so why can't we have a robot bear...?' I said, 'On that show, you're living in a world of bionics. To create a robotic character there wasn't really a stretch, because they weren't too different from our bionic people. Here, David Banner lives in the real world and a robot bear would be one buy too many.'"

RED RAGE

One important disagreement that Stan Lee won was the color of the character. Johnson wanted to make the Hulk *red* instead of green! "Well, sure — he should be red...The color of rage is red, not green — what is he, the Envious Hulk?" the producer jokes. "Stan wasn't upset about it or anything; he just said to me, 'The Hulk is green.' I said, 'Stan, why did you make him green?' He said that The Hulk started out gray and he couldn't maintain the color throughout the first comic. The printer who actually printed the comics, told him, 'I think we can give you a pretty consistent green' so Stan said 'Okay.'

"I said, 'Gee, Stan, that's not really too organic and doesn't make a lot of sense.' Stan said, 'It worked at the time and we were flying by the seat of our pants!' So, unfortunately, I was stuck with the green skin. I tried to make him red because I was trying to get him away from comic-book land."

Stan Lee smiles mischievously. "Everyone knows The Hulk is green. I love Kenny, he's a great guy and he did a wonderful job on *The Incredible Hulk* — but if he had made Hulk red, I would have had to kill him!"

As with the pilot, there are more nods to Boris Karloff's *Frankenstein*, the most obvious one having Hulk befriend a hermit.

RAGING SPIRIT

To set up the premise for the second *Hulk* TV movie, actor Ted Cassidy did a voiceover announcing, "Dr. David Banner: physician; scientist. Searching for a way to tap into the hidden strengths that all humans have. Then an accidental overdose of Gamma Radiation interacts with his unique body chemistry. And now when David Banner grows angry or outraged, a startling metamorphosis occurs. The creature is driven by rage and pursued by an investigative reporter. An accidental explosion took the life of a fellow scientist and supposedly David Banner as well. The reporter thinks the creature was responsible. A murder which David Banner can never prove he or the creature didn't commit. So he must let the world go on thinking that he, too, is dead, until he can find a way to control the raging spirit that dwells within him."

This was another nod to *The Fugitive*, where equally deep-voiced actor William Conrad did that show's *noirish* opening. 'The name: Dr. Richard Kimble. The destination: Death Row, State Prison. The Irony: Richard Kimble is innocent. Proved guilty, what Richard Kimble could not prove was that moments before discovering his murdered wife's body, he saw a one-armed man running from the vicinity of his home. Richard Kimble ponders his fate as he looks at the world for the last time, and sees only darkness. But in that darkness, fate moves its huge hand."

LOU FERRIGNO (Hulk): *"I remember, we were filming on the backlot of Universal Studios, I had the contacts in and I had to carry Laurie Prange down from the house and run into the woods. Director Alan Levi wanted me to do a practice run. I just started running through the woods carrying Laurie.*

I did a long run with her in my arms. With all the trees and a girl in my arms, I felt like Tarzan!

"*I was holding her and she was so small and light, it was fun. I was a little uncomfortable in the green greasepaint makeup and wig, but she felt really good to hold onto. Laurie's a very pretty girl and a lot of fun to be around — the only bad side was every time I carried her, I kept turning her green! Laurie was a sweet lady. The hardest scene was where I was in the quicksand and she has to pass me a tree branch to save me.*

"*The scariest thing I ever did on* The Incredible Hulk *was jumping off the roof of that house! In the second movie, I had to pick up Laurie and jump off. It was on the second floor and about 30 feet up. They had this big fireman's net for me, and I had the contacts in, so when you have the Hulk eyes in, you have to look straight ahead. When you jump into an airbag, you need to keep your legs in front of you.*

"*I had a stuntwoman in my arms doubling for Laurie. I was hesitating, when Bill [Bixby] walked over to me and said, 'The show's gonna be a hit, so jump…Jump! JUUMMPPP!' I almost wanted to cuff him! When I jumped, I couldn't see ahead of me and I made a nice landing, but I was really shaking; I was scared as hell…Thank God they got Manny Perry!*"

MANNY PERRY (Stunt Hulk): "*Louie wasn't a big fan of heights. I heard that when he had to do the jump on the second movie, it was the wrong jump. When you jump, a lot of people, out of inexperience or fear, like to go to their feet for security, rather than lying out front and back. That's how you get hurt.*"

JULIE ORSATTI (Widow of Stunt Coordinator Frank Orsatti): "*Bill Bixby and Frank Orsatti looked alike, although Frank was a little more built. You could always tell when Frank was doubling Bill in running scenes because Frank was pigeon-toed! David Banner was always pigeon-toed in chases and fight scenes because of Frank.*"

DOROTHY TRISTAN (Margaret Griffith): "*I was Laurie Prange's evil stepmother on* Hulk. *Bill Daniels played an evil doctor who was helping me. We had one line that neither of us could get out! My line was 'That must be the creature that the sheriff was looking for!' Every time I tried to say it, we just broke up. We did like 10 takes, because it was such a ridiculous line!*

"*It was fun watching Lou kick down the house! The first day I was there, I didn't know Lou was hearing impaired. I saw this big guy painted green walking ahead of me. Everything on the set was painted green, the garbage cans; the ashtrays were all painted what they called 'Hulk Green.' I saw this green sand can with a handle, so I picked it up, caught up with him and said, 'You forgot your purse, Sir' and he just looked at me. I said, 'Oops, I'm sorry if I offended you!' and somebody explained, 'He can't hear you.'*

"I got the part on Hulk *right after my husband [film director John Hancock] and I were fired off of* Jaws 2, *so I was still traumatized. I found it easy to be the bad stepmother! Bill Bixby was very nice. He said to me one day, 'Are you*

Dorothy Tristan and William Daniels see the creature The Sheriff was looking for!

angry with me, Dorothy?' and I said, 'No, not at all, Bill…It's just this Jaws 2 thing.' Losing Jaws 2 *was tremendously awful for us; it's Hollywood, after all. A costume designer on* Jaws 2 *also did my* Incredible Hulk *and I heard him say, 'I'm surprised they even let her on this lot again!' I really appreciated Kenneth Johnson hiring me and always wanted to thank him, for bringing me in when Universal was actively trying to destroy us."*

HULK FACTS

We see Hulk jump, one of his most impressive powers in the comics.

William Daniels (Dr. John Bonifant) would be a TV superhero in his own right as the voice of K.I.T.T. the talking car on the '80s incarnation of *Knight Rider.*

As noted, Dorothy Tristan and her husband, director John Hancock, had just been relieved of writing and directing duties on *Jaws 2*. They later made the film *Weeds*, with *Hulk* guest star Ernie Hudson and *Hulk* movie star Nick Nolte.

Laurie Prange (Juliet) would return as a different character with a handicap in *Hulk*'s fourth-season opener, "Prometheus."

Mills Watson (Sheriff) got mauled to death by a rabid St. Bernard in *Stephen King's Cujo* and played Claude Akins' clumsy sidekick Perkins on *The Misadventures of Sheriff Lobo*.

The first of Gerald McRaney's four *Incredible Hulk* appearances.

In 2008, Marvel Comics finally added a red-skinned Hulk. An enemy of the good Hulk, the red-tinged rampager is known as "Rulk"!

LAURA BANNER

Lara Parker played Laura Banner.
PHOTO BY PATRICK JANKIEWICZ

Although she dies in the first minutes of the pilot, Laura Banner looms large over the series. A stunning woman with high cheekbones and bright eyes, actress Lara Parker brought Laura to short, vivid life. As Laura Banner, David's beloved wife, it's losing her that makes him crash through the barriers of science and turn himself into a walking time bomb of monstrous rage. Laura has a posthumous popularity, with David mentioning her in all five seasons of the series. There are also flashbacks of the doomed Laura in several key episodes.

Director Johnson uses a lot of yellow in Laura Banner's scenes, "because it's warmth, like the sun — we see David lose that warmth when Laura dies," he explains. Because of this and her scarcity of screen time, she had to be indelible. To Lara Parker's credit, she is. The impressive Parker already had a cult following, thanks to her role as Angelique, the devious witch, on TV's *Dark Shadows*, as well as co-starring in the B-movie classic *Race with the Devil*. Lara Parker's red hair is dyed brownish blonde in this, probably to fit her character's sunny demeanor.

In later episodes, David reminisces about Laura Banner and reveals that she was a fellow scientist. "Okay, I didn't even know that I was a scientist," Lara Parker laughs. "All I knew is that I was Bill Bixby's wife in the pilot. They filmed Bill and I doing a bunch of cute couple things together, like kissing, crying, cooking and fishing." An impressed Kenneth Johnson says, "It was amazing to see Lara really throw herself into the middle of all these big emotional scenes, she pulled it off beautifully…"

Being married to Banner was a thrill for the performer. "I have always been very proud of the fact that my death is what causes him to become The Incredible Hulk," Lara Parker says coyly. "He literally turns himself into that monster because he misses me so much — I loved that!"

Although losing poor Laura is the reason Banner becomes obsessed with strength derived from Gamma Rays, "I was not credited for the part, which I have never understood to this very day," the disappointed actress frowns. "It has always puzzled me, because I didn't request that I *not* get screen credit. Not giving me a 'guest-starring' credit in that first TV movie makes it look like I'm just an extra in it. I would have been happy to have gotten a credit on *The Incredible Hulk*–are you kidding? The show was a big hit!"

"I really don't know how that happened," a puzzled Kenneth Johnson states. "Lara did a great job on the show. She should have been given credit."

HULK PROFILE

OLIVIA BARASH, HULK'S FIRST RESCUE!

As the Girl by the Lake, actress Olivia Barash has the distinction of being the very first person saved by The Incredible Hulk. The Hulk comes across Olivia Barash and her father's campsite.

Barash is the very first human Hulk comes across. She's a terrified little girl who panics at the sight of the green monster. Trying to flee him, she takes her canoe into the lake. It tips and she begins to drown. Hulk pushes a tree in to save her but is shot in the shoulder by the girl's father, who wrongly thinks he's attacking his daughter. A fixture in cult movies like *Repo Man, Doctor Alien* and *Tuff Turf*, where she co-starred with future Iron Man Robert Downey, Jr., Olivia Barash has fond memories of working with The Hulk as a child.

"Doing that pilot for *The Incredible Hulk* was funny. We shot that somewhere in the Malibu Canyon wilderness, at a lake. I had never seen The

Although afraid of Hulk, Olivia Barash becomes the first person he saved.

Hulk in live action, but I knew what he looked like from the comic books and cartoons. Of course, I wasn't prepared for how he would look in person," Olivia Barash says sheepishly.

"Instead of meeting the actor Lou Ferrigno before he went into makeup, we go right into the scene and they just brought him out as The Hulk! In full green makeup and wig. I was a little 10-year-old girl, so I really got scared! I was just terrified of him. Lou was hard of hearing so he talked funny and looking like that, I thought he *was* a monster! If my acting was realistic in that scene, it's because I really *was* scared!

"They also had me fall in the lake repeatedly and would dry me off to go in again. They didn't have a change of clothes for some reason. They would just throw me in the lake, get me out, dry me off and have the hair person blow-dry my hair to go again. While I was doing this again and again, one of the stagehands leaned over and said to my Mom, 'You know what the nickname for this lake is? *Polio Pond!*' They had been filming there for years and years and they said it was really diseased, but, thankfully, I didn't get sick.

"The guy playing my dad was sweet. I think we did all our scenes by the lake in two days. I was a fan of the *Hulk* TV show after I did that. I had loved Bill Bixby from *The Courtship of Eddie's Father* and I thought *Hulk* was cool…I was into it. I was also excited because I got to meet Bill Bixby at the cast and crew screening of the pilot."

The lake scene is also where Kenneth Johnson decided to let his first choice for Hulk, Richard Kiel, go and use Lou Ferrigno instead. "Was there another actor as The Hulk in my scene? I only remember working with Lou Ferrigno," Barash muses. "That's weird, though, because I vaguely recall that there may have been a second, taller Hulk. By the end of the second day, after he had been saving me from drowning in take after take, I realized Lou Ferrigno was a nice man — not a monster — and he was very sweet. He liked kids and we got along great."

Barash was impressed that "Kenneth Johnson and the crew were very nice to me, but everyone was kind of tense because it was a big action scene. There must have been a stunt double for me, but I did most of my own stunts. I was the only kid on the set and the water was pretty deep. When I auditioned for it, I told them I could swim because that was required for the role. I did the lines for the scene and I got the part! I thought it was cool that I was the very first person to meet The Hulk — that's kind of a big deal…

"The director, Kenneth Johnson, told me my scenes would be a little bit like when the little blonde girl meets the Boris Karloff monster in *Frankenstein*. I actually knew about that because when I did a *Little House on the Prairie*, I did two episodes as a girl named Sylvia who gets raped on the prairie and that director also mentioned the same exact scene from *Frankenstein*. I was literally playing with flowers in that, so that's an ongoing theme in my career!"

Her scenes with The Hulk were immortalized in an *Incredible Hulk* photo novel that Marvel Comics released. "Oh, I was amazed to be in that *Hulk* photo book! I wonder if I was supposed to get paid for it. Believe it or not, I haven't seen my *Hulk* in ages! I rented it when it came out on DVD and then forgot to watch it."

"I'm a producer now," Olivia Barash says contentedly. "I work with filmmakers like Jennifer Lynch. I am doing two films right now — *One*

Lucky Dog, about dog racing, and *The Bride Of El Charro*, which is a sequel to *The Curse Of El Charro* and stars Danny Trejo!"

HULK PROFILE
LAURIE PRANGE, DAMSEL IN DISTRESS!

Pale and pretty, Laurie Prange is a character actress who has guested on various classic TV shows, including *Kung Fu, Gunsmoke, Murder, She Wrote, TJ Hooker* and more. The petite, fragile-looking actress specialized in damsels in distress. She inhabits a special place in *Hulk* history: Prange starred in the series' second TV movie, *The Incredible Hulk: Death in the Family*, and returned as a new character in the show's fourth-season two-part opener, "Prometheus." Broken up for syndication, that meant she starred in four episodes of the show, one of the only guests to do that many. Putting her in the arms of the giant green Ferrigno made her look like a porcelain doll.

"I'm really proud to be linked to *The Incredible Hulk* TV show," Laurie Prange enthuses. "I'm happy for Ken Johnson that the show made such an impact — that series really was his vision. A terrific group of people were behind the *Hulk* TV series and they all had a great attitude. Ken Johnson had put his heart and soul into the series, that's what I remember the most about the show. Ken had a strong vision and something important to say.

"*The Incredible Hulk* was entertaining, but Ken got his point across with metaphors. You don't see that a lot on television. I feel doing a genre show with a message really elevates you. Ken wrote all four of my episodes. I felt an obligation and responsibility to make sure that he was pleased. Ken was very specific about what he wanted — he really wanted his vision fulfilled. He was the leader of that whole crew."

Prange plays two different women overcoming handicaps on *Hulk*. In the second TV movie, *Death in the Family*, she's Juliet, a crippled survivor who David Banner helps to overcome her fear and realize that she can actually walk again. For "Prometheus," she's Katie, a self-pitying, recently blinded violinist who befriends David, after he has transformed into a monstrous half-Hulk/Banner hybrid.

"In real life, I'm pretty resilient," the actress insists, "but I have this look that makes people think I'm fragile and will fall apart easily! I have played a lot of victims and I always try to find dimensions to them. I was really flattered when I landed the second *Hulk* TV movie that they did. I have four brothers, so I was already aware of who The Hulk was when I went in for the part. I had not seen the first *Hulk* TV movie when I did it, because I had just finished a short-lived Broadway musical from Hugh Wheeler, the man who wrote *Sweeny Todd*."

She was fond of the series' David Banner. "Bill Bixby was a sweetheart to me. I have nothing but good memories of him. Bill was very kind, caring and concerned. Working with Bixby was great; I really got along with Bill. Everybody called him 'Bix.' He was a very funny prankster —

Lou Ferrigno carries Laurie Prange.

Bill was so much fun. He was also a kibitzer. He came up to me wearing his Hulk Out contact lenses in his eyes and he goes, 'Rarrr!' I remember him teasing me when I went off by myself to get into character. Bill told me, 'You don't have to really feel it — it's acting! Just do it, just act.' There was a truth to that, but I like to transform and get into the psyche of the character.

"I remember they were lighting Bill and me for a scene when we heard that Elvis (Presley) had just died. Bill knew Elvis and I remember him saying what a shame that was and a sad waste. On the second *Hulk* that I did, in the show's fourth season, I found Bill very vulnerable. He had gone through a personal tragedy between the first *Hulk* I did with him and the second one. My heart went out to him. I had lost a brother in Vietnam, so I knew what that pain is like. We discussed that. I was only there for the weeks that we filmed and he asked me back on the show, which flattered me. He also had me audition for other things he directed that I wasn't quite right for."

She and the actor shared their personal grief over the loss of family members. "Whether it's parents losing a child like Bill did or a sibling losing a brother like me, it's very hard. I could feel his pain. We had a conversation and I mentioned specifically how it was for me and my parents losing my brother. Bill and I mutually acknowledged how horrific it was because life is so precious. It's really amazing to have our lives and we never know when that's it. You don't know what's gonna happen, so you wake up in the morning every single day and seize the day."

...And Bill Bixby carries Laurie Prange.

Prange remembers, "On the night we finished shooting 'Prometheus,' Bill Bixby gave me a hug and he just started crying. It was such a personal moment; he thanked me for being on the show. I choke up now just thinking about it. It was right after we shot the last scene.

"It was a wrap, I went out to my car and Bill said, 'Laurie...?' He came up, hugged me and said, 'Thank you for being on the show.' It was sad. I am moved just thinking about it — Bill was such a sweet man," she says, wiping away a tear at the memory.

During the shoot, when she came face to face with a green-skinned Lou Ferrigno for the first time, "I was amazed," Laurie Prange giggles. "He was huge and by 'huge,' I mean HUUUGE! I felt like I was in the arms of a flesh-covered 747 — he was just so...*huge*. Lou was so sweet. Here was this combination of this massive, hard-muscled specimen who could easily kill you if he wanted to, but he was as gentle as a lamb."

Doing stunts on the show "was amazing! I have done shows where I hung out of a sixth-story building and been around fire, but I really was amazed and impressed with what Lou Ferrigno would do. He was a

˻uct of that show, so I would watch him and think, 'Oh, my God — don't get hurt!' Even though he was huge, I really worried for him! That's probably the key to his Hulk's appeal. On my first *Hulk*, I was in a bed. Lou had to bust down a wall, come in, pick me up and carry me out. I remember lying on the bed after Lou was told exactly where he had to hit the wall so it would shatter and then I hear BAM! BAM! BAM! This continuous pounding, as Lou tried to knock that wall down! The wall wasn't rigged right, but Lou sure tried. Given 10 more minutes, he probably could have done it!

"I was carried by both Lou and Bill Bixby. Bill made little jokes that would make you laugh. When he carried me, he pretended to stumble. When Lou picked me up in his arms, it literally felt like when a 747 lifts you up! When Bill Bixby carried you it was bumpy, but when Lou carried you in his giant arms, it was effortless, you felt like you were floating! That was a wonderful feeling. My God, he is a massive man.

"On my first *Hulk* episode, I had 27 pairs of the same pajamas, because when Lou carried me as The Hulk, he would get them all green. A hornet went into my pajama pants and started stinging me — it kept stinging me. Everybody screamed, 'Take off your pants,' but I couldn't, I was too modest!

"We shot the second TV movie, *The Incredible Hulk: Death in the Family*, in two or three weeks. I had no idea that the show was gonna be such a hit. For years, people would come up to me and say, 'Omigosh — you're the little crippled girl from *Hulk*!' As a matter of fact, after doing my first *Hulk*, I was in Europe, at the opera to see Placido Domingo in *La Traviata*. After the opera, the singer John Denver walked right up to me and said, 'Excuse me, but my kids noticed you from across the room and they are huge *Incredible Hulk* fans.' That was a sweet moment, because his kids were smiling, excited to see me, while I was thrilled to meet John Denver!

"Dorothy Tristan played my wicked stepmother and she was actually very nice. She was an actress and screenwriter who had just come off of *Jaws 2*. Dorothy talked about that with others on the set, not with me. I was just this little actress, but it was mentioned on the set by the crew."

Every time she did the show, it was a new experience. "You never knew what to expect," Prange grins. "The next time I guested on *The Incredible Hulk*, it was in its fourth season, so I'm drowning in a dam when Banner saves me. We shot that off Tujunga, at Hansen Dam. Most of 'Prometheus' was shot in the woods behind the Magic Mountain amusement park.

"I'm drowning in quicksand on my first *Hulk*, but that was on the backlot of Universal Studios. The quicksand felt like talcum powder! The quicksand was my favorite scene of any of my *Hulks*; because I actually got to save The Hulk! 'Prometheus' was a better part for me, as the blind girl. I tried not to make her too filled with self-pity. In my own life, I have a low tolerance for self-pity! There are true victims in this world, so I have little patience for people who label themselves victims.

In her first *Hulk,* she's menaced by a brown bear. "Boy, do I remember that bear — he was a really big bear, but also a very gentle bear. They actually felt the bear was much gentler than they wanted him to be! The trainer had to make him seem meaner. I will say — when the bear actually stood up on his hind legs, he was pretty scary. During the Hulk/bear battle, I laughed so hard when Hulk threw the bear! I remember that big phony bear flying through the air! That was so funny. It is such a great moment, watching that bear in the air.

Laurie Prange on *Gunsmoke.*

"The director, Alan J. Levi, and I looked at each other when the bear goes into the air and we laughed. I also remember the real bear licking the green paint off Lou's face. I felt safe with the animals; we had a bear and a snake in my first episode. I suck the venom out in a scene where somebody got bit," she recalls shyly. "Alan Levi was a wonderful guy. Later, he actually came and saw me onstage in *A Streetcar Named Desire*. I was thrilled that he cared enough to come."

In her second *Hulk* two-parter, "I liked Ric Drasin, who played the half-Hulk in 'Prometheus.' He was very professional, very sweet and he really did look like a combination of Bill and Lou! As the blind girl, I'm afraid of him because he can't control his temper. I'm not a sun person, but I was outdoors on all four of my *Hulk* episodes…Between shots, I would find shade or go to my dressing room! It was such pleasant company, the whole crew was great. The only other crew I worked with that had such a family attitude amongst them was the crew of *Highway to Heaven*. On that show, you had guys who worked had with Michael

Landon since *Bonanza*. The *Hulk* crew loved Kenneth and he loved them in return.

"For some reason, I always played disabled people on TV; I have no idea why. I like character roles and how a disabled character thinks and moves intrigues me. My agent used to tease me, 'You're always on TV in hospital beds!' For *Hulk*, I prepared for the role of the crippled girl with study. My stepfather is crippled. He moves beautifully with crutches and I think I used that on my first *Hulk*. I really love the scene where David Banner helps me realize that I can actually walk. I drop the crutches and walk — it's a great moment. Sci-fi shows like *Hulk* or *Star Trek* really stir the imagination and are able to tell a message in their stories."

Was it harder to play crippled or blind? "They both had their challenges, but I think blindness is a little more intricate to do, because you're leading by a sense of sound," she says thoughtfully. "Your senses get heightened. I actually produced a one-woman docudrama about Fanny Crosby, who was blind, so I have thought a lot about blindness. Fanny was an 1800s Mother Theresa-type person who wrote a lot of hymns."

Studying her second *Hulk* character, "I realized very few people are solidly, completely blind. Most blind people can't see at all, but they do see a haze or shadows. I found that interesting. Because a blind person does not have a sense of sight to distract them, their other senses are heightened. Your hearing, sense of touch and feel of the world are on a different plane than just physical."

The actress "was born and raised in Southern California. I went to Venice High School. My dad's from Arkansas and my mom's from Illinois. My family of six kids put on plays in the backyards with a clothesline as our curtain. When my brother was killed in Vietnam, I was in the 10th grade. There was so much tragedy over his loss, I think what happened is I took a Drama class to do something about all that emotion and turmoil that I was feeling and funneled that into acting.

"I won first place at an acting competition at UCLA's Royce Hall playing Mary Tyrone in *A Long Day's Journey into Night*, beating 122 other kids. By the time I was a high-school senior, I performed *Antigone* at Universal Studios' Sheraton Hotel and got meetings with agents. My agent saw me perform onstage and said, 'Don't change a thing.' My very first job was a starring role with Julie Harris and Sal Mineo in the season-opener of the show *Name of the Game*, an episode written by Steven Bochco! I had a three-page speech on that, and my dialogue was 80% of the script. Steven was on set and said to me, 'It's really cool to see words you write actually being said.' He went on to do great things. I played a drug addict, even though I have always been drug free," she adds. "Sal Mineo was really amused by my innocence."

"From there, I got *Gunsmoke, Night Gallery* and all sorts of shows. I was Diane Keaton's good sister in *Looking For Mr. Goodbar* — I'm the peppy one who *doesn't* get stabbed to death. I even guest starred on Anthony Quinn's TV show, *Man and the City*. James Arness liked me so much on *Gunsmoke*; I'm one of the only people to do all three of his series, including *McClain's Law* and *How the West Was Won*. Of all these shows, *The Incredible Hulk* was a very special experience for me," Laurie Prange sighs. "I'm really pleased that it has stood the test of time and is still popular on cable and DVD to this day."

HULK GOES WEEKLY!

Airing 24 days after the original pilot, *The Incredible Hulk: Death in the Family* duplicated its ratings success and proved that Hulk's pilot was no fluke. When *The Incredible Hulk* was green-lit for a full-blown TV series, Kenneth Johnson had ambitious plans for the monster's weekly adventures.

"*Hulk* was about facing things inside yourself and learning to deal with them," Johnson explains. "When I did the series, we always tried to write from a standpoint of 'What is it about?' Not plots, but what is it *really* about? Is it about greed? Obsession? Our feeling was that The Hulk could be a manifestation of different things to different people. In Banner, anger brought out his demon. In others, it could be alcoholism, drugs or jealousy, any number of things. We were always looking for thematic ways to have our characters explore what their inner demons were. That was the way we approached the show: What is the episode really about *emotionally?* Every episode would have Banner helping someone else with their own 'Hulk.'"

The only regulars on the show would be Bill Bixby as David Banner, Lou Ferrigno as The Hulk and Jack Colvin as Jack McGee. *The Incredible Hulk* would have no fixed permanent set, as Banner moved from town to town every episode, rarely ever meeting the same people twice. Although sometimes, the same actors would pop up as new characters!

With *The Incredible Hulk* set for a series, the race was on to find writers who could churn out scripts quickly. Screenwriter RC Matheson became a valuable contributor to the show. He and his writing partner Thomas E. Szollosi wrote several important episodes. "We really enjoyed writing for *Hulk;* it was a great experience," says RC Matheson, who was credited on the show as "Richard Christian Matheson."

"Tom, my former partner, and I had written a couple comedy shows. A script we had done for a Jimmy Komack comedy had gotten to Ken Johnson. Ken heard we wrote dramas and comedy and had put word out that he wanted writers who could have a talent for both. That way, the writers could get the 'joke' of what *The Incredible Hulk* was and also bring a legitimate sense of drama and action. He also wanted a sense of irony,

Marvel announces the live-action adaptations of Hulk and Spider-Man.

because he didn't want it to be so earnest that the Banner character didn't realize the situation that he was in.

"We went in, met with Kenny and it was just a love fest — he was irresistibly funny, charming and quick," Matheson notes. "We laughed the whole time. It was like that from the very first time on the show. We had a meeting of the minds. From that first episode we did for *Incredible Hulk*, we were also brought onto Kenny's other show, *Cliffhangers*.

"Tom and I had worked for Harve Bennett, one of Ken's mentors, on *The Powers Of Matthew Star*...We did every Universal show except *Six Million Dollar Man, Baretta* and *Rockford Files*! Back then, Universal Television was broken into camps. There was Ken Johnson's camp, which included *Hulk, Cliffhangers* and *Bionic Woman*, and there was Glen Larson's camp, which included *Battlestar Galactica, B.J. and the Bear* and *Buck Rogers in the 25th Century*. Even though it was a big studio, it was like a big family tree with a familial group of writers. After we worked with Ken, Don Bellasario made us the head writers on *Quincy*.

"Tom and I were one-stop shopping, because we could do plot, dialogue and character, while writing scenes with cool hooks that kept you reading. We were under a seven-year contract to Universal, so The Black Tower [as Universal's executive office building was nicknamed] would periodically call you in and say, 'Glen Larson wants to meet you. He's doing an action show called *Knight Rider*, about a car that talks…'The only other idea that I thought was truly bizarre was Glen's *B.J. and the Bear*!

"I loved working on *The Incredible Hulk* because Ken Johnson made it so much about the character! David Banner is deeply conflicted. Other guys who could have developed that series would have gone a different way and had the character not as conflicted, but what Ken brought to it

Hulking Out always shattered David Banner.

is melancholy. There was already a melancholia in the character from the comics, but Ken fully embraced that for the show."

"Bill Bixby was the perfect guy for the series," Matheson declares. "To me, the moment that was most interesting was *not* when he became The Hulk, but when he would change *back* to David Banner. Becoming The Hulk was a moment of rage, but when he returns to Banner, you can see to some degree that he understood what just happened to him. He's acutely aware something terrible just happened and that he did some violent things. Even though it was a necessity given the situation he was in, he has a sense of woe, heartache and regret about it. I always thought that moment was very, very interesting, the big Jekyll and Hyde moment, and Bill Bixby would always play it beautifully.

"Sometimes when Hulk changed back to Banner, they would do something like have him holding a bird's nest or petting a cub, but I didn't think they needed that because I thought the transformation itself was lyrical. In my opinion when I was writing it, I always felt that Banner looked at every time he turned into The Hulk as losing another hour from his life. Every time Bixby came back, you could see he wasn't relieved to be back, he was just kind of shattered by what happened, knowing that he would have to pick up the pieces of his life again," the writer muses. "The violence was not the interesting part of it, David Banner's reaction to it was. *The Incredible Hulk* had those darker, more troubled moments that not a lot of TV shows did."

HULK PROFILE
ALAN J. LEVI, HULK HELMER

Bearded, thoughtful Alan J. Levi was an experienced pro at directing genre TV, with numerous episodes of *The Invisible Man, Six Million Dollar Man* and *The Bionic Woman* under his belt, as well as episodes of the original *Battlestar Galactica*. Levi even did uncredited work on that Cylon-filled show's acclaimed pilot after he directed the second *Incredible Hulk* telefilm.

The director feels "that *Six Million Dollar Man* and *Bionic Woman* were both similar to *Hulk;* all three were 'cartoon' shows, the only difference

in *The Incredible Hulk* was that we were dealing with a different being. The other two shows were about humans with these bionic superpowers, while The Hulk was a creature of rage, running amok.

"The genius of Kenny Johnson is that he was able to take these live-action cartoons and make them reality," Levi points out. "Kenny made all of these larger-than-life cartoon characters human. You really cared about David Banner."

Doing a show about a Gamma-irradiated giant had its own challenges. "As a director, there are always physical problems when you're dealing with a big green man — The makeup

Alan Levi. PHOTO BY PATRICK JANKIEWICZ

rubs off on everything! You also had to deal with stunts, fight scenes and the occasional bear or animal that Hulk would face."

Besides helming an occasional episode, director Alan Levi had an uncredited hand in the show. "Kenny, Jim Parriott and I were known as 'The Holy Triad.' I worked with Kenny on *Bionic Woman*, but I worked with Jim Parriott first, on the David McCallum show, *The Invisible Man*.

Alan Levi directing Bill Bixby.

Jimmy Parriott wrote almost every episode that I did. Jim Parriott and I paired up and when Kenny got *Bionic Woman* going, he asked us to come work on that. Jim wrote almost every script and didn't want anyone to direct them but me, him or Kenny. We were happy to help out on *Hulk*.

"I love and admire Kenny. Not just as a dear friend, but as a creator and an artist. I was doing a *Hulk* episode, directed about five days of it when my father got sick. Kenny said, 'Get on a plane — I'll finish the show!' The nicest compliment to me was people told us, 'I couldn't tell who directed what!'

"The hardest part about doing *The Incredible Hulk* was stopping short of doing full science fiction and trying to make it as humanly connected as possible," Alan J. Levi stresses. "We shot some of the *Hulk*s in six or seven days. Back then, you had more time to chat with an actor about it because you had fewer scenes, but the scenes you had went longer."

HULK PROFILE
BILL BIXBY, LONELY MAN

Of all the people connected to the show, the story of leading man Bill Bixby is easily the most tragic. His life came to resemble that of David Banner, the haunted hero he played for five seasons on *The Incredible Hulk*.

David Banner in *The Incredible Hulk* pilot. The ads declared "Bill Bixby is a scientist damned by his own brilliance!"

Bill Bixby, the son of a department store owner and a clerk, was born in San Francisco, January 22, 1934, with the unwieldy name of Wilfred Bailey Bixby, before he became one of TV's most beloved and versatile stars.

Bixby was a fifth-generation resident of San Francisco. He told *US Magazine*, this meant he had special responsibilities. "I'm from San Francisco. It's important for me not just to live, but to live in style."

The fresh-faced actor was in demand for network shows and TV movies most of his life, because he was equally adept at comedy and drama. When he started out as a guest star on shows like *The Twilight Zone* ("The Thirty-Fathom Grave," one of the Rod Serling program's rare one-hour episodes), *Dr. Kildare* and *The Many Loves of Dobie Gillis*, one could see that he was immediately worthy of his own series.

That came in 1963, with the hit science-fiction comedy *My Favorite Martian*. Bill Bixby played Tim O'Hara, an idealistic young reporter for *The Los Angeles Sun*, who befriends a cranky, eccentric Martian (Ray Walston). Tim takes the alien home, hides him from authorities and dubs

him "Uncle Martin." When that show ran its course in 1966, the actor then appeared on the big screen in the Elvis Presley movies *Clambake* and *Speedway*.

The charming Bixby had a nice-guy appeal.

"I went to City College with him and we dated," says actress and former Miss America Lee Meriwether. "I originally saw Bill when I was 11 years old, at Grace Cathedral in San Francisco. He was in a choir from one church and I was in another choir from a different church. I was so smitten by his handsome face. Segue to years later at City College, I'm going to my classes and I suddenly see Bill. I gasped and

Bill Bixby romances Francine York on *My Favorite Martian*.

thought, 'That's the boy that I saw in church!' So I followed him and he went to the City College theater department in San Francisco. I thought, 'I *have* got to get into these classes!' and I did.

"He was a year ahead of me, but I got to see him do a play. I became Miss America and came back to San Francisco after touring the country for a year. I went by a store and looked in a window and suddenly saw Bill Bixby working behind the counter! I went in and he said, 'May I help you?' so I decided to make the approach," giggles Meriwether. "I said, 'I thought your face looked familiar! Didn't you go to City College?' He looks at me for a minute and says, 'You're Lee Meriwether, aren't you?'

"We dated, and it was fairly serious. I moved to New York, did *The Today Show* and we corresponded. I met my first husband Frank [Aletter]. Bill then called me for a date and I had to do a 'Dear Bill' phone call. 'I'm sorry, Bill, I met someone…' and that was the end of our relationship. He borrowed three hundred dollars from me and that was the last I heard of Bill Bixby. He was a dear and I hoped that we would work together someday, but we never did."

Meriwether appeared on the *Batman* TV series and movie. Bixby also had a long, serious relationship with actress Yvonne Craig, which meant TV's Hulk dated Catwoman and Batgirl.

Yvonne Craig talked about dating Bill Bixby in her autobiography, *From Ballet to the Batcave and Beyond*. "Bill and I met the first time because I was doing a pilot for a series and he was visiting someone on the set. We seemed to hit it off and when he did *My Favorite Martian*, I was hired as the guest star on an episode. Toward the end of the show, he came to my dressing room and invited me out." When she accepted, "he handed me a press release on him, stating I'd get to know a lot about him if I'd read it. I thought this was a bizarre thing to do…At the time, I found it off-putting. We went out a few times and parted."

"We met again by chance in a restaurant two years later and began the process [*sans* updated bio] once again," Craig writes. "Bill was very competitive about everything and during the two and a half years of our relationship, I was often reluctant to tell him when I was working if he wasn't working as well at the time. Bill competed with everybody and in everything he did. It was ultimately this that led to our breakup. In explanation, I remember saying to him, 'Bill, the difference between us is this: If I'm on my way to an interview and I see a bird has fallen from its nest, I will pick it up and I'll take it to the vet…You, on the other hand, on your way to an interview could find your mother lying in the street. You would simply roll down the window and say, 'I'm on my way to an interview and I'll tend to you when I get back. Wish me luck!' Our priorities were just different."

Yvonne Craig had another encounter with Bixby after their breakup, when he was doing *The Incredible Hulk*. "My nephew Todd was obsessed with *The Incredible Hulk*," Craig laughs. "He was four and just loved Lou Ferrigno as the big green Hulk, smashing everything. I called Bill, who set it up so I could take Todd to the *Incredible Hulk* set. Bill would also have lunch with us. After watching the shoot several times, Todd said to me, 'I love Hulk but hate the boring guy he turns into. What are we going to do next?' I said, 'We're gonna have lunch with the boring guy!'"

In film, Bill Bixby played light comedic roles in fluff like Sandra Dee's *Doctor, You've Got Be Kidding!* He got to show another side when he played the sociopathic cowboy Johnsy Boy Hood in the underrated western *Ride Beyond Vengeance*. He returned to television with the hit series

The Courtship of Eddie's Father, an early "dramedy" where Bixby played Tom, a widowed magazine editor raising his precocious young son, Eddie (Brandon Cruz).

The Courtship of Eddie's Father was a surprise hit, with Bixby earning praise for both his performance and the chemistry with his young co-star. He was nominated for an Emmy for Outstanding Continued Performance by an Actor in a Leading Role in a comedy series. His portrayal of Tom Corbett, Eddie's father of the title, was so memorable that, in 2004, *TV Guide* ranked him #15 on their list of the "50 Greatest TV Dads of All Time."

"Bill was the nicest human in Hollywood! A real professional, you can't find anybody to say a bad thing about him," Brandon Cruz says fondly. "Every year we called each other the day *after* our birthdays as a joke. We always got it wrong, so it became a lifelong tradition to call each other the day after our birthdays."

Bixby married actress Brenda Benet on the 4th of July, 1971. A popular TV ingénue and guest star, the stunning Benet had also played Luan, the hooker with a heart of gold, in the cult revenge movie *Walking Tall*. It's easy to see that she and Bixby had an undeniable attraction to each other; it's on film. Although they met before doing the show, they were paired off on-camera when Benet was cast as his girlfriend Brenda on "The Lonely Weekend" episode of *The Courtship of Eddie's Father*.

"Brenda Benet was a sweet, beautiful girl with an interesting French background," remembers director Jeffrey Hayden. "I had worked with her on *Alias Smith and Jones* and just thought she was captivating."

Actress Jane Merrow "first met Bill when he came onto the set of a television movie I was doing with the edifying title of *The Horror At 37,000 Feet*. Brenda was in it with me, and since she and Bill were engaged at the time, he came to visit her on set. They were so happy."

The high point of the Bixby/Benet union was the birth of their son, Christopher Sean Bixby, on September 25, 1974.

"I remember when Christopher was born," Brandon Cruz says happily. "We were at his house in Malibu and Chris was in a bassinet on the beach. Bill loved that kid, just loved him, and he would sing to him. He sang him this 'Christopher Sean' song that he made up and Bill would sing it to him over and over. It was so sweet to watch. Bill told me, 'I learned how to be a dad by hanging out with you. Now I'm going to be a really great dad!'"

During *Eddie's Father*, Bixby became a director. After that series ended, he appeared in the TV movie *Steambath* on PBS. Based on the acclaimed play by Bruce Jay Friedman, about a group of people who have died and wind up in a steambath. The janitor turns out to be God. Tandy, Bixby's character, is a powerful man who refuses to accept that he's dead. The show was infamous, because it featured the first nudity ever seen on television, provided by the curvaceous Valerie Perrine. Despite this distraction, Bixby earned rave reviews for playing Tandy.

Bill Bixby then starred in *The Magician*, a short-lived cult series about playboy/illusionist Anthony Blake, who solves crimes for the police using magic. The gimmick was that Bixby would use actual stage magic onscreen, not special FX. While the show only lasted a single season, Bixby served as one of its directors.

He re-teamed with Rod Serling for episodes of *Night Gallery*, including one as a man who finds out he's a reincarnated sorcerer. To demonstrate his evil power, he tries to sacrifice a neighbor's cat on his backyard grill! Bixby also squeezed in two episodes of *Insight*, a theological *Twilight Zone*. One of his *Insight*s, "The War of the Eggs," written by *Jurassic Park* author Michael Crichton, cast Bixby as a man embroiled in a nasty divorce, a role he would soon be playing in real life.

After that, Bixby became a director on numerous episodic television programs that he was not involved with as an actor, including *Room 222*, *Kate McShane*, *Charlie's Angels* and William Shatner's *Barbary Coast*, in which he also helmed the pilot. He would soon be acting with *Barbary* co-star Richard Kiel, for the short time that Kiel spent playing The Hulk. A private person, Bixby lived with Brenda Benet in West Los Angeles, on an acre of land that used to be a lime orchard. Benet, a vegetarian, grew vegetables there.

Possibly because of the birth of Christopher, the actor started doing more kid-friendly projects, like appearing as a gambler saddled with three spunky orphans in the Disney comedy western *The Apple Dumpling Gang*, one of the studio's biggest non-animated hits of the '70s.

He also began hosting PBS's acclaimed *Once Upon a Classic* for four years. He would fly to Pittsburgh to shoot segments of the show. Bixby told the press that doing *Once Upon a Classic* was his way of giving back. "I work for PBS because it's my way of paying my dues to the entertainment industry. I owe show business a lot, and my PBS work is gratifying."

He then co-directed *Rich Man, Poor Man*, TV's very first miniseries, based on the popular Irwin Shaw novel, about the trials and tribulations of a family from World War II to the 1960s. Bill Bixby co-starred in it and watched *Rich Man, Poor Man* become an enormous hit and a trend-setting ratings blockbuster that showed the viability of that miniseries format.

Easily the TV event of the year, *Rich Man, Poor Man* swept the Emmy nominations, including one for Willie, Bixby's acting part. The same year, he was nominated for a guest shot he did on *The Streets of San Francisco*, playing a deranged department store clerk-turned-street vigilante who finds crimes with his police scanner.

With the bounce from *Rich Man, Poor Man*, Bixby could have done any-

thing, but he surprised everyone by taking the role of harried-scientist-on-the-run David Banner in the *Incredible Hulk* TV movie and the series that followed. This proved the actor's instincts were as sharp as ever, when *Hulk* also became a huge ratings monster.

The same year, he also appeared in another 1977 pilot that became a hit TV series. Bixby played Arnold Greenwood, one of the very first people to visit *Fantasy Island*. This was not the warm, cuddly dream factory of the weekly *Fantasy Island* TV series, but the pilot, where Mr. Roark and Tattoo were enigmatic, sinister figures. Every wish

Bill Bixby and Frank Orsatti.

granted turned out like *The Monkey's Paw*, where each guest ruefully realized they didn't really want their fantasy after all. Bixby played an older man — an age he would never live to in real life, sadly — who wanted to re-experience meeting an American girl he romanced in London during World War II. Shockingly, he wound up killing her, an act that he recreates in his fantasy.

On *The Incredible Hulk*, Bixby wasn't merely the star; the self-described "workaholic" also expressed interest in the direction of the series, storylines and situations. *Hulk* story editor Jill Sherman Donner remembers the late Bill Bixby "as a force of nature...Bill had an absolute force of natural energy, both for bad and for good! He did some great things, but he also could be a real pain in the tush! He himself would be the first to admit that."

To his credit, Bixby *did* admit that, telling reporter Merrill Shindler, "I'm a very high-intensity person in a high-intensity industry. I've tried to disguise it because people take it wrong. But it's better than trying to soothe people. That's a bore to me." In the same interview, he affirmed, "I'm very much a loner. There's never enough time for me to spend with me."

Bixby's "quality control" helped the show produce a large number of interesting, entertaining episodes. During the first season, he told the press that he intended to direct "three or four *Hulk*s." Ironically, he only

This page, facing page: Bill Bixby holds court on the *Hulk* set. PHOTOS BY VENITA OZOLS

directed one episode of the series, "Bring Me the Head of the Hulk." Actress Jane Merrow appeared with Bixby in that episode and on a previous series that he directed. "As both a director and actor, I loved his energy and enthusiasm. Bill became a great friend and I loved working with him on *The Magician* and *The Incredible Hulk*," Merrow says. "He was a very good director. We engaged professionally, i.e.: we could work quickly and were very much in tune, without a lot being said. The only thing I did not forget or forgive easily was when he directed me on *The Magician*. Bill made me go to the top of a clock tower, hundreds of feet up, or so it seemed to me, to wave to someone below. He had me go in front of the clock face, with *no* safety measures. Ah, vertigo!"

"I liked Bill a lot," testifies *Hulk* director Alan J. Levi. "Bill was very giving; he gave to everyone on the set, he was a good leader and he was kind to everybody. Kenny and I knew him as 'Bix.' Most of the stories about Bix are the good times that you had with him — and he always did a great job as David Banner.

"Bill's intelligence as an actor would show up a lot in his scenes. Bill really understood the Banner character. He understood what happened to him and, at certain times, he would come up with great ideas within

the scenes. He was a director's actor," Levi praises. "Bill was extremely intelligent; he'd sit down and talk with you about the psychology of a scene. That made the whole series better for all of us: the writers could write something more complex, knowing he would understand and Bill could pull it off. TV shows today are run more by the actors on the show than they were when *Hulk* was on the air."

Levi's wife, *Hulk* guest actress Sondra Currie, points out that "Bill Bixby was a fine director, a fabulous guy and a really good actor! Bill was well trained with wider parameters as an actor, so it was different working with him than your regular [TV actor]. He had a great background and was very much about 'actor speak.'"

Director Jeffrey Hayden notes that "Bill Bixby was a very talented guy, a director as well as an actor. With some actor/directors that can be a problem for a director like me, but every time I worked with him, he never interfered with my work or tried to direct scenes himself."

Hulk director Patrick Boyriven "loved Bill — but Bill's whole life was artificial. He wanted to create the perfect world around him. He was a control freak, but in a good way…To him, everything was controlled. If you were going on a boat trip with him, it had to be the *perfect* boat trip or else it didn't work for him at all. Bix only felt at ease if he was in control."

Bixby would not let his three-year-old son Christopher watch *The Incredible Hulk* because he worried in interviews that it would frighten the boy. He also would not allow his son to be photographed in many profiles done on Bixby, and fretted how his own fame would affect his child. "I don't want my son to hear people speaking to me in the different tones they use if you're a celebrity. I can't have him hearing those voices because he'll relate them to real life, which is not what they are. My responsibility to him as a father is to allow him to move through the world without affectation. I don't want him sacrificing his childhood because of my job."

While Bixby's directing career was thriving and *The Incredible Hulk* was a surprise hit, his marriage was falling apart. His relationship with his wife Brenda had turned acrimonious.

Hulk guest Deanna Lund found "Brenda Benet to be a nice lady — a girl, really, a baby, much younger than Bill and very immature. I think she was star-struck by Bill. To her, it was all a fairy tale. I don't know what happened, but he was a very bright man…Bill was extremely sharp and I imagine that he was hard to keep up with. Bill didn't have much patience for people who weren't as smart as he was. She was probably too young and naive."

Although the couple was breaking up, Bixby would reiterate in interviews how much they both loved their son, Christopher. Bixby's close friend, three-time *Hulk* guest Victoria Carroll, says, "The joy of Christopher's birth saved Bill, it really did. He loved that baby so much. Christopher became his whole world. He told me that he was very lucky in his career, but not so lucky in his personal life.

"During *Hulk*, he and Brenda weren't really getting along anymore. They had divorced and it was a pretty bad break. I met Christopher when Bill brought him to the set, a really cute child," Carroll continues. "On one of my *Hulk*s, Bill was picking out furniture for Christopher's room at Bill's house, but he was having a lot of trouble in his relationship with Brenda. Unfortunately, children get caught between parents and there were custody fights between them. I finally said to him, 'Why don't you just sue her for custody?' Bill felt that would enrage Brenda even more than she was and cause more trouble. At one point, he was even gonna remarry her and everybody said, 'WHAT?!?'"

The Incredible Hulk story editor/producer Jill Sherman Donner "knew that Bill and Brenda were having problems, everybody did. Bill was living in his bungalow on the Universal backlot. He also had a condo at the Marina, but I think he was spending a lot of time at his bungalow. He was always there, on the backlot."

Lou Ferrigno smiles at the memory of Bixby's child. "Little Christopher would come into my motor home and watch me get made up as The Hulk. He would sit in a chair and he was a miniature Bill Bixby! Chris even talked like Bill — this little kid would say to the makeup man, 'Hey, that eyebrow is crooked!' It was like having another director around!

"When he and Brenda started having problems, he spent a lot of weekends out on that boat of his," Ferrigno adds. "I felt bad about what was going on with Bill and Brenda because they had a son, and Bill was always filming on the lot. Brenda was sweet, but you could see there was a sadness about her, you could tell that she was damaged in some way."

A DEATH IN HIS FAMILY

In 1981, after Bixby and Benet had divorced, six-year-old Christopher joined his mother on a ski trip to Mammoth Lakes, California. Young Christopher Bixby came down with a throat infection. A worried Brenda Benet raced him to a local hospital. The child was having trouble breathing with his throat closing up. As the medical team tried to put a breathing tube down his throat, Christopher plunged into cardiac arrest and died on March 1, 1981. Understandably, this shattered Bixby and Benet's lives forever.

"Christopher died from epiglottitis, a sudden inflammation of the Adam's apple," director Patrick Boyriven explains. "He died of asphyxiation at Mammoth Hospital. It's very rare, only one in 5 million kids get it, but the hospital never understood it. Mammoth was a good hospital for ski injures, like sprains, broken legs or arms. Not for something like this. They said that a simple tracheotomy would have saved Christopher. To his credit, Bix never went after them for it. He could have won a huge settlement, but he also knew that would not have brought Christopher back. Bix knew that it wasn't deliberate; he knew that no one wanted to see a child die."

"I loved Bixby — he was a wonderful guy, but I think that he obviously became a very unhappy person because of what happened," *Hulk* producer Karen Harris asserts. "He was very angry and you wouldn't like him when he was angry. You really wouldn't. The absolute worst thing to happen on

Hulk was the death of Christopher Bixby. He was six and it was the most horrific thing. Christopher's death sent us all spinning on the set. It was really bad and put the whole crew in the doldrums.

"I'll never forget that day on the set," she continues. "Patrick Boyriven was directing. At that time, he was married to Mariette Hartley. Michael Conrad was guest starring. Kenny called all of us into his office to give us the bad news. It resonated through the day. When Bill came back afterwards, he tried to give the appearance that 'I'm here, I'm ready to work,' but you could tell it changed him. How could it not?"

Patrick Boyriven had been directing the episode "Interview with the Hulk" when the tragedy occurred. "Christopher died over the weekend, but we didn't know that," Boyriven remembers, still affected by it all these years later. "On Monday, I got word that Bix would not be on the set. Nobody told me what had happened, so I just shot everything that Bix was not involved with. On day two, they said he would not be coming to set, so I knew something was up. It was eerie–I knew Bix was too much of a professional to let two days pass without showing up for work unless he had a damn good reason. He was such a professional guy. It was announced on the set that Christopher had died. I don't remember who announced it; I think it was somebody from The Black Tower. All I remember is that a little '*No*' came out of my mouth.

"The next day, Bix came on set, very cheerful and friendly, but you could tell that it was not natural–he was actually heavily sedated and unfocused. I said to Bill, 'Are you sure you want to do this?' and he said, 'I'm fine, I'm fine.' I thought it was gonna be fine, this was the last day of my episode and it was finished," a horrified Boyriven notes. "But as he went through half the take, he would suddenly go into an unscripted exposition on pain. I kept looking at the guys with the ties from The Black Tower to see if we were going to continue and we did. We shot until midnight. I have seldom felt such compassion as I did for Bix."

Boyriven's then-wife, Emmy-winning *Hulk* guest Mariette Hartley, found the whole situation "was so tragic. Christopher Bixby was a beautiful little boy. My son Sean was the same age and he and Christopher were best friends. That was very hard on all of us, especially Bill…"

Director Boyriven interjects that "It was a dramatic moment, truly Bix's downfall. Poor Bix's life was lined with tragedy and that just destroyed him. Bix took chemicals after that, to slow him down and speed him up and to cope with what he had been through. Our son Sean was 5, Chris was 6, and they were best friends. Christopher died over the weekend and Sean was supposed to go on that trip to Mammoth, but Brenda was always a bit vague and Mariette and I didn't think it was a good idea to let him go on the trip.

"Two small rambunctious boys would have been too much for her. We didn't let him go, Thank God he didn't go. I can't imagine what it would have been like for Brenda, grieving over their son and still trying to look after ours. My son beat him at judo the day before, so when Christopher

Personal tragedy made Bixby's life resemble his famous TV character.

died the next day, my son thought he had killed him," Boyriven continues, with a catch in his voice. "Sean was a child, his best friend just died. You try to tell a five-year-old that it was nothing related to him, but they really don't understand it...Sean said, 'I killed him, I killed him!' It was horrible.

"There was a memorial service for Christopher Bixby. Chris' ashes were dispersed in the ocean. Sean came with me and that worried me; because the boys were the same age and best friends, I knew Bix would recall poor Christopher when he saw my son. Sean slowly walked up to him and asked Bix how he was doing. Bill Bixby told my son, 'I love to go the beach now, because whenever I put my feet in the water, I am next to him.'"

Lou Ferrigno was stunned. "The day Christopher died was terrible, just terrible. Bill had been out two or three days and the day he came back, they told me confidentially that his son had died. The day Bill came back on set, he came up to me and gave me a big hug before I was made up.

"I didn't know what to say to him; he just kept on filming and you could see that something had died in him. I don't know how he did it, how he could just keep filming…I know I *couldn't* do that," admits Ferrigno, the father of three. "I remember when Bill came back, he did a scene with Michael Conrad and he played it straight, but he had constant tears rolling down his cheeks."

For Benet, who was starring on the soap opera *Days of Our Lives* at the time, the grief over losing Christopher proved too much for her. On April 7, 1982, Brenda Benet went into the bathroom of her California home, laid down surrounded by a circle of lit candles and shot herself in the mouth with a Colt .38 revolver.

"That was so awful," says Jill Sherman Donner. "She killed herself — Brenda did it close to the one-year anniversary."

Patrick Boyriven remembers, "That very night we got a call from Bill… He said that Brenda had shot herself over Christopher's death. Mariette and I rushed right over to him. I never saw Bill again after that; he would only talk on the phone."

Karen Harris feels that "Brenda killing herself a year later was so terrible, because it just compounded the tragedy. Bill's family was truly gone now."

Lou Ferrigno "knew that Brenda could not handle the loss of her son — that was terrible for Bill's whole family. Bill was strong, he kept it on and then he went into complete seclusion."

Hulk guest Gloria Gifford realized "Bill's son had just died when I guest-starred on an episode and he was a wreck, just a complete wreck. Between scenes, Bill Bixby opened up to me about it. He said, 'No one will ever know — no one can ever know what this feels like.'"

Victoria Carroll "worked on the show right after Christopher died and it was very, very sad. How could anyone walk, talk or breathe after their child had died? I didn't have a child at the time when I did the show, but I remember thinking that. And then he lost his [ex] wife a year after that. She committed suicide. Poor Bill had an awful lot to deal with in such a short time.

"Bill really became David Banner after both deaths, because he had so much unfinished business with Brenda. He loved her very, very much and it may be unfair to compare it to this, but it was almost like the situation Phil Hartman had with his wife. [Carroll was in The Ground-lings with *Saturday Night Live* comedian Phil Hartman, who was shot by his unstable wife, Brynn Hartman, who then killed herself.]

"There was a lot of emotional illness there with Brenda; she was not a balanced person and she had a lot of problems," Victoria Carroll says in hushed tones. "By killing herself, those problems were never resolved and Bill never recovered from that. I think that ultimately affected his health. In fact, I know it did — how could it not? Bill was truly professional at work, but you could tell he was haunted. I cannot imagine any parent having to lose a child, especially now that I'm a parent myself. I don't know if I could go on living if something like that happened."

The actress "did a *Hulk* two-parter before Christopher passed away and one show after. On 'Mystery Man,' he was getting ready to take Christopher on a cross-country trip, just the two of them. Bill told me, 'This kid will never think that I didn't love him! He's gonna *know* that he's loved...' When we did the *Hulk* episode 'Fast Lane' after Chris died, he was restrained and somber. Bill went up and down in moods in a way that he hadn't before," Carroll confides. "He had such tragedy in his life. Television show shoots are so grueling everyday anyway, especially as the series lead, with 14- to 20-hour days."

"I called Bill when Christopher died," a saddened Deanna Lund remembers. "I was doing a soap opera in New York, *One Life to Live*. I was in the makeup chair when it was on the news and someone passed it on to me. I trashed my makeup crying and called him. We spoke and I knew what a terrible thing it was, because he adored that child. It turned out that he was really very bitter and angry about what happened. I think it was from his grief, but he was absolutely furious with his wife for taking Christopher into the cold when he had a cold. But it wasn't like the child was sleeping in an igloo — it was a really hard time for him and obviously, for Brenda, too. They both worshipped the ground that kid walked on."

Singer/actress Andrea Marcovicci guested on the show shortly after Christopher's death. "I, like every other woman in America, had a huge crush on Bill Bixby, so I was looking forward to meeting him. The minute I was with Bill, I saw that he was a man in profound grief over the death of his son," Marcovicci says, still saddened by Bixby. "He said to me that if his son had been with him that week instead of Brenda, it would not have happened. Bill felt if something like that happened to Christopher while around him, he would have taken him right to Cedar Sinai Hospital. He was so full of rage at his ex-wife Brenda and that led to a second tragedy, when she killed herself.

"Frankly, it surprised me that, even in grief, you could have shared that kind of anger with a temporary actress like myself," Andrea Marcovicci muses. "I was only there for one episode, but I feel all that bottled-up rage led to his own medical problems. If you don't release your own anger and grief, it will consume you and I feel in his case, it did. It really did. He couldn't face his grief and it was a very bad thing that he did to her. Brenda Benet Bixby had her own devastation — she lost her child — and to be constantly told that you killed your own son by your ex-husband, even in the media, was a cruel act. A cruel and profoundly sad act on his part. I could not say, 'Hey, Bill Bixby: I have had a crush on you since I was a kid, but you need therapy!' because they did not have that kind of grief counseling at the time."

Deanna Lund found that "Bill was pretty angry and not very diplomatic toward Brenda. I know when he talked about it, he blamed her. That may have had more to do with the way they broke up, which I am not privy to, but there was a lot of residual anger toward her from him. I don't think any mother could feel worse — or blame herself more — so that had to be really bad for her. Bill never got over Christopher's death. He had some problems over some of his own abuses, drugs, and I think that's how he coped with Christopher's death and that made him very mercurial. One minute very nice, and then he would get very angry. He was no longer the Bill Bixby I knew, which was a shame. He was a different person. Very bitter."

As a friend and confidante, Alan J. Levi "went through Bill's marriage problems with him, his son's death and then his wife's death. That was a very difficult time for Bill and he appreciated all the people who really loved him, Kenny, myself, Jim Parriott. I had left the show [before] his son died, but I still talked to Bill."

Bixby's protégé, Brandon Cruz, says, "When Christopher passed, it was so tough, because he lost his son and then he lost his ex-wife. No matter how they broke up, at one point, he had nothing but love for her. It changed him. Bill was devastated by Christopher's death, but when I talked to him about it, he was on the set of *Hulk* working. That's how he dealt with it. He handled the death of his father the same way on *Eddie's Father*.

"When his father died, Bill walked on set, said, 'Something went on, some of you may have heard, but I will speak to you all about it at the end of the day. Right now we have a job to do!' and he went right to work. Bill dealt with Christopher's death by golfing. He was a scratch golfer back in the *Eddie's Father* days; he and Sandy Koufax would hustle people at the country clubs. Bill once shot a 29 at the back nine on The Riviera! He could have gone pro. Grieving over Brenda and Christopher, he played 27 holes a day and got really good."

Hulk guest and Bixby golf partner Denny Miller eulogizes his friend as "a very good man and a wonderful golfer, but Bill had some very bad luck in his life. Injuries to people he loved, like his son. His son died shortly before we did my second episode, but he didn't seem to want to talk about it and you couldn't blame him for that. He loved that boy dearly."

Deanna Lund "dated Bill long after I did my *Hulk* episode and he was still very bitter. His mood had changed, but I could understand that; you can never get over losing a child. He dealt with his pain in a certain way, but alcohol was not his thing. I don't know if he was sick yet, but he may have been and not known yet. His illness was announced not long after and that would explain his hot and cold feelings on things."

Screenwriter Courtney Joyner spent time on the set of Bixby's next series, *Goodnight, Beantown*. "I had the pleasure of meeting Bill Bixby twice. The first time was on the Universal lot when I was working with [director] Virgil Vogel. Virgil introduced us, so I mentioned to Bill how much I loved *Ride Beyond Vengeance*. That really sparked him. We had a great chat about that, and he was also interested in what I was doing — writing — and Bill really took the time to be kind during this small chat with a total stranger. That impressed me greatly.

"Years later, I visited the set of his TV series, *Goodnight, Beantown*, and saw Bill Bixby again. The change in him was very sad. He had a great deal of tragedy in his life at that point, and it had been made public. What impressed me again was that he was on set, working on this show, instead of being home taking care of his severe illness. He looked frail, but he was right there, soldiering on. I was impressed by Bill Bixby as a person and a professional."

Going on to star and direct more TV shows and movies, the notoriously private Bixby remarried but it only lasted for six months. He did not even tell his friends when he was stricken with prostate cancer. "Bill kept in touch with me, but I only found out about it through the tabloids like *The National Enquirer*," marvels Brandon Cruz. "At the time, Bill was directing a Roseanne Barr Elvis movie. This was a silly TV movie-of-the-week, *The Woman Who Loved Elvis*, so I gave him shit about that. 'Bill, what are you thinking, doing this? Yeeeeck! Elvis was your friend, what are ya doing this for?!?' He laughed and said, 'Sometimes, we don't always make the best decisions.'"

Other friends of Bixby were horrified by the tragic turn of events his life kept taking. "When he went into the hospital, he found he had advanced cancer and his then-wife served him with divorce papers in the hospital. Isn't that cruel? I truly cared about Bill," Victoria Carroll says, shaking her head sadly. "Bill was a gentleman and a great friend. We remained friends until his death. He and my husband are the two men I loved the most.

"After Bill got sick, I talked to him on the phone because I felt he didn't want me to see him in the hospital. He would call me and we would talk. There was a last conversation that was very sentimental to me, but at the time I didn't know how truly sick he was. After we spoke, I suddenly thought, 'That sounded really final.' I didn't realize at the time that he was saying goodbye."

Patrick Boyriven says "Bix felt degraded by the cancer and he really didn't want anybody to visit him in the hospital and see him like that. He only wanted to talk by phone." Bixby married a third time, to artist Judith Kliban, the widow of cat cartoonist B. Kliban, in the last month and a half of his life.

Lee Meriwether grieved when she heard what happened to her former boyfriend. "It was just so sad; when he was ill, I found out where he was and sent him cards and tried to call. I left messages, but never got through to him. It was a woman's voice that always answered and I always felt that she might have decided that I didn't need to speak to him. I always felt what happened to him was just not fair. He was such a dear man and when his illness was announced, I kept him in my thoughts and prayers."

Brandon Cruz knows "Bill was a brilliant idea guy who knew about filmmaking. He started directing on *The Courtship of Eddie's Father* and he ended his career when his life ended; a week before he passed away, he was directing. People on *Blossom* [the sitcom Bixby was directing when he died] said that in the last week of his life, he was directing from a couch, laying down and wracked in pain. This meant a lot to him, this life that Bill chose. He passed away on a Sunday, but I have no doubt if it was a Monday, Bill would have gone to work. He was that tough a guy.

"I had lunch with him two weeks before he passed," Cruz confides. "Bill said to me, 'They haven't given me that much longer, but they have given me six months four times.' He'd always looked pretty good in the past, but this time he didn't look so good. It was very advanced. The only reason it was so advanced is Bill was a workaholic. He didn't even go to the doctor until it was Stage Three. Had he had early detection on prostate cancer, he would have beaten it. Bill was a fighter, but because it was discovered so late, no matter how badly he wanted to fight, it was a losing battle. He fought it for a few years after the first diagnosis."

As Bixby had told Merrill Shindler years before, "I have no scrapbooks or photos. I don't want to look back and say, 'That was me,' reliving what I used to be. That would mean I'm not living *that* day. The best thing that could happen to Bill Bixby is, when my demise comes, I have three unfinished projects. That would be happiness."

Bixby succumbed to his illness on November 21, 1993, with third wife Judith and his friend, *Laugh-In* star Dick Martin, at his side. A private funeral was held for him at Forest Lawn Hollywood Hills, as well as a memorial service at the Bel Air Hotel. Mourners included Mike (*Mannix*) Connors, Richard Crenna, Mariette Hartley, Kenneth Johnson and Lou Ferrigno. Cast and crew from both *The Incredible Hulk* and the sitcom *Blossom* also attended, as he was directing an episode of that when he died. Bixby's ashes were scattered off his Hawaii estate.

"I loved Bix. A lot of people didn't react to Bix passing the way they should have," Patrick Boyriven asserts. "Bix was the first guy to put me in the business and even took a chance on me by letting me direct. He set up a lot of people in the industry and I was very disappointed that so few people showed up for his memorial. People forget, you know? They forgot the man was a good guy."

"When Bill passed away, I was in Santa Barbara doing a movie with Barbara Carrera, who was also a friend of Bill's," Brandon Cruz sighs. "We got the news on set and Barbara said, 'Oh my God, I'm so sorry; I know you guys were close. Take as much time as you need.' I said, 'Are you kidding? Bill would want me to work.' It was really eerie; I assembled the crew and said, 'Something happened that you may have heard about, but I will speak to you all about it at the end of the day. Right now we have a job to do!' I got phone calls from Dick Martin and Bill's other friends because I missed his funeral. They were saying, '*Where are you?*' I was working, which Bill would have understood. Billy would work.

"I always listened to Bill. I actually turned down starring in the movie *Porky's* because Bill told me, 'Never do anything you wouldn't want your kids to see,'" Cruz laughs. "Now I kick myself in the head, I shoulda done *Porky's*, but I was following the advice of a beloved mentor and friend! Jimmy Komack [who produced *Eddie's Father*] was doing the *Porky's* movies and wanted me to do it, but I said, 'Billy Bixby told me not to' and he laughed and said, 'That's right, he did…'"

Jane Merrow still thinks of the late actor with great fondness. "Bill was a very intelligent man who was weighed down by the tragedy in his life. My son was the same age as his son, so I really felt for Bill when his son died. Needless to say, he was devastated and again, when his former wife Brenda Benet died. I think if these things had not happened to him, he would have lived a longer and very productive life, probably directing, which he really enjoyed. I really cared for Bill and miss him to this day." Bill Bixby's legacy lives on. The most touching tribute to Bixby came from his former co-star, Brandon Cruz: "I named my son after him," he says happily. "Lincoln Bixby Cruz — Bill would have liked him."

HULK PROFILE
LOU FERRIGNO, THE INCREDIBLE HULK

Lou Ferrigno learned to stop worrying and love The Hulk.

You are *not* an actor; you are a twenty-five-year-old bodybuilder who appeared as yourself in an acclaimed bodybuilding documentary. You are wearing contact lenses that make it hard to see. You are wearing oversized wax teeth that make it hard to speak. You are 85% deaf and cannot wear your hearing aids, making it hard to hear. Your nose and forehead are covered in prosthetic appliances. An unruly wig is painfully baby-pinned over your hair.

You have rags draped over your shoulders and wear nothing but tight torn pants. You are on the Universal Studios backlot and you are surrounded by a TV crew, all their lights and cameras upon you. Oh yeah, you are painted lime-green from head to toe. You are Lou Ferrigno and you are The Incredible Hulk, TV's unlikeliest star!

"That was something," Lou Ferrigno laughs at the memory. "I will never forget it — everybody on the set was just staring at me and I thought, 'This is really weird!'"

With his impressive physique and noble face, Lou Ferrigno looks like a superhero. And he has certainly played one on TV. While he has been an actor for over 30 years, he knows how the public at large sees him. "I'm The Hulk," he smiles. "And I'm happy to be The Hulk because it's the part that got me into show business! The Hulk will be something that will be with me for the rest of my life and I'm happy with that. Most actors end up on TV series that nobody remembers, they just fade away — but everybody knows and loves *The Incredible Hulk!*"

The man who would become The Hulk, Louis Jude Ferrigno, was born November 9, 1951, in Brooklyn, New York. Despite losing much of his

Lou Ferrigno about to enjoy a well-deserved 10-egg omelette breakfast.
PHOTO BY VENITA OZOLS

hearing to childhood illness, Ferrigno became a bodybuilder.

"Because of my hearing loss, it was hard for me to participate in team sports — although I did play a little football. I chose something where I could compete with myself," he elaborates. "Bodybuilding is a solo sport, so I got bitten by the 'iron bug' because I love competing with myself."

His drive and competitive streak made him a world-class bodybuilder, winning the title of Mr. Universe at age 21 and again at 22. Besides playing football for the Canadian Football League, the 6'5", 285-pound Ferrigno starred in the documentary *Pumping Iron*, about his noble but ultimately futile quest to best Arnold Schwarzenegger in the Mr. Olympia bodybuilding contest. Ferrigno comes off as the movie's underdog against an aggressive Arnold Schwarzenegger and Lou's own demanding father.

After that, he landed the role of The Incredible Hulk, and the rest is history. His *Hulk* was the only success Marvel Comics had with any of their characters in live-action, until the movie *Blade* opened in the late '90s and was followed by the one-two punch of the *X-Men* and *Spider-Man* film franchises. Ferrigno's Hulk is a large, intimidating beast, but *not* an evil monster. Through the actor's sensitive portrayal, viewers and the people he rescues can sense the creature's innate inner goodness.

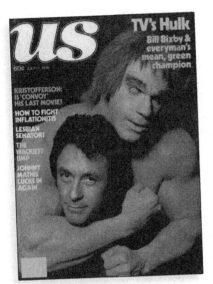

"I have never viewed The Hulk as a monster," he professes. "The problem is, people feel Hulk is a monster because of how he looks, so they judge him and they go after him. He's like Frankenstein's Monster who really isn't a monster either, just a human being with an abnormal brain. Poor Hulk can't help how people perceive him. As the series progressed, you could see that The Hulk was an intelligent creature who was just trying to hide from society."

Bill Bixby and Lou Ferrigno make the cover of *US* Magazine.

The crew admired their green-skinned star. "Lou really was not an accomplished actor when he started playing Hulk. When the series began, he was like, 'Oh my God, how did I land here?' but he really brought The Hulk to life," praises *The Incredible Hulk* story editor Karen Harris. "He had difficulties anyway due to his hearing problems, but because he was The Hulk, people on the set would ignore him and literally talk around him, having conversations like he wasn't even there. I remember him saying that once he was in the green makeup, people would just not notice him!"

The former Hulk remembers his producer and co-star with great fondness. "Bill Bixby and Kenny Johnson were like family to me. I couldn't wait to see them every morning. We were the perfect team. Bill Bixby and I were a great match. Bill was a wonderful guy, an entertainer and a real jokester. I loved working with him. He was a brilliant man who was also very funny. Bill was my mentor and I learned a lot from him.

"Being The Hulk changed my life and made my career," declares Ferrigno, a large and likable family man in the living room of his equally large and likable Santa Monica home. "My parents were proud of me, people everywhere were happy to see me and when I did the show, I experienced many things I wouldn't have otherwise. So many good things happened to me from the show. I met my wife Carla during *The Incredible Hulk*. She was a manager at TGI Fridays and I met her when she threw me out — I first met my wife when she threw me out of a restaurant!

Emerald City Comic Con devised a simple way to approach Ferrigno at Conventions. Do *not* shave him or dress him up as The Pharoah! JOHN AEGARD/BEN BATES/@ECCC

"She tossed me out because one of my friends didn't have their ID. I loved TGI Fridays, she was the manager and I laughed when I saw that they had a female manager! The next time I went, I had my stunt double, Manuel Perry, with me. I ran into Carla again and we hit it off. I would not have gone as far as I have without her — she was able to take my work from *The Incredible Hulk* and create a career out of it!"

Incredible things happened to him on the show. "Arnold Schwarzenegger came to see me on-set, as did Sean Penn and his brother Chris Penn from *Reservoir Dogs*. Their dad (TV director Leo Penn) brought them when they were kids. There was one person I will never forget. We were filming at Venice Beach; I was in full makeup having a cup of coffee when the door opened. A man was standing there with gray hair and black glasses," a still-amazed Ferrigno remembers. "He said, 'How are you?' I said, 'Hi' and he said, 'Excuse me, I have my niece from England with me. May I have a picture? My name is *CARY GRANT*.' My jaw dropped open, I was speechless: Cary Grant finally said to me, 'Are you okay?' Oh My God, that blew me away; *Cary Grant* was a fan of The Hulk!

"I loved being The Hulk," the actor raves. "With the wig, green paint and prosthetics on, I truly felt powerful. When I was on the set filming, there was only one Hulk — me! People would gather around me between scenes just to be near me. It made me realize how important the character was to everybody, which gave me the sense of power I needed to play the part."

A typical day for Ferrigno as The Incredible Hulk "was a long one," he groans. "Sometimes, I would arrive on the set at 4 a.m., then I would go straight to makeup. We would be ready to shoot at 8 or 9 a.m. They were long 12 to 14-hour days. The makeup was very itchy and I tried hard not to scratch…but it would start to peel and they would put on even more makeup.

"I still have nightmares of being in makeup. I really do," he laughs. "The beauty of all that makeup and those prosthetic appliances is that it helped me get into character. I wore a rubber nose, eyebrows and forehead. When they finished the makeup, wig and green paint, as soon as they put the eyes and teeth in, I *was* The Hulk. I just clicked into it."

Despite The Hulk's on-camera abilities, "I never hurt myself playing The Hulk, but I did have small, minor injuries. I would bang myself up, bruise my shoulder, get scratches here and there from all the running and jumping I did. I never broke anything because I had Frank Orsatti, an amazing stunt coordinator, and Manny Perry, a great stuntman who did The Hulk's most dangerous stunts! I am a great athlete, so I'm very flexible and agile, but I was safe because I had the greatest stunt coordinator in Frank Orsatti. Frank made sure I was safe — I felt very protected by him."

When Hulk rampaged, Ferrigno channeled his own personal Hulk. "For scenes where I was required to knock down a wall, fence or door, I

Wolverine namechecks Ferrigno.

would use my inner rage," he says shyly. "That would help me to Hulk Out because I have basically felt like The Hulk my whole life. I can relate to him and I was a huge Hulk collector as a kid. I just wish I had saved all those comics. Now they're worth a lot of money!

"Because I could relate to him, that's why I was able to show the sensitivity and anger of The Hulk, the parts of his personality that made him famous in the comics. I really got into the character and played The Hulk's soul, which is why the series was such a success. If Hulk was just an angry guy, I don't think the show would have lasted so long."

To make the creature look unstoppable onscreen, "I would work out for three hours to get pumped up for my close-ups." Hulk's arm gestures on the show look like modified bodybuilder flexes. "I loved the Hulk character and when I played him, I would just do these natural gestures because that's what I thought Hulk would make," Ferrigno volunteers.

ₒ after the series ended, Lou Ferrigno reprised The Hulk for a TV ₒovie reunion with Bill Bixby and Jack Colvin. "I had not been The Hulk for seven years when we did *The Incredible Hulk Returns* TV movie, but as soon as I got into the makeup, it was like it was yesterday. The most difficult part about being The Hulk was the constant touch-ups. Every time I did any physical thing, they had to re-touch me. Sometimes they took me to the motor home, stripped me down and put another three coats of paint on me because the touch-ups were showing onscreen. When it was warm, the makeup would run and I would have to spend all my time in the air-conditioned motor home because I didn't want to sweat it off."

Outside of The Hulk, he's a real-life hero. In 2006, Lou Ferrigno became a Reserve Los Angeles County Sheriffs Deputy. "It's an honor," he says. "I have always had a great deal of respect for police officers. My father was a New York police officer. I wanted to give something back to my community and I love it!"

His former competitor, Arnold Schwarzenegger, went on to become Governor of California. "That was exciting; I was happy for him. Arnold is a good guy. You never know," Lou Ferrigno grins. "One day I may put my hat in the political ring!" Hey, who wouldn't vote for The Hulk?

HULK PROFILE
KENNETH JOHNSON, THE MAN WITH THE PLAN

An alien spaceship model from *V* sits forlornly on a desk, while photos from various TV shows and movies hang on the walls. Johnny 5, the robot from *Short Circuit 2* guards a counter, while an ominous "Friendship Is Universal" from *V* hangs in the bathroom. Welcome to Kenneth Johnson's sanctum sanctorum.

Johnson's shows lead you in with a fantastic premise and then you stay to see the story with its message. Hulk may smash walls, but he also battles social ills. As writer/ director, Kenneth Johnson ran impressive genre shows where the fantastic elements are tempered with social commentary and a humanist message. "That was deliberate," Johnson comments. "Gene Roddenberry, bless his heart, had done something with *Star Trek* that made people want to look beneath the surface. He made shows like *The Incredible Hulk* and *Alien Nation* possible."

The wiry, bearded Kenneth Johnson is a charismatic, hard-working man. In jeans and a buttoned work shirt cuffed at the elbows, one can't help but notice that he dresses just like David Banner. "Actually, David Banner dresses just like *me*," Johnson laughs warmly.

"I have a lot of great memories from doing *The Incredible Hulk*," he says fondly. "Bix, Louie Ferrigno and all the great people who worked on the show made it a terrific experience."

Johnson "was born in Pine Bluff, Arkansas. My parents divorced when

Kenneth Johnson directs The Hulk. PHOTO COURTESY OF KENNETH JOHNSON

I was four and I moved to Washington, D.C., with my mother. I started doing radio plays on my tape recorder in 8th grade. That got me into theater and I found my calling. While in high school, I studied Shakespeare at Catholic University, and went to Carnegie Tech, now called Carnegie Mellon.

While in college, he turned down an offer from President Richard Nixon to do spots for his re-election campaign. "It wasn't what I had in mind," Johnson smiles. "People say to me, 'Gee, you could have written a book' and I say, 'Yes, or I could have gone to jail and been born again!' [like other Nixon aides.]

"I went in as a directing major and ran the film society. I liked doing theater, but it always made me a little sad because when it was over, it was gone. I realized with film, the work would be captured forever. I was trained at Carnegie in the Classics, from the Greeks on down to Ionesco, but I am something of a sci-fi fan. That was only natural, considering I grew up with any 1950s kid's interest in sci-fi, the same

Johnson with wife Susie and daughter Katie. PHOTO BY PATRICK JANKIEWICZ

as Spielberg and Lucas have. Those kinds of things were interesting to me. I never thought of myself as a sci-fi guy, but you create *The Bionic Woman* and do *The Incredible Hulk* TV series, pretty soon, people think that's what you do."

His career began when he came to California "and my friend Steve Bochco [co-creator of *NYPD Blue, Hill Street Blues* and *LA Law*] helped me start writing. He introduced me to a guy named Harve Bennett, who was anxious to have new ideas."

Writing for *The Six Million Dollar Man*, he created the hero's female counterpart. "I was inspired by *Bride of Frankenstein*. Since we had a bionic man, I felt he needed a mate, so I wrote the script for *The Bionic Woman*. I made Jamie Sommers the girlfriend of Steve Austin, the Six Million Dollar Man. For Jamie, I wanted a normal, accessible female who had some worldly experience before she suddenly faced this extraordinary circumstance. She was named for a water skier I'd met at Sea World. I loved her name."

Besides *The Bionic Woman* and the success of *The Incredible Hulk,* Johnson created the short-lived (but highly regarded) *Cliffhangers*, and then he had great success with *V*. His miniseries *V*, about an alien invasion from a man-on-the-street's point of view, was both audacious and interesting.

V Poster.

The alien invaders, in their jumpsuits, jackboots and sunglasses pretend to be friendly while Johnson focuses on humans eager to sell out their own race and planet to curry favor from their new alien overlords. "The whole idea of *V* was based on the Nazis rolling into Denmark in 1938," he explains. "The Nazis said, 'Hi, we're here to be your friends. We're going to protect you from the English and then we'll go away.' I carefully researched the rise of the Third Reich and the idea that the Nazis revealed their 'other face', as it were. I took their 'other face' literally and said, 'Okay, what's really under there?'"

As popular as it was domestically, *V* was an even bigger blockbuster overseas, with Europe appropriating the show's most famous image — a handsome, charismatic alien with a rip in his face exposing the lizard underneath — for various political cartoons and posters.

"It's really a character drama; an examination on how people are changed by power. Some people will collaborate with the enemy, like the Vichy French did, in order to enhance their own power, and how some are lifted to heights of power without wanting or expecting it, like the heads of the Resistance. *V* keeps coming back because it hits a primal core in people."

V inspired merchandising of toys, novels, tee shirts, costumes and comic books, as well as two spin-offs: *V: The Final Battle*, a sequel miniseries, and then a short-lived TV show. Neither was as successful as the original, nor had Johnson's involvement.

After that, he did *Shadow Chasers*, an unsuccessful mystery show with Dennis Dugan, *Short Circuit 2* and then a big sci-fi show, *Alien Nation*.

. the first TV shows to debut on the brand-new Fox Network, *Alien nation* is a loose adaptation of the failed James Caan/Mandy Patankin feature film. Johnson's series took the noisy, derivative cops-meet-aliens movie and turned it "into a compelling family drama; it just so happened that the family was from outer space."

His *Alien Nation* TV series was the polar opposite of *V* — friendly, non-aggressive aliens. "It came from a different place," he says. "Fox asked me to look at the *Alien Nation* movie and I didn't like it very much. I thought it was *Miami Vice* with Coneheads, but there was one scene where we glimpsed the alien wife and family that belonged to Mandy Patankin. I thought immediately, 'That's what the TV show is!' It couldn't be *Lethal Weapon* with aliens every week, because that would be really tedious and boring. *In the Heat of the Night* with aliens would be much more interesting — a societal drama about what it's like to be the newest minority on Earth. It came from a more humanist point of view." In a touching tribute, the matriarch of the alien family was named "Susan," after Kenneth Johnson's wife.

Alien Nation "was a gift from God; great people all the way around that still love each other to this day," he enthuses. "As a matter of fact, on the DVD set of the TV movies, I got 'em all together, sat them down in my living room and we just chewed the fat for an hour! They all loved being together. I wonder how many casts of TV shows still wanna see each other over 10 years later. Let alone, sit down to laugh and scratch? We all felt that *Alien Nation* was the best professional experience that any of us ever had."

The show was also true to one of Johnson's strongest beliefs: "Never work with an asshole": "It's true," he proclaims. "I have always tried to subscribe to that. Life is too short. Whenever I'm putting a crew together, I always tell them, 'We have two goals here — to make the most artistic project we can, given the time and money we've been given, and to have a good time.' If you're not having a good time, the hours are too long and the work is too hard. Life's just not worth it, so it's important to try to surround yourself with people that you love.' *Alien Nation* is a perfect example of that. From the get-go, it was perfect! *V* was that way, too. *The Incredible Hulk* was a great experience." *Alien Nation* was cancelled after a season, but was reborn as a long-running series of TV movies.

Johnson also directed episodes of *JAG, Easy Money, Seven Days* and the miniseries, *Venus Rising*.

HULK PROFILE
MANNY PERRY, THE INCREDIBLE STUNT HULK!

Stuntman/stunt coordinator/second-unit director and actor Manny Perry has done many amazing things onscreen; high dives, fistfights, driven cars in *Fast & The Furious*, caught bullets on *24* and dodged dino-

Manny Perry and Lou Ferrigno hold up Frank Orsatti.

saurs in *Jurassic Park III*. Onscreen, he's tried to kill Bruce Willis in *The Last Boy Scout*, joined Al Pacino for the slam-bam conclusion of *Heat* and stunt doubled Mr. T on *The A-Team*. "I wore a Mr. T bald cap with a pre-inserted mohawk," he chuckles.

Most impressively, Manny was The Incredible Stunt Hulk, who did all the dangerous things too risky for Lou Ferrigno on the series. When you see the Gamma-irradiated giant leap off roofs, wrestle wild animals, burst out of trucks, jets and doors or lift cars on the classic series, you are actually watching Manny Perry in action!

"Manny was a great guy and a great stunt double," Hulk Lou Ferrigno says admiringly. "Manny was impressive because he did a lot of stuff that I really didn't want to do, like jump off buildings!"

Every week, Perry stepped in as The Hulk for extremely unsettling situations. "Manny was the cement that held the Hulk together — he knew what Lou and The Hulk had to wear," praises *Hulk* makeup man John Goodwin. "He's a wonderful stunt guy and a real 'Salt of the Earth' person. It's funny, because he's black, but nobody ever knew it because he and Lou were both green!"

"Manny Perry is amazing. Talk about color blind; who knew Lou's stunt double was black?" *Hulk* producer Karen Harris laughs. "Manny was fun and a great stunt double for Lou."

He is also The Hulk you see exploding out of his shoes and tearing out of a shirt in the inserts used during transformation scenes every episode, while wrestler Ric Drasin doubles the mutating Banner. Perry looks back at his stint as the Stunt Hulk with great fondness. "As the Stunt Hulk, I would jump out of

Manny Perry on wires. PHOTO BY VENITA OZOLS

a 747 [in the episode '747'] and race across the runway. I jumped 80 feet without shoes," he boasts with justifiable pride. "No shoes because Hulk doesn't wear shoes…Then I had to immediately race down the runway and knock over a fence! Running as The Hulk was the easiest part of the job. The hardest was in one show where Bill Bixby gets thrown into a briar patch with a hornet's nest inside it. We did the zoom-in where Bixby's eyes start to turn green as he metamorphoses into The Hulk. Because of this, I had to be in the briar patch.

"In my shirt, I had a little box with a Queen Bee inside. At one point they released 10,000 bees who swarmed over me trying to get to the Queen. 80% of my body was covered by those bees! Lying there with those bees buzzing around your eyes, ears and nose is quite an eerie feeling," he shudders. "I got stung a couple times, but that's not bad considering the amount of bees they were using."

Doing stunts on a hit TV show "was exciting. I was very new, so I was overwhelmed by just being a stuntman. Still, I was impressed to see big stars on the show, like Loni Anderson and Gerald McRaney. Gerald was a great guy; he did a bunch of *Hulk* episodes as a bad guy, before he went onto his own series, *Simon & Simon*. He was terrific.

"I got the part of The Stunt Hulk because I was a competitive body-builder and I had just won the Mr. America and Mr. USA competitions. I was trying to get my foot in the door of Hollywood as a stuntman, but I didn't have any relatives in the business to say, 'Let me help you out...,' so I had to make my own way."

Hulk came into his life when "a buddy of mine said, 'They are looking for a guy to stunt double Lou Ferrigno as that Incredible Hulk character. I'm not sure if it's gonna work, because he's white and you're black, but...' I said, 'Okay, at least I have a shot at it!'"

On his *Hulk* audition, "There were 30 guys trying for it, most of them football player types, big shoulders, big waists, but they didn't have the chiseled neat physique like bodybuilders do. There were a couple of body-builders there, but most of those guys were short. At the time, I was 6'2" and weighed 260 pounds. I had just come off of competition, so I was in tiptop shape.

"When I walked into the office, all eyes went on me, but there was obviously concern because I was an African American looking to double a Caucasian guy! There was concern over the legality of that with the Screen Actors Guild. I worked my way through it and ended up being one of three finalists for The Stunt Hulk. We went onto the Universal Studios backlot and they took one guy 20 feet up the side of a building with a dummy in his arms. They told him to jump into an airbag, because The Hulk saves people. They explained for Hulk to save people every week, he'd have to smash through glass and brick.

"As the three of us gathered, we weren't painted green yet. We were in regular clothes just to see if we could handle it. The stunt coordinator briefed us on how to fall. I had already been practicing to be a stuntman, so I had some skills. The first guy jumped with the dummy in his arms, but he didn't do it properly. The guy landed on his feet, his knees buckled and hit him in the chin, sending his bottom teeth *through his lower lip*," Manny Perry winces. "He bled all over himself, the dummy and the airbag. He decided right away 'this isn't for me,' threw down the dummy and just walked off the backlot!

"The second guy went up the side of the building, crawled along the ledge with the same dummy in his arms. They screamed, 'Action — GO!' He just stood there contemplating. They repeated, 'Action — GO!' He still stood there, obviously thinking about what just happened to the other guy. After 90 seconds of standing there as they urged, 'Do something!,' he threw the dummy into the bag and climbed down, saying, 'I'm out of here!'

"Lo and behold, that left only me, myself and I! I went up, grabbed the dummy and jumped off the building with the dummy in my arms. I did what they call 'Layout,' where you go to your back and hit the bag. When you jump into an airbag, going to your feet is *not* the thing to do. Sometimes you will bounce right back off and land on the ground, or wind up like the guy I auditioned with, and have your knees slam into your face — which can break your nose or jaw. When you jump into a bag, you need to lie out, throw your head out and your body naturally follows in that direction or turns over and lands flat on the bag," he explains. "Everything was perfect. We did a couple of other little Hulk things with that great stunt coordinator, Frank Orsatti.

"Frank told me, 'When you walked in, you were my first choice, but I had to look at everyone… There may be a problem with your skin color.' I said, 'Okay, we made it past the first round; let's see if we can go through the second.' He went back to the studio and talked to his producers. A week later, they brought me in so the producers and directors could take a look at me.

"I did the same type of Hulk things. They said, 'That looked good. Manny seems to have all the abilities we need and obviously, the look is there. Let's do a more serious test. Take Manny to makeup and hair, have him painted green and get him and Lou together in makeup. We'll have them run through a *Hulk* obstacle course and see if he works as a double.' They had me come to Universal Studios at 3 a.m. and it took them four and a half hours to do me in the Hulk makeup and wig.

"They took Lou Ferrigno and me up to the Saugus Racetrack, to run an obstacle course. Louie ran it and I ran behind him. If Louie jumped over something, I jumped over it the same way. We went left to right, up and over. There were some things that Louie could not do, because he's an actor, not a stuntman. At the end of the day, they decided, 'We like this guy, it's gonna work, so let's do a really close makeup test in the studio on stage, with proper lighting.' We did that and I got the job.

"My [skin color] was a problem because at that time in the late '70s, there were a lot of Caucasian stuntmen being 'painted down' to look like

African-American actors they were doubling. At that point, the NAACP was at the top of their game, so they called the studios and complained they were taking jobs from black stuntmen. That became an issue, because I was in the same situation, but in reverse. Here I was, a black guy, doubling a white guy. Even though we were green, that was the case.

"My buddy Frank Orsatti said to the stunt community, 'Hey, if anybody

Manny Perry's Stunt Hulk in action.

would like to complain and think that they have someone better suited for the job, I have an open invitation: bring yourselves down here and we'll take a look at you.' Obviously, nobody came because nobody had that type of physique. Stuntmen weren't developing their bodies to be muscled up like a competitive bodybuilder. I used bodybuilding to get into show business. I got the job and our show went on for five years."

Because of the difference in their skin pigmentation, there was a concern it would alter the green color of The Hulk. "In automotive classes, you learn that when you had a base coat, the 'primer' is the color underneath your top coat of paint on your car. If you had a gold or tan base — the top coat of color is influenced by that bottom base coat of color. As my base coat was black and Louie's primer was white, would that top coat of green have a different texture, a different tint, a different color? That would be a problem if the camera caught Louie as one shade of green and me as a different shade of green. If it was a problem, that meant they would have to alter the makeup. Were they willing to do that to have me as a stuntman? Happily, the top coat didn't show any difference of tone between Louie and myself."

Turning into a Hulk was a painstaking process. "While doing the show, I lived in Marina Del Rey and left my house at 3:30 a.m. to be in the makeup chair by 4:00 a.m. I would sit in that chair for three or four hours having that Hulk makeup put on. To become The Hulk, you had a wig to put on, a forehead piece that had to be blended in, a nose, all latex material and on top of all that, you had to be painted green," he moans. "Then they added the eyes and teeth. All the hair on my body had to be shaved off and it was quite time-consuming, but it was all worth it.

"The makeup didn't bother me at all. When you perspire, you do it through your pores and 60% of your body temperature is released through your scalp. Having a wig on made it kind of tough to cool the body down," Manny Perry grimaces. "We worked in the summer when it was hot; 99 degrees through 105! The makeup was a water-based clay makeup, so Lou and I would sit in the motor home, cooling our bodies down until everything was set. When the lights were perfect and the cameras ready to roll, that's when they would bring us out to do whatever we had to do…Louie to do the acting and me to rescue a kid, crush a car or jump off of something!

"We couldn't spend too much time on location under the hot lights; because our bodies would start to heat up and you would perspire, dripping off the green paint. I never had any side effects from the makeup, but we could only shoot for short periods of time before it would start running off on camera. In the winter months when it was cooler, we could shoot for longer periods of time."

Before he got the show, "I was aware of Louie Ferrigno from bodybuilding. He was winning big competitions at 16 and 17, so I would see him in the magazines. When he came to California, we all worked out at the world-famous Gold's Gym. I would see him there and we were both from back East. When he walked in to work out, he was the biggest thing any of us had ever seen!

"I immediately teamed up with him. I told him, 'Louie, you're gonna do real well in competition.' He was gonna go up against Arnold [Schwarzenegger], because that was the guy Louie was trying to dethrone," the stuntman recollects. "Louie had won all of the competitions below Mr. Olympia, so that was his target. I was 'Mr. America.' Louie and I became buddies, he got the call to play The Hulk and a month after that, I got the call to be his stunt double. We hung out and trained together while doing *Hulk*. Eventually, they opened a gym on the Universal Studios backlot for us."

As for Hulk's alter ego, Bill Bixby, "I liked Bill a lot — he was very warm and open," Perry declares. "He took me in; he knew I was new, so Bill gave me good encouragement. A true gentleman, Bill was always very gracious and kind. We got to be very close. Before *The Incredible Hulk*, my first job was playing Big Jim Slade in John Landis' *Kentucky Fried Movie*. Ironically, Bill Bixby had a part in that movie, too. Both Bill and John

Landis were great to me. Six months later, we were working together on *The Incredible Hulk*. I knew Bill from loving his TV show, *My Favorite Martian*."

Hulk producer "Kenny Johnson was a great guy. A really nice man and good director/producer. Kenny was one of the first guys to give me an opportunity. He could have said yes or no to me being The Stunt Hulk. By saying 'yes,' he changed my life and put me on the map! I had a five-year job as the top stuntman on a hit TV show. He would walk up and give me a hug every day on set. I also met his wife, Susie, a sweet lady. Kenny is a great family man. I owe a lot of my career to Kenny Johnson."

Hulk battled a lot of animals on the show…It's hard for Perry to pick the toughest one he worked with. "When you work with animals, you have to be careful. I remember I had to fight this bull [in the episode 'Jake']. We were shooting in Pico Rivera, California, and we had this Brahma bull, an 1800-pound animal who was six feet tall at the hump. So in the episode, Hulk is at the middle of the arena and this bull is set loose to charge after him. We did all the coverage of the camera over the Hulk's shoulder as the bull ran at him, then we had the wranglers come in to divert the bull. Finally, we had to do a shot where the bull approached The Hulk and Hulk is more powerful than the bull.

"We tried to use an animatronic bull, but we just could not make it look convincing. The bull looked fake; the angles for the camera just would not work, so we brought the real bull in and sedated him, because he was a wild animal and we could not contain him. In the middle of the arena, we set all our cameras up and I literally got the bull by the horns. I had one horn in each hand as I try to muscle him down, so it would look like his head was being twisted to the ground.

"The wranglers said, 'Whatever you do, do *not* let the bull get under you…' Meaning do not let him bring your bodyweight up over his head. When you lean into bulls like that, they are so strong; they will just flip you like a flea! I was Mr. America, 6'2", 260 pounds, so I said, '*Bull get me?* Hah — No way!' We did two or three set-ups with the bull, I was comfortable and my confidence level was getting up.

"Suddenly, the bull looked up at me intensely: his eyes were right on mine. I said, 'That's a peculiar look' and then he dipped his head under me with his horns and got me over him, my entire bodyweight was laying on his horns. He did one little flick with his 30-inch neck and that flick hurled me eight feet into the air and threw me back 25 feet, right on my butt!

"His strength was unbelievable," an astonished Manny Perry whispers. "I never thought anything could do that to me, with me being so big. I wasn't hurt, the arena sand is soft — but it shook me up. For take two, I was on my toes, determined not to let him get me over again.

"Animals are unpredictable. In the second *Hulk* TV movie, we did a scene in a river bed with a bear who was supposed to wrestle The Hulk. The Hulk and the bear have this little scuffle. The animal trainer, Monty Cox, had different bears, but the director [Alan J. Levi] and producer [Kenneth Johnson] liked this one brown bear named Pooh Bear.

"Lou and I wrestled Pooh Bear a little bit on land and then in the water. I remember, during one take, he put one of his paws in between my legs, wrapped the paw around my thigh and then pulled the paw and my leg into his body. I never felt so helpless or so scared…The enormous strength of this animal put real fear into me! Whatever he decided to do to me, there was nothing I could have done to defend myself against this bear's power."

Ferrigno loved carrying women on the show. Manny Perry enthusiastically agrees. "Oh yeah; it's part of being the hero; you're rescuing a beautiful lady or little girl. If she's menaced by an animal or something, Hulk would come in, handle the threat and carry her away. Fight scenes on *The Incredible Hulk* weren't too bad, because you were working with experienced stuntmen who would help me throw them. The Hulk would not punch people because he didn't have those kinds of skills. The Hulk was a menacing character who would grab you by the back of your collar and toss you."

To hurl his enemies away, The Hulk had help. "We had an apparatus called an air-ram, which is a nitrogen-charged platform with a trap door. You stand on it, press a button and the trap door would throw you! The guys I roughed up as The Hulk would hit the button as I was throwing them and with the air-ram, I could throw them 20 feet! One of our best stuntmen, Dennis 'Danger' Madalone, was always a punk I would rough up on the show. Being thrown by air-rams is one of Dennis' specialties. He'd come in as an MP in a helmet, Hulk would grab his gun from him and wrap it around his neck like a bar. In another episode, Dennis would be a gang member who gets backhanded by The Hulk. We had him on a ratchet that would make him fly backwards. When Hulk was in a hurry, we just had him quickly backhand somebody."

As The Incredible Stunt Hulk, Perry knew how to bash through brick. "The walls I would smash through as The Hulk were always made out of balsa wood. They would lay a light thin coat of concrete on one side covered by fake brick. "When The Hulk was in a position where he was trapped in a building by men with weapons, the quickest way out is a straight line. Hulk would not walk around a table, open a door and walk out. No, Hulk would go straight *through* the nearest table and wall. There was a certain way you would have to go through a wall. You protect your face as your forearm actually breaks the wall! As you go through, you open yourself up to keep debris from cutting up your face or getting in your eyes. Once you were on the other side of the wall, they would put Louie over there and he would step out and pick up the action."

His wardrobe was pretty specific. "Hulk wore cut-off shorts and a ripped-up shirt. I also did all of the inserts on the show. When you saw Banner's shirt rip as he Hulked Out, that was my arm! I used my chest to pop out of the shirt and used my back to tear a seam. I did all of the inserts on a separate stage on a separate day. They did all of the close-ups, while Louie would be acting as The Hulk in another episode.

"For the scenes where Banner is going from Bill Bixby to The Hulk, I brought in Ric Drasin as someone we could cut to in-between, once the metamorphosis started happening and we could see a full-body figure who was not as big as Ferrigno or myself, but certainly bigger than Bixby. That would bring in a little transition. I brought in several guys from the gym. Ric Drasin is a friend from the gym and he got the job."

In one of the more ambitious episodes, "Blind Rage," Manny Perry doubled Hulk as he battles a tank. "Oh, I do remember that *quite clearly*," Perry laughs nervously. "It was one of the highest-rated shows of the entire series. I remember fighting that tank and thinking, 'This is pretty challenging for The Hulk...Is The Hulk gonna win over the tank? Tank's pretty tough, but The Hulk is tougher!'

"Whenever we had stunts of that magnitude, you don't just go out and do it. We take that action sequence and rehearse it pretty thoroughly. You never do a stunt unless you're gonna feel that all safety issues have been totally addressed. You get to a point where you're pushing the envelope, as safe as you can get it without crossing the line. Now you're standing in front of a tank and pushing against it, as you think, 'Maybe the driver is gonna miss the brake and hit the throttle — that could be the end of it — and the end of me!'"

For Hulk's weekly adventures, "Frank Orsatti stunt coordinated the show, Ernie Orsatti would work the show, he was Frank's younger brother, and Rex Pierson, who was a half-brother to the Orsattis. Rex was The Hulk's stand-in. My mom, dad, aunts and uncles would come visit me on the set of *The Incredible Hulk*. They left their little town in Cape Cod to visit their son, the lead stuntman on a hit TV series...It was almost like a fantasy for them! Of course, I would never tell my mom when I had to do the more dangerous stunts. I would get them chairs on set, they sat next to the monitors and got to watch me run and jump, smash and crash. That was a proud moment for me, seeing them watch me on the show.

Manny Perry is happy. "My young son knows I was The Stunt Hulk. My son, Quinn Hugh Perry, is a huge Hulk fan; he's got Hulk pictures all over the place, the Hulk doll, the comics, he has it all."

HULK PROFILE

DANGER DENNIS MADALONE, FALL GUY

With his long hair, jeans and locket photos of his deceased dogs around his neck, stuntman Danger Dennis Madalone is one of a kind. As a stunt coordinator, he set up the violence of Quentin Tarantino's *Pulp Fiction*, been eaten by monsters, beaten up and killed on various *Star Trek* spin-offs, including *The Next Generation, Deep Space Nine* and *Voyager*.

Madalone also doubled William Katt for so many hair raising stunts as *The Greatest American Hero*, the show's creator, Stephen J. Cannell said, "We would see him do these things and think, 'Oh My God — we killed Dennis!'" Madalone did various stunts on *The Incredible Hulk*, including falls, throws and fights. He occasionally doubled Bill Bixby.

Hulk stuntman Dennis Madalone also doubled William Katt's *Greatest American Hero*. PHOTO BY PATRICK JANKIEWICZ

"I loved doing *Hulk*," Dennis Madalone offers. "I was the stunt double for a lot of the bad guys. Frank Orsatti was stunt coordinator on *Hulk*. He loved his crew and he took care of all us stunt people who worked on the show. Frank Orsatti actually let me double Bill a few times…That was an honor! My hair was shorter then, so I could pass for Bill's double. I also played a lot of punks and goons on the show. Lou Ferrigno's stunt double, Manny Perry, and I have known each other a long time. Manny would toss me around as the Stunt Hulk!

"I met Manny when he was a bodybuilder and I helped him get an interview to double The Hulk and the rest is history. Manny, Frank and Tommy Huff are truly the best! Great guys and great stuntmen. I worked with Lou Ferrigno all the time on the show. Hulk threw me around a lot; so I did a lot of falls on the show.

"When Lou threw you, you stayed thrown," Madalone jokes. "In one show, Lou threw me down a flight of stairs and let me tell you, *that* was a crazy ride! It was my very first stairway fall and I think I was trying too hard to hide my face after Lou threw me. I'm flyin' down the stairs, I should have paid more attention to the fall!

"Bill Bixby was the greatest…I actually bought his van from him when we were doing the *Hulk* show," the stuntman adds. "Frank Orsatti said, 'Would you like to buy Bill's van?' This big yellow van, it used to be Frank's van. Frank sold it to Bill and Bill sold it to me. I loved it; that was a nice, hip van!"

HULK PROFILE
JACK COLVIN, ROVING REPORTER

Jack Colvin played hard-nosed reporter Jack McGee of supermarket tabloid *The National Register* in the pilot for *The Incredible Hulk* and all five seasons of the series. He reprised McGee for the 1988 TV movie *The Incredible Hulk Returns*. As McGee, Colvin relentlessly hunts Banner and The Hulk for the run of the series.

Jack Colvin, whose wonderful reporter had hangdog eyes and a perpetual sneer, made McGee alternately threatening and sympathetic to Banner. McGee is not evil; the series takes great pains to show he simply recognizes The Hulk's existence as the story of the century and he wants to be the one to tell it. He is as obsessed with finding The Hulk as David Banner is with curing himself.

Kenneth Johnson found "Jack Colvin to be a fun guy. He was a contract player at Universal. A good actor, Jack used to joke that he only had one line per episode: 'I'm looking for a large green creature?'" *Los Angeles Times'* TV critic Kevin Thomas praised Colvin for doing "more with this character than it probably deserves."

Because McGee was not in every episode or starring like Bixby, Jack Colvin wound up directing numerous episodes of the show. Hailing from Lyndon, Kansas, Colvin's family moved to California when he was a boy

Jack Colvin and Don Marshall.

and he became a stage actor. He was a pupil of acclaimed acting teacher Michael Chekhov. He later taught Chekhov's acting technique himself. Colvin also partnered with actress Yvonne Wilder as the comedy duo Colvin and Wilder. He was seen in numerous films alongside stars like John Wayne, Robert Redford, Paul Newman, Burt Lancaster, Bill Cosby and Charles Bronson.

On TV, he guested on *Rat Patrol, Kojak, The Six Million Dollar Man* and *The Rockford Files*. Outside of *The Incredible Hulk*, Jack Colvin is best known for dying at the hands of Chucky the killer doll in the original *Child's Play*. Colvin had been a popular actor in Los Angeles stage productions.

He told *The Los Angeles Times* that he was uncertain when *Hulk* first came his way. "When they told me the title, I laughed...But then they gave me two scripts to read and I knew the series would go. People identify tremendously with the frustration, the rage and the anger that breaks out in a man."

McGee grows as the series goes on. In the pilot, McGee is unlikable, suspicious and untrustworthy. He becomes protective of Hulk in later seasons. For episodes like "No Escape" and "Bring Me the Head of the Hulk," he refuses to let someone kill the creature, even blocking their shot to save Hulk's life.

"Jack Colvin was an important part of the team with Bill and me," insists Lou Ferrigno. "Jack was a good guy. I'm sad that I lost touch with him before he died. He was so fun as McGee. He directed some great episodes as well. Besides Bill and me, he was the only other 'regular' our show had!"

Frequent *Hulk* guest Don Marshall remembers Colvin as "a nice guy, but he was always trying to make something happen for him as an actor. Jack was kind of hungry for that. It's understandable, because when you get a part like McGee, you really want to make the most of it, but Jack was really into Jack at that particular time. It wasn't so much the character, he was into his career. He was looking out for himself, while Bill Bixby looked out for everybody."

"Jack Colvin was great," enthuses Karen Harris. "A wonderful actor, a wonderful person — there was never any trouble with him. There are no bad Jack stories. He even directed some of the best episodes! He was a wonderful guy and is sorely missed.

"Poor Jack had a really tough time at the end of his career," Harris continues. "He had a stroke and no family to take care of him. Actress Sharon Gless stayed fairly close to him. Before her hit show *Cagney & Lacey*, she had been a contract player at Universal and she and Jack had been together for many years. Sharon met Barney Rosenweig on *Cagney* and they got married, but she and Jack had remained friends. It's my understanding that she actually helped Jack out a lot. In fact, I know the girl who was Jack's neighbor and she took his dog in when he passed away."

Colvin died in 2005 at the age of 71, from complications after another stroke.

Stunt Hulk Manny Perry found "Jack Colvin to be a real gentleman. He directed a few episodes. On the show itself, his Jack McGee was the guy always trying to run down The Hulk, but he was always a day late and a dollar short. When he came into town thinking he had The Hulk trapped, Bixby's Banner had already left. Jack was a nice, kind man and personally, he was very helpful to me. I had a few little acting roles on the series outside of the green as a stunt performer. I would be a thug or a crook, so Jack and Bixby always helped me get motivated."

HULK PROFILE

KAREN HARRIS & JILL SHERMAN, STORY EDITORS/PRODUCERS

One of the biggest success stories to come out of *The Incredible Hulk* TV series was the writing team of Karen Harris and Jill Sherman. They jumped from obscurity — before *Hulk*, Sherman was literally scrubbing toilets on the Universal backlot that she would later use as a *Magnum P.I.* writer! The duo first rose to story editors/producers on *The Incredible Hulk* TV show.

When *The Incredible Hulk* became a series, the show needed writers in a hurry. "My friend Karen Harris and I decided to team up as writers," beams Jill Sherman Donner, who became co-story editor with Harris. "Karen and I heard that Ken Johnson had such a hit at CBS with *The Incredible Hulk* TV movies, they wanted *Hulk* scripts faster than the speed of light.

"We didn't know who The Hulk was, but we certainly knew what starvation was. They needed scripts quickly, so they agreed to see us! Ken met with us, we did a couple of freelance scripts and we were made story editors right away. I would have been thrilled to write anything, but *The Incredible Hulk* was really my niche; I loved sci-fi, so this was great!"

Just as *Hulk* was becoming a series, Karen Harris remembers, "I was typing scripts for a living for other people, but I wasn't a writer. I got the process of writing from typing other peoples' scripts. Jill was editing a skateboard magazine, so together we almost made one good writer! Jill was also reviewing movies for a Palm Springs TV station. We went to a screening of *Star Wars*. We sat through that opening shot of the spaceship being so huge that it went on and on with our mouths hanging open and said, '*That's* what we want to do!' My brother, Robert Harris, was an executive at Universal, who became president of the studio in the late '80s.

"My brother told us, 'There's a pilot that's just been made, the executive producer likes to work with women and young writers, and he's looking for people.' That was Kenny and *The Incredible Hulk*. We went to a screening of the pilot in a room with 15 other writers watching it. After that, we went in and pitched, 'The Hulk in a zoo' to Kenny and got our first assignment," Harris says happily. "That became the second episode of the series, 'The Beast Within.' At the start of the series, Bill Bixby would act angry to keep you on your toes. On 'Beast Within,' the first time we met him was when he had us come to his trailer to give us notes on the script…And instead of giving us notes, he tore us a new one!

"Bill essentially said, 'When I met with writers on *The Courtship of Eddie's Father*, I wasn't happy until they left in tears!' Jill cried at the drop of a hat, but I wasn't gonna cry in front of him," Karen Harris points out

Jill Sherman, Jim Hirsch and Karen Harris. PHOTO COURTESY OF KENNETH JOHNSON

proudly. "I wasn't gonna give him the satisfaction. Kenneth Johnson was a great teacher and mentor. We learned a lot about writing from him. One thing we learned from him that I have since passed on to many other writers is 'Don't write down to your audience. Don't write a comic book, write a good story.'

"When the show was going on, I would tell someone all the stuff that was happening to Karen and me on *Hulk*," adds Jill Sherman Donner. "All these crazy things that we did on a weekly basis and somebody once told us, 'You will be chasing this experience for the rest of your career.' And he was right — we have!"

Banner and The Hulk from the opening credits.

THE INCREDIBLE HULK TV SERIES

Upon its debut, *The Incredible Hulk* became CBS's highest-rated series, running on Friday nights at nine o'clock. A month later, it was joined by the popular soap opera *Dallas* at ten, which was about the squabbles between an oil rich Southern family and their most ruthless member, J.R. Ewing. Both became huge hits, with *Dallas* morphing into a full-fledged cultural phenomenon.

Hulk's ratings tenacity was impressive, as genre shows outside of *The Bionic Woman* and *Six Million Dollar Man* were not doing that well. The expensive, heavily hyped *Battlestar Galactica* crashed and burned that same season, as did *Fantastic Journey, Logan's Run* and *Lucan*, which was a preposterous *Six Million Dollar Man* rip-off about a guy who has super powers simply because he was raised by wolves!

The Incredible Hulk series followed the pattern of the second TV movie, with David Banner chasing a cure across the United States, inadvertently coming into a situation every week where the people helping him out really needed his help. He works a series of odd jobs and uses pseudonyms, usually beginning with his own first name, David.

Whether it was your first or 50th episode of the *Hulk*, the opening credits set up the premise beautifully. As with the second TV movie, we hear the narrator explain who David Banner is and why he becomes The Hulk over a series of visuals from the pilot. For the ongoing *Hulk* series, the opening narration was altered and perfected:

> *"Doctor David Banner, physician, scientist, searching for a way to tap into the hidden strengths that all humans have. Then an accidental overdose of Gamma Radiation alters his body chemistry. And now, when David Banner grows angry or outraged, a startling metamorphosis occurs. The creature is driven by rage and pursued by an investigative reporter. The creature is wanted for a murder he did not commit. David Banner is believed to be dead, and he must let the world think that he is dead, until he finds a way to control the raging spirit that dwells within him."*

"THE FINAL ROUND"

Season 1, Episode 1
Airdate: March 10, 1978
Directed By Kenneth Gilbert
Written By Kenneth Johnson
Banner's alias: "David Benson"

Cast

Dr. David Banner .... Bill Bixby
Jack McGee.. Jack Colvin
The Hulk ....Lou Ferrigno
Henry "Rocky" Welsh .... Martin Kove
Mary .... Fran Myers
Mr. Sariego .... Al Ruscio
Wilt... Paul Henry Itkin
Bill Cole .... Tony Brubaker
Man in Audience................................. Paul Micale
White Mugger.................................... T. Miratti
Black Mugger .... Ron Trice
Tom.. John Witherspoon

"Final Round" opens with David Banner in Delaware, where he's mugged. Before he can get angry, he's saved by Rocky, a good-natured boxer. Rocky lets David stay with him and even gets him a job at the gym as a medic/trainer. David notices Rocky is sent on mysterious errands by the gym's unfriendly owner, Mr. Sariego.

Mary, Rocky's girlfriend, tells David that Rocky has dangerously high blood pressure. When the gang of muggers attack David and Rocky again, Sariego's package rips open and the pair find that it's full of cocaine. Upset the two men know his secret, Sariego plans to have Rocky killed in a deliberate ring "accident" and murder David after the bout.

A nice, perfectly paced start to the series. Although David's story is secondary compared to the two telefilms, where David's problems are front and center, it's fun to see his character going into "TV series lead character" mode. The episode really centers on Rocky's problems, so it's the template for the series that follows. David Banner is a tormented guardian angel who insinuates himself into the life of a troubled person, family or town and proves better equipped at solving others' problems than his own. In the end, he solemnly moves on.

The climax, where Banner is held prisoner on a platform high above the arena as the fatal fight begins, was actually used previously on Kenneth Johnson's *The Bionic Woman* episode, "In This Corner, Jamie Sommers." Martin Kove is likable as the dim but noble Rocky, who is obviously based on Sylvester Stallone's iconic movie character. John Witherspoon is good as a sympathetic boxer.

Hulk stops the fight in "The Final Round."

MARTIN KOVE (Rocky Welsh): *"I did that* Hulk *in January 1978 and it was the very first episode of the series! I was excited, because The Incredible Hulk was the largest guest-starring role I ever had at that point, just a huge part. I had gotten into town a couple years earlier, met my ex-wife and brought her to the set. Bill Bixby was really cool; he was a great teacher to me. Bill was warm and very personable, a lovely man, and I was very sad when he passed away. A great guy to work with.*

"Whenever my future ex-wife came to the set, Bill was a charming guy and he was very much the host; showing her around. For a guy who had been in the business forever, he was a very gracious star and I appreciated that! It was a huge role for me and I was living in Agoura. One day, I remember being late because the alarm clock didn't wake me up and we were shooting at The Marina.

"I had the greatest time on that show because it was all about this boxer who talks like 'dis' and he was named Rocky...he was a direct rip-off of Sylvester

Stallone's Rocky! *A complete rip-off! They wanted the character's speaking style to be just like his in that movie, too. Sylvester is a friend, but we never talked about* Hulk *because there was a lawsuit over it.*

"*When I guest-starred on* Hulk, *Sly knew about the imitation, because he was at Universal making the movie* F.I.S.T. *Our guy on* The Incredible Hulk *bore a very strong likeness to* Rocky. *Because it was such an obvious*

Banner helps a young boxer named Rocky.

rip-off on Rocky, *they sued and it was settled.*

"*Lou Ferrigno was great. I enjoyed working with him and we still see each other, we're friends. Lou's a lovely guy, we go trap and skeet-shooting together. His speech is so much better now, much more fluid than it was then.*"

KENNETH JOHNSON: "*I had already left* The Bionic Woman *by the time I did* The Incredible Hulk *television series. Lindsay [Wagner] had gotten into a really bad place by the second full season, personally, emotionally and medically. Our relationship had deteriorated, because when you're a big star overnight after being a contract player living in a small hovel on Benedict Canyon, it begins to work on you. She went from unknown to being a person who couldn't go to Disneyland without being mobbed.*

"You unfortunately attract a lot of sycophants, who surround you like Erlich and Haldeman surrounded Nixon. I was the only one being straight with her and she didn't want to hear it.

"I went to Frank [Price, then head of Universal TV] and said, 'This is a train heading for a wall, I gotta get off before it hits!' He asked me to please stay onboard a little while longer, and finish the season, but one day Lindsay announced, 'I'm not coming to the set until he's gone'–'he' *meaning me! I said, 'Great, I'm out of here.' At that point, I had already done the* Hulk *pilot, so the timing was perfect. Frankly, I was glad to be gone. I went and did* The Incredible Hulk *and had a great time! I left* The Bionic Woman *before they brought in Maximillian [The Bionic Dog]. It was truly symbolic — the show had really gone to the dogs!"*

HULK PROFILE

It's the first time Jack McGee and The Hulk really meet face to face. In the pilot, he only sees Hulk from a distance. As Hulk exits the stadium at the climax, he recognizes the reporter and stops to roar angrily at McGee!

HULK FACTS

Nice opening fake-out; when David is set upon by muggers. We think he'll Hulk Out, but instead he's saved by Kove.

Another surprise has one of Sariego's boxers knock David unconscious before he can Hulk Out.

Hulk gets cocaine all over his foot.

David claims to have been a medic in Vietnam.

The first of director Kenneth Gilbert's four *Incredible Hulk* episodes.

Martin Kove, who usually plays villains in films like *Rambo, Death Race 2000* and *Karate Kid,* gets to be a good guy here.

This is also the first time we see Hulk smash through a wall and run down an alley: Pay attention to this shot, because it will be re-used throughout the series, in the episodes "Captive Night," "Kindred Spirits" and "Metamorphosis."

Comedian John Witherspoon, best known as the dad in the *Friday* comedies, plays it straight here in one of his first roles.

Shot at the Olympic boxing arena in downtown Los Angeles. The Olympic was also used as the setting for another Marvel Comics superhero, in the movie *Daredevil*.

"THE BEAST WITHIN"
Season 1, Episode 2
Airdate: March 17, 1978
Directed By Kenneth Gilbert
Written By Karen Harris & Jill Sherman
Banner's alias: "David Bradburn"

Cast

Dr. David Banner . . . . Bill Bixby
Jack McGee. . . . . Jack Colvin
The Hulk . . . . .Lou Ferrigno
Dr. Claudia Baxter. . . . . .Caroline McWilliams
Carl . . . . Richard Kelton
Dr. Malone . . . . Dabbs Greer

David works at a zoo to find out about an anti-aggression compound being used on the animals there. The compound's creator, Dr. Claudia Baxter, is doing anti-rage research that David hopes will free him of The Hulk. To demonstrate her drug's success, Claudia has Elliot, a giant gorilla, roaming around her office in an attached enclosure. Although he looks menacing, Elliot is docile as a lamb.

As David and Claudia start to get romantic, her colleague Carl gets jealous and injects Elliot with a rage compound. He locks David in a cage with the now antagonistic Elliot, who brutally attacks the put-upon scientist. David changes and The Hulk immediately beats Elliot down. Zoo animals keep dying mysteriously. Claudia and David learn that Carl is helping Dr. Malone needlessly kill the animals to use them for other purposes. Jack McGee shows up looking for The Hulk. Malone and Carl inject David with a full dose of the Rage Drug and it's up to the power of The Hulk to save him and Claudia.

Although the gorilla costume is ridiculous, Hulk's punch-out with Elliot is pretty satisfying. "The Beast Within" has some nice moments, the best being Claudia telling David that she has studied Banner's work on aggression. He's amused when she complains that the late Dr. Banner "can be terribly long-winded," unaware that she's talking to the man himself. Humorously, David agrees with her! Hulk also changes back to David in a tiger pen, petting a cub, which soothes him. When he's David again, he gently lifts the cub off his lap and it spontaneously crawls back on.

Bill Bixby at the zoo in "The Beast Within."

JILL SHERMAN DONNER: *"I have always been a science-fiction buff, so I loved* The Incredible Hulk *because it was* Dr. Jekyll and Mr. Hyde. *It was our first job and the series went almost five years. 'The Beast Within' was our 'Hulk in a zoo' pitch. As an animal rights activist, I was glad they didn't use a real gorilla to play Elliot."*

KAREN HARRIS: *"Our pitch was 'The Hulk is in a zoo and he faces off with a gorilla' — they loved that! The guy in the gorilla suit is pretty obvious, but we were just happy to have our script filmed, it was so exciting! I remember specifically, Jill and I wrote "INT. ZOO LAB. The walls are covered with shelves of multicolored bottles, filled with unknown liquids.' We walk onto the set and there's a shelf of multicolored bottles. We almost wet ourselves — we made it up and there it is. To be honest, it looked pretty absurd! It just looked silly, like an apothecary. We thought, 'Uh oh, we have to be careful with what we put on the page, because it's gonna actually show up.' "*

HULK HIGHLIGHT
The green one fights a gorilla!

HULK FACTS
First episode written by Karen Harris & Jill Sherman, the series' most prolific writers.

The zoo tour buses are actually repainted '70s Universal tour trams.

Elliot the Gorilla is obviously there because of the success of Dino De Laurentiis' then-recent *King Kong* remake. Lynda Carter's Wonder Woman battled a gorilla for the same reason that season.

Richard Kelton (Carl) starred in the sci-fi comedy series *Quark.* He died within months of doing *Hulk.* Kelton asphyxiated from a carbon monoxide leak in his trailer in a bizarre accident while shooting the miniseries *Centennial.*

Character actor Dabbs Greer played the elderly version of Tom Hanks' character in *The Green Mile.*

Caroline McWilliams (Claudia) is no stranger to superheroes; she was married to movie Batman Michael Keaton.

"OF GUILT, MODELS AND MURDER"
Season 1, Episode 3
Airdate: March 24, 1978
Directed By Larry Stewart
Written By James D. Parriott
Banner's alias: "David Blaine"

Cast
Dr. David Banner . . . . Bill Bixby
Jack McGee. . . . . Jack Colvin
The Hulk . . . . .Lou Ferrigno
James Joslin . . . . Jeremy Brett
Sheila Cantrell. . . . . Loni Anderson
Girl . . . . .Jane Alice Brandon
Jackson. . . . . Bill Baldwin

Collins . . . . Ross Durfee
Elkin . . . . .Rick Goldman
TV Reporter . . . . Doug Hale
Security Guard . . . . .Vince Howard
Policeman . . . . .Art Kimbro
Terri Ann. . . . . Deanna Lund
Ellen . . . . Nancy Steen
Dr. Elaina Marks (Flashback footage). . . . . .Susan Sullivan

David Banner is in the final seconds of changing back from The Hulk. Banner sees that he's in a swanky mansion which The Hulk has torn apart. Splashing water in his face in a bathroom sink, he turns to leave. To his horror, he suddenly sees the body of a murdered woman in the corner. Banner checks her pulse. She's dead from a broken neck. Did The Hulk kill her? He can only remember bits and pieces of the night. Responding to a woman's cries for help, Banner remembers charging onto the grounds of a private estate when he's attacked by savage doberman pinschers. Slipping into the California night, David hears the LAPD issue a manhunt for The Hulk. During a live press conference on every channel, The L.A. Police Chief announces, "As long as this creature is on the loose, everyone's life is in danger."

The victim was Joslin Cosmetics Spokesmodel Terri Ann Smith. David goes to work as a valet for Terri Ann's boyfriend, makeup millionaire James Joslin, to find the truth. Joslin, who expresses no genuine grief over Terri Ann's death, claims an enraged Hulk broke in and snapped Terri Ann's neck after she pretended to call for help. David only hazily recalls rushing up the driveway as he heard the beautiful Terri Ann crying for help. Before he can reach her, he's attacked by vicious guard dogs. Everything else is a blur to Banner.

The Dobermans bit and mauled him until his change was triggered. Because of The Hulk's involvement, Jack McGee is also nosing around. As Joslin's valet, David hopes to find out who really killed Terri Ann. Wandering the estate, he sees beautiful model Sheila Cantrell doing a photo shoot in a karate outfit. Fearful of Joslin's wrath, the scared Sheila confides to David that The Hulk is innocent. Joslin himself murdered Terri Ann for trying to blackmail him. When David seeks her help in going to the police, he then realizes that Joslin and Sheila are in cahoots. Sheila, a black belt, snapped Terri Ann's neck herself with a single blow, and then she lured David into a trap.

Joslin recognized David post-transformation in the mansion the night of the murder and wanted to tie up all loose ends. Joslin gloats, "I don't know where that creature came from, but he made the perfect scapegoat!" Now that David knows too much, he's going to be crushed alive in a car compactor.

"Of Guilt, Models and Murder" is a fantastic episode, a *Rashomon* scenario where we see a crime committed from every possible angle — including Hulk actually killing Terri Ann — and we're left to draw our own conclusions. The opening reveal is a creepy shock, with Banner's slow realization that he's alone in a mansion with a dead woman he may be responsible for killing. Using Banner's lack of memory from his Hulk Out to place him in a murder mystery is really clever.

Because Jeremy Brett plays Joslin as so autocratic, British and cold, we naturally assume he's the murderer. Instead, the third-act revelation that Loni Anderson's doe-eyed, seemingly innocent, Sheila is a kung-fu killer is a real surprise. But the show plays fair every step of the way, even showing her in the karate outfit

Despite being a sweet lady, Deanna Lund is murdered several times in the show — once by The Hulk!
PHOTO BY PATRICK JANKIEWICZ

snapping boards to establish she had the power. Loni Anderson is quite good, revealing at the end how and why she did it. Terri Ann's death, and Banner's guilt at the very real possibility of The Hulk being her murderer, is driven home by actress Deanna Lund's resemblance to Lara Parker, the redhead who played the late Mrs. Laura Banner in *The Incredible Hulk* pilot. While wondering if he killed Terri Ann after Hulking Out, David has a flashback of the late, great Elaina Marks from the pilot, reminding him that The Hulk is not a killer because "David Banner is *not* a killer."

Bixby conveys guilt and remorse beautifully in the show and when he finds the real killer, he exudes a palpable sense of relief. As the LAPD and other credible authorities acknowledge the living presence of The

Hulk, it makes later episodes where regular people scoff at Jack McGee by calling The Hulk a tabloid hoax somewhat dubious.

DEANNA LUND (Terri Ann): *"I remember getting killed several times in that show during the flashbacks of what everyone claims happened, even being killed once by The Hulk! He's innocent, of course, because Loni Anderson really broke my neck with a kung-fu kick. That was funny!*

"I knew and liked Bill Bixby and his late wife, Brenda Benet, from when I worked with them both on the TV show Search. *My favorite part about doing* The Incredible Hulk *is when Lou Ferrigno comes in as The Hulk to save me, but I've already been killed. For the rest of the show, he's not sure if he killed me or not. Being held by The Hulk was actually a lot of fun! Lou is a nice guy, very big and very gentle, I liked him a lot! It was really amazing and fun being carried by The Hulk. For the scene where he cradles my dead body, he lifted me up like I was a baby!*

"To be honest, I kept thinking Bill Bixby was the director of my episode instead of Larry Stewart, because he called all the shots in my scenes. Bill knew what he wanted and really didn't hesitate to make sure he got it. I remember thinking, 'If he isn't a director, he should be!' He could do the camera shots and angles, but he could also deal with actors and their performances."

LOU FERRIGNO (Hulk): *"I was very nervous around those Doberman pinschers; even though they were very sweet dogs. When it comes to animals, being in makeup with the way I looked as Hulk, I always worried that the animals would perceive me as a dangerous predator. We had an animal trainer who worked very hard to make sure that didn't happen with any of the animals, but one day, doing this particular episode, one of those Dobermans suddenly growled at me...We kept shooting with that one dog and I was just hoping to go home in one piece!"*

KENNETH JOHNSON: *"I was lucky to have writer/producers like Jim Parriott. We worked together on* Bionic Woman *and on every script for that show, Jim or I would always do the final pass, just to keep her character consistent."*

MANNY PERRY (Stunt Hulk): *" 'Of Guilt, Models and Murder' has one of the most frightening stunts I ever did on the show. In the junkyard, you have this thing called a 'Car Crusher.' It takes cars and turns them wafer-thin. We had a scene where Bixby is thrown into a trunk. A forklift throws the car into the crusher as we zoom-in on Bixby's eyes through a crack in the trunk to show the metamorphosis start. The Hulk jumps up, stops the crusher and blows the hydraulic line. To be inside that car when the crusher was coming down,*

I suddenly thought, 'If this crusher malfunctions and I hit the STOP button, but it doesn't stop that's it!' To be in the car hearing and feeling that thing coming down on you is quite unnerving. It was very scary!"

HULK HIGHLIGHT
The Hulk fought a bear and an ape in previous shows. Here, he goes up against Dobermans.

HULK FACTS
Whether or not he may have killed or harmed someone as The Hulk is a constant fear of the comics' Bruce Banner.

Nice bit between David and teenage runaway Jane Alice Brandon, who sees him as a kindred spirit of the road.

Hulk loses his prominent "Frankenstein brow" in this episode, for a more toned down one.

David gets the killers' confession with Jack McGee's tape recorder.

Art Kimbro (Policeman) co-starred in *Beverly Hills Cop* and voiced the demonic Lamia in Sam Raimi's *Drag Me To Hell*.

In the 1980s, Jeremy Brett went on to play the world's greatest detective in the incredibly popular PBS series *Adventures of Sherlock Holmes*.

Within months of her *Hulk*, Loni Anderson became a national sex symbol and CBS star on the sitcom *WKRP In Cincinnati*.

Deanna Lund starred in the sci-fi cult series *Land of the Giants*.

Nancy Steen (Ellen) became a big writer/producer on shows like *Roseanne*, *Night Court* and *Caroline In The City*.

Doug Hale frequently plays newscasters and worked on *Bionic Woman*'s "Fembots in Las Vegas" two-parter.

There's a bright-yellow 1977 Honda Civic prominently displayed in an establishing shot. This exact same Honda is also seen in an establishing shot in "Final Round."

HULK PROFILE
LONI ANDERSON

Blonde and beautiful, Loni Anderson is a TV icon. Before her sitcom success, Anderson was a popular guest star on TV shows like *The Love Boat, Three's Company, S.W.A.T., The Bob Newhart Show* and *Barnaby Jones.*

Lou Ferrigno with Loni Anderson, Venita Ozols, and other members of the HULK crew. PHOTO BY VENITA OZOLS

Loni Anderson also played it serious when she guest starred on *The Incredible Hulk* as the murderous model Sheila.

"I loved Bill Bixby," Loni Anderson coos. "He was a really inventive director. Bill had directed me in a TV movie called *Three On A Date.* It was the first blonde thing I had ever done and everything took off after that. When I was doing that, he asked me to 'come be a killer with me on *The Incredible Hulk* '. Of course I said 'Yes'."

"I break Deanna Lund's neck and frame The Hulk for her murder in the episode 'Of Guilt, Models and Murder'," she boasts. "Everyone thinks The Hulk did it and no one, not even Bill, knows I really killed her! Because I was a blonde for Bill on *Three On A Date,* he said 'As the killer, I *don't* want you to be a blonde. I want you dark haired.' I put a dark rinse back in my hair before we shot it, so in the episode, it's kind of brown. I had a great time on the show! The crew was very nice. Lou Ferrigno was a dear. His stuntman (Manny Perry) actually showed me how to do a stunt where I break something in a scene demonstrating my kung-fu prowess. Lou was so sweet and gentle as The Hulk. He and Carla came to my wedding party.

"Jeremy Brett played the owner of the cosmetics company. I pretend to be afraid of him to set Bill Bixby up. Jeremy was a nice man and after we did *The Incredible Hulk,* he went on to become my favorite Sherlock Holmes in his brilliant PBS series. It was fun to play a killer…I look and act innocent to get Bill Bixby to trust me and then he learns that I really killed Deanna, not Hulk! Because I was a killer on the show, my grandmother back in Minnesota actually refused to watch my *Hulk* episode," the actress smiles. "She said, 'I don't want to watch you as a killer…What will I tell my bridge club?!?'"

"What comes to mind the most is Bill Bixby," Loni Anderson says reverently. "I saw Bill again at the very end. My show *Nurses* was shooting next door to the sitcom *Blossom,* which Bill was directing. I went over to see him and poor Bill looked so weak, he could hardly stand. I loved him and gave him a big hug. That was the last time I saw him, but he was truly a great person."

HULK FACTS

Loni Anderson worked with Lou Ferrigno's friend/competitor Arnold Schwarzenegger in *The Jayne Mansfield Story.*

Ferrigno wasn't the only Hulk she worked with. She starred with Hulk Hogan in *3 Ninjas: High Noon At Mega Mountain.*

"TERROR IN TIMES SQUARE"
Season 1, Episode 4
Airdate: March 31, 1978
Directed By Alan J. Levi
Written By William A. Schwartz
Banner's alias: "David Blake"

Cast

Dr. David Banner . . . . Bill Bixby
Jack McGee. . . . . Jack Colvin
The Hulk . . . . .Lou Ferrigno
Jason Laird . . . . Robert Alda

Norman Abrams . . . . Jack Kruschen
Leo Kahn . . . . Arny Freeman
Carol Abrams . . . . Pamela Susan Shoop

    In New York, David is working at a Times Square arcade as a change
provider for pinball machines. He also repairs broken machines for the

Hulk takes a bite of the Big Apple.

owner, Norman Abrams. David is also seeing Norman's pretty doctor
daughter, Carol. Leo and other local business owners urge Norman to
go light on his monthly payment to Jason Laird. Laird, the seemingly
friendly lender who Carol fondly calls "Uncle Jason," is actually a ruthless
loan shark leaning on them. Because his fees are so exorbitant, Leo feels
Jason will back down if they all stand up to him. Jason decides to make
an example of Norman and Leo
    To prove his loyalty and protect Carol from Jason's vowed retribution,
Jason demands Norman shoot his friend Leo, who suggested holding back.
This will destroy Norman and scare all the other men into backing down.
Norman thinks the only way to end this oppression is by killing Jason.

David realizes poor Norman doesn't have a prayer and his 4:00 meeting with Jason is a suicide mission, so he resolves to stop it. When his cab is caught in Manhattan's nightmarish rush-hour traffic jam, he realizes he can't save Carol's father. "You don't understand, I have to be there by four o'clock," David groans to the uncaring cabbie. Finally, David Hulks Out, smashes the cab door off its hinges and races through a snow-covered Times Square, reaching Norman at the showdown before Jason can have him killed.

Hulk outraces a cab in "Terror In Times Square."

This is a fairly conventional *Incredible Hulk* TV episode, handled by one of *Hulk*'s best directors, Alan J. Levi. The show is enlivened by a slam-bang fight between Hulk and Jason's warehouse worker goons, as well as The Hulk's climactic charge through Manhattan. The actual New York footage was shot by series creator Kenneth Johnson. There's really no terror in Times Square to speak of, because the main villain is utterly ineffectual. Robert Alda plays Jason Laird so sweetly, that when his loan shark realizes the local store owners have short-changed him, he seems more hurt than angry. Also funny is when a thug gives David a variation on his own catchphrase, telling him, "You really don't want to make *me* angry!"

In terms of jobs, David Banner might as well be working at a buggy whip factory or a record store, as the pinball arcade has gone the way of the Dodo bird. Poor Hulk takes a real beating in this episode. Besides going up against numerous thugs and destroying a cab and a car, he also gets rammed in the back of the leg by a forklift. Because of this, David limps for the rest of the episode, a nice touch.

HULK HIGHLIGHT

The Hulk racing through a snow-covered New York. Of course, one can't help notice *he's wearing slippers!*

LOU FERRIGNO (Hulk): *"When we shot that, it was only 10 degrees and I wore [slippers] because I was running in the street. Don't forget that this is Times Square in the late '70s, so those streets were full of broken glass and other things. I had to wear slippers! There are some places even The Hulk won't go barefoot! It is kind of funny to see Hulk running around New York in fuzzy slippers, though."*

JILL SHERMAN DONNER: "It was tough, because Lou had to run in places that you couldn't have swept up for him beforehand, like Times Square! It looked to your eye like the green slippers matched him perfectly, but then you would get the film and go, 'Oy!' To color correct it we had a choice: Lou could either have yellow hair or yellow feet!"

KENNETH JOHNSON: *" 'Terror In Times Square' was fun — I shot all the New York City footage and had a good time doing it."*

ALAN J. LEVI: *"I directed everything, except the New York exteriors. Kenny took Lou and went back to New York and shot that while I was shooting here. Kenny was laughing when he returned. He said, 'You're not gonna believe what happened.' He ran Lou Ferrigno down the middle of Fifth Avenue and said he looked around and not a single soul looked at The Hulk! It was just New York as usual. I said, 'I missed it, Kenny, because you left me here to handle the drudge!' "*

PAMELA SUSAN SHOOP (Carol Abrams): *"I loved doing* The Incredible Hulk! *I was sort of Bill Bixby's love interest. She was a cool character, this wisecracking New Yorker who's also a doctor. It was a great role, a very strong character, and I didn't usually get to play people that strong. There was a lot riding on that episode, because it was the first one shot after the pilot, so Kenneth Johnson was very involved with it. I liked my performance in that and I really liked working with Bill Bixby. He was a very professional, giving actor. Bill was wonderful to other actors, which I appreciated. He later directed me in the pilot for* I Had Three Wives. *Lou Ferrigno was nice and huge! Hulk saves my father at the end of the episode. Poor Lou Ferrigno had to be freezing in New York, as there was snow on the ground!"*

BILL BIXBY (in *The St. Petersburg Times*, "Hulk has competitors Turning Green with Envy"): *"We were filming a show in New York where the Hulk had to run down a city street. It was about 35 degrees and damp. We hadn't blocked off the street or anything, so Lou runs by a bunch of startled people, turns a corner and stops in front of a jewelry store. The filming stopped and Lou was cold, so he went inside the store. Well, this little old lady sees him, lets out a scream and calls the cops. She told them she had been attacked by The Hulk!"*

HULK FACTS

The show sneaks in a risqué double entendre, when flirtatious Carol tells David, "How 'bout I go for your sack?" He's carrying a bag of change.

Look for a giant billboard for Dino De Laurentiis' 1976 *King Kong* remake, as Hulk races through the city.

Guest villain Robert Alda was father to *M*A*S*H* star Alan Alda and also guested on the '70s TV *Spider-Man*.

No stranger to comic-book characters, Pamela Susan Shoop was an Amazon on Lynda Carter's *Wonder Woman*.

In '70s Times Square, The Hulk passes long-gone grindhouse theaters showing *Saturday Night Fever* and *The Boys In Company C.*

New York is home to Hulk's publishers, Marvel Comics.

"747"
Season 1, Episode 5
Airdate: April 7, 1978
Directed By Sigmund Neufeld, Jr.
Written By Thomas E. Szollosi & Richard Christian Matheson
Banner's alias: "David Brown"

Cast

Dr. David Banner	Bill Bixby
The Hulk	Lou Ferrigno
Phil	Edward Power
Stephanie	Sondra Currie
Denise	Denise Galik
Kevin	Brandon Cruz
Mr. Leggit	Howard Honig
Cynthia Davis	Susan Cotton

Pilot. . . . . Del Hinkley
Mr. McIntire . . . . Don Keefer
Nurse. . . . . Barbara Mealy
Mrs. McIntire . . . . Shirley O'Hara
Captain Brandes . . . . Ed Peck
Controller . . . . J. Jay Saunders

"This is your Captain growling..." Hulk takes the helm in "747."

On a lead to a possible cure, David catches a flight on a crowded 747 transporting the riches of King Tut. Unfortunately for him, Stephanie, a slinky stewardess (this is long before they coined the PC term "flight attendant"!) helps her pilot boyfriend drug the co-pilot to rob the treasure. When the crooked pilot is also knocked unconscious and no other pilot is onboard, David must stay calm to land the plane or everyone aboard will die! In an exciting climax, he tries to prevent his transformation as long as he can. He even steers in mid-transformation, with dilated eyes. When it finally happens, Hulk follows braking instructions as best as he can.

Shot on the backlot in Universal's legendary Stage 747, a set resembling the interior of a 747 used for the *Airport* movies. Because of this, every '70s Universal television adventure show would do an episode set on an airplane—*McCloud, The Six Million Dollar Man, Kolchak: The Night*

Stalker, McMillan & Wife–and *The Incredible Hulk* is no exception. What makes this *Hulk* episode different than those other shows is that "747" is more than a perfunctory "We gotta use the *Airport* set" exercise, because it focuses on Banner and his attempt to hold back The Hulk in a highly-stressful situation. It's a character episode, where Banner is in a race against time and against himself. Can he get the plane down safely before the situation triggers his body chemistry?

"747" is an exciting episode, one of the very best of the first season. Banner is placed in an intense event, and tries not to Hulk Out. The show has great suspense as David fights mounting anxiety, because he's forced to try to land this jumbo jet. As with the *Airport* disaster movies of the era, "747" sets up a diverse group of airline staff and passengers, all archetypes of the genre (The Thief, The Kid, the nervous passenger, etc.), and builds to a satisfactory conclusion. The treasures of King Tut were such a late '70s obsession, they were even ridiculed in a novelty song by comedian Steve Martin, so it's amusing to see them used here as the McGuffin. This episode drew a lot of media attention because Kevin, the kid on board, is played by Brandon Cruz, Bill Bixby's young co-star from *The Courtship of Eddie's Father*.

Writing team Thomas E. Szollosi & Richard Christian Matheson frequently did episodes where Banner has to use his brains and medical knowledge before Hulking Out. Their later show "The Snare" is one of the five best episodes of the entire series.

HULK HIGHLIGHT
The Hulk lands the plane (with help), which hints that the creature is more intelligent than we suspect.

RC MATHESON (Writer): *" '747' was kind of a bottle show. They were always looking for a bottle show at Universal where the episode inexpensively takes place on only one or two sets. They were always trying to play economic catch-up with a bottle show. At Universal, if you were on-budget, you were overbudget and a bottle show could be done for less money because Universal already had the 747 sets from their* Airport *movies.*

"There's an amazing amount of stuff going on in our episode! The Hulk's got to land a 747, the flight attendant drugs the flight crew, the King Tut exhibit is on board, so there's just an operatic amount of plot. I remember the whole King Tut exhibit phenomenon was a very big deal at the time, so we threw that into the story, too. Of course, reuniting Bill Bixby and Brandon Cruz again after The Courtship of Eddie's Father *was a real crowd-pleaser.*

"We [co-writer Thomas E. Szollosi and himself] were on set as they shot it. The 747 set was really massive; it was 50% of a fuselage and just took up most of the stage. In the corner is a green man on a pay phone fighting with somebody... That's one of my favorite memories; watching Lou Ferrigno completely done up as the Hulk on the phone, and it sounded like he was quarreling with his agent! Seeing him pissed on a set payphone was just great. How many chances

Thomas E. Szollosi and RC Matheson flank Bill Bixby. PHOTO COURTESY RC MATHESON

does one get to watch Hulk fight with his agent? That was hilarious! Sadly, I never got a picture with The Hulk.

"I did think having The Hulk land a 747 was pretty cool. It was such a big moment, because it was so crazy! Banner's a deeply tormented guy. Both becoming the Hulk and phasing out of it equally tormented him. It took something from him each time he turned into Hulk and turned back. Therefore, when he's concentrating, he has to make sure he doesn't fully transform into The Hulk, because if he totally transforms, he couldn't land the plane. His eyes could go white, but he needed some lucidity to do the task he was doing. He doesn't fully Hulk Out until he needs the brute strength at the very end to set the brake. Until that moment, the eyes could change, but he had to retain Banner's intellect."

BRANDON CRUZ (Kevin): *"On the episode, I was excited to see Sondra Currie, who played the villainous flight attendant...I immediately noticed that*

Sondra was extremely hot! Thank you, Bill Bixby for having her on my episode of the show! I was a hormonal teenage boy and she was gorgeous."

SONDRA CURRIE (Stephanie): *"Err...How sweet of Brandon to say!* The Incredible Hulk was *an interesting show and a lot of fun to do. Before* Hulk, *the only real comic-book shows were* Batman *and* Wonder Woman, *but neither had the humanity that* Hulk *did. I really liked Lou Ferrigno; I thought he was a very sensitive guy and a sweet person."*

DENISE GALIK-FUREY (Denise): *"Don't have much to tell about that episode, except that I really enjoyed working with Sondra Currie, and Bill Bixby was very nice. Working on the Universal lot back then was great because it was always so busy!"*

HULK FACTS
The plane footage is from Universal's *Airport 1975*, as are the sets.

Sondra Currie starred as part of a heart-removing, Mummy-worshipping cult on *Kolchak: The Night Stalker.*

Denise Galik is in Roger Corman's drive-in classic *Humanoids from the Deep.*

Stage 747 is still very much in use today, seen in numerous films like *Jurassic Park III* and TV shows.

HULK PROFILE
SONDRA CURRIE

Beautiful redhead Sondra Currie is Stephanie, the deceptive stewardess in "747." The actress sees her *Incredible Hulk* character as greedy and a thief, but *not* a murderer — or a genius!

"In the show, my scheme is pretty dumb...I actually drug the co-pilot with Cabitrol, because the pilot and I are in cahoots, so I can steal King Tut's treasure," laughs Sondra Currie. "Of course, I left out an important element of my master plan — Who's gonna land the plane?!? I thought about that after I was doing it, *'Where's the logic in this script?'*

"We used the great big airplane set at Universal, Stage #21, which they call 'Stage 747.' It was this enormous 747 stage that *Airport* was shot on. I stepped into that role literally overnight, because they originally cast a very close friend of mine in my role, Morgan Fairchild.

"Morgan got a pilot for Quinn Martin Productions and asked to be replaced on *The Incredible Hulk*. I think they called me at eleven o'clock at night the day before they actually started shooting that *Hulk*, and they asked if I could step in. I could and was happy to do it — I had a great time making it. It was a really good show for me. I was working quite a bit in episodic TV, so I was very excited to be on *The Incredible Hulk*, because it was a fun role. I didn't know who The Hulk was, but it was a hit show and I loved Kenny [Johnson]. My husband, Alan Levi, directed the second *Incredible Hulk* TV movie — but we never worked together on the show!"

Sondra Currie. PHOTO BY PATRICK JANKIEWICZ

Currie co-starred in Todd Phillips' comedy hit *The Hangover* — her opening the blinds is literally the first shot of the film. "That whole film was a lot of fun and I was stunned that it became so huge (Grossing over $200 million), but I have to say, Todd knew. One day on the set, he said 'This is my *Star Wars!*' He was right."

HULK PROFILE
BRANDON CRUZ

As Kevin, a precocious teenage boy watching Hulk on a plane, Brandon Cruz is reunited with his former TV Dad, Bill Bixby.

"It was gonna be a surprise cameo in '747' when Bill first called me for it," remembers Brandon Cruz. "My appearance on the show was just gonna be for *Hulk* publicity, because we were on *The Courtship of Eddie's Father* together. But once I actually got onto the set, it turned into a lot more than a cameo. I was suddenly a big part of the episode, which I thought was really cool, because I had not worked with him since *Eddie's Father*.

"I had fun being reunited with Bill on *The Incredible Hulk*. When *The Courtship of Eddie's Father* ended, the producers, directors and everyone

else was coming up to me and saying, 'We'll work together again!' Bill
saw my excited reaction to being told that. He came up and Bill was very
honest with me — Bill was always very honest. He said, 'You know what,
kid? I don't want to burst your bubble, but I don't know who is gonna
work with who again. That's the way the business works...Everybody
is so, 'Yeah, we've gotta do this again,' but we may never see each other

Brandon Cruz helps Banner land a plane in "747"

again. We'll do something; maybe not today or tomorrow, but we'll do
something.' He told me this in 1972 and *The Incredible Hulk* was 1978. It
took a while, but we *did* work together again! He called me up one day
and said, 'Hey, do you want to do this new show I'm doing?'

"Doing the show was exciting. I went in to do it and I met Lou
[Ferrigno], Frank Orsatti and a bunch of other people working on *The
Incredible Hulk*. I had fun, because I was not supposed to do as much in
the show as I did. Bill said, 'Brandon, you've got to hang around...Let's
write you in a little more and have you come in when Lou is flying the
plane and you see him and flip out!' Bill shot from the hip on this episode
and it was a lot of fun to do. I actually got to help Hulk land the plane!
I tell him to step on the brakes."

"THE HULK BREAKS LAS VEGAS"

Season 1, Episode 6
Airdate: April 7, 1978
Directed By Larry Stewart
Written By Justin Edgerton

Cast

Dr. David Banner . . . . Bill Bixby
Jack McGee. . . . . Jack Colvin
The Hulk . . . . .Lou Ferrigno
Wanda . . . . Julie Gregg
Ed Campion . . . . Dean Santoro
Lee. . . . . Don Marshall
Cathy. . . . . Simone Griffeth
Tom Edler . . . . John Crawford
Charlie. . . . . .Paul Picerni

When Ed Campion, a reporter friend of Jack McGee's, tries to tip him off to mob corruption in Las Vegas, he's brutally attacked and slammed by a car into a coma. David Banner is the only eyewitness and Campion entrusts him to get his tape-recorded evidence against the mob to McGee.

As an added twist, he has to be careful not to let his nemesis Jack McGee or anyone else discover that the dead David Banner is actually alive and well. McGee hits Sin City, so Banner repeatedly dodges him. Jack McGee realizes the witness is deliberately avoiding him, so that makes him a person of interest to the wily McGee. The scientist and the reporter continue their cat-and-mouse chase through Vegas, until both are captured by the mob...cleverly tied back to back — so Jack never actually sees who he's going to be killed with!

The two are going to be buried alive in a landfill in the middle of the desert, where only The Hulk can save them! As the dirt pours on them, David Hulks Out and sends the mobsters scattering.

"The Hulk Breaks Las Vegas" is fun, using the Vegas setting to great advantage. A nice moment comes when McGee talks to David by courtesy phone in a casino as he's trying to see what he looks like. Jack McGee tells David, "Your voice sounds familiar — are you sure I don't know you?" Through a door and over a phone, this marks the first time David Banner directly talks to Jack McGee since the pilot...Not counting when he growls at him as The Hulk in "The Final Round."

ɪn between all the Vegas action, David has a romance with stunningly beautiful card dealer Cathy, as mob hit men pursue him and McGee. This is a great episode, clever, well-written, nicely directed, with plenty of Hulk action. It's exciting for the way David Banner has to avoid danger at all costs — the physical threat of the gangsters and the potential exposure by Jack McGee.

Jack McGee realizes that the Hulk is more than just a monster.

HULK HIGHLIGHT

While Banner's desert Hulk Out is cool, the true Hulk Highlight comes when McGee realizes that the Hulk isn't some generic monster on the loose, but an unknown man who actually changes into The Hulk. After saving the reporter in the climax, McGee watches as Hulk starts to revert to Banner. This alters McGee's hunt for The Hulk to include the man he turns into.

Another Hulk Highlight comes when McGee tries to reason with The Hulk. "'Doctor David Banner', does that name mean anything to you? Banner, do you understand," Jack McGee cajoles, before noticing The Hulk is going into his transformation back to Banner. "What's happening to your face?!? Something's changing!"

At the end, McGee notes, "The only missing link is the name of the man who becomes The Hulk!" Without a doubt, "The Hulk Breaks Las Vegas" is the biggest Jack McGee episode of the first season.

SIMONE GRIFFETH (Cathy): *"I was one of the last contract players at Universal Studios, along with Kim Cattrall. I ended up on* The Incredible Hulk *because it was a Universal show. My story about* Hulk *is I had to be a blackjack dealer in Vegas. I got the part and thought, 'This is gonna be great' — and then I realized I didn't know how to play cards!*

"A friend taught me how to play blackjack over the weekend, but I realized that as a dealer, I had to be an expert! It was terrifying to have the dialogue with Bill Bixby and have to deal the cards at the same time…I was so scared because I really didn't know how to play cards at all! I spent most of the show agonizing over the rehearsals with the cards. That's all of what I really and truly remember about The Incredible Hulk!*"*

DON MARSHALL (Lee): *"I played Lee, a bad guy in Vegas trying to kill Banner, when* The Hulk *comes after me! Lou Ferrigno was one of the most gentle big men that I have ever met in the business. He was very concerned with how an actor may feel when he might have to pick you up and throw you. We did some of it in Las Vegas, but I think we did most of it here in Los Angeles. That was a good part as a heavy. I liked being a bad guy. It's very seldom a guy like me gets that kind of part…I got to beat up Bill Bixby! I hadn't gotten to play a heavy like that since I did* Dragnet *with Jack Webb. At the end, we're burying Bill and Jack Colvin in the desert, which was a real bad guy thing to do."*

PAUL PICERNI (Charlie): *"I remember my second* Hulk *episode, 'Captive Night,' really well, but I have no memory of doing this one. I know I didn't get to go to Las Vegas for it — that I would have remembered!"*

HULK FACTS
Hulk lived in Las Vegas for a time in the comics.

Hulk gets shot in the shoulder again, for the first time since the pilot!

Julie Gregg was Sonny Corleone's wife in *The Godfather*.

Simone Griffeth appeared with fellow *Hulk* guests Martin Kove and Louisa Moritz in *Death Race 2000*.

Dean Santoro co-starred in the pilot for *The Man from Atlantis*.

After Deanna Lund, Don Marshall is the second cast member of *Land of the Giants* to guest on *The Incredible Hulk*.

"NEVER GIVE A TRUCKER AN EVEN BREAK"

Season 1, Episode 7
Airdate: April 28, 1978
Directed By Kenneth Gilbert
Written By Kenneth Johnson

Cast

Dr. David Banner . . . . Bill Bixby
The Hulk . . . . Lou Ferrigno
Joanie. . . . . Jennifer Darling
Ted. . . . . Frank R. Christi
Mike . . . . Grand L. Bush
Woman at Gas Station . . . . Peggy Doyle
Man at Gas Station. . . . .

Charles Alvin Bell
Storekeeper . . . .
Don Starr

On his way from Las Vegas, a hitchhiking David is picked up by Joanie, a flighty, treacherous girl who uses David as a distraction so she can steal her truck back from two crooks, Ted and Mike. David, Joanie and the thieves keep switching cars with each other, so you see them chasing each other in a truck and a Plymouth.

This goofy chase episode shows the influence of *Smokey and the Bandit*, 1977's second highest grossing film. Unfortu- Bill Bixby and Jennifer Darling.
nately, *Dukes of Hazzard* would

have a similar effect on later episodes of *Hulk*. "Never Give a Trucker an Even Break" is the notorious episode of *The Incredible Hulk* that managed to anger Steven Spielberg. The director was offended by use of footage from his classic telefilm *Duel*, as well as the actual *Duel* truck. Reportedly, after catching this episode, Spielberg had his contract amended so that Universal Studios could not use any of his movies for stock footage.

One can only imagine his surprise that, after directing the blockbusters *Jaws* and *Close Encounters of the Third Kind*, Steven Spielberg suddenly found himself retroactively shooting second-unit footage for *The Incredible Hulk* TV series! Seeing the *Duel* footage and vehicles being used in a wacky episode with twangy country music is more than a little surreal. It may have also been a little embarrassing for Spielberg, as he announces on the *Duel* DVD that the one and only truck he used to shoot the film was utterly destroyed so he could obtain the telefilm's dramatic final shot, but here it is, seven years after *Duel*, completely unscathed. The *Duel* truck could be seen in the '80s, sitting in the backlot motor pool, by any tourist on the Universal Studios Tour.

A comedic episode, "Never Give a Trucker an Even Break" is the most lighthearted script *Hulk*'s Kenneth Johnson ever wrote for the series. The most amusing scene has a shirtless, post-Hulk Out David grousing, "I really have to buy shirts that stretch," which shows Johnson and Bixby are having fun with the concept. Jennifer Darling is spunky as Joanie, Grand L. Bush and Frank R. Christi are amusing as the thugs.

HULK HIGHLIGHT

The Hulk demolishing the pay phone is one of the most satisfying scenes of the entire series! The funny bit has David Banner in a phone booth, on a pay phone, when he calls for help from the police, his pupils dilating as he tells the uncooperative telephone operator, "I...don't... have...25 cents!"

LOU FERRIGNO (Hulk): *"I really liked when Bill Hulked Out and I smashed the phone booth, because everyone wants to do that!"*

JENNIFER DARLING (Joanie): *"The episode upset Steven Spielberg? Oh no — I hope he liked my performance! It was fun to work with Kenny on* The Incredible Hulk *as a different character from Peggy the secretary on* The Bionic Woman!*"*

KAREN HARRIS: *"They shouldn't have used footage from* Duel. *Ken wouldn't like it if someone took his material and used it in something else, but what could he do? The studio is telling him, 'You have to make this one for half the budget, because you went overbudget on five others!' He was doing a bottle show, using stock footage because that kept it all on one location."*

HULK FACTS

The first Kenneth Johnson *Hulk* script since "The Final Round."

Jennifer Darling co-starred as Peggy, Oscar Goldman's secretary, on both *The Six Million Dollar Man* and *Bionic Woman,* on two different networks!

Grand L. Bush later played Agent Johnson in the blockbuster *Die Hard.*

Duel author Richard Matheson's son, Richard Christian Matheson, was an *Incredible Hulk* writer.

"LIFE AND DEATH"
Season 1, Episode 8
Airdate: May 12, 1978
Directed By Jeffrey Hayden
Written By James D. Parriott
Banner's alias: "David Barnard"

Cast

Dr. David Banner	Bill Bixby
Jack McGee	Jack Colvin
The Hulk	Lou Ferrigno
Ellen	Julie Adams
Dr. Stan Rhodes	Andrew Robinson
Crosby	Carl Franklin
Carrie Taylor	Diane Civita (as "Diane Cary")
Trucker	Al Berry
Man in Elevator	Ben Freedman
1st Detective	Gilbert Garcia
Chief Nurse	Mitzi Hoag
2nd Detective	Judd Lawrence
Tina	Lilah McCarthy
Police Officer	James Remar
Young Woman	Sara Rush

David volunteers as a guinea pig for an unconventional, highly experimental DNA test with renegade scientist Dr. Stan Rhodes at The Matrix Labs. On the way over, he befriends Carrie, a young pregnant girl. To David's horror, he learns that Rhodes and his assistant Ellen are brokering babies.

"Life And Death" is a fascinating *Hulk* episode because the villains are actually practicing a form of eugenics, with strange plans for infants, dealing with issues which are commonly discussed in the news now, but were mere conjecture when James D. Parriott wrote this episode over 30 years ago. An interesting episode, unafraid to explore a complex subject.

As with "Of Guilt, Models and Murder," Parriott adds a little levity to a serious subject. When Carrie hears David is heading for the hospital, she tells him, "Hope it's nothing serious." David gives her his pained grin and says, "Well, it's nothing to *get worked up* about."

JULIE ADAMS (Ellen): *"I remember Hulk was very, very green! I try to have Andy Robinson beat up The Hulk, but I didn't have much luck with that. I liked doing it very much. The Incredible Hulk was a very pleasant show to work on. I liked the fella who played The Hulk and Bill Bixby was a sweet guy. Bixby was delightful and very professional. He was just a really good actor. It was well directed by Jeffrey Hayden, so what's not to like?*

"Jeffrey is a good director and married to my friend, Eva Marie Saint. I had known him socially a bit before Hulk, *through Eva, so it was very nice. My then-husband Ray Danton had directed a bunch of* Incredible Hulk *episodes, but he didn't do mine. Ray directed a bunch of episodes of* Quincy — *I did three of his episodes of that — and I did a* Cagney & Lacey *that he also directed."*

ANDREW ROBINSON (Dr. Stan Rhodes): *"It was an episodic, so I don't remember very much about it, but Bixby was nice, Julie Adams was in it and I seem to remember slightly hurting my back in a fight scene with The Hulk and that's about it!"*

LOU FERRIGNO (Hulk): *"Oh man, I remember that fight scene with Andrew Robinson…I had to grab Andrew by the tie and throw 'im. As long as I live, I will never forget this…When I grabbed his tie, it tightened up around his neck! I remember him walking away pissed, as he was trying to open his tie. I thought, 'Oh shit!' and felt so bad. I loved Andrew Robinson and Julie Adams, so it was a thrill to work with them together!"*

JEFFREY HAYDEN (Director): *"Andy Robinson was a lovely actor and Julie Adams is always wonderful — I had worked with her years before, at Universal. I had also worked with Bill Bixby on* The Courtship of Eddie's Father. *The Incredible Hulk was an interesting show to do, because you had FX, makeup and stunts. It usually took two days just to prep it and six days to shoot a* Hulk.*"*

HULK FACTS

Julie Adams starred with another big green monster, in *The Creature from the Black Lagoon*.

Popular character actor Andrew Robinson is best known as serial killer Scorpio in the original *Dirty Harry*.

Carl Franklin (Crosby) is the acclaimed director of *One False Move* and *Devil in a Blue Dress*.

Diane Cary is a popular member of Kenneth Johnson actors. She's also in his *The Bionic Woman, V* and *Alien Nation*.

Look for film heavy James Remar (*48 Hrs*, the serial killer show *Dexter*) as a police officer.

David Banner mentions Helen, his younger sister for the first time. We later meet her in the episode "Homecoming."

"EARTHQUAKES HAPPEN"

Season 1, Episode 9
Airdate: May 19, 1978
Directed By Harvey Laidman
Written By Jim Tisdale & Migdia Chinea Varela
Banner's alias: "Robert Patterson"

Cast

Dr. David Banner	Bill Bixby
Jack McGee	Jack Colvin
The Hulk	Lou Ferrigno
Hammond	Peter Brandon
Diane Joseph	Sherry Jackson
Paul	Kene Holliday
Nancy	Lynne Topping
Martha	Pamela Nelson

David poses as safety expert Robert Patterson to gain access to a nuclear plant's Gamma Ray equipment, specifically a Gamma Inversion Laser that may cure him. Jack McGee and a group of reporters are also inspecting the plant. When David finally reaches the Gamma chamber, Dr. Diane Joseph gets suspicious. Robert Patterson needs a cane to walk and David isn't using one. Away from prying eyes, David Banner straps himself in for a Gamma Ray bombardment from the Laser to finally rid him of his hulking alter ego. When Diane sees what he's about to do to himself, she's horrified.

Stopping the countdown, Diane thinks she has saved his life while David feels his cure slipping away. She calls security. Before David can be arrested, the plant is rocked by a massive earthquake and several jolting

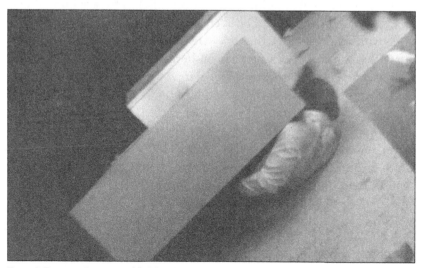

David Banner's stunt double Frank Orsatti learns the hard way that "Earthquakes Happen." PHOTOS BY VENITA OZOLS

aftershocks. Now the plant is full of scalding steam, when the Gamma Rays begin firing from the laser David primed, further worsening an unstable situation. Because of David tampering with the Gamma Inversion Laser, the plant is now heading for a full nuclear meltdown.

Considering that "Earthquakes Happen" is concerned with accidents at a nuclear power plant almost a full year before the horrific real-life incident at Three Mile Island and the Jane Fonda/Michael Douglas film *The China Syndrome* makes it startlingly prescient. This episode is a cool *Poseidon Adventure* scenario, as a bunch of diverse characters are thrown together in a dangerous situation and have to form an uneasy alliance if they hope to escape.

What's also amazing is that all the characters are in danger because of David's misuse of the Gamma device. This fits into what Kenneth Johnson feels is David's biggest problem: obsession. Banner is so obsessed with finding his cure that, in this instance, everyone else almost dies because of it! David's single-minded desire to purge himself of The Hulk has led to a terrible carelessness in this episode, where Banner almost triggers a nuclear accident. Diane, the hot-tempered Turner, and others are forced to join Banner, despite their mutual mistrust of him

When Turner angrily snarls, "We ought to take that guy [David] and push him into the steam! It's *his* fault we're trapped in here…" You have to agree with him; he's right…*It's totally David's fault!* It's also a nice turnaround; usually, David Banner is in a dangerous situation that The Hulk has accidentally put him in — now Hulk has to save himself and others from a problem that David created.

As with other episodes, this uses extensive footage from the Universal movie *Earthquake. Hulk's* first season borrowed footage liberally from Universal films like *Earthquake, Two-Minute Warning, Airport 1975* and *Duel.* There's a lot of clever throwaway bits in this episode, like when Mrs. Waverly, the woman who creates Banner's fake ID, arbitrarily raises the price he's paying for it when she realizes he's a desperate man on the run. David guilting her out of it is also a nice character detail.

It's great to see Sherry Jackson, a popular guest on every major sci-fi show of the '60s and '70s, like *Batman, Star Trek, Lost in Space, The Twilight Zone,* finally make it onto *The Incredible Hulk*!

David gets to do some actual doctoring here, taking care of the security guard's broken leg.

Dr. Diane Joseph, thinking Banner is suicidal for putting himself in the Laser's path, is interesting. In any other episode, she would be the love interest, but here she is suspicious of Banner and his motives. When Jack

McGee realizes that the nuclear plant emergency story may turn into a Hulk sighting, he gets excited.

When the plant holds a press conference, Jack immediately has a question. "We understand that, ah, somebody spotted a large Hulking creature down there. Could you describe exactly — "

"Come on, Jack," another reporter snaps, "we're trying to cover a *real* story here!"

KAREN HARRIS: *"The show was expensive and that stock footage from movies like* Earthquake *is how we made it work…We couldn't afford to rent a real 747 for '747' or stage a horse race at Santa Anita for 'Rainbow's End.' We could only do bits and pieces and without those film clips, the whole series would have been prohibitively expensive."*

JILL SHERMAN DONNER: *"Using that footage kept costs down. The footage belonged to Universal, so they said to us, 'Just take it!' "*

SHERRY JACKSON (Dr. Diane Joseph): *"Bill Bixby is gone now, so I don't want to say anything bad, but he was under a lot of stress when he did the show. His marriage was coming apart and he was not in a good place. We have this big table in the lab in the episode. Bill actually Hulked Out on set, climbed on that table and screamed and berated the entire cast and crew!*

"If you saw the show, we have papers, files and things on this table as we try to deal with the earthquake and the meltdown — Bill was grabbing these files and props off the table and actually throwing them at the crew like a four year old having a tantrum! Bill was mad about everything. He was screaming at everyone, so we were all hiding from him. It was a complete psychotic break and not a pleasant experience.

"It was a control issue — I don't think he liked the director (Harvey Laidman) and this was his way of showing it. Lou Ferrigno was a sweet guy, quiet. I am covered with rubble after the earthquake and when he picked me up, I was as light as a feather!"

"Make Up and Hair warned me the first day how Bill Bixby would try to pick me up. On the first day, he would ignore me. Second day, he would be nice to me, third day he would invite me to his trailer for a drink and on the last day, he would sleep with me. To prevent this, I took a guy I used to date and my mother. After that outburst attacking the crew, I had no interest.

"I did not realize that we did that episode before Three Mile Island. That's strange That's also what happened in Japan, too — an earthquake triggered a meltdown."

HULK FACTS

This is the first time David uses an alias that doesn't start with his first name.

Original title for this episode was "Nuclear Cave-In."

Two of the nuclear scientists try to bring the plant back online by doing a playful variation on the opening dialogue of *The Six Million Dollar Man*. ("I've got a blowout in Damper Three — " "Get your pressure to zero...")

Co-writer Migdia Chinea Varela was the first Latina to join the Writers Guild of America West (WGAW), and founded its Latino Writers Committee.

There's a cool shot of David Banner on '70s Hollywood Boulevard.

Dr. Elaina Marks makes a flashback appearance.

On *Batman*, Sherry Jackson gasses Robin the boy wonder while dressed as Little Bo Peep.

There's a funny outtake when Sherry Jackson tells Banner "I'm not going to let you kill yourself" with the Laser, Bixby jokingly responds, "You don't have to be so shitty about it!"

Harvey Laidman, a successful TV director, never did another *Incredible Hulk* episode. Sherry Jackson remembers the director and star clashing.

"THE WATERFRONT STORY"
Season 1, Episode 10
Airdate: May 31, 1978
Directed By Reza Badiyi
Written By Paul M. Belous and Robert Woltersoff
Banner's alias: "David Barton"

Cast

Dr. David Banner	Bill Bixby
The Hulk	Lou Ferrigno
Josie	Sheila Larken

Tony	Jack Kelly
McConnell	James Sikking
Sarah	Helen Page Camp
Marty	Ted Markland
Vic	William Benedict
Nancy	Lynne Topping
Marsha	Pamela Nelson

Working in a waterfront tavern, David helps Josie, a brave young widow standing up against local thuggish Union dockworkers. "Waterfront Story" is your prototypical *Incredible Hulk* episode — a woman in need, aggressive bad guys and a chance for Banner and the raging spirit that dwells within him to even the odds.

Look for Lou Ferrigno in his green slippers when Hulk runs through the shipyard! Also amusing is when Sarah tells The Hulk, 'You remind me of my second husband; the strong, silent type. Only talked when he had something to say. Except he usually wasn't green!'"

How an anti-Union episode, where the widow even shouts, "If it wasn't for the Union, Frank would still be alive!" was shot on the Teamster-filled Universal backlot is anyone's guess!

KENNETH JOHNSON: *"We used stock footage of a lightning bolt in the* Hulk *pilot from the Universal library, for the scene where he's in the rain and begins his first transformation. It was a perfect lightning bolt; I think it was from* Bride of Frankenstein. *When we went to series, that lightning bolt was used in* The Incredible Hulk *television series' opening credits and we had to cut a check for it every single week!"*

HULK FACTS
Sheila Larken also appears in another *Hulk* episode, "Nine Hours," but she is best known as Scully's mom on *The X-Files*.

James Sikking went on to co-star on *Hill Street Blues* and *Doogie Howser, M.D.*

HULKAMANIA!

The Incredible Hulk was an immediate hit. The show was immortalized in bubblegum cards, tee shirts and posters. The Mego Toy Corporation's Incredible Hulk action figure became the company's biggest seller. There lso toys like *Hulk* "Inflatable Muscles" for kids, a Stretch Armstrong ...1 of The Hulk, a Hulk bank in the shape of his head and a "Hulk Rage Cage," where a rubber Hulk toy would fill with air and, once inflated, burst from a flimsy plastic cage.

In the late '70s comic-book TV explosion that came after *Wonder Woman*, *The Incredible Hulk* was the only hit, as his Marvel Comics' compa-

Hulk's TV stardom goes to his head. ART BY MARIE SEVERIN

triots *The Amazing Spider-Man* and *Captain America* were disappointing failures. An attempt to launch *Dr. Strange* also flopped, because, like Spidey and Cap, the show had no respect for the source material.

Johnny Carson made *Hulk* jokes on *The Tonight Show* and Lou Ferrigno was a guest on T*he Dinah Shore Show* and appeared as The Hulk on *The Mike Douglas Show*. True to The Hulk's TV conceit, he charged through the audience wordlessly! There were jokes that CBS would renew *Hulk* just to keep Ferrigno on their team for *Battle of the Network Stars*! Robin Williams parodied the Bixby/Ferrigno transformation in the "Mork In

Wonderland" episode of *Mork & Mindy*, while John Belushi actually played the Ferrigno Hulk on *Saturday Night Live*.

In a skit with Margot Kidder spoofing her Lois Lane role, Belushi walks in as The Hulk. Laraine Newman was Hulk's wife, Cookie. Hobbling in on crutches, covered in bandages, she announces to Hulk, "Come Monday: Separate beds!"

Hulk stinks up Lois Lane's apartment and snaps, "What's a bathroom supposed to smell like, roses?"

In his book *Outside The Ring*, obscure wrestler Terry Gene Bollea remembers when he appeared on a local Tennessee talk show and was inspired. Sitting on camera "next to Lou Ferrigno...the guy who played The Incredible Hulk, who was all over people's TV's with his green body makeup at that time. He was a real nice guy, and everyone was so impressed by how huge he looked with those big bulging muscles. The thing was, sitting next to me at that point in my life, the guy looked kinda small....I got back to the dressing room after the show and (my friend) was like, "Good God, Terry! You were sitting on TV and you were bigger than The Hulk!" From that point on, Bollea re-christened himself after Ferrigno's character and became World Wrestling Federation superstar, *Hulk Hogan*.

Bixby and Ferrigno on the cover of *Crazy*.

Ferrigno also guested as The Hulk on *Billy*, a Steve Guttenberg-starring CBS sitcom that attempted to be a modern '70s re-telling of *Billy Liar*. The Guttenberg character's loud, angry father transforms into Ferrigno's Hulk as Guttenberg walks the creature out. The *Hulk* TV show was covered in *Us, Time, TV Guide, People, Starlog, Creem, Circus* and *Dynamite*, while it was being simultaneously spoofed in magazines like *Mad, Cracked* and *Crazy*.

Wolverine creator and longtime Hulk writer Len Wein teamed with one "Joseph Silva" — actually comic writer Ron Goulart — and Marv Wolfman to produce the first Hulk novel, *Stalker from the Stars*. In the story, Hulk, Bruce Banner and Rick Jones do battle with a sentient slimy blob from outer space that has enslaved a small town in a plot loosely cribbed from *It Came from Outer Space*. Because of his increasing TV popularity, Ferrigno's Hulk was also added to posters and flyers advertising the Universal Studios Tour, alongside *Jaws, Frankenstein* and *The Wolf Man*.

In *The Count Dracula Live Show* that ran in the Castle Theater on the Universal backlot, the evil Dracula is only defeated by The Incredible Hulk! Hulk was actually played in some shows by Manny Perry and future *Body by Jake* fitness guru Jake Steinfeld, while "David Banner" was a rube plucked from the audience at every show. There was also a fake smashed wall on the backlot tour, where kids could stick their heads through it and have their picture taken with a painting of the Ferrigno Hulk.

Hulk creator Stan Lee and his brother, illustrator Larry Lieber, launched a *Hulk* newspaper comic strip to join his popular *Spider-Man* strip that launched in 1977. Imitating the TV series format, Bruce Banner was drawn to look like Bill Bixby and The Hulk noticeably resembled Ferrigno. As with the show, Hulk didn't talk, he only growled. Hulk's rogues' gallery of monsters, Toad Men and super-villains were nowhere to be found. A silent Hulk is a boring

On the Universal backlot, dorks can pretend Hulk punched them through walls. PHOTO BY PATRICK JANKIEWICZ

Hulk and the strip was soon cancelled. This is an important lesson. When Stan Lee launched his *Spider-Man* strip, he refused to alter it other than re-tooling Spidey's origin to resemble that of the '70s TV show. By trying to do his Hulk in the Kenneth Johnson manner, Lee muted what made his own creation so enjoyable on paper.

Marvel launched a more mature *Hulk* magazine, simply titled *The Hulk*, for older readers who were lured in by the TV show and didn't want to see the character fighting those pesky Toad Men or The Abomination. In this book, The Hulk would confront controversial issues like nuclear power, spousal abuse and drugs. Sometimes the book went overboard trying to be controversial — it drew criticism for a story where Bruce Banner Hulked Out after being propositioned by a gay man in a shower at a Times Square YMCA!

The comic-book Bruce Banner also sported Bill Bixby's hairstyle. The words "MARVEL'S TV SENSATION!" were added to the cover of every *Hulk* comic published. Marvel released a photo novel of the show pilot, complete with comic-book word balloons containing Kenneth Johnson's dialogue. Marvel Comics also did a funny commentary on Hulk's TV triumph. An issue of *Marvel Two-In-One* ran a story called "Battle in Burbank!" As he does in most stories, a confused Bruce Banner is running shirtless and shoeless through a small town, when he sees a commercial for the TV show in an appliance store window...And is highly offended by it!

"What?!?" Banner exclaims. "Now...Now they've turned my tragedy into some sort of...of soap opera? My God, have they no decency?? No respect for privacy? No...no." So upset with the show, he changes into The Hulk, who spots Lou Ferrigno on TV and snarls, "That is NOT the Hulk! Hulk is NOT on any TV show...Hulk is HERE!! Who is making fun of Hulk this way?! Now Hollywood makes fun of Hulk!"

Destroying the appliance store, Hulk announces, "Hulk will smash dumb studio!" He hops to Hollywood, punches through several sound-stages, clashes with The Thing from The Fantastic Four and eventually confronts the show's producer, who is *not* drawn to look like Kenneth Johnson. The producer vows to do a better job on the show, but Hulk never meets the actor playing The Hulk, which seems like a missed opportunity. An angry Hulk even tells the producer, "Just be sure Hulk doesn't look so stupid — or Hulk will be back!"

CLIFFHANGERS

Kenneth Johnson used his clout from the success of The *Incredible Hulk* to create another fantasy-tinged TV show. Instead of ripping off *The Incredible Hulk* and grabbing another Marvel character, he went in a different, ambitious direction, with the underrated, short-lived *Cliffhangers*. This series told three separate stories in 15-20-minute chapters, like '40s Republic serials. Each week would end with an amazing cliffhanger for each story.

The first segment had the vampire Count Dracula (Michael Nouri) find love and danger in modern-day San Francisco. The undead Dracula teaches night school under an assumed name and even plays "Peg O' My Heart" in a jazz piano bar. The second segment had Susan Williams, a globe-trotting Brenda Starr-like reporter (Susan Anton). The third was about a cowboy (Geoffrey Scott) trapped in a futuristic civilization. "*Cliffhangers* was great fun," Kenneth Johnson says fondly. "My Dracula was played by sexy Michael Nouri, one of the funniest human beings on Earth. The Susan Anton segment was patterned after *The Perils of Pauline*. For the third segment with the cowboy, I was inspired by the *Phantom Empire* serial made in the '30s."

The show was his attempt to revive serials three long years before George Lucas and Steven Spielberg did it with *Raiders of the Lost Ark*.

Michael Nouri as Dracula in *Cliffhangers*. PHOTO COURTESY KENNETH JOHNSON

"George, Steven and I had all grown up watching the same great Republic serials," he smiles. "It was only inevitable that we would all gravitate to trying to recreate that same genre. Note that one of my heroes used a bullwhip *before* Indiana Jones! I did not have a favorite segment of the show, because they were all a hoot in their own way. It's like asking, 'Which is your favorite child?'"

Sadly, the show only lasted one season. "Fred Silverman [then head of NBC] loved the show. He was very proud of it, so proud he put us on Tuesday nights against his toughest competition and *Happy Days* killed us with a 45 share," Johnson says ruefully. Except for *Curse of Dracula*, a TV movie culled from the *Dracula* segments to capitalize on Nouri's sex symbol status after the movie *Flashdance*, *Cliffhangers* sank without a trace and is not available on DVD.

SEASON TWO

For its second season, *The Incredible Hulk* had become CBS TV's number one primetime show. A true breakout hit, Friday nights at nine o'clock would not be a successful timeslot for any other sci-fi show until *The X-Files* came along fifteen years later. CBS formed a hero sandwich around *Hulk*: new show *The Dukes of Hazzard* at eight, about two Southern brothers and their hot cousin Daisy Duke doing battle with the corrupt leaders of Hazzard County, and *Dallas* at ten.

Dukes was more or less action and stunts in search of a story. The show's big moments would come when the Duke brothers' car, The General Lee — which had the old South's Civil War "stars and bars" painted on the roof — would jump over something that week, or cause a police car to crash. Having leggy Daisy Duke leaning in cut off shorts didn't hurt, either. *Dukes'* star John Schneider would go on to play Pa Kent in *Smallville*.

Ironically, *Dukes of Hazzard* would have a detrimental effect on *The Incredible Hulk*. Some *Hulk* episodes would now have completely gratuitous car chases, a pointless distraction for a show centered on a hitchhiking hero and a big green monster who runs around barefoot!

Despite working on the equivalent of three TV shows in one with *Cliffhangers*, Johnson was still able to oversee an ambitious second season for *The Incredible Hulk*. This time around, David Banner and The Hulk come across social issues, specifically exploring the Dark Side of others, including teenage drinking ("Alice In Discoland"), violence in sports ("Killer Instinct"), depriving the mentally challenged ("Ricky," "The Quiet Room"), exploiting one's community ("Like A Brother") and, in an especially controversial episode, a man who abuses his own wife and young son ("A Child In Need"). To the show's credit, it never gets too preachy and there's plenty of doors, walls and cars for Hulk to smash.

Story editor Nicholas Corea was made into a producer for the show's second season. He told *Starlog* magazine that his favorite episodes for the new season "include a battered child and a professional football player.

Instead of the usual mustache-twirling villains, we have a father with definite psychological problems and a player concerned with the violence of the sport. The violence in both these shows builds until the men have their own 'Hulks' inside them."

Corea added that "the people David will be dealing with are going to be allegories to his own problems — people with beasts inside them or things they must deal with. At the same time, we're really going to confront what it means to change. Rather than just have David get involved with something and Hulk Out three times, we'll have shows dealing with his fight against the inner beast." Bill Bixby was excited about the show's turn toward social commentary, telling *Us* Magazine in 1978, "This is not a message show, but we plan to deal with some very interesting subjects next season — child beating, teenage alcoholism, even psychosurgery. We make the show for adults, but we make it so that children can watch, too. They're not afraid of [Hulk] because they can see anger manifested as something tangible. Listen, Carl Jung would have loved this show..."

"MARRIED"

Season 2, Episodes 11 and 12
Airdate: September 22, 1978
Directed By Kenneth Johnson
Written By Kenneth Johnson
Banner's alias: "David Benton"

Cast

Dr. David Banner . . . . Bill Bixby
Jack McGee. . . . . Jack Colvin
The Hulk . . . . Lou Ferrigno
Dr. Carolyn Fields. . . . . Mariette Hartley

David travels to Hawaii to seek medical help from specialist Dr. Carolyn Fields. When he arrives at her home, he finds her convulsing in the throes of a grand mal seizure. He breaks in and saves her life. When she awakens, David finds that she's dying, with only six to eight weeks left.

As they discuss her condition, Carolyn casually mentions that the late Dr. David Banner was doing breakthrough work on curing people with her affliction. David tells her he might be able to help, because he worked with Banner "very closely." Intrigued that he actually knew the late Banner, she asks about him.

Carolyn: Why did he suddenly abandon work on diseases such as mine?
David: His wife died and his life took on other priorities.

David wants to give her hope, so he reveals his secret identity to her in a well-written way. When she says, "David Banner was killed in a lab fire," David tells her, "No," and sums up his state by asking her if she's

"Married" is the only time Banner confronts his raging alter ego on the series.

ever read Robert Louis Stevenson. Puzzled, she asks, *"Treasure Island?"* David responds, *"Dr. Jekyll and Mr. Hyde."*

The two fall in love as Banner tries to get Carolyn's illness to go into remission. She uses her hypnotherapy to suppress The Hulk, to see if she can cure David of his anger problem. Before she hypnotizes him, David warns her that "there is a very real danger here — I don't know what might happen."

In several sessions, The Hulk is temporarily subdued in David's subconscious by nets (which he easily tears through), a vault and other impenetrable objects. The creature breaks through each time, but some of the traps take longer for him to get through — a positive sign of hope. David has nightmares of Laura Banner and Elaina Marks' deaths. Carolyn makes a credible love interest, one who interacts with The Hulk more than any other woman in the series before or since Elaina Marks. When her condition worsens, Carolyn runs off to a swingers' bar and leaves with two guys. David tracks her down, but she refuses to leave. When David insists she go, the guys beat him up for crashing the party. He Hulks Out, destroys their 'pad' and carries Carolyn out. Jack McGee is now on the island, looking for The Hulk, whose path leads straight to Carolyn. When the reporter arrives at her door, David successfully avoids McGee. David and Carolyn impulsively marry. He and Carolyn work up a plan to use Hulk's regenerative cells to cure her condition. A little boy is drowning and Carolyn saves him, but is considerably weakened by the ordeal. Hurricane Kevin is blowing into Hawaii and David must get Carolyn to the hospital if he hopes to save her life.

The Hurricane is making the trip difficult, with trees blocking the road as Carolyn's pain increases. She finally jumps out and races down the street. Chasing her, David is battered by debris, desperately trying to save the woman he loves. As the wind and rain slam him back in his attempt to save her, the raging storm triggers his transformation. He Hulks Out, reaches Carol and carries her to safety, only to find that the storm has taken its toll.

She dies in Hulk's monstrous arms, but before she goes, Carolyn kisses him and says, "I'll miss you, David." The next day, David sits alone on the beach, amongst the wreckage of both the house and life that they shared. The little boy she saved comes over to ask David about Carolyn. They make small talk and the boy says that he intends to become a doctor in honor of her.

A sad, impressive two-part episode from series' creator Kenneth Johnson, "Married" renews the mandate of The Incredible Hulk pilot — a solitary hero, hurt by life and lost love, trying to find a cure for himself and helping others.

Despite his mute status, Ferrigno does an amazing job of displaying grief as The Hulk. His scenes with Carolyn are obviously meant to echo those with Elaina in the pilot, and he pulls it off beautifully. We see Banner's late lovers in the show, Laura Banner and Elaina Marks are back, through the magic of flashbacks.

You sense the frustration the creature feels; he can't crush or throw a hurricane like his usual opponents, nor can he save a dying woman from a terminal illness. "Married" introduces the show's "classic Hulk" look, which Ferrigno sports for the next four seasons, complete with the creature's shag haircut.

It also gives us the first and only time on the series that David Banner meets his raging alter ego — who he tries to restrain in his subconscious. While Banner and Hulk are separate characters, Kenneth Johnson queries, "Wasn't Mr. Hyde always lurking within Dr. Jekyll?" The Hulk evades and breaks through every trap Banner sets and devises to capture him. An exasperated David finally admits that The Hulk "is too damn strong to be contained, even in my imagination!"

Shooting these desert confrontations between David Banner and The Hulk in Brawley, California, temperatures soared so high that Lou Ferrigno's makeup began melting and separating! There are several images reminiscent of William Friedkin's horror classic *The Exorcist* on display in "Married," from both David and The Hulk within him being hypnotized, to their confrontation in the desert, which recalls the panoramic shot between the priest and a demon statue from the film. Another *Exorcist* echo is the dream sequences of David running after the woman he loves as she leaves him. In one creepy shot, she even boards a bus being driven by a hooded Grim Reaper. This recalls the Father Karras dream sequence in *The Exorcist*. The most amazing achievement of "Married" is that it won Mariette Hartley an Emmy Award for Best Actress. To say this was a long shot because it was on a fantasy show is an understatement. Ironically, Johnson had also written an Emmy-winning character for Lindsay Wagner on his previous fantasy show, *The Bionic Woman*. Hartley gives a credible, touching performance while going through the five stages of grief. She also admits she should have had kids because she always wanted them, saves a child from drowning, and then dies a noble death. These are all typical components of an Emmy-win, but the fact that Hartley did it while emoting to a big green monster made her victory all the more impressive.

Another incredible feat is seeing how this *Hulk* two-parter uses the Hawaii setting to its full advantage. This is especially impressive because they *never actually went there*, but instead faked it all in Southern California! All the surfers off Diamondhead are stock footage, the waterfall where Banner marries Hartley is actually on a college campus in Pasadena, California, and the place he first meets her is the Pasadena Convention Center. The beach luau that Hulk crashes is actually indoors on the Universal backlot and the rest is Malibu. The only time you can really tell it's California is when Banner chases Carol to a Hawaiian swingers' bar... There's really no way to disguise The Pacific Coast Highway!

HULK HIGHLIGHT

We finally get to see Hulk and Banner confront each other — a common image in the comics, but this is the one and only time they come face to face on the series! The next time Bixby and Ferrigno meet is the episode "King of the Beach," but Ferrigno isn't playing Hulk.

MARIETTE HARTLEY (Carolyn): *"Where else but in Hollywood would you get an award for* The Incredible Hulk*?! I did not expect to win the Emmy, so when they called my name, I was just stunned! All I could say was 'Holy Cow!' The night I won, I was nursing my baby daughter at the time, but the building The Emmys were held in was freezing cold. I was so surprised at winning and I was so cold, I mentioned nursing my daughter and said, 'All she's getting [out of me] tonight is ice cream!'*

"It was a fun show. I actually go to bed with Bill Bixby and wake up with Lou Ferrigno...I especially remember at the end of 'Married,' where I literally die in his arms. When he carries me, Lou Ferrigno says, 'God, you're so heavy!' Thanks, Lou — I needed that! I became very close to Bill and Ken and the director of photography, John McPherson, who we lost. I adored Bill Bixby and I loved Lou, too. How can you not love Lou Ferrigno?!"

KENNETH JOHNSON: *"I'm very proud of 'Married,' for which Mariette Hartley won a Best Actress Emmy. Banner marries a woman, but she dies at the end. 'Married' gave me a chance to finally have a shot where Banner and The Hulk are in the same frame at the same time, because we're inside Banner's head. He's trying to cage The Hulk in his mind. That was a great episode and it was released in Europe as a theatrical feature,* Bride of The Incredible Hulk. *Dear God, that title! Universal called me one day and said, "Congratulations, you have the top-grossing film in Europe!"*

LARA PARKER (Laura Banner): *"Even though I died in the pilot, I liked that Bill Bixby's character had flashbacks of me in later episodes — it showed that he missed me!"*

JULIE ORSATTI: *"In the episode, Kenny Johnson had this chamber built to trap Hulk in. He had to show The Hulk hit the wall of the chamber and leave an imprint. Frank [Orsatti] kept hitting it with his fists until it made an imprint. He did it, but he had to break his knuckles and hand to get it! Frank used to work all the time with broken arms and broken hands. The doctor always made fun of Frank because he usually had casts that went up his arms. Frank couldn't work with casts on his arms, so he would cut the casts down to his wrists and painted them black! The doctor always teased Frank about that. He'd say, 'Nice work, Dr. Frank — glad to see you know what you're doing!' He would always rip the casts down to his wrists when he got home."*

HULK FACTS

Although Hartley's character is billed as "Carolyn," David only calls her "Carol."

When Carol sees a picture of The Hulk in *The National Register*, it's from the climax of "Terror in Times Square."

David and Carol's "Herro/ah so" nonsensical Asian impressions could charitably be described as "politically incorrect."

Look for Diane Markoff, the sexy girl at the swingers' pad, from Season One's "Earthquakes Happen."

David mentions his father for the first time on the show, but we won't meet him until Season Three's "Homecoming."

Split into a two-parter for syndication.

Look for *Star Trek*: *Deep Space Nine*'s Rosalind Chao as a receptionist.

Bixby and Hartley were re-teamed on the flop sitcom *Goodnight, Beantown*.

In his director commentary on the DVD, Kenneth Johnson reveals that Bill Bixby told him he thought of these episodes, where Banner ponders the meaning of life, visualization and the story of the cliff, when he was dying.

Meeno Peluce (Boy) went on to star in *Voyagers*, a short-lived show created, directed and guest-starring many people from *The Incredible Hulk*.

Hulk had confronted grief in his comic book the year before these episodes aired, when Jarella, his green-skinned girlfriend, is killed by CryptoMan, an evil robot.

Most Dated '70s Line in the Episode: "Dig that sound? It's quad!" When the creep picks up Carolyn in a bar and takes her to his bachelor pad, he tries to impress her with his now-archaic sound system.

Second Most Dated '70s Line in the Episode: "Far Out!" Uttered by the creep's friend when The Hulk smashes in.

Mariette Hartley was starring in a popular series of camera commercials with *Rockford Files'* star, James Garner. Although she was married to *Hulk* director Patrick Boyriven, the public thought she was with Garner. To solve this misconception, she wore a shirt reading 'I AM NOT JAMES GARNER'S WIFE.'

"THE ANTOWUK HORROR"
Season 2, Episode 13
Airdate: September 29, 1978
Directed By Sig Neufeld
Written By Nicholas Corea
Banner's alias: "David Barton"

Cast

Dr. David Banner . . . . Bill Bixby
McGee . . . . Jack Colvin
The Incredible Hulk. . . . . .Lou Ferrigno
Harlan Bates . . . . Bill Lucking
Samantha Bates. . . . . .Debbie Lytton
Brad. . . . . Lance LeGault
Buck . . . . Dennis Patrick
Sheriff Colton . . . . .Myron Healy
TV Reporter . . . . Bill Diez
Mayor Claire Murphy . . . . Gwen Van Dam

David winds up in Antowuk, California, a dying tourist town. He's working for local shopkeeper Harlan Bates. Harlan is jealous of David's relationship with his 10-year-old daughter, Samantha. At one point, he snarls, "People think you're her father!" He drunkenly attacks Banner and gets tossed around by The Hulk. This Hulk sighting brings in tourist dollars and national press coverage, so Harlan and the town seek to profit from it. "This creature is exactly what Antowuk needs," rationalizes

Harlan. "A tourist attraction that won't stop, it's bigger than a Bigfoot. Harlan vows to "bag this monster and stuff him!" He searches for the creature with his friend Brad. The attention also attracts several hunters out to kill themselves a Hulk. Big game hunter Buck Hendricks plans to shoot The Hulk, with or without Jack McGee's help. Buck settles in for a Hulk hunt, noting, "It'll show itself again — the big ones always do!" Brad

Bill Lucking is The Antowuk Horror.

returns alone, saying the creature got Harlan. This leaves Harlan's young daughter Samantha heartbroken over her missing father. Banner, who was looking after the girl and literally minding the store, is appalled at this blatant attempt to frame The Hulk and carelessly frighten Samantha.

Brad riles the townsfolk into chasing The Hulk. When another Hulk hunt proves fruitless, a Sasquatch-like creature suddenly appears, flips a jeep and attacks the town fair. With news of two monsters on the loose, the town is suddenly besieged with hunters and looky-loos, bringing much-needed money.

David realizes Harlan is posing as the other creature and resolves to stop him before he gets shot. This leads to a confrontation between The Hulk, Harlan's fake 'Antowuk Monster' and all of the hunters.

A fun, fast-moving action episode, "The Antowuk Horror" is especially welcome coming after the sad, somber conclusion of "Married." One suspects that "Antowuk Horror" was meant to air at a later date of the season, but was moved up because its story is so much lighter in tone. "Rainbow's End" and "A Solitary Place" both deal directly with Carolyn's death. David's grief over her is central in both those shows, but it's never mentioned in the zippy "Antowuk Horror." Those episodes are both set in Mexico and Southern California, places closer to Hawaii than this Pacific Northwest town. The first two seasons of *Hulk* were quite careful in the geographical accuracy of Banner moving from place to place, so one can only assume this show was moved up for its jauntier tone.

Nice acting by Bixby and William Lucking. As drunken bully Harlan Bates, there's a great scene where Lucking as Bates lords over David. Showing he sees David as worthless, Lucking crushes a beer can while David grips his broom tighter and tighter in a desperate effort to repress his rage. Bates is smart enough to realize Banner is better than the menial labor he's been forced to do and mockingly calls him "College Boy." As Harlan's precocious daughter, child actress Debbie Lytton complains to Bixby at one point, "Don't you know anything about First Aid?'

Lance LeGault and his actress daughter, Mary. PHOTO BY PATRICK JANKIEWICZ

When Buck the hunter wants McGee to help him kill The Hulk, we see that the reporter would actually like to keep the monster alive. We also realize McGee has no desire to harm Hulk at all. He tells Buck, "Five years ago, you wouldn't even consider shooting something worth more alive than dead!" McGee makes it clear that he doesn't want Hulk hurt in any way; he just wants to land the story of the century. Jack's anti-shooting stance toward Hulk would be the central plot of the fourth season's "Bring Me the Head of the Hulk." Somebody on *The Incredible Hulk* staff obviously had issues with big game hunters, as they show up as villains in this, "The Snare" and "Bring Me the Head of the Hulk." Deep Voiced character actor Lance LeGault, who plays Brad, was no stranger to the Hulk's "chasing the innocent hero" format. He played the Jack McGee role on *The A-Team*, as a military man hunting the wrongly convicted heroes. He also played another hunter on the *Hulk*-inspired show, *Werewolf*.

The town of Antowuk is loosely based on Willow Creek, California, the real Pacific Northwest town that was put on the map in October 1967, when hunter Roger Patterson shot credible footage of what appeared to be the elusive Bigfoot in nearby Bluff Creek.

BILL LUCKING (Harlan): *"Bill Bixby was always generous with me and we had several laughs about my attempts to be The Hulk from the country in that episode...I was 'The Antowuk Horror' of the title, and we laughed about how sensitive Lou Ferrigno's feet were. As The Hulk, he had to be barefoot and he really didn't like it. I wouldn't have either, but it struck me as incongruous that The Hulk would have sensitive feet. The show was silly, but what I remember most about it was that was the week that I had quit smoking. We were shooting the show up in the Angeles National Forest and the director kept insisting that The Antowuk Horror run up every steep hillside that he could find. I decided that if action characters were in my future, it would be best to have a useful set of lungs. Sorry I don't have more exciting memories of the show, but it was an episode of television!"*

LANCE LEGAULT (Brad): *"It was an incredible show to do. Bill Bixby was a longtime friend of mine. I liked him a lot, having worked with him on two Elvis Presley movies. Not many actors did two Presley films, so we knew each other really well. I knew him from a long way back. He also directed me in the* Jesse James *television series for ABC.*

"I had a great time working with Bill Bixby in 'The Antowuk Horror'! Bixby was a good guy. Before he ever got to play The Hulk, Bill did a lot of good work. Bill Lucking, who played my pal Harlan, is still a friend of mine to this day. We shot our Incredible Hulk *episode in the summer and it was hotter than hell! We were running around the mountains in these wool plaid shirts because we were supposed to be mountain men, trying to hunt down some beast over rocky terrain...I was going uphill and downhill in this itchy wool shirt and nobody was servin' Jack Daniels and water, no girls were visiting the set, so we were getting underpaid and overworked. Other than that, doing* Hulk *was a real pleasure!*

"We shot most of it on the Universal backlot. That was the extent of my big Hulk *contribution. In the episode, I try to kill Lou Ferrigno's Hulk. You couldn't kill Lou — he's too big! Lou is a nice guy; a gentle soul and sweet creature. An artist, not a fighter. I remember Lou Ferrigno didn't like running around barefoot! Lou is a baby, a big, gentle baby. About as tough as my sister, he's sweet, not tough."*

NICHOLAS COREA (in *Comics Scene* magazine): "*The Incredible Hulk* series was very thematic. The TV *Hulk* stories were all based on themes like love, hate and greed. We were always able to make a moral point at each story's end."

HULK FACTS

The title is a parody of the then-popular literary bestseller *The Amityville Horror*. The IMDb claims frequent *Hulk* guest Christine Belford and her family actually lived in the Amityville Horror house before the murders.

Poor Hulk is shot in his shoulder for the third time, after the pilot and "Hulk Breaks Las Vegas."

William Lucking's characters are fathers with daughter issues in both his *Hulk* episodes, "The Antowuk Horror" and "Dark Side."

Lucking got green himself, as an Orion Slave Trader on the *Star Trek: Enterprise* episode "Bound."

"Uncle Nic's Traveling Fair," which the fake monster attacks, is named after episode writer Nicholas Corea.

If the courthouse looks familiar, it should — it's the clock tower on the Universal backlot, later used for *Back to the Future*.

We finally see Hulk in purple pants — his color of choice in the comics.

"RICKY"

Season 2, Episode 14
Airdate: October 6, 1978
Directed By Frank Orsatti
Written By Jaron Summers

Cast

Dr. David Banner . . . . Bill Bixby
The Hulk . . . . Lou Ferrigno
Ricky . . . . Mickey Jones
Buzz . . . . James Dalton
Irene . . . . Robin Mattson

Ted Roberts . . . . Eric Server
Sam Roberts . . . . .Gerald McRaney

Working as a mechanic at a racetrack in West Valley, New Mexico, David meets Ricky Detter, the sweet younger brother of Buzz Detter, one of the derby's star drivers. Ricky is mentally retarded, and eager in his

David Banner helps a young retarded man (Mickey Jones) find acceptance in "Ricky."

efforts to help his big brother. Jealous racing rivals The Roberts Brothers use Ricky to break his brother's concentration, at one point, even putting him out on the track. Buzz is clearly ashamed of his brother and keeps shunting him aside, which hurts the impaired Ricky's feelings.

Banner realizes that Ricky is high functioning and wants Buzz to place him in a special school to help him learn to develop his creative tendencies. Buzz resists, but David resolves to help the two. When Ricky is playing in Buzz's car and accidentally starts it in a locked garage, he passes out as the engine runs. A horrified Banner sees this and Hulk saves him from asphyxiating. Unfortunately, he also smashes up Buzz's car to do it. After Ricky revives, he teaches The Hulk how to open a soda can. Ricky and Hulk bond over their similar circumstances.

"Ricky" is one of the best examples of when *The Incredible Hulk* took social commentary and used it to strong story effect. There's a great sequence where Ricky sees Lou Ferrigno's Hulk as something of a kindred spirit. Unlike "normal" characters, Ricky isn't afraid of The Hulk and even tries to help him do some basic things. Mickey Jones plays Ricky in a realistic manner, which makes his performance that much more moving. The

A shirtless Frank Orsatti leads Lou Ferrigno, Mickey Jones. PHOTO COURTESY OF JULIE ORSATTI.

evil racing siblings provide a counterpoint to Buzz and Ricky's brotherly relationship. The scene of Ricky pretending to drive in the parked race car is touching. Mickey Jones holds your attention through the scene, displaying childlike wonder. It's a truly great moment, despite having some of the sappiest music of the entire series being placed needlessly over it.

Jaron Summers' script is emotionally involving, but also doesn't skimp on Hulk action. The scenes of The Hulk with Ricky are sensitive, genuine and interesting. Although inarticulate, Ferrigno's Hulk clearly recognizes that Ricky is special and is gentle around him. The two characters form a friendship in a credible fashion.

One of the show's big success stories was director Frank Orsatti. He started out as Bill Bixby's stunt double for the first ten episodes of *The Incredible Hulk* and then went behind the camera with this episode. While he easily pulls off the smashing, crashing stock car sequences and Hulk bashing, the true surprise is how well he invests the retarded brother's story with such emotion.

Orsatti went on to direct a lot of the show's big action episodes, like "Mystery Man" and what is arguably the show's best Hulk-centered episodes, "The First," in the fourth season, but it's impressive to see a stuntman-turned-director get to the emotional heart of the story.

HULK HIGHLIGHT

Hulk drinks pop! Breaking into a garage where Ricky has been over-come by carbon monoxide, David cuts his hand on a piece of metal trying to save Ricky the same way he cuts his hand on a tire iron in the pilot. Turning into The Hulk, he saves Ricky, who teaches him how to open a soda can.

MICKEY JONES (Ricky): *"It was a great script and Kenny Johnson was a great guy. 'Ricky' was my big acting breakthrough — after the episode ran, everybody started calling me for roles. I received many letters from parents of retarded children thanking me for the way I played Ricky."*

KENNETH JOHNSON: *"I liked The Hulk as a character, particularly when we began to explore more of him in later episodes — seeing Hulk in the moments after the anger had passed and before he metamorphosized back into Bill Bixby. The moments of childlike simplicity and innocence that he had. There's a wonderful scene in 'Ricky' where Mickey Jones tries to show him how to open a soda can. The Hulk doesn't understand stuff like that. Hulk himself is a little like dealing with someone who is mentally handicapped or primitive. I loved finding little moments like that to play with. It helped broaden the scope of the show."*

LOU FERRIGNO (Hulk): *"When I drank the soda, that's how I felt The Hulk would behave and drink. He lets Ricky show him how to do it."*

STAN LEE: *"That was one of my favorite episodes of the show; it's a real tearjerker!"*

KAREN HARRIS: *"Frank Orsatti was Bill's stunt double and paid dearly for a lifetime of stunts…He had hurt himself so much in his career that he would lash himself to the handlebars of his motorcycle to go home!"*

JULIE ORSATTI (Frank Orsatti's widow): *"Frank told me he loved doing* The Incredible Hulk *and he admired Kenny Johnson so much. Frank thought*

Bill Bixby was a great guy and felt Lou was just incredible. Frank was a stunt coordinator on Hulk *and he wanted to direct. He had been doing second unit, so Kenny Johnson decided to take a chance and let Frank direct 'Ricky.' When Frank started casting, he found Mickey Jones. Frank fought for him because Mickey was a new, unproven actor. Frank said, 'I promise you, he'll do great. Mickey is perfect for this part.' Everybody doubted Frank's vision for the episode. It turned out well, Mickey was great and Frank got all the praise for the tenderness in the show. Mickey and his wife Phyllis are nice people and still close friends today."*

JARON SUMMERS ("Ricky" screenwriter in *Starlog* magazine): *"Basically, it was the story of a mentally retarded kid who wanted to be a race car driver, but it got out of hand because he wasn't very good on the track. One of the things I liked was that they always have The Hulk Hulk-Out. I've always wanted to destroy a Coke machine that wouldn't return a coin, so I had The Hulk do it."*

HULK FACTS

The Harris School for Special Education that Ricky is sent to is named after Karen Harris.

Kenneth Johnson was so impressed with the show and the huge ratings it garnered, he put a full-page ad in the trades praising newly-minted director Orsatti.

Ricky watches *The Wolf Man* on TV, which helps him understand The Hulk's transformations.

James Daughton was evil Greg Marmalard in *Animal House*.

This is Gerald McRaney's first appearance on *Hulk* since "Death in the Family."

Mickey Jones, a frequent *Hulk* guest, also appears in Kenneth Johnson's *V.*

"RAINBOW'S END"

Season 2, Episode 15
Airdate: October 13, 1978
Directed By Kenneth Gilbert
Written By Karen Harris & Jill Sherman
Banner's alias: "David Bishop"

Cast

Dr. David Banner . . . . Bill Bixby
Jack McGee. . . . . Jack Colvin
The Hulk . . . . .Lou Ferrigno
Kim Kelly . . . . .Michelle Nichols
Thomas Logan. . . . . Ned Romero
Jimmy Kelly. . . . . .Gene Evans
Lawrence Henry Carroll III . . . . Craig Stevens
Man on Bus. . . . . John Myhers
Security Guard . . . . Warren W. Smith
Andy Cardone . . . . .Larry Volk

David seeks out Native-American Thomas Logan, who has created an herbal compound that calms rage in racehorses. Thomas intends to use it on troubled racing stud, Rainbow's End. David is hoping to use it to calm The Hulk. He also tries to help Kim, a girl jockey, whose drunken father may destroy her life. When David learns the man is going to assassinate the jockey on Rainbow's End, he must stop the gunman before he accidentally kills his own daughter!

"Rainbow's End" is an underrated episode where the subplot of David's search for a cure is far more compelling than the tired father/daughter main story. One suspects this was to be the episode originally meant to follow "Married" as the loss of Carolyn Fields is front and center. Banner even has flashbacks of Carolyn's death from "Married."

David meets the enigmatic Thomas Logan, one of the best characters ever created by writers Karen Harris & Jill Sherman Donner. Actor Ned Romero makes Logan a credible person. Logan witnesses David's transformation and tries to convince him of its positive aspects. The scene of David Banner and Logan discussing the pros and cons of being The Hulk easily trumps the main storyline about the female jockey and her embittered alcoholic father. You wish the show had brought Thomas Logan back.

'hen he sees the change, Thomas Logan doesn't freak out like other people on the show do, but instead has a rational discussion about it later with David, after he's changed back.

Thomas: You possess a powerful force.
David: No, it possesses me! And I can't control it, even in my sleep.

That line is yet another callback to "Married," where Banner changes after a nightmare while in bed with Mariette Hartley. When his herbal compound successfully blocks David from Hulking Out, Thomas notes, "My grandfather's tribe would have treated you like a god." David quickly shoots back, "I don't want that kind of power."

The show also has one of David's funniest Hulk Outs. At the crowded racetrack, he's carelessly tripped, stepped on and kicked by an oblivious crowd of racing fans and gamblers, until it sets off his transformation.

Amazingly enough, *Hulk* writer/producer Nicholas Corea borrowed this episode 18 years later for an episode of *Walker: Texas Ranger*, with the exact same horse doping plot and even kept the horse' (and episode's) name, "Rainbow's End."

"Nicholas Corea was one of my closest friends and a mentor to me and Jill," says Karen Harris, co-writer of the *Hulk* episode. "When we did 'Rainbow's End' for *The Incredible Hulk*, Nic was our immediate supervisor. He helped us through the process, breaking story, supporting our work, giving notes and helping us to make it better.

"In 1997, Nic was working as a consultant on *Walker: Texas Ranger*. He was also diagnosed with cancer. I knew work was what kept his spirits up and kept him going. He mentioned 'Rainbow's End' and that he wanted to do a horse-racing story for *Walker*. I said, 'As long as Walker doesn't Hulk Out and turn green, where's the conflict?' Truthfully, giving Nic permission to pay homage to our work was the least we could do for a man who had given us both so much. Jill agreed. Nic died in January of 1999."

"Rainbow's End" is one of the very best episodes of the second season..

KAREN HARRIS: *"They loved our first episode, 'The Beast Within,' so we pitched them 'The Hulk at the races,' which became 'Rainbow's End.' I like how Thomas Logan thinks Banner being able to become the Hulk is great! Thomas Logan was a good character because he thought Banner's transformation was cool. He's also a trainer for the horses and he honestly tries to help Banner. That character might have had his genesis in The Writers' Room. On* The Incredible

Hulk, *we had a writers room where you would sit with Kenny, Nic Corea or whoever we had to answer to, and one of them would come up with a concept like, 'Hey, what if the guy* likes *the idea that Banner is The Hulk?' and you would incorporate that into your script."*

JILL SHERMAN DONNER: *"We mentioned this horse illness, Sickle-hoffs, that we had researched for this episode and Bill [Bixby] insisted that it did not exist! Bill said, 'You're putting me in the position of giving false information to the general public; children are watching!' He was furious and he was being completely serious. We made sure Sickle-hoffs was real. We brought in our research to show that it was real, but Bill still didn't believe us!*

"[Producer] Robert Steinhauer was a very big horse guy, so we made sure we depicted the racing accurately. Because Robert loved racehorses, we knew he'd go for our pitch — doing the episode meant that he could spend a week at the track!"

HULK FACTS

After battling animals throughout the season, Hulk saves a horse from a fire.

That's Santa Anita racetrack playing the fictional "San Remo."

Writers Karen Harris and Jill Sherman also have David look into plants to cure him in "Kindred Spirits."

David describes his Hulk Outs in clinical terms, as "an illness which is not unlike hyperactivity, followed by blackouts."

"A CHILD IN NEED"
Season 2, Episode 16
Airdate: October 20, 1978
Directed By James D. Parriott
Written By Frank Dandridge
Banner's alias: "David Baxter"

Cast

Dr. David Banner . . . . Bill Bixby
Jack McGee. . . . . Jack Colvin
The Hulk . . . . Lou Ferrigno
Jack Hollinger . . . . Sandy McPeak

Margaret Hollinger . . . . Sally Kirkland
Mark Hollinger . . . . .Dennis Dimster
Mary Walker . . . . .Rebecca York
Reporter . . . . .Marguerite DeLain
Kid. . . . . Nyles Harris
Middle-aged Man . . . . Thomas Middleton

Banner protects an abused kid in "A Child In Need."

While working as an elementary school gardener, David believes one
of the students, Mark Hollinger, is a victim of child abuse. When he
brings his concerns to the school nurse, he's met with resistance. "Are you
a nurse, Mr. Baxter, or a doctor?" As a man on the run, David obviously
can't tell her that he's a doctor.

David takes it upon himself to intervene in the family's problem and
finds that Jack Hollinger is an alcoholic who abuses his wife and son.
In denial, wife Margaret Hollinger refuses to acknowledge the family's
problem. After David changes into Hulk to save Mark, The Hollingers
decide to blame the boy's bruises on him. The school nurse tells David,
"The news said he was beaten and carried off by some kind of creature.
Do you know anything about that?" "Only if the creature was his father,"
David responds. Jack decides to shut David up once and for all.

In the exciting climax in the school gym, The Hulk finally confronts
the abusive Jack Hollinger — who first tries to punch the creature. Hulk

has had enough and starts shoving Jack backwards. Jack unexpectedly has flashbacks of his own father beating him when he was Mark's age. He breaks, sobbing and begging his "father" to stop. Confused by this reaction, The Hulk leaves. Jack agrees to seek help.

After writing one of the best shows of the first season ("Of Guilt, Models and Murder"), James D. Parriott directs one of the series' most

Hulk takes on the brutal wife/child beater.

acclaimed episodes of its entire run. To *The Incredible Hulk's* credit, the show doesn't soft-pedal the child abuse issue and there are several disturbing scenes where the father starts an incident to hit the boy. Having the angry, hateful father (Sandy McPeak) suddenly snap and lapse into his own unhappy childhood at the hands of The Hulk is truly disturbing. McPeak does a great job giving the father a volatile personality. Sally Kirkland stands out as the helplessly fragile, frightened mom.

SALLY KIRKLAND (Margaret Hollinger): *"Playing this poor Mother in a bad situation was a great role on a great show. I love emotional roles, so having a husband who was abusive to me and my child on the show was what I live for. Bill Bixby was the best. I love the scene where I'm getting upset with him when he's urging me to get help. We had this great dramatic scene, where Bill accidentally blew the line and said that my husband is an 'eggbeater'. I thought it was hilarious when it happened. They later used it for a comedy show,* Foul Ups, Bleeps & Bloopers, *where they had to get my permission or pay me to use that clip.*

"*I used a method acting technique called Emotional Recall to put me in the right mindset for the episode, how I would feel in a similar situation — I have been beaten up before in real life and used it for* The Incredible Hulk. *When I get emotional with Bill was my favorite scene, so many different emotions at once. Bill treated me like gold. He was extremely respectful of me on* Hulk. *I had the good fortune of being directed by Bill in* The Woman Who Loved Elvis. *I played Roseanne Barr's best friend. Because I was also an acting coach, Bill trusted me to teach Roseanne how to cry on camera. I taught her Emotional Recall for that.*

"*Mark Dimster was a wonderful kid, a good young actor and I spent time with him between the scenes to make our on-camera connection as mother and son more realistic. The director, James D. Parriott, trusted me and encouraged me while I was playing this woman.*

"*I remember being fascinated when Bill put in his contact lenses as he changed into* The Hulk. *I was blown away when Lou Ferrigno came through the wall — that was amazing to watch!*

"*The child abuse episode got me a lot of attention and a lot of work. I could not get arrested as an actress in the '70s, but television jobs like* Hulk *saved me. I did an ad campaign to get an Emmy for it — buying these ads wiped me out financially, but it did lead to a lot more work.*

KENNETH JOHNSON: "*When we did this child abuse episode, we were exploring another type of monster…What is the monster that comes out of a person and makes him abuse an innocent child? I wanted to do the wifebeater/ child abuser show, but the network said to me, 'That's not a* Hulk *episode — there's no bad guy!' I said, 'NO BAD GUY?!? Get a grip, fellas!' That actually became one of the episodes people remember most fondly.*"

LOU FERRIGNO (Hulk): "*The child abuse episode, where the father is hurting his young son, is great. I love the ending where The Hulk confronts the father and pushes him against the wall as the guy remembers his own father beating him. What a great show!*"

RON STEPHENSON (Casting Director): "*We cast Sally Kirkland as the boy's mother. She did a great job, but Sally danced to her own music. A nice gal, but her foibles and personality quirks are legendary!*"

JAMES D. PARRIOTT ("A Child In Need" director, in *Starlog* magazine): *"At that time, those types of shows worked. Ken [Johnson] had a real gift for finding a true human side that made those shows successful. He knew that you had to play these superheroes as real people and give them some real problems and issues to deal with. I directed an episode about physical child abuse. I'm proud of that and* The Incredible Hulk *was a really smart show. The first season was a little fluffy, but I think* Hulk *continued to improve. After I left, they started doing more shows that were relevant and wonderful."*

HULK FACTS

As noted above, there's a hilarious outtake of Bill Bixby blowing a line to Sally Kirkland. When she tells him, "Stop It! Jack is a good man — " Bixby looks at her in serious concern, and states, "He's also an eggbeater and that makes him dangerous!"

After Hulk, Sally Kirkland was Oscar-nominated for her title role in the film *Anna*.

Dennis Dimster, who plays the abused Mark, is now a TV director.

After this episode, *The Incredible Hulk* comic books retroactively added Bruce Banner's tragic backstory of being an abused child.

"ANOTHER PATH"
Season 2, Episode 17
Airdate: October 27, 1978
Directed By Joseph Pevney
Written By Nicholas Corea
Banner's alias: "David Braemer"

Cast

Dr. David Banner	Bill Bixby
The Hulk	Lou Ferrigno
Li Sung	Mako
May Chuan	Irene Yah-Ling Sun
Grandma Loo	Jane Chung
Frank Silva	Tommy Lee Holland
Mr. Fong	Joseph Kim
Simon Ming	Richard Lee-Sung

Receptionist. . . . . Helene Nelson
Driver . . . . Eric Stern

When David finds an old man freezing to death in the back of a refrigerated truck, he rescues him. The man is Li Sung, a blind Asian martial arts master. Banner gets him back to the school he started in San Francisco. Li Sung is saddened to find a former pupil of his has the neighborhood in a grip of terror. "Another Path" is a nice combo of action and grim ideas, a trademark of all the Nicholas Corea episodes. Mako is interesting as the wise but not boring Li Sung. This episode is so good, it actually got a sequel, "The Disciple," that was intended to be a backdoor pilot for a TV series. David references "Married" in this episode, when he tells Li Sung, "My wife Carolyn and I we were trying to reverse my disease. [Li Sung knows he's The Hulk] We were almost successful, but, ah, she died. I've tried to control it many times." Li Sung also confesses that he had an anger problem, "When I was young and first blinded, there was a terrible rage in me. A tiny rage compared with yours, but it has taken half my lifetime to control it."

HULK FACTS
Mako went on to appear alongside Lou Ferrigno's friend Arnold Schwarzenegger in *Conan the Barbarian.* He also voiced the rat Splinter in the animated *Teenage Mutant Ninja Turtles,* his final role.

Actress Irene Yah-Ling Sun returns as a new character in the episode "East Winds."

"ALICE IN DISCOLAND"
Season 2, Episode 18
Airdate: November 3, 1978
Directed By Sigmund Neufeld Jr.
Written By Karen Harris & Jill Sherman Donner

Cast

Dr. David Banner . . . . Bill Bixby
Jack McGee. . . . . Jack Colvin
The Hulk. . . . . .Lou Ferrigno
Alice Morrow . . . . .Donna Wilkes
Louie. . . . . Jason Kincaid

Joan Roberts . . . . Julie Hill
Ernie . . . . Marc Alaimo
Molly . . . . Beth Anne Rees
Waitress . . . . Rori Gwynne
Art Philbin . . . . Dennis Holahan
Al . . . . Brion James
Girl at Disco . . . . Jennifer Joseph

Working at the bar in the Pandemonium Disco, David recognizes
Alice, who he knew as a child. She was the daughter of a deceased friend.
Now fatherless and lost, poor Alice has grown into a teenage alcoholic.
David attempts to get her away from destructive friends, which leads
to trouble that only Hulk can handle. As part of the second season's
social issues, David explores teenage drinking. In many episodes, Banner
befriends a young kid or teen, usually a girl, and changes her life for the
better, as he does in "Antowuk Horror," "Like A Brother," "A Child In
Need" and "Metamorphosis." Here, Harris and Sherman reverse the formula. Banner was a role model for Alice and when he disappeared from
her life to find a cure to his Hulk, poor Alice sees her own life spin out
of control over feelings of loss and abandonment.

Because of his inadvertent role in Alice' downfall, Banner seems to be
even more involved in the situation than he usually is. Donna Wilkes is
quite touching as Alice, while bad guy Marc Alaimo chews up the scenery
as a creep named Ernie.

Yikes — look at those awful clothes! The gaudy Discoteque setting and
that generic disco music all scream, "Welcome to the late '70s, kids!" The
only thing not dated about this episode is The Hulk himself — happily,
green skin and torn pants never go out of style!

HULK HIGHLIGHT
Hulk trashes a disco!

JILL SHERMAN DONNER: *"One of the most important things Ken ever said
to me was, 'No one's gonna die.' When there would be a mistake, I would spend
most of my time writing on the set or crying. My life was divided into those
two things, it was my first job, so what did I know? I cried for five years on
The Incredible Hulk. Ken finally sat me down and said, 'No one is gonna die.'
The very next day, Broadcast Standards & Practices sent me a memo about
the 'Alice In Discoland' episode. We used a strobe light and I didn't know this,
but they said a strobe light can trigger epileptic seizures in viewers. They said,*

'You have to do something about the film, because that strobe light is at just the right meter. I went to Ken crying, 'Someone really could have died!'"

KAREN HARRIS: *"That episode is sooo '70s, but we had a great time with the subject; it was about teenage alcoholism. 'Alice In Discoland' was the last episode we sold by pitching an arena for the story to take place in. They said, 'No more pitches, we need actual stories.' We sold them on that with 'Hulk in a zoo' and 'Hulk at the races.' They didn't want to do any more big arenas, like discos or zoos, because the first AD did not handle crowds of extras well. Donna Wilkes, who played Alice, was a good little actress. She did a TV movie of the week that I wrote for Lynda Carter. It was called* The Baby Brokers, *but they retitled it* Born To Be Sold!"

HULK FACTS
Donna Wilkes starred in *Jaws 2* and the '80s cult movie *Angel*, where she played another teenage girl in trouble, this time a "high school honor student by day...Hollywood hooker by night!"

Marc Alaimo and Dennis Holahan are frequent *Incredible Hulk* guests.

Brion James (Al) became a popular movie actor in films like *Tango & Cash, Southern Comfort* and *48 HRS.* James made *Frogtown II* with Lou Ferrigno.

"KILLER INSTINCT"
Season 2, Episode 19
Airdate: November 10, 1978
Directed By Ray Danton.
Written By William Whitehead
& Joel Don Humphreys & Richard H. Landau
Story: Richard H. Landau
Banner's alias: "David Burnett"

Cast
Dr. David Banner . . . . Bill Bixby
The Hulk . . . . .Lou Ferrigno
John Tobey. . . . . .Denny Miller
Dr. Byron Stewart . . . . Rudy Solari
June Tobey. . . . . Barbara Leigh

Coach Haggerty	Pepper Martin
Security Guard	Mello Alexandria
Mitch Adams	Bill Baldwin
Drunk	Wally K. Berns
Bob Turner	Paul Coufos
Tony Bowers	Wyatt Johnson
Kurt Donahue	Frank Orsatti
J.P. Tobey	Herman Poppe
Kermit Connelly	Pat Studstill
Young John Tobey	Tiger Williams

David comes to work at The Coliseum in Los Angeles as a sports medic, so he can learn more about Dr. Stewart's work with hypnosis and rage therapy. Unfortunately, this treatment is only making angry star quarterback John Tobey more violent. David realizes Tobey's brutal competitive streak is driving a wedge between Tobey, his teammates and even his wife. It's building to the "Killer Instinct" of the title. "Killer Instinct" is a great episode, exploring the beginning of rage and explosive tempers. Denny Miller did two *Incredible Hulk* episodes as two diametrically opposite characters — an aggressive football player here and a disheartened paraplegic in "The Harder They Fall". He's excellent in both.

Beautiful Barbara Leigh seeks Bixby's help with her raging husband in "Killer Instinct."

As the quarterback John Tobey, he's like David Banner's Hulk without the Gamma Rays, animalistic and volatile. When he deliberately hurts a fellow player, he's only apologetic afterwards. David sees this Jekyll & Hyde personality and hopes to help him overcome it. We glimpse Tobey's childhood and see where all his rage began. Despite the seriousness of the episode, "Killer Instinct" also has a playful side. When David tries to sneak into the stadium to stop Tobey from killing someone during the big game, he's thrown into a security cell with a bunch of drunks and troublemakers, who are suitably stunned when he transforms.

Humorously, Coach Haggerty is excited to hear about The Hulk, when his recruiter tells him, "I'm telling you, Coach, the guy had to go 290 [yards] and there wasn't an ounce of fat on him!" "So where is he?" Haggerty snaps. "He was green, right? Playing for Green Bay? Let me know when you get his name on a contract! In the meantime, stop taking whatever you're taking before the commissioner's office gets wind of it!"

There's also a fun bit where the work of Dr. David Banner is referenced. David asks Dr. Stewart about his unusual hypnosis therapy and tells him, "I read your earlier books. I was very impressed. The seeds of aggression lie deep in the subconscious mind. Aggressive behavior is nothing more than acting out of the subconscious thoughts…" "That's very good," Stewart tells him, adding, "Of course, others have said the same thing; Waldheim, Marshall, Banner." David says, "Ah yes, but Banner was talking about strength, not aggression. The ability to find a well of hidden strength at a moment of crisis." Stewart responds, "Perhaps Dr. Banner failed to see that the source of that hidden well is the same for both things." "Perhaps," David concedes, now knowing firsthand the connection between strength and aggression.

DENNY MILLER (John Tobey): *"I had played football in college and the Army as an offensive end, so when I got the script, I was excited because it was a great part, a really great part! My character was based on [NFL legend] Dick Butkus. They even used footage of Dick as me. Butkus and I actually worked together on the old Vega$ TV show a couple times and his knees were bad. Really bad. His knees had been operated on so many times, when it came time for us to do something simple, like just walk across the street, they had to get a double for him.*

"I like that scene where I bring a gift to a guy I deliberately put in a wheelchair and he throws the box back at me. It's really hard to do those parts, where it's kind of awkward and uncomfortable, because I always thought I was much better at comedy, but I was pleased that I had such a great part on The Incredible Hulk. *I thought Pepper Martin was good as the coach and Barbara Leigh was great as my wife."*

BARBARA LEIGH (June Tobey): *"When I did that show, I liked everyone on it. I loved the director [Ray Danton] dearly and was very sorry that we lost touch. He was nice and I liked Denny Miller, who was impressive as my husband. I really thought Bill [Bixby] was a good actor with a sad heart over the loss of his son. The only thing that really stands out for me during the filming of 'Killer Instinct' is that I spent a lot of time with Bill and listened to him talk about his son, who later died. I think he tried drowning his sorrow from his son's death and then his ex-wife taking her own life. Honestly, I don't think he was ever happy after the loss of his son. Bill Bixby was very nice to me, so I only have fond memories of him, but that's what I remember most about him."*

MITCHELL DANTON (Emmy-winning editor and son of the late Ray Danton): *"My dad was always very proud of 'Killer Instinct.' He loved sports and he thought it was an episode that came together very well. There was a scene where the football player with anger issues spots The Hulk in a crowd and someone at the network said to him, 'How would that guy spot him?!' Dad said, 'Wait a minute, you are making a show about a guy who turns into a large green monster…And you're worried that no one is gonna believe you can see him in a crowd?!'"*

HULK HIGHLIGHT
Hulk crushes a football helmet, carries Tobey down the field and bats aside players who try to stop him.

HULK FACTS
Pepper Martin (Coach Haggerty) is the truck driver who beats up a powerless Clark Kent in *Superman II.*

Gorgeous Barbara Leigh was the first actress to portray Vampirella in posters, comic-book covers and appearances. She's been in *Playboy* twice and now works for the company.

Tiger Williams co-starred in the "Secret Empire" segments of Johnson's *Cliffhangers.*

The crowd scenes are stock footage from *Two-Minute Warning.*

Director Ray Danton was married to *Hulk* guest star Julie Adams.

Wally K. Berns (Drunk) specialized in playing drunks in various movies and TV shows.

William Whitehead wrote and acted for the *Swamp Thing* TV series, which starred *Hulk* guest Dick Durock.

"STOP THE PRESSES"
Season 2, Episode 20
Airdate: November 24, 1978
Directed By Jeffrey Hayden.
Written By Karen Harris & Jill Sherman & Susan Woollen

Cast

Dr. David Banner	Bill Bixby
Jack McGee	Jack Colvin
The Hulk	Lou Ferrigno
Jill Norton	Julie Cobb
Karen Weiss	Mary Frann
Fred	Pat Morita
Charlie	Art Metrano
Joe Arnold	Sam Chew Jr.
Mr. Roberts	Robert O'Brien
Game Warden	Tom Bodkin
Lenette Logan	Janet Brandt
Printer	Sandy Champion
Mr. Geller	Mike Griswold
Copyboy	Donald Petrie

Working as a restaurant dishwasher, David has grown quite fond of the sweet, ditzy owners, Jill and Karen. The girls can't quite believe that someone so smart and good-looking is working as their dishwasher. Joe Arnold, an unscrupulous reporter from Jack McGee's tabloid, *The National Register*, is planting roaches in their kitchen for an expose.

While spreading the bugs in a food area, Joe accidentally photographs David, who surprises him. Arnold escapes, planning on running the shots, not knowing he's got the scoop of the year: a certain fugitive Gamma Physicist alive and well. David realizes the only way to keep his photo from running is to go into *The National Register* and get them back himself. Meanwhile, it's the worst day of Jack's life, as his editor, Mr. Roberts, tells him, "The publisher is thinking of killing your weekly 'Creature Report.' The Hulk Hunt is getting too expensive; plane tickets, wrecked cars…" The climax, with The Hulk running amok at the printing presses of *The National Register*, manages to solve Jack, David, Jill and Karen's problems all at once!

"Stop The Presses" is a great episode, a fun lark from one of the series' best directors and two of its best writers. Jack Colvin obviously realized the

script's quality and stepped up to the plate as Jack McGee. Funny, tragic and principled, Colvin gives his best performance before "Mystery Man." Julie Cobb and Mary Frann are flat-out adorable as the naive restaurant owners, while Pat Morita hilariously plays off the stereotype of the Asian cook. Sherman and Harris even have the two female leads named after themselves. "We did stuff like that all the time," laughs Jill Sherman Donner. The show's two female writers use their namesake characters to playfully poke fun at the series conventions, particularly the way that, while working menial jobs, the intelligent, handsome and thoughtful

Julie Cobb. PHOTO BY PATRICK JANKIEWICZ

David Banner changes the lives of those around him, meets beautiful women, solves their problems and then disappears into the sunset.

Deconstructing the show in the last ten minutes, Jill notes that David the dishwasher "is great at helping us with the books!" Karen White sighs, "I love brainy dishwashers!" At the end of the episode, David has hitchhiked out of town, while Jill notes, "The place sure has lost a lot of its magic since he left. I mean, men like David just don't come into a girl's life very often. He was so special. We'll never see him again. Another town, another name. Wasn't he wonderful?" Karen agrees, "He was perfect."

JILL SHERMAN DONNER: *"That was a really fun episode to do. Basically, the Mary Frann and Julie Cobb characters are based on us. The actresses do a great job; we had run out of names, so we used our own!"*

KAREN HARRIS: *"'Stop The Presses' had been written by a freelance writer, Susan Woollen. Susan was told that it would be about these two dingy girls who run a restaurant and she was told to call them 'Jill and Karen.' We had just been hired officially on staff and the first show Jill and I are asked to do a rewrite on had two main characters named 'Jill and Karen.' We were excited at first to have characters named after us, but then we saw that they were dingy broads! We wanted to change their names, but Ken said, 'No, it's Jill and Karen.' After he said that, we really had fun with it. Both our characters have huge crushes on David Banner, saying, 'He's so mysterious; I wonder what his secret is!' That was fun. 'I love brainy dishwashers!' is such a Jill line, because she really does! Brainy dishwashers are her thing. Julie Cobb is wonderful in the show and she's still a close friend."*

JULIE COBB (Jill): *"I had a wonderful time! My partner in crime was the late Mary Frann, who was a lot of fun to work with. We later did another pilot together, but I had an absolute ball doing* The Incredible Hulk! *Karen Harris and Jill Sherman, the writers, said it was going to be a spin-off, a backdoor pilot for a series of the two of us running a business together. I got cast and was allowed to read with other actresses who were up for the Mary Frann part. There were a lot of good actresses up for it, like Erin Gray, but Mary Frann got the part. I didn't know Mary and I were playing Karen and Jill. Bill Bixby was bright, friendly and very sweet — I thought Bixby was quite charming. Lou Ferrigno was a nice guy. I didn't have too much to do with them, because most of my scenes were with Mary!"*

JEFFREY HAYDEN: *"Julie Cobb and Mary Frann were delightful. Being around them for six days was just a pleasure."*

ALAN J. LEVI: *"*The Incredible Hulk *always did fun stuff, like using the names of the crew...I remember one Hulk where there's a heist and every character is named after a crew member!"*

PAT MORITA: *"I enjoyed doing fantasy shows like* Hulk *and* Man from Atlantis *— it beat playing generals on the losing side of the war!"*

HULK FACTS

Donald Petrie (Copy boy) became a director. He cast Julia Roberts in her first big role, in *Mystic Pizza*.

In this show, Hulk producer Robert Bennett Steinhauer is listed as the publisher of *The National Register.*

Sam Chew, Jr. was a regular on Johnson's *The Bionic Woman.*

Pat Morita was Mr. Miyagi in *The Karate Kid*, where he battled fellow *Hulk* guest Martin Kove.

Art Metrano was Lt. Mauser in the *Police Academy* movies.

Mary Frann (Karen) became a CBS star in her own right, as the bemused wife on *Newhart.*

Julie Cobb (Jill) co-starred in the *Salem's Lot* and *Brave New World* miniseries. She was the first female 'Red Shirt' to die on *Star Trek.*

"ESCAPE FROM LOS SANTOS"
Season 2, Episode 21
Airdate: December 1, 1978
Directed By Chuck Bowman
Written By Bruce Kalish and Philip John Taylor
Banner's alias: "David Brown."

Cast

Dr. David Banner	Bill Bixby
The Hulk	Lou Ferrigno
Holly Cooper	Shelly Fabares
Jim	W.K. Stratton
Mike Evans	Lee de Broux
Sheriff Harris	Dana Elcar
Mexican Man	Ben Frommer
Mrs. Mallard	Toni Hancock
Jill	Desiree Kearns
Forrest	Kerrigan Mahan
Mr. Mallard	Al Valleta
Chase	Vernon Weddle

Passing through Los Santos, Arizona, David and Holly Cooper, a woman he's never met before, are framed for the murder of her husband by

...corrupt sheriff. Handcuffed together, the two try to escape the town and prove their innocence. This has a great opening, where David is befriended by the seemingly friendly Los Santos cop, only to learn that he's been selected as the fall guy for killing a local woman's political gadfly husband. A fast-paced "chase" episode where David finds himself literally on the run, but unable to get out of town. There's crisp dialogue, such as when Holly asks, "How do you know I didn't kill my husband?" "Easy," David replies breezily, "I'm your accomplice and I'm innocent!"

"Los Santos" has a couple of decent Hulk Outs, although it stretches credibility when Holly (Shelly Fabares) asks David where Hulk came from because she *was handcuffed to him when he changed!*

The growing popularity of *Hulk*'s fellow CBS show, *The Dukes Of Hazzard*, can be felt in a long and painfully unnecessary chase scene where David drives an old truck that easily outraces the Los Santos Sheriffs' Department. Behind the wheel, Banner

The Dukes Of Hazzard was having a detrimental effect on *Hulk*.

even forces the cops off the road and into a ditch. This is pretty good stunt driving — and totally out of character for a hitchhiker who is rarely ever behind the wheel! Besides, the first time we ever see David behind the wheel in the pilot, his wife dies when he has a simple blowout.

HULK FACTS

There's a surprising racial slur in this episode, when Los Santos' Sheriff Harris asks a Mexican man driving a truck full of people, "Can you prove they're not wetbacks?" It's what a racist bad guy would say, but still surprising to hear.

Lee de Broux is a *Hulk* two-timer, appearing in this and "Fast Lane." He also starred in the first and last episodes of sci-fi show *Quantum Leap*.

For the first time since the second *Hulk* pilot, *Death in the Family*, David is chased by bloodhounds!

Shelly Fabares appeared in *Clambake* with Bill Bixby.

"WILDFIRE"

Season 2, Episode 22
Airdate: January 17, 1979
Directed By Frank Orsatti
Written By Brian Rehak
Banner's alias: "David Blakeman"

Cast

Dr. David Banner	Bill Bixby
The Hulk	Lou Ferrigno
Linda Calahan	Christine Belford
Ray	Billy Green Bush
Mike Calahan	John Anderson
Frank Adler	Dean Brooks
Phil Haze	Ernie Orsatti

David works on Mike Calahan's wildcat oil rig. He's also dating Mike's beautiful daughter Linda and things are getting serious. Mike bets all his money on one last claim and it pays off; he strikes oil. When they discover it, Mike and Linda's problems are only beginning, as competitors and traitorous employees decide to put them out of business by any means necessary! Christine Belford elevates what is an otherwise uninspired, run-of-the-mill *Hulk* episode. Her performance as a lonely girl surprised to run into someone as sophisticated as David working as a rigger gives the episode a touch of melancholy. As usual, action director Orsatti pulls off the gushers, explosions and fistfights.

KAREN HARRIS: *"Christine Belford and I are still in touch with each other. She was really good on the* Hulk *episodes that she did."*

MARK A. BURLEY (Unit Production Manager): *"Frank was Bill Bixby's best friend and he didn't want anyone to outshine Frank as* Hulk's *action director. When Orsatti directed, Bill would work extra hards to make Frank look good."*

HULK HIGHLIGHT
Hulk smashes a CB radio (also the most dated '70s moment in the Episode)!

HULK FACTS
Ted Cassidy, the uncredited voice of the Hulk and opening narrator, died the night before this episode aired. His narration was kept for the run of the series and character actor Charles Napier became the new voice of the Hulk.

We learn in this episode that David can write in French. Not coincidentally, so can Kenneth Johnson!

Billy Green Bush will return as a sheriff for Frank Orsatti in *Hulk*'s excellent fourth-season entry, "The First."

"A SOLITARY PLACE"
Season 2, Episode 23
Airdate: January 24, 1979
Directed By Jeffrey Hayden
Written By Jim Tisdale & Migdia Chinea Varela
Banner's alias: "David Baily"

Cast

Dr. David Banner . . . . Bill Bixby
McGee . . . . Jack Colvin
The Incredible Hulk. . . . . .Lou Ferrigno
Gail Collins. . . . . Kathryn Leigh Scott
Raul. . . . . Hector Elias
Ramon. . . . . .Jay Varela
Joey Malone. . . . . Bruce Wright

Opening "Somewhere in Baja, Mexico," David has been able to keep from Hulking Out for 32 days, a new record for him. He feels that isolation is the key to holding back the change, with no one else around to cause him stress.

On a bus heading into the jungle to look for The Hulk, who was last seen in that area, Jack McGee recognizes fellow passenger Gail Collins, another fugitive doctor from the United States. She is wanted for questioning in the death of a patient. Realizing he has two stories in the area — Gail Collins and The Hulk — McGee wants to solve them both.

Gail stumbles across David's encampment and helps herself to his medical supplies. David catches her, but also recognizes Gail as a fellow doctor, a neurosurgeon, and the two form a friendship. They start falling in love, until the father and brothers of Gail's 'victim' show up to hunt her. They saw her in the National Register article. David's admission at the beginning of the episode that "I find myself missing Carol more and more…," means "A Solitary Place" is a direct sequel to the season-two opener, "Married." We see flashbacks to "Married" as "A Solitary Place" hits some of the same emotional themes as those episodes. Kathryn Leigh Scott is a credible love interest, essentially playing a female version of David Banner in an above-average episode.

Kathryn Leigh Scott. PHOTO BY PATRICK JANKIEWICZ

KATHRYN LEIGH SCOTT (Gail Collins): *"I really enjoyed doing the* Hulk *TV show. I thought 'A Solitary Place' was good, interesting and well written…I worked with Lou Ferrigno, so it was great fun being saved by The Hulk! I played a doctor, who flees after a medical mishap. I go to Baja, where I meet David Banner, another doctor on the run. When we shot it, there was so much illness on the show, with a flu going around. Everyone seemed to be getting sick on it — including Bill Bixby! When Bill got sick, that meant I was on it longer than I would have been otherwise for a single episode. Due to that crew-wide illness, I ended up working on* Hulk *for three weeks, because we had to keep shutting down as poor Bill and other people were recuperating. I don't remember where we shot it, but it was a fun episode. I found Bill Bixby to be very warm and friendly."*

JEFFREY HAYDEN: *"Kathryn Leigh Scott was a nice lady. Lou Ferrigno was a very nice guy who worked very hard, even though he was not an actor. I liked him a lot. Toughest thing on that show was when Bill Bixby put the contact lenses in his eyes for the transformation. It took 20 minutes, as you waited with 75 other guys on the crew. We shot 6-8 pages a day and those contact lenses always slowed things down."*

HULK FACTS
We see a gentle side to The Hulk in this episode, when he pets a rabbit as he transforms back to Banner.

"Somewhere in Baja, Mexico" actually means "The Mexican Village" set on the Universal Studios backlot.

With his articles on Gail Collins, we see that McGee doesn't just cover The Hulk.

Jim Tisdale & Migdia Chinea Varela wrote the first season's exciting "Earthquakes Happen."

"LIKE A BROTHER"
Season 2, Episode 24
Airdate: January 31, 1979
Directed By Reza Badiyi
Written By Thomas E. Szollosi & Richard Christian Matheson
Banner's alias: "David Butler"

Cast

Dr. David Banner	Bill Bixby
The Incredible Hulk	Lou Ferrigno
Taylor George	Tony Burton
Lee	Ernie Hudson
DJ	Michael D. Roberts
Oscar	Carl Anderson
Rev. Jack Williams	Austin Stoker
Mrs. Dennison	Maidie Norman
Mike	Stuart K. Robinson
Mother	Elizabeth Chauvet
Jimmy	Jesse Dizon
Fantine	Rana Ford
Bobby	Dale Pullum

Working at an inner-city car wash, David tries to take care of two orphans. He runs afoul of Taylor George, a drug dealer, who runs the neighborhood like a dictator. His rule is enforced by his goons and a savage black panther. George now expresses an interest in the two boys and a dangerous contempt for David Banner.

"Like A Brother" is an exciting episode. Putting Banner in a black com-

In "Like A Brother," the imposing Taylor George (Tony Burton) threatens Banner.

munity, up against a villain of color, is daring. Tony Burton plays Taylor George as charming but deadly, with a pre-*Ghostbusters'* Ernie Hudson as his lead muscle, Lee. Austin Stoker is a sympathetic Reverend, who hits the social commentary button when he tells Taylor George, "Your name is tattooed in needle marks on arms all over this neighborhood."

As with "747" and "The Snare", writers Thomas E. Szollosi & Richard Christian Matheson come up with an offbeat episode and even work in some genuine doctoring for David Banner to do…He discovers that one of the orphans is diabetic. This applied medical knowledge is probably because of their work as story editors on *Quincy, M.E.*

HULK HIGHLIGHT
In his latest animal battle, Hulk scares off a panther.

TONY BURTON (Taylor George): "*I loved having a black panther as a pet on that* Hulk! *This savage panther on a leash made my bad guy kind of cool. Bill Bixby was nice, I liked him. Austin Stoker and Ernie Hudson are great guys, but the only thing about* Hulk *that stays in my mind was the panther. That black panther was actually a big leopard they painted black, because real black panthers are dangerously erratic — you don't know what they are gonna do! So the black panther-who-was-actually-a-leopard was nice all day, but toward the*

end of the day, he must have gotten tired. We came into this scene and he suddenly said, 'RRROOOAAR- RGGH!' *Everybody jumped! It scared the dookie out of me.*"

ERNIE HUDSON (Lee): "*I really did that episode of* The Incredible Hulk *for my sons, because they loved the show. They thought seeing their dad get thrown by The Hulk was great. Of course, I was a little surprised to see that they were rooting for The Hulk over me, their own dad! I was a little nervous around the panther, but I had a great time on the show otherwise. Tony Burton, Bill Bixby and Lou Ferrigno were all fun!*"

Ernie Hudson. PHOTO BY PATRICK JANKIEWICZ

AUSTIN STOKER (Rev. Jack Williams): "*I did the episode in a couple of days. I remember doing scenes with Bill Bixby, showing him around the neighborhood as Banner. It was fun to see Tony Burton, who I did a movie with previously. I didn't have any scenes with The Hulk, unfortunately!*"

RC MATHESON: "*I recall a black guy who was either a story editor or a producer on* Hulk *and he and Nicholas Corea had a great banter together. They would playfully razz each other about things. Nic was a bit of a bohemian thinker. He had the idea of doing a* Hulk *episode with a black backdrop; where every character but Banner is black and that really appealed to him. It's interesting to go back and look at these old* Hulk *shows, because there are guests on the show that went on to become really significant actors, like Ernie Hudson.*"

HULK FACTS

As noted, guests Austin Stoker and Tony Burton played cop and convict in the John Carpenter cult classic *Assault On Precinct 13*.

Tony Burton was also Duke, Apollo Creed and Rocky Balboa's trainer, in all six *Rocky* movies.

Carl Anderson was Judas in *Jesus Christ Superstar*.

We see a flashback from this in the episode "Proof Positive."

"HAUNTED"
Season 2, Episode 25
Airdate: Feb. 7, 1979
Directed By John McPherson
Written By Andrew Schneider
Story by Karen Harris & Jill Sherman

Cast

Dr. David Banner	Bill Bixby
The Incredible Hulk	Lou Ferrigno
Renee Stevens	Carol Baxter
Bernard	John O'Connell
Fred Lewis	Johnny Haymer
Renee as Child	Randi Kiger
Woman	Iris Korn
Dr. Rawlins	Jon Lormer

David works as a mover for Renee Stevens, who goes back to her childhood home for the first time since the death of her twin sister. Once back in the homestead, Renee is haunted by Becky, the child ghost of her dead twin.

"I don't believe there's a ghost in this house and neither do you," David tells Renee. In the climax, David must help her overcome the spirit's fatal call, as The Hulk does some ghostbusting. "Haunted" sets up an intriguing question: how would David Banner and The Hulk deal with a ghost? Of course, there's no ghost here, it's just Renee's guilt and the revelation that she isn't Renee at all — Renee drowned at the old mill and wild child Becky took her place.

"Haunted" is a slow, plodding episode that feels like bad Nancy Drew; a ghost (who is not really a ghost), an old mill and a bunch of red herrings. It all add up to one of the worst episodes of the second season. Both Hulk Outs are for arbitrary reasons — David is trapped in a locked room or smashing a water wheel, so there is really no one for Hulk to confront. Incredibly, Carol Baxter, the star of "Haunted", wrote a virtual remake of this episode for the fourth season's equally terrible, "Wax Museum".

One funny bit comes when David offers to be Renee's moving man. When she doesn't think he's up to the task, David smiles and says, "Believe me, I'm stronger than I look!"

HULK FACTS
In the comics, The Hulk can see ghosts and astral projection, while others can't.

Besides *Hulk*, John O'Connell guest-starred with TV superheroes *Wonder Woman* and *Buck Rogers*.

Carol Baxter starred in "The Curse Of Dracula" segments of *Cliffhangers*. She and "Haunted" guest John O'Connell both return as new characters in the fourth season's "Prometheus."

"MYSTERY MAN" PART ONE & TWO
Season 2, Episodes 26 and 27
Airdate: March 2 and March 9, 1979
Directed By Frank Orsatti
Written By Nicholas Corea
Banner's alias: "John Doe"

Cast

Dr. David Banner	Bill Bixby
McGee	Jack Colvin
The Incredible Hulk	Lou Ferrigno
Rose	Victoria Carroll
Doctor	Don Marshall
Bob Cory	Howard Witt
1st Man	John C. Colton
Nurse #1	Nadieda Klein
Hospital Guard	John McKee

2nd Man . . . . Norman Merrill
Hal Pollock . . . . .Michael Payne
Pilot. . . . . Skip Riley
Dr. Elaina Marks. . . . . .Susan Sullivan
3rd Nurse. . . . . Barbara Tarbuck
Nurse Phalen. . . . . Alin Towne

Banner and McGee bond in "Mystery Man."

Accepting a ride from Rose, a very drunk, heartbroken country singer, turns out to be a very bad idea for David. Her cowboy husband ran off with a rodeo girl. "I don't make a habit of picking' up riders," she slurs, hitting on David, before lapsing into rage at her cowboy.

"You ain't ever really been mad have ya," Rose asks, then steers the car into a fiery crash. Rose is injured, but David Banner is badly burned. Trapped in a burning car like his late wife, David Hulks Out and bursts from the vehicle. Lifting the wreckage, it explodes, setting Hulk's hair on fire. Two samaritans see his burned form and call an ambulance because he's "hurt bad."

His face swathed in bandages, David has no memory of who he is, sustaining amnesia from the accident. The doctor believes the traumatic experience he's suffered has left him with temporary amnesia. Dubbed "John Doe" by *The National Register*, the tabloid does a series of human

...st stories on poor David. When the bandaged David meets Jack McGee, he tells the reporter "I know you — " and has hazy flashbacks of him. McGee thinks he recognizes his face from his column in The Register.

The paper magnanimously sends David with Jack McGee to see a specialist to help recover his memory. The plane crashes in the wilderness and McGee's leg is broken.

Using the plane's broken wing, David sets the reporter's leg in a splint and then pulls the injured man along on a makeshift litter. After Hulking Out, Banner remembers who he is. He then must save McGee from wolves and a raging brushfire without letting the reporter know who *he* is.

"Mystery Man" is two of the most action-packed episodes of the series; one of Nicholas Corea's most ambitious stories, with non-stop cliffhangers. Frank Orsatti keeps the episode fresh and fast. Only someone as perpetually unlucky as David Banner could go through a car crash and plane crash in the same week.

As with previous Corea episodes, there are a lot of nice character moments. The scene where David recovers his memories — with a painful flashback of the late Elaina Marks — is especially moving. It also takes the time to remind viewers that David Banner is a doctor, using his skill to help Jack McGee.

We learn more about Jack McGee in these two episodes than in all five seasons of the show combined, from McGee's time in the Korean War to why he is so suspicious of people. McGee confirms his hunch from "The Hulk Breaks Las Vegas" that The Hulk is not a full-time monster, but someone who changes *into* a monster. "Mystery Man" also takes great pains to show that McGee is a sympathetic man. He describes himself as "kind of a hunter and The Hulk is what I hunt..."

McGee speculates that "John Doe" is also after The Hulk for another reason. "The Hulk is rough, he's a killer, he could have hurt somebody you know, somebody you love." Talking with Banner, the reporter feels that exposing The Hulk will be his personal salvation. When he and Banner — whose face is hidden under bandages — begin talking about his quest to find Hulk, Banner finally asks him what he's wanted to know since the series' pilot. "*Why* do you want The Hulk so badly?"

Mulling over Banner's question, McGee finally says, "Because The Hulk means escape. Get it? It's the biggest story of the twentieth century! I could win a Pulitzer for journalism. More importantly, I could get off *The Register*. I could stop banging out pap for the supermarket masses. I could get my column back, write real stories. Important stories — I could be somebody!" Much like Carl Kolchak, beloved hero of Universal's previous fantasy show, *Kolchak: The Night Stalker*, we find that the earnest, intrepid Jack McGee is a down-on-his-heels reporter looking for a break.

After hearing McGee's revelation that he's hunting Hulk for his career, Banner confronts him. "But The Hulk saved your life. You told me so yourself. Don't you think you should help It?" "Yes," McGee readily agrees, "but you gotta choose. That's all life is, you know, my friend, just choosing. It's you or the other guy." This gives viewers a unique insight into Jack McGee. David seems to respect his honesty, if not his integrity. You get the impression that under different circumstances, Banner feels that he and McGee could be friends. It's also obvious to Banner that here, helpless in the wild, McGee is "the other guy."

This two-parter demonstrates why Orsatti was *Hulk*'s action director, with plane crashes, brushfires and even wolves. "Mystery Man" also seems to be a loose homage to Saki's classic short story "The Interlopers," where two lifelong enemies are trapped in the wilderness, bond and find they have much in common. Once they pledge eternal friendship upon rescue, they realize what they think are their saviors are actually wolves.

JULIE ORSATTI (Frank Orsatti's widow): *"On 'Mystery Man,' Frank was proud to have gotten Monty Cox to work on the show. Monty was a guy who provided exotic animals for rent in movies and TV. Universal said, 'No, no, don't use Monty Cox, he's too expensive,' but Frank got him to do it for an acceptable price because he was his friend. He got wolves and all these other exotic animals into the show."*

HULK FACTS

Guest Victoria Carroll (Rose) was the first actress to play She-Hulk, in the 1980s *Incredible Hulk* cartoon.

Jack McGee confirms that Hulk is a man who changes into a monster

His list of animal attackers grows as Hulk faces off against wolves.

Don Marshall returns, for his first appearance since "The Hulk Breaks Las Vegas."

The late Elaina Marks puts in an appearance, via flashback.

Nicholas Corea wrote *The Rare Breed*, a book about his adventures as a cop in St. Louis after his return from Vietnam.

In St. Monica's Hospital, where the burned David is taken, we hear a "Dr. Sherman" being paged…This is a tribute to the show's Story Editor, Jill Sherman.

HULK PROFILE
DON MARSHALL

Actor Don Marshall showed up in three episodes of *The Incredible Hulk*. He was a thug in "The Hulk Breaks Las Vegas," a kindly doctor who tries to save David Banner's burned face in "Mystery Man" and a misguided member of a lynch mob out to kill Banner in "Deathmask."

The thoughtful actor considers "Mystery Man" "to be my favorite *Hulk* episode ever. I liked it because I was playing a doctor, trying to help David Banner with his facial injuries, instead of someone trying to hurt him! When I did 'Deathmask,' Bill told me, 'There's a good part coming up that you would be perfect for,' which turned out to be the doctor in 'Mystery Man.' I did all my scenes with him while he was lying in the hospital bed.

Don Marshall's best shot as a Doctor In "Mystery Man."

"There's an amazing shot of me in 'Mystery Man,' truly generous for a guest actor on a television show," Marshall proclaims. "Bill Bixby had the director Frank Orsatti do a really tight close-up of me. It's a great shot where I'm telling him about the damage he sustained in the fire. He gave me that amazing close-up, a type of shot I have not seen very often. Bill really worked with me and tried to help me out as an actor. You don't

Don Marshall roughs up Banner in "The Hulk Breaks Las Vegas."

have many actors or directors willing to do that for somebody and Bill was both. That was so beautiful of him…Bill was one of the most beautiful people I ever knew, willing to help and work with actors."

Marshall was truly moved by the star's generosity. "Bixby was a very loving person. When you become very secure in your craft, you can help other people and that's what Bill Bixby did. I had never met anybody like him before or since, someone who was that generous. In acting, when you work, you see other actors, but they are mostly into themselves. They don't have time to help anyone else. When you do run into someone like Bill Bixby, who was so secure in his acting and directing that he wanted to help someone else, it's really beautiful."

He also enjoyed working with — and occasionally battling — Bixby's alter ego. "As The Hulk, Lou Ferrigno would come up to the actor he was gonna fight on camera and tell them not to worry, he would be very careful so they would not get hurt! That meant a lot to me as an actor, for Lou to let you know that he was concerned about your well being and that you wouldn't be hurt. This is what my experience with Bill Bixby, Lou Ferrigno and Kenny Johnson was like on all three of *The Incredible Hulk* episodes I did! Caring and concern is all you got from these nice guys. All I can say is thank you, gentlemen, for the work and great experience you have given me!"

"THE DISCIPLE"
Season 2, Episode 28
Airdate: March 16, 1979
Directed By Reza Badiyi
Written By Nicholas Corea & James G. Hirsch

Cast

Dr. David Banner	Bill Bixby
The Hulk	Lou Ferrigno
Mike Roark	Rick Springfield
Colin Roark	Gerald McRaney
Joe Lynch	George Loros
Man	John Fujioka
Li Sung	Mako
Police Sargent	Brian Baker
Mike's Mother	Anne Bellamy
Newscaster	Bill Dietz
Lynch's Doctor	Fredric Franklyn
Tim Roark	Stacy Keach, Sr.
Policeman	Rene Le Vant
Al	Doug McGrath
Jo Lee	Lina Raymond
Lynch's Henchman	Fred Ward

David calls Li Sung from "Another Path" and finds that The Master has become severely ill. Banner returns to his side. Realizing he doesn't have much time left, Li Sung grooms a protégé, police officer Mike Roark. Unfortunately, Mike finds it hard to reconcile Li Sung's teachings with his work as a cop. Mike is also having problems with his tough cop brother Colin.

Reunited with Li Sung, David tells him, "Nothing that I've tried has succeeded in helping me control my problem. I came closer with your teachings than ever before."

This is another episode featuring recurring *Hulk* guest star Gerald McRaney and the welcome return of Mako's Li Sung from "Another Path."

Rick Springfield. PHOTO BY LISA ORRIS

The first direct "sequel" to another episode since the pilot, "The Disciple" was reportedly a backdoor pilot for a series about Rick Springfield's zen/karate cop. A fairly slow-paced episode, because David Banner is on the sidelines watching Li Sung and Roark bond — when he was more intimately involved in "Another Path". Because of this, it isn't as interesting as the previous show, "Another Path." Nevertheless, Bixby has some nice Banner scenes, including one where he actually refers to himself as "The Hulk." Usually he just says "It" or "the creature."

HULK HIGHLIGHT
The Hulk has a skirmish with the police, where he lifts up and smashes their searchlight.

RICK SPRINGFIELD (Mike Roark): *"I guest starred on a lot of big Universal shows like* Rockford Files, The Six Million Dollar Man *and* The Incredible Hulk. *That episode I did of* Hulk *was going to be a spin-off for a series about my character, this police officer trying to reconcile his police work with his mystic beliefs. I was really into martial arts at the time so the show was going to reflect that. The cop I played was a martial artist. All I really remember about doing the show is that Lou Ferrigno had to sit around in a refrigerated room so his makeup would not melt. Lou was a really great guy who was just miserable in all the green paint and prosthetics, stuck in that cold room."*

RON STEPHENSON (Casting Director): *"Rick Springfield was a very hot singer and soap star at the time. We were thrilled to get him and he did a very nice job."*

HULK FACTS
Yes, that *is* the great Fred Ward, the gruff character actor from *The Right Stuff, Remo Williams* and *Tremors*, as Lynch's henchman.

Guest star Rick Springfield brought another comic book hero to life, when he starred in the short-lived *Human Target*.

The only episode co-written by *Hulk* producer James G. Hirsch.

"NO ESCAPE"

Season 2, Episode 29
Airdate: 6 April, 1979
Directed By Jeffrey Hayden
Written By Benjamin Masselink
Banner's alias: "David Barren"

Cast

Dr. David Banner	Bill Bixby
McGee	Jack Colvin
The Incredible Hulk	Lou Ferrigno
Tom Wallace	James Wainwright
Kay Wallace	Mariclare Costello
Dr. Robert Scanlon	Skip Homeier
Dep. Chief Harry Simon	Thalmus Rasulala
Robert	Sherman Hemsley
1st Officer	Howard Brunner
2nd Officer	Jerry Fitzpatrick
Mathews	Tom Lowell
Steve	Chris Peterson
1st Reporter	Lynne Randall
Voice	Michael Santiago

David is arrested for vagrancy in the town of Santa Maria, California, when police find him sleeping on a bench. In the back of the paddy wagon, he's meets Tom, a wild-eyed crazy man who keeps calling David "Ramon." When Tom starts having flashbacks of electro-shock therapy, David calls for the cops to help him in the front of the van. They blow David off. "Lousy fascist traitor," snarls the lunatic, who immediately attacks David for "betraying" him. This triggers his transformation into The Hulk. Tom saw the cops arresting David as '30s fascists because he believes himself to be Ernest "Papa" Hemingway and David to be his friend "Ramon."

When David changes into Hulk, he smashes out of the police van and escapes. Tom Wallace, the delusional mental patient, also flees. As the man believes himself to be Ernest Hemingway, David realizes he's responsible for Tom being loose and must find him before he hurts himself or someone else. Detective Harry Simon is determined to get both men back.

After seeing The Hulk in person, Wallace keeps having delusions of the creature, even seeing him when a jogger runs by in a green track suit.

Concerned, David calls Tom Wallace's doctor and claims to be a "Dr. Johnson." He goes to see Kay, Tom's wife, and discovers Tom is a claims adjustor who had a nervous breakdown and thinks he's Ernest Hemingway while showing paranoid schizophrenic tendencies. Jack McGee suddenly barges in as David talks to Kay. McGee sees David, seated in front of blinds, backlit, but recognizes his silhouette.

Tom's friend Robert balks at helping David find him. David explains, "His Hemingway hallucinations and his delusions about his wife and doctor have finally come together…You know how Ernest Hemingway died? He put a gun in his mouth and he pulled the trigger!" David must stop Tom on his houseboat before he kills his wife or reenacts the famous writer's last suicidal act.

At the end, David gets onto the houseboat with Tom's wife and doctor, who the delusional Tom believes are having an affair. The houseboat is surrounded by Harry Simon and the police, as well as Jack McGee. David convinces Tom to release the doctor and Kay, but cannot leave himself. McGee realizes why, telling the cops, "The man on the boat with Wallace, he's the creature…*He's The Hulk!*"

Everything works out as David correctly deduces that Wallace has a benign tumor affecting his behavior. At the end, a police sketch artist attempts to draw Banner and McGee realizes that Tom is deliberately misleading the description to protect David, telling the artist "he was very big boned."

Once again, Jack McGee saves Hulk's life, spoiling a cop's aim when he tries to shoot the creature. As with "Of Guilt, Models and Murder," credible authorities see The Hulk, as he knocks over the cops who put David in the back of the wagon. At a press conference, Dep. Chief Harry Simon reports the suspect who destroyed the paddy wagon is "a 7-to-8-foot green man and the police who identified him have been given blood alcohol tests."

Guest star Thalmus Rasulala is quite good as Simon, a dogged cop — the same role he played in the horror classic *Blacula*. Every time we see Tom Wallace have a flashback, they play the stinger used when David's transformations begin. It's distracting and Wainwright doesn't make Tom or Hemingway very compelling.

In one scene, David collects recyclable bottles and takes them to a place onscreen called "Hot Dog Stick," which is unmistakably "Hot Dog on a Stick," the female clerk is even wearing their famous rainbow-colored Hot Dog on a Stick hat! More importantly, what you see is not just any Hot Dog on a Stick — this is the very *first* Hot Dog on a Stick ever, which opened at Muscle Beach in 1946. The founder was David Barham, which could easily be used as a David Banner pseudonym.

MANNY PERRY (Stunt Hulk): *"At the end of the episode, I did a big dive into the water as Hulk. When we had water, we had an oil-based makeup instead of the water-based one that we usually used. Coming out of the water with our usual green makeup meant that you had to be re-painted. Working around water, the oil-based makeup wouldn't run off, but it was very time consuming."*

LOU FERRIGNO (Hulk): *"Jack Kirby was in this episode, so I recall being excited about that."*

JEFFREY HAYDEN: *"Nothing really comes to mind about doing this episode. Having a guy running around thinking he's Ernest Hemingway is funny, though."*

HULK HIGHLIGHT

Hulk smashing out of the police van is pretty cool, but the scene where he enters a Laundromat and is at first soothed, then angered, by the spinning washer and the buzzing when the load is done, gives insight into Hulk's tortured psyche. Ferrigno plays The Hulk like a dog — at first relieved by the washer, but also apprehensive of the possibility of sudden attack.

HULK FACTS

David calling himself "Dr. Johnson" is an homage to the series' Kenneth Johnson.

As noted above, look for legendary comic book artist and Hulk co-creator Jack Kirby, as a police sketch artist.

Michael Santiago, a popular voiceover artist on numerous Universal shows, can be heard in 14 different *Hulk* episodes, as well as *Six Million Dollar Man*, *Bionic Woman* and *BJ and the Bear*.

"KINDRED SPIRITS"

Season 2, Episode 30
Airdate: April 6, 1979
Directed By Joseph Pevney
Written By Karen Harris & Jill Sherman
Banner's alias: "David Barton"

Cast

Dr. David Banner . . . . Bill Bixby
McGee . . . . Jack Colvin
The Incredible Hulk. . . . . .Lou Ferrigno
Gabrielle White . . . . Kim Cattrall
Rick. . . . . .A Martinez
Professor Williams . . . . Whit Bissell
Frank. . . . . .Eloy Casados
Little Jim. . . . . Don Shanks
Lone Wolf. . . . . Chief Dan George
Security Guard . . . . Melvin F. Allen
Reporter . . . . .Brian Pevney
Michael . . . . .George Gonzales
Elaina Marks. . . . . .Susan Sullivan

When evidence is found that seems to suggest the existence of a pre-historic Hulk, David investigates. He learns a plant may have cured that Hulk. Banner looks for the plant, only to get caught in a showdown between Indians and scientists. Yes, 'Indians'. This is pre-"Native American" terminology. If you can get past the silly first five minutes of the episode, where a primitive Hulk — Lou Ferrigno dressed like Tonto — is seen chasing cavemen, "Kindred Spirits" is a very good episode, with strong characters and some cool Hulk action. The hunt for the prehistoric Hulk's remains takes them to Native American land, where the scientists find themselves at odds with the locals. The local agitators have a grudge against the Government's BIA: Bureau of Indian Affairs.

A nice bit comes when Jack McGee faces down the Indian activists, who demand he drop The Hulk story he's covering and report their griev-ances. "That story's been told," Jack McGee notes. He calls the activists "a bunch of troublemakers crying exploitation!" Gabrielle White explains before she got her doctorate, "I was Gabrielle White Cloud — I was raised on that reservation with those troublemakers!" Confused, McGee asks, "When did I get to be the bad guy?"

Another fun line comes when a Native American activist tells McGee, "Isn't the missing link as big a myth as The Hulk? Or should I say 'Hoax'?"

"Kindred Spirits" is a good outing, a confrontation between two groups in which both have a valid point of view. Kim Cattrall is great as Indian Dr. Gabrielle White, a devotee of the work of David Banner…Although Cattrall looks about as Native American as Minnie Mouse!

Sex And The City's Kim Cattrall.

In "Rainbow's End", a Native American tells David Banner that his tribe would have worshipped him as a god. We see that in the opening to "Kindred Spirits", where the prehistoric Hulk is treated like a vengeful god by the tribe of cavemen.

After The Hulk forces both parties to stand down and hear each other out, David Banner learns the only plant that could cure him has actually gone extinct, a cruel and ingenious deterrent to Banner's quest.

If you can buy *Sex and the City*'s Kim Cattrall as an Indian, then swallowing the "prehistoric Hulk" sequences shouldn't be too traumatic. The Native American characters here aren't as interesting as the enigmatic Thomas Logan in Karen Harris and Jill Sherman's superior "Rainbow's End."

Once again, Banner seeks herbs as a cure for The Hulk, as he does in the Harris and Sherman-scripted "Rainbow's End." This is the same way Henry Hull tries to cure himself of lycanthropy in the classic Universal horror film, *Werewolf of London*.

KAREN HARRIS: *"I forgot Kim [Cattrall] was a member of the tribe. I loved Kim's conflict; her ambition and search for information vs. the traditional preservation of her culture. I developed such a crush on A Martinez and Eloy Casados during that shoot because they played rebels with a cause. As for the plant cure being influenced by* Werewolf of London, *I can't speak for Jill, but I guarantee you, if the idea of plants as a special cure was an homage to anything by me, it was to the fact that we were children of the*

'60s. We were also pretty progressive about homeopathic medicine. I thought the plant that could cure him going extinct was a great twist. We were very proud of that!"

WHIT BISSELL (Professor Williams): "*Kim Cattrall was a nice girl, Bixby was a good actor and nice man, so was the guy playing Hulk, but to be honest, I was a little intimidated by The Hulk himself. I did several Hulks, but I remember this one really well because we were shooting at night. We were in this cave, trying to escape. There was a scene where I was trapped in a cave-in and The Hulk was supposed to pick me up and carry me out. Once I saw the size of him, I thought he was going to break my ribs! When The Hulk had to pick me up, he put his giant arms around me and I lost my breath! He was tremendously strong. My God, he was strong. He was also quite gentle and careful and I'm quite happy to say that he didn't break me!*"

RON STEPHENSON (Casting Director): "*We did cast Kim Cattrall in the show. She was a lovely girl and a capable enough actress at the time, but as for breakout stars, we turned down Demi Moore, [Academy Award winner] Anjelica Huston and Michelle Pfeiffer. We used Sally Kirkland early on! Back then, the studio had a talent program run by Monique James and her colleague, Claire Miller. They would have people under contract whose salaries were paid off by working on the studio's films or TV shows. At that time, actresses under contract included Kim Cattrall, Jamie Lee Curtis, Delta Burke and Sharon Gless, to name a few.*

"*This talent group started in the days of Rock Hudson, Julia [Julie] Adams, Piper Laurie, George Nader, etc, and carried on until the mid-'80s. We were asked to use these future stars in our shows to pay off some of their $50,000-$100,000 contracts. A lot of producers felt pressured into using these actresses, so we used Kim, but they never warmed up to Jamie Lee Curtis, who later became a huge film star.*"

HULK HIGHLIGHT
Mercifully, this is the only time in the series we see a prehistoric Hulk chasing cavemen!

HULK FACTS
Kim Cattrall went onto stardom with *Mannequin*, *Big Trouble In Little China* and *Sex and the City*.

A Martinez later starred in several TV shows.

Whit Bissell is the second *Creature from the Black Lagoon* actor to appear on *Hulk*, after Julie Adams.

"THE CONFESSION"

Season 2, Episode 31
Airdate: May 4, 1979
Directed By Barry Crane
Written By Deborah Dean Davis
Banner's alias: "David Beeman"

Cast

Dr. David Banner	Bill Bixby
McGee	Jack Colvin
The Incredible Hulk	Lou Ferrigno
Harold Milburn	Barry Gordon
Pamela Morris	Markie Post
Waitress	Elaine Joyce
Gladys	Fritzi Burr
Harry	Earl Colbert

Pamela, Jack McGee's beautiful and perky assistant at the *National Register*, is intrigued by Harold Milburn, a sad little nebbish who announces, "I came to confess. I...am The Hulk!" Pamela believes Harold's claims to be The Incredible Hulk, especially when he offers proof, a torn shirt. While Pamela believes Harold, Jack is disgusted.

"I can't believe you actually fell for the old torn shirt routine, Pamela," McGee says snidely. "There are Hulk groupies in every city in this country; the only difference [is] this little guy is a bit crazier than the rest." When Banner gets involved to make sure his identity is not compromised, the chase is on! "The Confession" is a goofy, enjoyable, McGee-centered episode.

Markie Post is delightful as McGee's assistant Pamela, sexy and funny as she gives him grief every time he tries to brush her off. When she snaps at him, "I asked to apprentice at *The New York Times, The Washington Post, The Los Angeles Times* — real newspapers. *The National Register* was NOT my first choice." "Well," Jack replies dryly, "at least we have something in common!" *The National Register* provides fodder for yet another funny episode. Colvin really rises to the occasion in these shows and his byplay with the female guests is quite clever.

HULK FACTS

Markie Post was a popular guest on shows like *Hulk* and *Buck Rogers In The 25th Century*, before starring in her own sitcom, *Night Court*.

Guest Barry Gordon later became president of the Screen Actors Guild.

Fritzi Burr's first of two *Hulk* appearances. We see her again in Season Three's "My Favorite Magician." She was also in the classic film *Chinatown*.

"THE QUIET ROOM"

Season 2, Episode 32
Airdate: May 11, 1979
Directed By Reza Badiyi
Written By Karen Harris & Jill Sherman
Banner's alias: "David Balin"

Cast

Dr. David Banner . . . . Bill Bixby
The Incredible Hulk. . . . . .Lou Ferrigno
Dr. Hill . . . . .Joanna Miles
Dr. Morrow . . . . Philip Abbott
Kathy Allen. . . . . Sian Barbara Allen
Sam . . . . .Robert F. Lyons

Working as an orderly at the Valley View Sanitarium, David learns that a doctor is conducting illegal mind control experiments on the patients. When he's caught snooping around, David is turned into a patient himself. Basically *The Incredible Hulk* meets *One Flew Over The Cuckoo's Nest*, "Quiet Room" has some fun stuff — like when a mentally ill bully tries to muscle The Hulk, or when Hulk jumps out a window and runs to freedom, as patients delightedly follow him, but overall, an average episode.

"Quiet Room" does give Bill Bixby a nice scene, where he desperately tries to convince someone, anyone that he is sane and should not be in there.

MARK A. BURLEY (Unit Production Manager): *"Lou Ferrigno was a super nice guy. He was hearing impaired. Because he had been deaf as a child, he did not talk very much. He wore two hearing aids and when he spoke, Lou's speech was that of a deaf person. Lou would have a 10- or 12-egg omelette every morning!"*

HULK HIGHLIGHT

The patients happily following Hulk to freedom is an homage to the classic film *King Of Hearts.*

HULK FACTS

Philip Abbott voiced Colonel Nick Fury, head of US security organization SHIELD, on the *Spider-Man* and *Iron Man* cartoons.

Robert F. Lyons is a *Hulk* two-timer, also appearing in "Fast Lane."

Joanna Miles appeared in *Bug!* with *Hulk* guest Bradford Dillman and the Yul Brynner post-apocalyptic thriller *The Ultimate Warrior.*

"VENDETTA ROAD"
Season 2, Episode 33
Airdate: May 25, 1979
Directed By John McPherson
Written by Justin Edgerton & Michael McGreevey
Banner's alias: "David Brennan"

Cast

Dr. David Banner . . . . Bill Bixby
McGee . . . . Jack Colvin
The Incredible Hulk. . . . . .Lou Ferrigno
Ray Floyd . . . . Ron Lombard
Cassie Floyd . . . . .Christina Hart
John Fielding. . . . . Howard Morton
Ben Madrid. . . . . .Morgan Woodward

David winds up a reluctant 'passenger' with Ray and Cassie Floyd, a young couple who fancy themselves a modern Bonnie & Clyde. Once he's stuck with them, Banner becomes their unwilling accomplice, as the pair drive around the country, throwing sticks of dynamite into Westco gas stations. Ray and Cassie do this in an attempt to avenge the death of Ray's father. Banner becomes concerned when he realizes Cassie may be pregnant, as the two refuse to be deterred from their vengeance.

Another episode showing the insidious influence of *The Dukes of Hazzard* on poor *Hulk*. Here, our intelligent, eloquent hero is stuck with two moronic hillbillies driving around the Universal backlot, blowing up gas stations — a perfect metaphor for what *Dukes of Hazzard* was doing to *The Incredible Hulk!* This is especially disappointing, as writer Justin Edgerton did one of the best episodes of the first season, "The Hulk Breaks Las Vegas."

CHRISTINA HART (Cassie): "I have done a lot of shows, but with *The Incredible Hulk* there was nothing of interest for me, unlike many other shows I've done. I do remember that both Bixby and Ferrigno were very nice to work with."

HULK FACTS
Howard Morton guest-starred with Bixby on three episodes of *My Favorite Martian*.

Directed by *Incredible Hulk* cinematographer John McPherson.

Nice to see Morgan Woodward, a classic character actor who has done every major genre show from the original *Star Trek* to *The X-Files*!

Lou Ferrigno was on the CBS Team for *Battle of the Network Stars V* and *VI*.

HULK PROFILE
MICKEY JONES

Entering character actor Mickey Jones' Simi Valley home, you are confronted by his two careers. Besides photos of him, wife Phyllis and their five kids, there's a shot of him with all four Beatles, which they autographed, as well as gold records on the wall, representing his career as a musician with Bob Dylan, Kenny Rogers and others.

As a drummer, he performed on many rock classics, like "Just Dropped In (To See What Condition My Condition Was In)," which he played with Kenny Rogers and the First Edition. The song was used memorably in Jeff Bridges' *The Big Lebowski*.

"As a musician, I have been around the world 40 times. When I met The Beatles, they asked me for an autograph, so we swapped — I gave them mine and got all four of theirs! I spent a lot of time with those guys. That's a copy — I sold the original on ebay," he laughs.

"I played with Trini Lopez for eight years and three years with Johnny Rivers. I did the drumming on 'Secret Agent Man,' which is what that first gold record on the wall is for. I have a bunch of gold records from my work with Trini…I played on 'If I Had a Hammer.' I was with Bob Dylan for a couple years, including his first electric tour, but I always wanted to be an actor."

Bearded Mickey Jones with Lou Ferrigno in Hulk makeup. PHOTO BY PHYLLIS JONES

His switch to acting paid off when he played Ricky, a young mentally retarded man on *The Incredible Hulk* episode of the same name. Wanting only to help Buzz, his older brother and hero, Ricky finds everything goes wrong. After he befriends "The Big Green Man," as he calls The Hulk, his beloved brother and others accuse him of lying.

Jones' performance as Ricky is heartbreaking, so it's a shock when he returns in "The Long Run Home" as Doc, a brutal member of a biker gang. Doc is as scary as Ricky is lovable. He returned again in *Hulk*'s final season, as a logger who tries to make David leave town in "Triangle."

The humble Texas-born Jones is memorable as the mechanic who shakes Chevy Chase down in *National Lampoon's Vacation* ("All of it, boy!"), a Martian miner in *Total Recall* who tells Arnold Schwarzenegger, "I used to work in that mine." He also had recurring roles on both

Home Improvement and *Dukes of Hazzard*, "because at one point, I was gonna replace Cooter, when he left over money!" The actor also did a popular Breathsavers commercial that ran for six years. He covers all of it in his entertaining autobiography, *That Would Be Me: From Rock & Roll Survivor to Hollywood Actor.*

"'That would be me' was my catchphrase on *Home Improvement*, but I owe everything I have to *The Incredible Hulk*. My career really goes back to 'Ricky' — that episode of *The Incredible Hulk* was truly a gift from God, it changed my life," Mickey Jones says reverently. "Up until 'Ricky,' I had only done very small parts like security guards with one line of dialogue. I would say, 'Nobody came through here' and that was my whole part! My wife Phyllis was working two or three jobs to keep the rent paid while I was struggling to be an actor. I was at an interview in Century City and my agent called the office. The secretary handed me the phone and said, 'Your agent wants to talk to you.'

"I got on and my agent Carrie said, 'As soon as you get out of there, go over to Universal Studios, Producer Building #3. You have an interview for *The Incredible Hulk*!' I thought it was gonna be another one of those one-line parts. So I get out of there and drive over to Universal, go up to the room and there are two or three guys there who I saw on TV all the time. One of 'em was Dirk Blocker, Dan Blocker's kid, and they were all waiting to audition for the role of Ricky.

"The sides were three or four pages, which was better than the one line parts I usually got. I went in and read it. The way I read it is the way he was described in the script, 'Ricky is 19 going on 9.' The choice I made for Ricky is that he is a little kid in a big body. The funny thing is, when I auditioned, I was actually 37! I was 8 years older than James Daughton, the guy playing my big brother," Jones chuckles. "I was clean-shaven with short hair, which makes you look young, and I have always been baby-faced.

"To me, this guy Ricky was right up my alley. I could absolutely relate to who Ricky was, because growing up as a kid, I knew what it felt like when my dad yelled at me or when my mom got in my face. I also knew how I felt when one of them would give me a pat on the back. I knew I could do this role, I just didn't know if I would get the opportunity to do it. There's an intensity to Ricky that is sort of like Lenny in *Of Mice and Men*. He's just a little boy in a big body. I truly got inside that character. I knew exactly how Ricky felt and why he was here.

"We all know if you reprimand a little kid and you're angry, it breaks their heart. If you give 'em just a little pat on the back, 'Hey, you did a great job,' it makes them feel 10 feet tall. I took those two extremes when I read for Frank Orsatti, the man who directed 'Ricky.' I made Ricky heartbroken when he got reprimanded and 10 feet tall when he got a compliment!

"So I go home and don't think much about it. All I thought was, 'I read those three lines pretty good, so I hope I get the job.' My agent calls me that night and she says, 'You got *The Incredible Hulk!*' I wasn't too

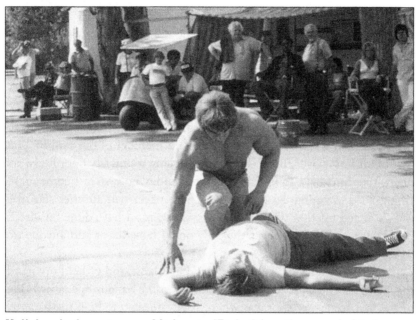

Hulk bends down to save Mickey in "Ricky" (see the crew behind them?) PHOTO BY PHYLLIS JONES.

excited, I said, 'Oh good. What day does it work?' She said, 'It isn't what day it works. *You* are the main guest star on the show; the name of the show is 'Ricky,' you *are playing Ricky!* You'll get the script tonight.' When that script arrived, I jumped so high, I hit the ceiling! I read the script and then read it again and realized that I had 52 pages of dialogue in a 56-page script! I was in every set-up and every shot of the episode — I even interact with The Hulk."

After his initial excitement, fear set in. "Quite honestly, I was very nervous about this. I was scared to death, I had not done anything this major before," Jones admits. "Here I was, getting a shot to do something that we all pray to get a shot at. I show up on the set the first day and walk up to Frank Orsatti. This was his first directing job. He had been stunt coordinator on the show and doubled Bill Bixby. I said to Frank, 'I just want to tell you how much I appreciate this and how grateful I am that you were willing to take a chance on me.'

"Frank looked at me and said, 'Mickey — I did *not* take any chance on you. I read 70 people for the role and when you walked out of the room, I knew it was your role because you nailed it, hands down. You had me so emotional when you walked out. I saw the other guys, but I knew you had the job.' I said 'Really?!' It was hard for me to believe I made that kind of impression on Frank."

He also made an impression on the show's star. "During the first day, there was a knock on my dressing room trailer door — my room was attached to the honeywagon [the crew bathroom]. I thought it was the wardrobe guy, so I said, 'C'mon in.' *Bill Bixby* walks in and says, 'Mickey, I just wanted to introduce myself. I'm Bill Bixby.'

"I said, 'I know who you are!' He said, 'I just want to welcome you to our show. You are, from this day forward, a member of our family. That big motor home over there? That's my dressing room. My door is always open. You don't have to knock; you're my buddy now, so just come on in. If you need anything, let me know.' I have never had another star of a TV show tell me that when I did their show, and I have done hundreds of TV shows! Bill Bixby was the only one. I have never had anyone do what Bixby did.

"Making the episode, I was nervous, but Bixby kind of held my hand through this whole process. We shot 'Ricky' at the Saugus Speedway. One of the first scenes we shot was where Ricky goes up to help the bad guy after his car catches fire. Ricky gets reprimanded by that guy, so I played Ricky as if it broke my heart. I was trying to help and he jumped all over me! I had my little badge on that said 'Ricky' and Bill, as Banner, comes to my aid. When I walked out on that set the first day, I believed that I was Ricky. I didn't have to fumble for my lines, I just did it and it was dead-on.

"I remember one of the early shots was me sitting alone in the race car in the garage, pretending to be driving it. Frank was talking me through that. 'Okay, start the engine up — you're really excited sitting in this car.' As Ricky, I looked all around like I was really on the track in the race car and took it all in. I looked at every gauge — I did it slow. Frank said, 'Let's take it out on the track.' I pretended I was driving on the track slow and made an engine sound. Then, we're in the middle of the race and my energy level is at maximum speed! When it was all over, and Frank said 'Cut,' I almost collapsed; I had expended so much energy. I remember saying to Frank, 'Hey, Frank — please don't let anything go past you that you think I can do better! Nobody wants this show to be better than me.'

"Frank said, 'Don't worry about it. If I think you've got more in you and can do it better, we will do it again. I have all the film in the world.' That made me feel secure. The first day goes well and I am feeling pretty good that I'm there. Still, I was nervous that they will find out my secret; that 'Ricky' is my first real acting job. Well, sure enough, the next day, Frank comes up to me and says, 'I got a call last night from The Black Tower.' When The Tower calls, it was usually bad news."

Sure enough, The Black Tower had Bad News for Mickey. "Frank says, 'The Tower is pretty upset with me. I got two calls from the big brass. They said, 'Who is this guy, Mickey Jones? We've never seen this guy before, never even heard his name, don't know him and don't even know what he looks like. Why are we going with a total unknown?' The next day, Frank gets another call from The Tower. 'We're gonna be looking at dailies — we're not sure we want to continue this. We don't know anything about this actor, we don't know if he can pull this off and it's an important episode.' I'm now nervous that I am going to lose my job, they might even re-cast this and start over.

"Third day I come in, Frank says, 'Mickey, I need to talk to you.' I say 'Sure. What's up, boss?' 'I got another call from The Tower last night.' I thought to myself, 'Oh, gosh — I'm getting fired...' Frank says, 'The Tower thinks I'm a genius for casting you in this role after seeing the dailies from the first day!' I said, 'Are you serious?' Frank laughed and said, 'Yes! They think I am the best director they have ever come across because I cast you and nobody had ever seen you before! You are a complete unknown and when they saw the footage, they said, 'Oh My God, we've got a winner!'

"Frank Orsatti means the world to me. He knew me from no one, but gave me an opportunity and stuck with me, even when The Tower was breathing down his neck. He was wondering, 'Am I gonna get fired?' Then Frank told me The Tower wanted him to sign a long-term directing deal because of 'Ricky'! Frank Orsatti is the reason I'm acting. He took a chance on me when no one else would. I can't give any credit to anyone else. He was a great stuntman, a great director and more importantly, he was an all-around great guy."

Making the episode was a family affair. "During shooting, my wife Phyllis brought all five of our kids — four girls and a boy — to the set. The makeup man put a scar on one, a bad burn on another, while our daughter Jennifer got a bullet hole! She wore it to her doctor's appointment and the doctor was startled by it, asking her, 'Are you okay?' That meant a lot, that the makeup man and crew were so nice to my family on the set of *The Incredible Hulk*."

On the show, Jones remembers, "I was the first person to meet The Incredible Hulk and not run away screaming. Ricky likes The Hulk. When he first comes up to me, I say, 'Oh. You're green.' Ricky is an innocent. The scene where Ricky meets The Hulk after Hulk saves him from asphyxiating is really cool."

The highlight of the entire episode comes when Ricky shows the big

Mickey and Bill Bixby on the set. PHOTO BY PHYLLIS JONES.

green brute how to open a can of soda. "Oh, I really like that scene. Kenny Johnson told me he thought that scene of me opening the pop can for Lou's Hulk was very important. It's nice to do something that people remember. The way it was scripted was relatively broad.

"I was the one who decided to give it a real detail. When I hand Lou's Hulk the can, he starts to crush it and I go, 'No, no, no — not like that! What you do is take this finger, put it right here and then you pull it back!' Hulk imitates me and puts his finger there. I go, 'That's the way ya do it — you got it! Then you drink it.' I try to show Hulk how to open a can of pop step by step. I look back at that scene and I can honestly say that was a magical moment. Ricky meets The Hulk and doesn't run away, but, instead, makes friends with him. Ricky tells his brother and friends about 'The big green man,' but they think he's crazy."

This leads to a great character moment where Bixby's Banner fears that he may have hurt Ricky as The Hulk. "When I tell Bill Bixby about the big green man, he doesn't call me a liar, he gets worried. 'Did he hurt you? Are you okay?' I tell him, 'No, he's nice!' The Bixby character, David Banner, is relieved to know that it's okay. I don't like most of what I did in the show because I always feel I could do it better, but I can look at that scene and say it's pretty good! I always think I can do it better."

The "Ricky" episode features a lot of up-and-coming stars. "Eric Server and Gerald McRaney played the bad guys. The girl who starred as my brother's girlfriend, Robin Mattson, went on to become a big soap star. Eric and I are still friends. During filming, we called Gerald McRaney 'Mackie.' Mackie and I were friends even after he became a big star on *Simon & Simon*. Gordon Jump was also in 'Ricky' and then he went on to do *WKRP In Cincinnati* right after it"

When "Ricky" aired, Jones found a warm public reaction. "It was very cool…I have to tell ya, I got tons of fan mail from people who were parents and teachers of retarded children. Those letters meant a lot to me. Basically what they said in those letters was 'Thank you for not making him an idiot, because they are not idiots.' Frank and I had talked about that; Frank said, 'The majority of guys who read for this role played him as a dumb punch-drunk fighter, 'duhhh,' or a complete imbecile and he's neither of those.'

"I told him, 'My choice was to wear my feelings on my sleeve and play him as a little kid in a big body.' Frank goes, 'That's exactly what I was looking for in casting this role! This role was pivotal to my career, too.' One day, I get a call from Kenneth Johnson's secretary and she says, 'Please hold for Kenneth Johnson.' I think, 'Oh no, I am in trouble! I wonder what I did…?' Kenny Johnson got on the phone and says, 'Mickey, I just wanted you to know that we submitted you for an Emmy for 'Ricky'. We submitted four Emmys this season: one for Bill, one for Lou, one for Mariette Hartley and one for you, because your performance is Emmy-worthy.' Well, I didn't get nominated, but the fact that the creator of the show called me up to say that he submitted me for an Emmy for my first real acting job meant the world to me.

"I went to Universal a week before 'Ricky' ran, for a cast and crew screening. I went in; I was really nervous and sat in the very back. When I came onscreen as Ricky, I just hated myself in it! I *hated* what I did, because I knew I could do it better," Mickey Jones confides. "That's the problem with acting for me. It's very difficult. I will go to a cast and crew screening one time and I usually won't look at the film again because it's very difficult to look at something you did and not say, 'I could have done that better.' If that's the case, it's a shame you didn't do it better at the time. I didn't like myself in it. I was not happy after it started, so I slipped out the back door because I knew I was gonna get reamed for it. I'm walking across the parking lot and, just as I get into my truck, I hear this voice yelling, 'Mickey — Mickey, wait!' I thought nobody saw me leave. It was Dwayne Hickman, the guy who played Dobie Gillis [on the TV series *The Many Loves of Dobie Gillis*), he was now a CBS bigwig.

"He said, 'I need to talk to you. I'm Dwayne Hickman — ' I said, 'I know, you're Dobie Gillis!' I was so new — you don't say that stuff, especially to network execs! He said, 'I'm now a producer at CBS and I just came out of that screening of The *Incredible Hulk*. Believe me, we want you!' I thought, 'Did he see something I didn't see? Because I didn't like it!' I looked at it a couple years ago with my granddaughter and liked it. I can watch it now and accept where I was at that time. When I did it, I knew nothing. I have learned how to hit a mark and what words to play up since then, but I was really young and green. The episode got me a lot of work. My wife was working three jobs to support me while I pursued my acting career. After that *Hulk* episode 'Ricky,' I started getting jobs. She came to me and asked if she could quit one of her jobs. I said, 'Baby, quit 'em all!' She hasn't worked since."

Wearing a hat, straggly beard and sunglasses, Jones returned to *The Incredible Hulk* as Doc, the leader of The Barbarians motorcycle gang, California Chapter, in "The Long Run Home."

"That was wild, to come on the show as a bad guy! Now you can't come back in the same season, especially after you played a character as memorable as Ricky, but *Hulk* would bring you back later on," Mickey Jones explains, "The next season, I came back with Paul Koslo and Bob Tessier as an evil biker. I love riding motorcycles. I got my first cycle in 1966 and I just love riding. I have played a lot of bikers. Me and Bob Tessier were the two main bad guy bikers in 'Long Run,' the rest of our gang was all stuntmen! Monty Cox, Carl Ciarfalio, Julius Fleur, and the rest were all motorcycle ridin' stunt guys! Monty was dating Susan Backline, the girl who gets eaten by the shark in *Jaws*.

"Because Tessier and I were the only two actors, if you watch the episode, you'll notice that we're the two guys up front and the two of us did all the dialogue! We also did all our own riding, too, which Frank Orsatti loved, because Frank did that one, too. Frank liked that he didn't have to cheat us on the bikes. Bob Tessier and I became good friends. Bob's gone now, but he was an Algonquin Indian and during the war, he spent a lot of time in Japan. He actually owned land there. Every time I talked to him, he would open a new door and you would learn something else fascinating about him. A great guy — he played Shokner, the baddest guy in the prison who they kept locked in chains in Burt Reynolds' *The Longest Yard!* He also boxes Charlie Bronson in *Hard Times*. Played a lot of American Indians in movies like *Last of the Mohicans*, but they would have to cover up all his tattoos!

"One of my gang, Carl Ciarfalio, is a stuntman who went on to become my stunt double in several movies! We first met on *Hulk* and he doubled me later. That's Mick Rogers in the photo with me, Bob and Carl. We're chasing Paul Koslo, who is on the back of the bike that Bill Bixby is driving. We shot 'The Long Run Home' on private oil reserve land off the 5 freeway by Magic Mountain! They had private roads that this oil company, Atlanta Richfield, owns, so there was no traffic at all. We did all that riding on these rugged dirt roads and paved private streets. The only part we didn't shoot there is the scene in front of a barn where we decide what we're gonna do with Paul Koslo and we all give thumbs down. We shot that on the Universal backlot. Because the bikers were pretty memorable, that was it for me on *Hulk* that season! I came back in the fifth season episode, 'Triangle,' where we beat David Banner up because he won't stop seeing Andrea Marcovicci, who our boss wants for himself."

For 'Triangle,' Andrea Marcovicci jokes, "I cannot imagine any thugs as charming as Mickey Jones and Charles Napier." Hearing that, Mickey Jones blushes. "Awww, that's cool to hear! Andrea was a really sweet gal and fun to work with. Peter Mark Richman was our boss and he was nice, too. I have known Charlie Napier since we did the 'Triangle' episode of *The Incredible Hulk* and I have done a couple of other films with Charlie. He's a truly great guy. He did a beautiful watercolor for Phyllis. Charlie also did the voice of Hulk when he got angry! Charlie's had a helluva career; he got his start in soft-porn movies for Russ Meyer and he's still working today. Charlie's done everything from commercials and *Philadelphia* to *Silence of the Lambs!*

"On the 'Triangle' episode of *The Incredible Hulk*, we work for Peter Mark Richman, who uses Charlie and me to intimidate Bixby. My favorite scene is when Bixby and I are working in the trees, sitting side by side as we finish up our day as lumberjacks. That little time of us riding on the back of the truck, taking off our gloves and hardhats, getting settled for having fun after work was just great. Bill Bixby was a genuinely nice guy. He was as sweet as a guy could be. You could tell that his heart was always in the right place. Every episode I did, Bixby always treated me like a king. He was unique among actors. I'm a regular guy and I try to treat people that way, too. When I come onto the Warner Brothers or Universal backlot in my truck, people think I'm a teamster or driver, not an actor. I consider that a huge compliment! Bixby acted like a regular guy, too. He wasn't a snob or anything."

As for The Hulk himself, "I didn't get to know Lou Ferrigno too well in the beginning. Lou had a hearing problem and you had to really look at him and talk loud so that he could read your lips. He would walk by and you would say, 'Hey, Lou, Good morning!' and he might not hear you and would just keep walking! On 'Ricky,' I got pictures of Lou in his green face with none of the body greened up yet. They would always do Lou's face first. He played with my kids and could not have been nicer.

"I don't remember as much about 'Triangle' as I do my other two *Hulks*, because it was not a huge role. Do you remember the scene where me and Bill Bixby are fishing? That's a cool scene — we're pals, enjoying it, when Andrea Marcovicci shows up and ruins our whole day. I look at her, realize it's the girl my boss wants, and say to Bixby, 'Hey, man, I don't wanna be here with *her!* I'll see ya later.'"

"Triangle" was shot after the death of Bill Bixby's son, Christopher. Did he notice any change in Bixby? "You know, I can't honestly say that I did…I think that's because Bill was so professional at what he did… Bill said something to me that made a lasting impression. On 'Ricky,' I told Bill, 'You probably don't remember meeting me before — I was an extra on *Speedway!*' On the Elvis Presley movie *Speedway*, Bill co-starred and I was in the bad guy's pit crew. Bill said to me, 'Early in my career, I had a decision to make. I could either be an *actor* with my nose in the air and only do films and not piddle with television or I could do television and if a film comes along, great, but if it doesn't, I'll do television. I chose television.' Bill said, 'You are not aware of how your life can change once you do a television series.'

"I have had a pretty good career. I have done over 500 TV shows, 80 feature films, hundreds of commercials and I tell people to this day, Frank Orsatti gave me a career! If it hadn't been for Frank Orsatti, who knows if I would have been able to make a living as an actor," Mickey Jones muses. "I have a career because of Frank Orsatti. This guy, in his very first directing job, took a shot on a completely unknown person and we both got rewarded for it. "

HULK PROFILE
VICTORIA CARROLL

A vivacious blonde with a lilting voice, actress Victoria Carroll made a memorable guest on three episodes of The *Incredible Hulk.* Besides playing a serious role in "Fast Lane," Carroll is Rose, a sexy drunk driver David Banner

Victoria Carroll and Bill Bixby.

is unlucky enough to hitch a ride with. She crashes, burning Banner's face off in the process, which takes the Gamma scientist two episodes to grow back! In "Mystery Man" Part II, she's seen in flashback, crashing again.

"Playing Rose, the alcoholic country singer in 'Mystery Man,' was so much fun," Victoria Bell enthuses. "I didn't meet Bill Bixby when I auditioned; I was actually cast by the director, Frank Orsatti, who I read for. Frank Orsatti was a wonderful fellow — he came from a stuntman family and was a good director.

"I was in The Groundlings at the time, and because of that, I had a lot of costumes, so I went into the audition wearing an outfit that is almost the exact same costume I wear on the show. I came in wearing my cowgirl hat and ah did mah Oklahoma accent for Rose's lament when she's driving. I said, 'Oh, rodeo, rodeo — if it weren't fer the damn rodeo, this never woulda happened!' I was so uninhibited from working with The

Groundlings, that I would go into an audition and just *know* I had it. I came out of my *Incredible Hulk* audition thinking, 'Oh, I know I got this one' — and I did! I went to Hollywood's master of dialects, Robert Easton, to help me get the right accent for Rose.

"We shot it in Valencia, California, by Magic Mountain. I'm drinking as I drive and I added some things that were not in the script, like when I spilled my drink on Bill Bixby. That was an ad-lib, but he actually loved that! Waiting on set to film my scenes with him, I was in one of those wobbly little trailers that they give you on location and I heard Bill doing a scene outside. They were on walkie-talkies, and I heard the director say to Bill, 'We'll pick you up in a minute, we're waiting for a truck' [to pass by, because of the noise] and Bill said, 'I hope one comes by!' He was there by himself and I started to laugh, because it was a funny remark.

"I introduced myself to Bill and we had a great time doing that episode! We were friends from that day on. He said that we became lifelong friends at that moment. Bill was a mentor to me, always encouraging me and he came to the house," the actress happily recalls. "The two men I love most are my husband Michael [voiceover king Michael Bell] and Bill Bixby, and I met both of them through *The Incredible Hulk!*"

"Michael voiced Bruce Banner on the '80s *Hulk* cartoon when I came onto that show to play his cousin, She-Hulk and we started dating. Bill Bixby was on the live-action *Hulk* and he was an absolutely wonderful man. Michael and I built a theater, The West End Playhouse, and Bill came to see all of the shows that we did there. I said to Bill, 'I hope you don't mind, I have so many wonderful actors that I would love you to meet…' Bill said, 'Victoria, if you send me a really good actor, you're doing me a favor!' He meant that, because he was also a director. Bill was so in love with actors. He was a joy on the set and he had me on three episodes of *Hulk*, a variety show, a *Sledge Hammer* he directed and an episode of *Goodnight, Beantown*, with Mariette Hartley. Basically, when Bill worked, I worked! "'Mystery Man' was such great fun. I was the comic relief and then they kill me off! I weep, laugh, crash the car and kill myself, badly burning David Banner. By the time Hulk lifts up my car, poor Rose is long dead! I watched myself die, as the stuntman doubling me crashed the car. He climbed out of this totaled car and just brushed himself off. When the stuntman walked away from the crash, I said, 'How do you do that?' and he said, 'The car has roll bars!' I had a '67 Mustang hardtop at the time that I just loved. I said, 'Could you make my car safe, too?' He said, 'Sure!' and put a complete roll bar in my Mustang! When I finished the show, Bill said, 'Victoria, whenever you're on the lot, come visit me!'

As for The Hulk, "I met Lou Ferrigno on my episodes, too. He was always around shooting his Hulk stuff. Nice guy. They were shooting a Hulk scene while Bill and I did our scene. Hulk carried me in my next episode, 'Fast Lane.' Every time Lou Ferrigno touched you or carried you as The Hulk, you were green! They were constantly touching him up. He left green everywhere on the set!"

Venita Ozols on set.

HULK PROFILE
VENITA OZOLS

Today, Venita Ozols is a busy, in-demand first assistant director (AD). The multi-tasking Ozols keeps big shows on schedule, wrangles talent and basically operates as the directors' and producers' extra set of eyes and ears. "First AD schedules a show, hires extras, runs the set, establishes call times for cast and crew, directs extras on set and generally guides production all day," she explains.

Being a genre fan, she has worked on numerous sci-fi shows, including *Star Trek: Deep Space Nine, Alien Nation* and *The X-Files.*

"I loved working on *X-Files*," Ozols admits. "My very first episode of the show started with a naked man in a cave who vomited up what looked like Pepto Bismo into a mold. The mold then became the last person he had eaten. Shooting it was a challenge; the first take the vomit wouldn't

't and the second take splashed vomit all over and scared the hell
out of the actor! I thought to myself, 'I'm on *X-Files* and this is great!!'

"Because I genuinely liked science fiction, as a first AD I made it be
known, 'If you need a first AD for a sci-fi show, I'm your girl!' I knew so
much about green screen and visual FX from years and years of doing it,
I even worked on Robert Urich's *Ice Pirates*, which was Angelica Huston's
first starring part. It was a great movie that I'm actually in, wearing a
jumpsuit and delivering a line of dialogue."

As a young college girl, Venita Ozols left New York for Hollywood.
Rooming with her friend Francine Selkirk (now a famed casting director,
back then she was "Francine the Teenage Dream" on Chuck Barris' *The
$1.98 Beauty Show*), Venita became an assistant director trainee. Working
for Kenneth Johnson on *The Bionic Woman*, the tireless young Ozols was
transferred over to *The Incredible Hulk*.

There, fresh-faced Ozols found herself around TV star Bill Bixby,
fellow newbie Lou Ferrigno and even rising TV stars like Loni Anderson. She even found herself dating the show's stunt coordinator/male
model, Frank Orsatti.

"On *Hulk*, when I was a trainee, I had to tell actors when we needed
them on set, give them their call times, get them breakfast, lunch, dinner
and give them scripts and page revisions. I was really happy to be on *The
Incredible Hulk*, because I had read *Incredible Hulk* comic books as a little
girl and it was a great show with great people," Venita Ozols sighs.

"Working on many shows and movies, there are definitely people
deserving of being trashed, but there are also people who are incredible
and many of them were on that show. Kenny Johnson is an amazing
human being. The tone of a show is really set by the producer and star.
If the star of the show walks on set and everybody freezes and tenses up,
it's not a pleasant experience. I have been on shows like that and it's a
horrible working experience. It wasn't like that on *Hulk*.

"Kenny Johnson ruined me and many other people for enjoying this
business. After working with him, you immediately find out how rare he
is. He creates a family atmosphere where everyone feels loved, trusted
and encouraged to contribute, from the craft service guy to the executive
producer...If anybody has a good idea, he wants to hear it — a lot of
producer/directors say that, but in Kenny's case, he really means it. Kenny
says, 'Do your very best' and everyone on the set is glowing. But then, you
finish a Kenny Johnson show, then go off to work on something else, and
come across egos, assholes and uptight people. You get all bent out of
shape, thinking, 'W-what happened to my wonderful work experience?!'

It's tough! All of us can't wait for Kenny to get another show going so we can all get back together as a creative family. Kenny is a truly unique human being — a humanitarian/feminist who genuinely loves people."

As for the show's Dr. David Banner, "I, like any other girl, loved Bill Bixby from *The Courtship of Eddie's Father*. The first thing you immediately learned working on *Hulk* was that Bill was *not* Eddie's Father," she

Venita learns that Bill Bixby is *not* Eddie's Father.

grins. "He was nothing like Eddie's Father…We shot one episode at an elementary school ('A Child In Need') and the kids had all watched *The Courtship of Eddie's Father* reruns, so they were outside his trailer, calling for him to come out. I asked Bill to go outside and give them a quick wave so they would go away and Bill said, 'No, Venita, I am *not* going to do that. They want to see Eddie's Father and that's not me. I would like to take the mantle of that character off of me, hang it on a coat hanger and stick it in the closet.' Bill didn't want to wave to kids because he was tired of being Eddie's Father after all those years. He knew they wanted to see Eddie's Father, not him, and he was exhausted at the end of a long shooting day and simply didn't feel like putting it on for them. He was a kind and generous man, but he really *wasn't* Eddie's Father in real life.

"Bill was a nice guy. As a young hot girl, what was funny to me about Bill Bixby is that I had absolutely no attraction to Bill whatsoever. I always assumed it was because he was Eddie's Father — even if I wanted to take that mantle off him," Ozols jokes. "But looking at it objectively, that was not it! Bill was not to me a masculine man. He was very delicate, impeccably groomed, elegantly dressed just right, not a hair out of place, almost eerily so. He never looked less than perfect, which was a little odd.

"When things weren't going so well with Bill and his wife Brenda, I

Venita advises Lou Ferrigno.

remember Bill talking to Frank [Orsatti] about being lonely and how he liked Frank's boat a lot. Frank occasionally took me out on his great boat. Bill liked Frank's boat so much, he got a yacht of his own and he spent a lot of time out alone on that. Bill Bixby was a man looking for a home. There was an intense loneliness to him."

As for crusading, Hulk-hunting reporter Jack McGee, "Jack Colvin was a total sweetheart. He reminded me of working with Richard Anderson on *The Bionic Woman* — a total pro. Super nice, always had a smile, knew his lines and ready to go. I really liked him. He seemed a little sad, but sweet. I was fond of Jack. He directed episodes after I left the show.

"My favorite thing on *The Incredible Hulk* was The Hulk himself. I'm in this business for the magic. I love special FX and The Hulk himself was a great special effect! To see Lou's Hulk as a big, misunderstood gentle giant. I liked how even though he looked like this giant green Cro-Magnon man that first season, there was something immediately sympathetic and relatable about him. My favorite scene on *The Incredible Hulk* was in the pilot, when he saved that little girl. As someone with a lifelong love of special FX, I loved watching Hulk break stuff."

Lou Ferrigno was beloved by the crew. "He really was," Ozols recalls. "Lou was very easygoing. I loved Lou, but there was a running gag on the show about Lou's hearing disability. Everybody believed Lou's hearing came and went selectively; Lou heard what he wanted to hear and didn't hear what he didn't wanna hear!"

During the first season, Hulk had a problem that he couldn't solve by smashing. "Because Lou was a bodybuilder, he would work out before going on camera so The Hulk would look totally pumped up," the AD says with a smile. "The pace of the show really sped up during the first season to get episodes done. They cut off Lou's workout time, working him to death on camera, so he didn't have adequate time to work out that much and pump up for appearing on camera…I'm at dailies one day, halfway through the first season. Lou likes to eat because that's what he normally does, to build up his muscles. I would bring him his ten egg omelets, which he ate everyday. The producers are watching dailies of him as The Hulk and somebody says, 'Ahhh, um…anybody notice his middle?' There's a big gasp in the room and somebody else looks and says, 'Oh, God, we're gonna have to change the name of the show to *The Incredible BULK*!' Lou was getting a paunch like a middle-aged man!

"To fix that, they said, 'Okay, we need to adjust his schedule so he gets a couple hours a day to work out.' In Lou's defense, he had been asking for that, but they cut down his workout time to get him into makeup and on camera faster, so we started making sure he had workout time every day."

Ozols chose her profession because she was a movie buff since childhood. "When I was an 8-year-old little girl, I sat through *Hush…Hush, Sweet Charlotte* twice so I could figure out how they cut the guy's head off with the axe. I came home and told my parents over dinner, 'I figured out how they cut the guy's head off in a movie...They used a dummy, with a pre-cut dummy head!' and my parents were looking at me, going, 'What?! You saw a movie where they cut a guy's head off?'

"I loved movie magic and sci-fi shows like *The Outer Limits* and *Twilight Zone*, so when I came to Hollywood, my very first day in the assistant director training program, they sent me to Universal, where there was a room run by a guy named Paul Gaherra. Paul had all the names of all the stages and shows that he would assign the trainees to. I walked into his office and saw normal stuff like *Kojak*, when I spotted *The Bionic Woman*. I said, 'I'm the new trainee for *Bionic Woman*.' Paul said, 'That's pretty funny. You should know I assign where trainees go.' I said, 'Yeah, but I thought you should know I'm perfect for it!'

"Happily, I get *The Bionic Woman* and I'm on it for five months. I'm supposed to rotate from a TV show to a movie and I go to Paul and say, 'Please, you've got to get me off *Bionic Woman*. You've had me on it too long and I need to go somewhere else!' Nothing happens. After my sixth month on the show, Lindsay [Wagner, The Bionic Woman herself] comes up to me and says, 'Good news: they were gonna take you off the show and put you somewhere else. So I called them up and said, 'You *can't* take Venita off our show! This is Lindsay Wagner and we need her for the rest of the season!' In my head, I'm thinking, 'Oh My God!' so I spent two and a half years on *The Bionic Woman* and when it ended, I went over to *The Incredible Hulk!*

"A lot of the *Hulk* series was shot on the backlot, but we also went on location to neighborhoods and San Pedro, to shoot at an Elks Club or a school. We went all over the place. You would do an episode at the zoo and another on the mock-up of a 747 on the backlot. A lot of *Hulk*s were shot in the woods behind Magic Mountain.

"You can actually see me in a bunch of episodes from the first season," Ozols admits. "On *Hulk*, I was often strategically on camera in the background, without my walkie-talkie. When you're in an episode, I was always on the peripheral. During the zoo episode ['The Beast Within'], we were shooting at the zoo. I was walking across the field from base camp to set, looking down at a production report I was working on, when I heard a serious growl. I looked up and realized I was a foot away from walking straight into an unhappy lion that was tethered to the ground on a chain. Another step and he would have had me!

"There were some great guest stars on the show. Loni Anderson was sweet and a lot of fun. A great girl with a good sense of humor — meeting her, you knew she was gonna be a star, no matter what. When Loni got *WKRP In Cincinnati*, I wasn't surprised at all. Kim Cattrall also did a *Hulk*. I liked her, she was funny gal. She brought a good vibe to the set

"I remember when Loni did that show; she played a kung fu killer [in "Of Guilt, Models and Murder"]. Loni and Bill were in Bill's trailer and it was…rocking," she notes, her cheeks blushing. "They needed Loni on set, so I came to get her and the trailer was *rocking!* Bill's driver stopped

Venita Ozols with her hands full on *Hulk*.

me and said, 'Give him five minutes, will ya?' and five minutes later, they both came out. Loni Anderson was a sweetheart — she told me that she was normally dark haired like me, and because of that, she was stuck playing Mexicans and Indians…But when she went platinum blonde, she became a sex symbol who never stopped working!"

For a young girl in her first big adventure in Hollywood, Ozols had a major highlight from *The Incredible Hulk* series. "I was dating Frank

Orsatti, and it was wonderful," she says with a beatific smile. "I remember the first time I saw him, I was sitting in the production office and this amazing looking man walked in and stood right in front of me, so I was just looking at his butt. I remember going, 'Wow' and he turned around and I said, 'Whoa' because he was totally gorgeous.

"I was in my early 20s, Frank was a decade older, and he was so completely professional, all business, a serious stuntman. Through working together, we developed a friendship that grew into a fire. We realized we really liked each other and started dating up a storm. We tried to hide it from the crew, but I don't know how successful we were. The only way people on *Hulk* would know I was dating him was whenever he came near me on the set, I always lit up," she blushes. "It was just Frank, me and 3,000 other girls!

"I dated Frank Orsatti, but I had moved on from *Hulk* to a different show, while Frank was still stunt coordinator on *Hulk*. There was a knock on my door one night after work, it was Frank, but he was knocking in a weird way, like he was kicking the door. I open and he holds up both hands to show me that his knuckles were completely swollen and bloody. I said, 'My God, Frank — what happened to you?!' He said, 'Get me some ice, will ya? I think I broke a couple knuckles on each hand.' I said, 'FRANK, WHAT HAPPENED?' Frank says, 'We were shooting this scene where The Hulk is in a metal box in the desert and he's trying to break his way out of it. (From the episode "Married") I'm using brass knuckles, and all this stuff, to simulate Hulk punching his way out, but nothing seemed to be working. We weren't getting the shot; Kenny was getting all upset, so I said, 'Okay, ya got one take. Ready? When they rolled the cameras, I just punched the shit out of it with my knuckles.' I said, 'YOU IDIOT!' but Frank goes, 'We got the shot.' Frank was all man.

"He played himself in a shaving commercial, where Frank drove a boat through a wall and broke both his legs. They dragged him out of the boat as the director said, 'Frank, we have one shot left.' For the last shot, he had to stand there and say, 'Hi, I'm Frank Orsatti, Hollywood stuntman, and I call this fun.' He said, 'Okay, put boards behind my boots to prop my legs up!' He did the line, the director yelled cut and they raced him to the hospital!"

Ozols loved her time on *Hulk*. "There were great people like Werner Keppler. Werner was Lou's makeup man. The crew nicknamed him 'Our friendly little Nazi!' A good-natured guy, with a German authoritarian way. I especially enjoyed being around Kenny. On *The Bionic Woman*, I was amazed to see that Kenny Johnson made a point of meeting me and introducing himself, so I truly thought the world of him. He was incredibly knowledgeable, friendly — everyone on the crew was in awe of him, but also loved him. He's a brilliant man who expects everything done very quickly, because his schedules were so tight. That gave him a rep as a guy who had ADs going through the turnstiles.

"Through the years, I lost touch with him and then he was doing a

pilot called *Alien Nation*. I got a phone call to come interview for the job. I knew we'd get along. He didn't know I was four and a half months pregnant and he was doing a show that would conclude with me in my ninth month, but I wanted to do the show so badly; I didn't tell him I was pregnant.

"I had a lot of energy, I wasn't showing yet, everything was great, no problem. We got along. He tested me by asking me if certain things were done. 'Already done, Kenny!' After the second or third day, he came up to me and said, 'You passed the test — I'm not gonna ask you anymore questions.' We had a wonderful

Venita Ozols. PHOTO BY PATRICK
JANKIEWICZ

working relationship. Finally, I was about eight months pregnant and having a hard time hiding it, so I thought, 'I gotta let him know! I told him I was pregnant. He asked, 'How far along?' I lied and told him seven months, because I didn't wanna scare him off," Ozols giggles.

"He said, 'Okay.' Kenny took a moment and then added, 'You know I *would* have hired you even if you told me you were pregnant, right?' I said, 'I know that now — I didn't know that then.' He didn't treat me any differently, always had that same great respect. Kenny really isn't much of a yeller — if he yells, there's usually a good reason for it!

"My daughter Brigitte Graham is an actress. She was on *Alien Nation* as a five-year-old. Brenda, Kenny's assistant, played her mother on an episode, and that was her start! I was one of the only crewmembers on *Alien Nation* who never played an alien conehead on the show, because I was one of the few on the crew who *didn't* want to play one. Too many horror stories. One of the alien actors told me to put my hands 'tightly over my ears and try to hear what people are saying to you — that's what being an *Alien Nation* alien is like.' No thanks! I didn't want to be green like *Hulk* either," she laughs.

HULK PROFILE
RON STEPHENSON
HULK CASTING DIRECTOR

"On *The Incredible Hulk*, my work was nuts-and-bolts casting," explains casting director Ron Stephenson. "In 1979, I was brought into Universal to finish the last five episodes of season two of *The Incredible Hulk* due to the fact that the producers had fallen out of love with their current casting director, Phil Benjamin. Sometimes the chemistry turns sour on a show and people need to adjust things. Phil was doing a fine job, but they didn't feel like he was part of their family.

"A production like *The Incredible Hulk* was a very close-knit group led by executive producer Ken Johnson. Ken, along with his producer, Nicholas Corea, was wonderful to work with. I was immediately welcomed and felt right at home. After season two finished, I was put under personal contract to Universal Studios and finished out the next three years casting *Hulk*. I began casting it and learned the rhythm of the show very quickly. I would read a script, send it to Breakdown Services where they broke down each character in the guest cast and sent it out to agents. The agents in turn would submit headshots and resumes that I could look through to see who was available for the show and the process began again with every episode.

"I would either choose from my own personal list or lists from the agents, about four or five people to bring in for each role. They would receive the script in advance or just their scene if it was just a one- or two-line part and we had a casting session that would run three or four hours. The producers, director and sometimes the writers would attend the session. Afterwards, we would collectively pick the right person for the role. It was very straightforward.

"*The Incredible Hulk*'s guest cast did not demand any stunt casting. It was a theme-driven show and we just needed good actors to fill in the puzzle. This was in contrast to other shows I cast, like the TV detective show *Simon & Simon*, which had a particular pace and humor, so the casting was more specific. The two guys in that show performed best with actors who could fall into their comic rhythm.

"That was a little tougher. On *Murder, She Wrote*, we had an even more unique situation. We chose the actors as needed from old movies as we needed stars from the old movies and TV shows. *Murder, She Wrote* was a star-driven show. Each role needed a familiar face, no matter how small the part. If we needed to convince an actor to do it, we did have the advantage of baiting the hook with Angela Lansbury and an above-the-average payday for guest stars. Many times, the directors of each episode found out who they were working with only a day before the show shot. *The Incredible Hulk* was much more straightforward casting."

SEASON THREE

Season Three has *The Incredible Hulk* jump wildly between two gears: "Lighthearted" and "Very Dark." For every romp this season, like "My Favorite Magician" or "The Lottery," there's several dark ones, like the *Night of the Hunter*-esque "Sideshow," with women being chased by a religious fanatic, or the season's darkest entry, "Deathmask," where Hulk goes after a serial killer. Season Three keeps these two major differences in tone for the whole season, lurching back and forth.

"My Favorite Magician" marked a reunion with Bill Bixby's *My Favorite Martian* co-star Ray Walston, while "Homecoming" finally introduces David Banner's family — his farmer father and scientist sister. The Hulk himself gets several interesting challenges, including blindness in "Blind Rage," while "The Snare" shows how the Hulk would handle himself in a "Most Dangerous Game" scenario.

There's a fun variation on the "Evil Twin" storyline in "Broken Image," where Banner literally confronts a dead ringer. Because Kenneth Johnson was busy working on both *The Incredible Hulk* and *Cliffhangers*, this was the first season where the first *Hulk* episode was not written and directed by him. It was done by the great Alan J. Levi.

"METAMORPHOSIS"

Season 3, Episode 34
Airdate: September 21, 1979
Directed By Alan J. Levi
Written By Craig Buck & Frank Dandridge

Cast

Dr. David Banner . . . . Bill Bixby
McGee . . . . Jack Colvin
The Incredible Hulk. . . . . Lou Ferrigno
Jackie Swan . . . . Katherine Cannon

Greg . . . . Gary Graham
Ken . . . . James Reynolds
Lisa Swan . . . . Mackenzie Phillips
Diane Markon. . . . . Jennifer Holmes

   David meets and saves the life of rock star Lisa Swan, a self-destructive
singer and drug abuser dominated by her manager/sister, Jackie. Banner
sticks around to help Lisa, which makes Jackie and her goon, Greg, suspicious. When they drug Banner, Hulk has hallucinations, but still refuses
to flee. And then they decide to get rough...
   The plot with the jealous sister bears some resemblance to the Kevin
Costner film *The Bodyguard.* The script for *Bodyguard,* by *Raiders of the Lost
Ark* writer Lawrence Kasdan, had been floating around Hollywood since
1977, so it's entirely possible that it was an influence on this episode. *Hulk*
director Alan J. Levi does some inventive things, like showing us what The
Hulk sees in his drug-altered state. Not being able to move his feet and
seeing microphone cables turn into cobras are the cool/cheesy highlight.
   Mackenzie Phillips, singing generic '70s rock in a neo-Kiss outfit and
makeup is pretty funny! Even more amusing, we see Hulk high on drugs!
The Hulk absorbs so much electricity in one scene, he shoots lightning
bolts from his fingers. Ironically, a much smaller jolt gives him psychic
powers in the fourth-season episode "Deep Shock."
   Actress Mackenzie Phillips was a big CBS star at the time, for her
hit sitcom *One Day at a Time.* Missing work due to substance abuse, she
was fired from that show and reportedly had the same problems on *The
Incredible Hulk.*

   GARY GRAHAM (Greg): *"It was a crazy episode; I'm the first guy in history
to dose The Hulk! I dose David Banner with acid while he's Hulking Out, so
he throws me into some drums. He's seeing things because I slipped something
into his drink.* Hulk *was a great experience for me, because it was one of my
first big parts and I made a lifelong friend in Kenny Johnson, who I did* Alien
Nation *with. When I met with him later for* Alien Nation, *neither of us
remembered working together before, so I got the show on my own merits! "On
my last day of filming* Hulk, *I was apparently due to start work on [cult film]*
The Hollywood Knights, *which was supposed to start shooting that same day.
They held me up on* Hulk, *and I was five hours late for work on* Hollywood
Knights, *so they tried to sue me for $20,000 until they dropped the lawsuit!*
   *"Bill Bixby was a lot of fun; a sweet guy who liked to joke around. I really
wish I had known him better! Lou Ferrigno was cool. It was fun watching*

Lou throw my stunt double into a drum kit again and again! The director of photography, John McPherson, worked hard, God rest his soul. Alan J. Levi, who directed the episode, was wonderful — very high energy and extremely cool! Alan is also a technophile who designs programs and installs mega sound systems and computer programs…Alan really is an amazing guy.

"*Working with Mackenzie Phillips was an interesting thing. It was the late*

Gary Graham with his *Alien Nation* co-star Michelle Scarabelli. PHOTO BY PATRICK JANKIEWICZ

'70s, so everybody was doing drugs on set. I wasn't, of course, but at the time, it was sort of 'Don't ask/don't tell.' That led to precarious situations, so they started clamping down on it."

ALAN J. LEVI: "*We shot that concert scene at The Santa Monica Civic Auditorium. Mackenzie Phillips had her ups and downs, drug-wise, as is well known now. I had my hands full on that show; I had to get The Hulk high and then deal with Mackenzie, who was already high! I knew she was having trouble with drugs at that time, and she did have one incident during the shoot. It was ironic, because she was playing a rock star who was having problems with drugs — that was what the subject of the show was, but she showed up one morning three hours late.*

"In the script, Mackenzie's character was high. She didn't have to act that day because Mackenzie was really high. She had partied the night before and showed up that way to work. That was the roughest day. I just went with it, what else can you do? She was very sweet and apologetic, but when you're in this business, you're around drugs a lot. Neither my wife [actress Sondra Currie] nor I have ever been druggies, we escaped it for whatever reason, but I understood it.

"I was very patient with Mackenzie and talked her down. The problem was when she was high, her study habits were very poor, so we had some dialogue problems. She didn't know her lines. On film, you can shoot one line at a time and cut back to her and it looks great. The problem was we were shooting at a location that we couldn't go back to the next day, Gull's Way. We were only at Gull's Way, a famous house on the top of a cliff in Malibu, for one day, so we had to get it all done that single day. It's a beautiful house; I also shot a Columbo there."

SONDRA CURRIE: "I have to add a little bit of trivia! My sister [rock star Cherie Currie], who at that point was lead singer of The Runaways, wanted to do that Incredible Hulk episode really bad, so she went in to read for the rock star/Lisa Swan part. She actually read for her future brother-in-law! Alan and I didn't really know each other at the time, but Mackenzie got it... They were all having trouble with the drug scene at that time."

RON STEPHENSON (Casting Director): "Of course, the whole world was aware of Mackenzie Phillips' problem with drugs, but she was perfect for the role and she accepted it gladly. I never felt she had any qualms about doing that kind of part. I later used her on both Simon & Simon and Murder, She Wrote, and she was excellent. Those parts had nothing to do with drugs, and she was fine."

HULK FACTS

Besides starring in every TV incarnation of Kenneth Johnson's *Alien Nation*, Gary Graham also did the cult film *Robot Jox*, with *Hulk* guests Paul Koslo and Michael Aldredge.

"BLIND RAGE"

Season 3, Episode 35
Airdate: September 28, 1979
Directed By Jeffrey Hayden
Written By Dan Ullman
Banner's alias: "David Blair"

Cast

Dr. David Banner . . . . Bill Bixby
The Incredible Hulk. . . . . .Lou Ferrigno
Col. Drake. . . . . .Nicolas Coster
Dr. Anderson. . . . . .Jack Rader
Carrie Banks . . . . Lee Bryant
Lt. Jerry Banks. . . . . Tom Stechschulte
Sergeant. . . . . Dennis Fimple
Ambulance Driver . . . . Michael Horsley
M.P.. . . . . .Mesach Taylor
Brubeck. . . . . Leonard Lightfoot

David is staying with The Banks Family. Jerry Banks is an officer at a Chemical Research Post, where they do chemical warfare research. Hitching a ride home with a transport truck, Banks helps the driver dump his load. A bright yellow cannister containing the chemical compound X202 leaks, spraying both Banks and the driver. Later that night, Jerry falls through his doorwall, completely blind.

Instead of helping Banks and the driver with their affliction, Colonel Drake and military brass quickly form a cover up. The base doctor insists Jerry's blindness was caused by the fall. The compound that sprayed him causes blindness and a complete collapse of the central nervous system, giving victims "four days, maybe less." When nobody on base wants to help him, Jerry asks David to retrieve the cannister to prove what happened. David, wearing a gas mask, goes to the government dump. He finds it easily (which is why it was the only canary yellow canister in the dump!), works his way up out of the landfill of trash and chemical waste, only to come face to face with a soldier in a biohazard suit, who punches David back down. Losing his mask, Banner is also exposed to the X202 and Hulks Out, smashing a crane. David then goes blind. Drake orders David imprisoned, planning on finishing the cover up after all the victims are conveniently dead. When Carrie, Jerry's wife, helps David escape, it's up to the blind Banner to get the truth out. David Banner's luck being as bad as it usually is, he blindly wanders into a chemical research training area. When he gets blasted with tear gas, Banner Hulks Out, while Drake and his men decide to capture the creature. "Don't kill him, let's capture him," shouts Drake. When a soldier says, "He's getting away," Drake shoots poor Hulk in the arm.

Can a blind Hulk defend himself from the military and solve the problem? This and the fourth season's "Prometheus" are the closest you come in the series to seeing Hulk actually battle the military, as he does on a regular basis in the comics. Hulk battling soldiers is fun, through not on the scale of carnage he usually creates in the comics.

Hulk's shoving match with a tank is a cool bit, clearly the big moment of the episode. There is so much action in this outing, with Hulk smashing a crane, throwing soldiers, that he doesn't even battle the tank until the last five minutes. Seeing Hulk coming their way, the tank commander sneers, "Flatten him — run him down!" Hulk mangles the turret and breaks the tank. He escapes and Drake faces a court martial.

Once again, The Hulk's healing factor, which was introduced back in the pilot, plausibly helps combat his blinding dilemma. "I know a great deal about metabolism," David tells the Military doctor and higher ups. "The substance we were exposed to, I think you'll find, has altered our baso metabolism. I think the cure, the antidote, is in the metabolism. If you can increase it to 20, 30 times normal…" Basically, David is suggesting the same metabolic surge he goes through as The Hulk that purges his injuries to overcome the chemically induced blindness.

Jeffrey Hayden always brought interesting little touches to his *Hulk* episodes, and 'Blind Rage' shows a lot of them. There's an atmospheric shot of Hulk alone on a hilltop and David staggering around blind is also effective. A scene where David goes blind with the camera-as-David's POV looking at a blackboard that slowly goes blurry is impressive directing by Hayden. He also finds time for some levity, as the rest of the episode is grim, with blindness and death. A funny moment has Hulk run an obstacle course in his own unique way. When two Privates see the big green creature face to face, they wonder if he's "a NonCom — or a secret weapon?"

Composer Joe Harnell does an ambitious drumming, cadence style military score, befitting the setting. The militarized version of Joe Harnell's "Growing Anger" is especially good. The Banks' family lives on the suburban *Leave It To Beaver* street on Universal's backlot.

JEFFREY HAYDEN: "Hulk shoving with the tank was very hard to do! CG effects did not exist yet. Believe me, if they did, they would have made my life so much easier! Instead, it was Lou and Manny wrestling with a real tank."

MARK A. BURLEY (Unit Production Manager): "We always had two Hulk Outs per episode. We only had two per show because they were so expensive and time consuming to do. People would actually tune it at the end of the second and fourth acts just to see the Hulk Outs!"

HULK HIGHLIGHT
As noted above, a blind Hulk tackles a tank!

HULK FACTS
Mesach Taylor (M.P.) later co-starred in *Mannequin* with fellow *Hulk* guest Kim Cattrall and became a CBS star on *Designing Women*.

Jack Rader (Jerry) was an Imperial Guard in the infamous *Star Wars Holiday Special*.

This episode's guests, Nicolas Coster (Col. Drake) and Leonard Lightfoot (Brubeck), later co-starred together in "The Offspring," a touching episode of *Star Trek: The Next Generation*.

Tom Stechschulte went back to superheroes after *Hulk* when he narrated *The Watchmen* motion comic.

Look for popular '70s child actress Michelle Stacy, the little girl from *Airplane!* and *Day of the Animals*, as Banks' daughter.

Hulk suffers tear gas again when a bailiff maces him in *Trial Of The Incredible Hulk*.

David working as "the best counterman at Ken's Dry Cleaners" and the hospital paging "Dr. Matheson" are homages to the series' Kenneth Johnson and Richard Christian Matheson.

"BRAIN CHILD"
Season 3, Episode 36
Airdate: October 5, 1979
Directed By Reza Badiyi
Written By Nicholas Corea
Banner's alias: "David Barnes"

Cast

Dr. David Banner .... Bill Bixby
The Incredible Hulk. .... Lou Ferrigno
Elizabeth Collins. .... Lyn Carlin
Jolene Collins .... Robin Dearden
Mr. Arnold .... Joseph Mascolo
Dr. Bruno .... Henry Rowland
Dr. Kate Lowell. .... June Allyson
Ramon Alvarez .... Tonyo Melendez
La Bruja. .... Madeline Taylor Holmes
Cop .... Stack Pierce

16-year-old Joleen Collins (Robin Dearden) is a prodigy who excels at language, music and physics. While the Kirkland Institute needs her for its research, all she cares about is finding her mother. Joleen has no real friends, outside of her computer, M.A.X. To build a talking computer with clunky late '70s technology proves she's a genius! She sneaks out of the top-secret research facility and hits the road to see her mother in Los Angeles.

David befriends the teenage genius and impresses Joleen when he recognizes her quote Anna Hempstead Branch. He's picking grapes with migrant workers and promises to take her to Los Angeles when she fixes his car. Joleen finds being around normal people refreshing. The workers are being exploited by La Bruja, a local witch woman.

When Joleen sees La Bruja perform "psychic surgery" on one of the crop pickers, she exposes her as a fraud and shows how she did it. Instead of rallying behind her, the workers run away in fear after Bruja's henchmen beat up David and pull Joleen into her trailer. Hulk tosses La Bruja in a water barrel and kicks over her trailer. This frees the local migrant workers from her influence and they laugh at her.

Seeing him change back to human form, Joleen tells David, "I know about your rather extraordinary problem." Meanwhile, the Kirkland Institute discover Joleen is missing and report her as being kidnapped to retrieve her faster.

"We've got to get her back," snarls menacing Institute head, Mr. Arnold. "Joleen Collins was working on a classified project. Joleen Collins *herself* was a very classified project!" They go to recover Joleen themselves. When the mother leaves on a bus and the Institute tries to reclaim Joleen, the sad, angry girl threatens suicide. David Hulks Out and brings the mother to her, forcing a reconciliation in the process. Poor June Allyson gets the worst exposition of the episode when The Hulk enters carrying Joleen's mom. Playing a scientist in big glasses, she announces: "That's the girl's mother in It's arms!"

"Brain Child" is a great episode — mother/daughter relations through the dark prism of Nicholas Corea. The episode bears a resemblance to Stephen King's bestseller *Firestarter*, where a little girl is abducted by a top-secret government agency as she tries to get reunited with her father. While the novel wasn't published until 1980, it was being serialized in *Omni Magazine* in 1979, when this episode aired. King's influence is also felt in "The Psychic."

After seeing David change, Joleen wants to know what happened to him. Banner describes, "My problem…It's Gamma Radiation poisoning. Extreme emotion, [of] any kind, rage, frustration, fear, anger…I don't know, they somehow seem to promote a molecular change, a cellular generation that is uncontrollable, an actual reversion to the primal state."

When Joleen's mom is finally found in a sleazy LA hotel, we see one of Corea's favorite motifs surface, as many of his episodes display a fondness for seedy hotels populated with lowlifes. Look for the Hotel Rosslyn in several shots of David running through downtown.

The mother/daughter confrontation where the mother rejects her and slaps her is touching. It's also the second time a woman slaps Joleen in the episode, the first being La Bruja. A big problem of this episode's mother/daughter storyline comes at the end. Hulk wanders away. If Hulk himself doesn't care about the mother/daughter relationship, why should we?

When his used car, which he bought for "$50 and a handshake," breaks down, David Banner makes a reference to the car he smashes in the pilot. "Car, you're making me angry," a frustrated David tells the jalopy. "Now if you get me angry, do you know what I'm going to do? I'm gonna turn you into a tin sandwich!"

DAMN YOU, DUKES

David Banner once again outraces, outdrives and evades police in an old station wagon. At least after a 20-foot jump (*in a station wagon?!*), it finally blows a gasket and ruptures.

HULK HIGHLIGHT

Director Reza Badiyi does a really cool upward shot where you see The Hulk jump from one building to the next; clearly Stunt Hulk Manny Perry in action!

RON STEPHENSON (Casting Director): *"One of my favorite shows was 'Brain Child.' It starred June Allyson and Robin Dearden. Robin was a beautiful young actress who married the brilliant actor Bryan Cranston from* Breaking Bad *and settled down to enjoy motherhood."*

HULK FACTS

Befitting its Mexican heavy setting, the show goes with a mariachi score.

For once, David gets shot, not Hulk, as he's mistaken for a kidnapper. Don't worry — it's only a flesh wound!

Robin Dearden resurfaces in the later *Hulk* episode, "Danny."

Dearden came out of a five-year hiatus to guest on her husband's show, *Breaking Bad.*

Hulk two-timer Stack Pierce was a ballplayer for The Cleveland Indians and an alien captain on *V & V: The Final Battle.*

Joseph Mascolo appeared in *Jaws 2.*

Lyn Carlin starred in the horror cult classic *Deathdream*, with John Marley, David Banner's father in the *Incredible Hulk* episode "Homecoming."

There is a funny blooper from the episode, where Bill Bixby asks Robin Dearden, "Do you fool around? How about your mother?"

Although a big movie star in the 1940s and '50s, poor June Allyson is best remembered dubiously…as the first celebrity to do commercials for Depends Adult Diapers.

"THE SLAM"
Season 3, Episode 37
Airdate: October 19, 1979
Directed By Nicholas Corea
Written By Nicholas Corea
Banner's alias: "David Barnes"

Cast

Dr. David Banner . . . . Bill Bixby
Jack McGee. . . . . Jack Colvin
The Incredible Hulk. . . . . .Lou Ferrigno
John Blake. . . . . Charles Napier
Doc Alden. . . . . Julius Harris
Captain Holt. . . . . .Marc Alaimo
Rader. . . . . .Robert Davi
Roth . . . . Skip Riley
Sheriff . . . . .Brad Dexter
Harris . . . . Charles Picerni
Old Convict. . . . . John Steadman
Reporter . . . . Linda Lawrence

When a hungry David grabs an apple, he is busted for vagrancy and is taken to a hellish prison work camp. The corrupt authorities are trying to break the will of John Blake, a charismatic convict that the others look up to and rally behind. Although The crazed Sheriff (who has a giant picture of Napoleon on his wall) has been unsuccessful in his efforts so far, Blake suddenly finds the lawman one step ahead of him. Blake realizes his plans are being thwarted because one of the men in the prison camp is a snitch. As the new prisoner, suspicion naturally falls on David.

Every TV action show does a *Cool Hand Luke* episode and this one is *Hulk*'s. "The Slam" is a veritable character actor convention, where past and future James Bond villains like Julius Harris, Tee Hee from *Live and Let Die*, mix it up with Robert Davi, Bond's enemy Franz Sanchez in the later *License to Kill*. Charles Napier, who at this point was voicing Hulk, gets to do a rare turn as a good guy!

There is a hilarious moment where the real informant, Harris, accuses David of being the traitor. All these hardened, mean-looking, sweat-stained convicts confront David Banner. Coming closer, ever closer, one of them suddenly begins the chant of "Fink! Fink! Fink! FINK!" *Fink?* That's the best they could do? Not even "Rat" or "Squealer"?

Jack McGee has a funny sequence when the work camp has a press conference. McGee immediately asks about "reports of a giant man involved in an escape attempt," when another reporter says, "Knock it off, McGee! We're not here to investigate your Hulk theory!"

When the corrupt Sheriff drives David in, he gloats that he has spared him a trial, so there will be no mugshots or fingerprinting of the fugitive scientist. He tells David, "I may not look like much...I may not be much, but I can still spot a man on the run." He only calls David by his prison number, 1124.

Charles Picerni. PHOTO BY PATRICK
JANKIEWICZ

CHARLES NAPIER (John Blake): *"Being friends with Nic Corea, it was fun to do this episode and actually play somebody sympathetic, not a bad guy. I always enjoyed seeing Bill Bixby and Lou Ferrigno when I did the show. Lou and I did* Frogtown II *together, which is my favorite bad movie!"*

CHARLES PICERNI (Harris): *"I liked doing* The Incredible Hulk *because I got to work with the great Frank Orsatti. An incredible stuntman, Frank was a wonderful guy who went way too soon. Nicholas Corea was a real gentleman, too. I'm the snitch in jail who tricks the other convicts into attacking Bill Bixby!"*

LINDA PAWLIK (Reporter): *"I remember when I got the part, my agent told me that it was a possible recurring role as Jack Colvin's sidekick...I think every actor gets this story! Anyway, at the time, my mother was visiting me. I got clearance to bring her to the set. We shot at a work camp outside of Los Angeles — a long drive, but I think we met at a base camp and they vanned us in, but I'm not really sure. I remember two things: 1. Girls against the boys: I was outnumbered — haha. 2. Bill Bixby saw that I had brought my mother, and he could not have been more gracious — he got her a chair and asked her if there was anything she needed. I was so impressed by his graciousness toward her.*

"Jack Colvin was very nice to me but beyond that, I remember very little, except that it was so hot up there you could fry an egg on my forehead. I have a

vague memory of actually filming my part. Time is a funny thing. It just feels so distant. Maybe it's because I hated having short hair. Sorry I cannot offer more. Unfortunately, I have no photos. Never even occurred to me that there was a set photographer. Oh, we filmed it in one day. The irony is that I became friends with Bill years later."

HULK HIGHLIGHT

David has a suspenseful change, when a group of cons give him a midnight beating for being a suspected snitch. Will he change before they kill him? *(Spoiler alert: Of course he will, or the series would be over!)*

HULK FACTS

Hulk stuntman Charles Picerni is two-time *Hulk* guest Paul Picerni's brother.

"Harris," the camp snitch, is named after *Hulk* story editor Karen Harris. "We did that all the time," laughs Karen Harris. "That was probably Nic teasing! He loved to get in his digs — especially with me, because I would call him on his shit. We quite loved each other."

"MY FAVORITE MAGICIAN"
Season 3, Episode 38
Airdate: October 26, 1979
Directed By Reza Badiyi
Written By Sam Egan
Banner's alias: "David Barker"

Cast

Dr. David Banner	Bill Bixby
The Incredible Hulk	Lou Ferrigno
Jasper Dowd	Ray Walston
Lily Beaumont	Joan Leslie
Kimberly Dowd	Anne Schedeen
Edgar McGee	Scatman Crothers
Giancarlo Corleone	Robert Alda
Rose Brown	Fritzi Burr
Ben	Bill Capizzi
Earl	Bob Hastings

David becomes the reluctant assistant to failed magician Jasper the Great. Just when he thinks things couldn't get any worse with Jasper, David finds himself at a wedding on Mafia don Giancarlo Corleone's estate, where Jasper has an old score to settle.

One of *Hulk*'s "funny" episodes, "My Favorite Magician" is actually an amusing show. Watching it, you know if you see a guy in a tux, The Hulk

This episode reunited *My Favorite Martian* stars Bill Bixby and Ray Walston!

is going to toss him into a wedding cake. As the title implies, it features Bixby's reunion with his *My Favorite Martian* co-star Ray Walston. It's fun for the viewer, because the two truly appear happy to be working together again. Robert Alda plays the bad guy much more broadly here than he did in "Terror In Times Square" and is great. "My Favorite Magician" also refers to *The Magician*, the show Bixby did between *Martian* and *Hulk*.

HULK FACTS

Bob Hastings was a recurring character on the live-action *Amazing Spider-Man* TV show and voiced Commissioner Gordon on *Batman: The Animated Series*.

Guest Scatman Crothers played a superhero in his own right, when he voiced cartoon super dog, *Hong Kong Phooey*.

Anne Schedeen is best known as Kate, the hot mom on *ALF*.

The Magician is the TV show that Fox Mulder is watching as a child the night his sister is abducted by aliens on The X-Files.

"JAKE"
Season 3, Episode 39
Airdate: November 2, 1979
Directed By Frank Orsatti
Written By Chuck Bowman
Banner's alias: "David Barnes"

Cast

Dr. David Banner . . . . Bill Bixby
Jack McGee. . . . . Jack Colvin
The Incredible Hulk. . . . . .Lou Ferrigno
Jake White. . . . . .LQ Jones
Leon White. . . . . James Crittenden
Tibby. . . . . .Jesse Vint
Marvin. . . . . Fred Ward
Maggie . . . . .Sandra Kerns

David is in Gastin, Texas, working as a rodeo medic. The king of the rodeo, bullrider Jake White is having problems. Weary, Jake is saving up to buy two trucks. David finds that tough, noble Jake is weak and suffering from Addison's Disease. His weasely younger brother Leon is a rodeo clown and a gambler being blackmailed into helping steal cattle. Despite his illness, Jake is planning on riding Killer Instinct, the meanest bull in the circuit.

Leon is ashamed to be a lowly rodeo clown, to which David replies, "Why? Rodeo clowns save lives everyday!" Leon's criminal partners attempt to run David off, first by lassoing him and dragging him behind their horses. This is thwarted when Hulk yanks them out of their saddles and drags them through the creek!

A nice *Hulk* episode from the show's action specialist Frank Orsatti and producer/writer Chuck Bowman. It's fun to see Hulk in a western setting, protecting good cowboys from black hats. Orsatti plays with the concept, including a scene where Hulk bumps into a cowboy hitch-hiker, who runs away at top speed in his boots when he sees the creature. The music of the episode also playfully riffs on *The Magnificent Seven* score, befitting its western theme. One can't help but notice that the newspaper David reads about the rustling in has no bylines. Props to Bixby for delivering the line "Rodeo clowns save lives everyday" with a straight face.

Hulk producer Nicholas Corea gets a funny shout-out when the P.A. speaker mentions, "We have another lost child. This one is a little boy 8 years old, says his name is Nicky Corea. Come all the way from East Monroe, Louisiana, with his family."

HULK HIGHLIGHT

In this episode's animal attack, Hulk wrestles a bull to the ground and chases it off.

LOU FERRIGNO (Hulk): *"'Jake' was the episode where Manny got thrown by the bull; I will never forget that! Manny Perry was pinning the bull by the horns and it got under him and threw him. I screamed when I saw it, because I thought Manny had been killed. Frank Orsatti and Bill Bixby grabbed me, pulled me aside and said to me, 'Never do that again. You never scream like that on a set. He's a stuntman; he's trained to take such risks.' That's when I said to them, 'I don't care, he's my friend.'"*

HULK FACTS

Killer Instinct the bull is named after *Hulk*'s classic Season Two football episode.

Classic Western actor LQ Jones appeared in *The Wild Bunch* and directed the cult movie *A Boy and His Dog*. Besides Bixby and Colvin, he's the only other actor to appear on the show and direct an episode ("On the Line").

Jesse Vint starred in Roger Corman's *Forbidden World*.

Hey, let's hear it for Fred Ward in his second *Hulk* appearance!

"BEHIND THE WHEEL"
Season 3, Episode 40
Airdate: November 9, 1979
Directed By Frank Orsatti
Written By Rick Rosenthal, Todd Susman and Andrew Schnieder
Banner's alias: "David Barnes"

Cast

Dr. David Banner . . . . Bill Bixby
Jack McGee. . . . . Jack Colvin
The Incredible Hulk. . . . . .Lou Ferrigno
Colleen Jensen. . . . . Esther Rolle
Swift . . . . Michael Baseleon
Sam . . . . Jon Cedar

David becomes the sole driver for the Majestic Cab Service and its struggling owner Colleen, as a gangster tries to put her out of business. Meanwhile, Jack McGee realizes that Majestic's phantom cabbie may actually be his longtime quarry, The Incredible Hulk! This is actually another funny episode, similar to the earlier "Never Give a Trucker An Even Break" — but it actually surpasses that, by taking full advantage of Banner trying to remain calm while performing the frustrating, thankless tasks of a cab driver.

"Behind The Wheel" is highlighted by Esther Rolle, who knows gangsters are after her driver, but decides to avoid telling David Banner that crucial bit of information so he's not scared off. David is repeatedly thrust into highly stressful situations as a cabbie, as he tries not to Hulk Out... Besides, he already did that in a cab, during the first season's "Terror In Times Square"! Problems include a woman giving birth in the back of his cab and mob-intimidated gas stations that won't fill his tank.

RICK ROSENTHAL: *"I had this idea that driving a cab would make a great episode. I thought Banner could do a great Hulk Out from under a car. I love the shot of Hulk's green foot popping out of the shoe. It was a funny show. My* Hulk *episode came about in a very curious way. I met Ken Johnson, the producer of* The Incredible Hulk, *at a dinner. I had just gotten out of the American Film Institute as a director. Ken and I hit it off, Ken's a really bright guy. Later, Ken called me up and said, 'How would you like to be story editor on* The Incredible Hulk?'

"I said, 'I'm flattered, but honestly, I'm kinda close on a couple things and want to stick with directing.' He says, 'Great, okay.' A year later, out of the blue, I get a call. 'Hey, Rick — it's Ken Johnson. I'm producing a new series called Cliffhangers and want to know what you would think of being a producer on the show?' I think to myself, 'Self, you turn him down for story editor and he offers you producer — Good move!' I meet with him at Universal. Ken says,

'Just so we get to know each other better, can you write an episode of The Incredible Hulk?'

"So I sit down to write a Hulk and I come up with this idea of Banner as a cab driver. In college, I had driven a cab. I did it for Town Taxi, who had the catchy slogan, 'For the best in town, call Town.' I wrote 'Behind the Wheel,' turned it in and never heard a word. A year later, I get a letter from the Writers Guild telling me that they are arbitrating the credit determination on 'Behind the Wheel.' I had no idea they had even produced it, I never heard a word — I didn't even know they shot it! Six years later, I get a call from Ken Johnson. Never heard from him about producing Cliffhangers after I turned in that

In this episode, Rick Rosenthal gives Hulk his old college job.

PHOTO BY PATRICK JANKIEWICZ

Hulk script. When Ken said, 'How's it goin'?' I said, 'It's going pretty well, Ken, but not particularly with you.' He said, 'What do you mean?' I said, 'I wrote this little Hulk episode for you before I was supposed to start producing your show and I never heard from you again.' Ken said, 'Oh, sorry; I've been really busy.' For six years?!"

HULK FACTS

As noted above, this episode is co-written by film director Rick Rosenthal (*Bad Boys*), actor Tod Susman and one of *Hulk*'s best writers, Andrew Schneider.

Rosenthal's *Halloween II* starred *Hulk* guests Cliff Emmich, Gloria Gifford, Jeffrey Kramer and Pamela Susan Shoop.

"HOMECOMING"

Season 3, Episode 41
Airdate: November 30, 1979
Directed By John McPherson
Written By Andrew Schnieder

Cast

Dr. David Banner	Bill Bixby
Jack McGee	Jack Colvin
The Incredible Hulk	Lou Ferrigno
D.W. Banner	John Marley
Dean Eckart	Regis J. Cordic
Elizabeth Banner	Claire Malis
Crop Duster	Steve Burns
Dr. Helen Banner	Diana Muldaur

Unable to endure the loneliness of the road anymore, David goes home to Grail Valley, Colorado for Thanksgiving with his sister and estranged father. Both believe he died when The Culver Institute blew up in the pilot. Instead of peace, he finds The Banner Family farm is being targeted for destruction inside and out…by a greedy real estate developer who wants the land and the crops are being devoured by voracious bugs.

His scientist sister Helen hopes David can find a way to save the family homestead. We realize David vowed to become a physician as a child because of the death of his mother, Elizabeth. He and his farmer father, D.W., also have unresolved tensions, from when he accused his dad of not caring about the dying Elizabeth.

David finds a way to keep the bugs from destroying his father's crops, while Hulk handles the evil developer and his goons. Seeing Banner use his scientific mind to save his family shows another side to the character. It also demonstrates that Banner loves his family and, even though he can't solve his Hulk dilemma, he is a genius.

"Homecoming" is a great episode. We finally meet David Banner's family and learn what motivates him. The same obsession David Banner felt in the pilot over the death of his wife is on display here with the death of his mother. His interest in becoming a doctor stems from being unable to save his mother. His sister Helen, after being happy that her brother isn't really dead, accuses David of being selfish for the way he drops in and out of his family's life. "You've always done that," she complains. A climax with The Hulk going up in a crop-dusting plane is exciting.

Casting the terrific John Marley and the equally impressive Diane Muldaur as David's father and sister contribute to a great show from writer Andrew Schnieder and director/d.P John McPherson. A nice coda has Banner see McGee coming, so he flees before joining his family for the Thanksgiving dinner that he had been longing for. D.W. and Helen invite a starving and grateful McGee to dinner. Sitting down with The

Hulk with his Father (*The Godfather*'s John Marley) in "Homecoming."

Banners, we see Jack is just as much a lonely man as David.

The only thing that mars this otherwise perfect episode are flashbacks to David's childhood. Marley is good as a younger D.W., but child actor Reed Diamond is annoying as a young David Banner. Worse, though the flashbacks are set in an unnamed '40s farmbelt era, Diamond has that stupid '70s bowl-head haircut popularized by Nicholas on *Eight Is Enough*! One dumb haircut on a whiny '70s child actor means that period verisimilitude flies right out the window.

Johnson had intended to bring back Helen Banner in the fifth season with a blood disease. Her situation can only be stopped by a transfusion from a relative. David gives her Hulk blood and sets her up as a middle aged She-Hulk. This is what Johnson did in spinning off *Bionic Woman* and that is why Marvel and Stan Lee felt it was important to create a female Hulk first.

MANNY PERRY (Stunt Hulk): *"In that episode, I had to go up in a crop-duster plane...on the wing! The stuntman doubling Bill Bixby grabs the wing of the plane and he changes into Hulk in mid-air. We took the wing onstage, and then we had to go to the actual airfield, with cameras on the wing and the ground to show me in the air standing on the wing of the fuselage, growling and tearing my shirt off. I had to hang on as the plane is bobbing and dipping! There was no airbag, no safety devices, because we were 70 feet in the air, so it was pretty frightening!"*

HULK FACTS
John Marley will always be remembered for waking up with his racehorse Khartoum's head in *The Godfather*.

Diana Muldaur starred on multiple episodes of both the original *Star Trek* and spin-off *Star Trek: The Next Generation*.

To Bixby's credit, he manages to make David Banner seem extra lonely for this episode.

"THE SNARE"
Season 3, Episode 42
Airdate: December 7, 1979
Directed By Frank Orsatti
Written By Thomas E. Szollosi & Richard Christian Matheson
Banner's alias: "David Bennet"

Cast
Dr. David Banner . . . . Bill Bixby
The Incredible Hulk. . . . . .Lou Ferrigno
Pilot. . . . . Bob Boyd
Michael Sutton . . . . Bradford Dillman

Stuck at an airport, David winds up in a lively game of chess with the enigmatic Michael Sutton. Accepting a ride from Sutton, a pilot with his own plane, David find himself trapped on his private island. The deranged Sutton intends to hunt David like an animal, something he has apparently done on the island many times before. Stressed out by the chase, David Hulks Out. Seeing the green creature only makes Sutton more excited to stalk his prey — the hunter has no intention of abandoning his mission.

When Sutton sees him as The Hulk, he is not the least bit int'
Instead, he is truly excited to finally have a worthy adversary, น.
of his usual helpless victims. Banner goes through a battle of wits with
the hunter. All attempts David makes to evade him, hide his scent or
counter-attack fail. Finally, he Hulks Out again, as Sutton pursues The
Hulk tirelessly through the island wilderness. As he comes in to finish the

Crazed hunter Bradford Dillman goes Hulk Hunting.

beast off, the relentless Sutton accidentally kills himself with a crossbow
in mortal combat with Hulk. Banner finds a boat tied to a dock the next
morning. David climbs aboard and sees a tape recorder. Hitting "PLAY,"
Banner hears Sutton congratulate him on his victory. If he reached this
boat, Sutton acknowledges that he must be dead. David leaves the tape
recorder on the dock and speeds away in the boat. As Sutton goes on
about the joys of the hunt, the tape concludes and the recorder explodes,
obliterating the dock…Sutton's final attempt to kill his greatest opponent.

Every TV adventure series has a certain number of plots that they
recycle — and all of them do a variation on Richard Connell's classic short
story, *The Most Dangerous Game*…Even *Gilligan's Island* did an episode
inspired by it! Taught in English classes across the country, *The Most
Dangerous Game* was the first story to create that "hunter-stalking-people"
plot, with aristocratic madman Count Zaroff deliberately trapping people
on his private island and hunting them like beasts.

"The Snare" is an excellent example of how good a show can be when they do the classic story right. Banner and Sutton go through several clever reversals as they try to outwit each other. Writers Thomas E. Szollosi and Richard Christian Matheson contribute a Hulk episode that is action from start to finish. As a former stuntman, Orsatti makes sure the physical action is impressive. Bradford Dillman is an interesting, above-

Bill Bixby discovers Dillman's previous victims in "The Snare."

average psychotic. Unlike many TV villains, he has a perspective and an agenda, which makes for a thrilling hour. Dillman also makes Sutton perversely likable. Unlike most of Banner's human attackers on the show, he doesn't flee at the sight of The Hulk, but doubles down, resolving to kill the creature. Bill Bixby does a fine job in the episode — Banner is realistically stressed, afraid and then angry with resolve. He clearly realized it was a superior script with a great guest star and rose to the occasion. By adding Hulk's best action director, Frank Orsatti, the show goes from an impressive episode to a classic one.

RC MATHESON (Writer): *"I just watched 'The Snare' again recently on The SyFy Channel and enjoyed it. I always like a story about two characters; it's challenging and interesting to watch the psychology between those two... You know that one of them is definitely up to something.*

"The two actors, Bill Bixby and Bradford Dillman, were really having fun with it. Both were at the height of their powers and I think they really got into it. You can see that in the scene where they are playing chess together and having dinner. You can tell something's afoot, because there are a lot of fun surprises in it.

"Ken Johnson said they had always wanted to do The Most Dangerous Game on The Incredible Hulk. They told Tom and me that they had tried to do a Most Dangerous Game-type episode before, but couldn't figure out a way to do it. We figured it out by saying, 'Banner's at an airstrip, trying to get somewhere…This guy offers to give him a lift and he has his own island…' We didn't overcomplicate it. When we pitched it, Ken and the other producer just looked at each other and said, 'Shit! Let's do it that way.' We were off and running! That was the easy part, the hard part was coming up with all the tricks and setbacks Banner and the hunter pull on each other. We tried to make the situation as difficult for Banner as we possibly could. I never thought of The Hulk as a character, because he's Banner's Id, and the Id is the absence of Superego. The Superego is the detail that gives a person specific characteristics. The Id is sort of formless survival and aggression; it's a primary. When you get into the Superego, that's the nuance and behavior. Hulk is clearly The Id.

"The punch line with the tape recorder blowing up the dock is a really cool ending! I don't remember if that was me, Tom or something they did in-house, but it was a nice surprise. Killing Bradford Dillman's hunter was also fun. They didn't give us any grief over doing it, even though the show ran in the family hour, because Ken and the producers loved any cool idea that you could bring to the table."

RON STEPHENSON (Casting Director): "'The Snare' was one of our most wonderful shows ever! A two-character script based on The Most Dangerous Game that starred Bradford Dillman as this maniacal killer chasing Bill. It was really unique and Brad was brilliant."

JULIE ORSATTI: "Frank [Orsatti, director] got malaria while shooting 'The Snare' in the woods behind Magic Mountain! He had malaria before, but he got it again filming that episode. Frank was really sick. He worked his heart out on every gig and never slept, so he was always sick after he directed."

HULK FACTS
Bradford Dillman starred in the B-movie classic *Piranha*. He also appeared in *Escape From The Planet Of The Apes* with fellow Hulk guest, William Windom.

Frank Orsatti designed a map of the island and showed where every incident occurred before he directed the show.

The Most Dangerous Game angle is explored again in the episode "Bring Me the Head of the Hulk."

"BABALAO"

Season 3, Episode 43
Airdate: December 21, 1979
Directed By Richard Milton
Written By Craig Buck

Cast

Dr. David Banner	Bill Bixby
Jack McGee	Jack Colvin
The Incredible Hulk	Lou Ferrigno
Dr. Renee DuBois	Louise Sorel
Antoine Moray/Babalao	Bill Henderson
Luke	Michael Swan

In New Orleans during Mardi Gras, David helps beautiful Dr. Renee DuBois face down The Babalao, a witch doctor who holds the neighborhood and her most vulnerable patients in the grip of terror! Renee is his only obstacle, David is her only defender, so the witch doctor has her abducted for an unholy voodoo sacrifice. The Babalao tries to kill David in the middle of a crowded Mardi Gras celebration.

What could be a cool premise — David and The Hulk facing a supernatural menace — is completely undercut in the first ten minutes when Babalao's assistant immediately notes that he doesn't have magical powers, telling him, "I don't believe that voodoo stuff of yours any more than you do," so it becomes a routine "Hulk vs. Con man" episode. La Bruja in "Brainchild" was far more intimidating than this Babalao, and she wasn't even the main storyline!

Whether this was mandated by Broadcast Standards & Practices to keep *The Incredible Hulk* from scaring younger viewers or just sloppy writing, it removes all suspense. When Renee is kidnapped for a voodoo ceremony, we know nothing bad will happen to her because The Babalao has immediately been revealed *not* to be a Babalao! This is especially unfortunate as it immediately follows "The Snare," one of the best episodes of *The Incredible Hulk.*

Director Richard Milton deserves props for cheaply recreating Mardi Gras on the Universal Studios' backlot New Orleans Square set. Being a TV show, it's a New Orleans where no tourist reveals anything to earn beads or any public intoxication is seen. There's also a weird action scene where David gets beaten up by a guy in a gorilla suit, who then tries to roll him under a Mardi Gras float.

Louise Sorel brings an earthy sexiness to her doctor in an otherwise marginal episode. To the show's credit, it adopts a bluesy jazz score for the N'awlins location. It's humorously easy to tell where the New Orleans stock footage ends and the very cheap backlot recreation begins.

LOUISE SOREL (Dr. Renee DuBois): *"I was incredibly nervous about shooting the voodoo sacrifice ceremony, because I was in this long, diaphanous gown. When The Babalao is going to sacrifice me, they put me on this flat table surrounded by candles. What an insane thing to do; they had lit candles all around my body in this long, flammable dress!*

"Since The Hulk was going to have to come up to me, pick me up over all these lit candles in all his greenness, and then carry me through a wall, I asked a crew guy, 'Can he do it?' The guy just looked at me and shrugged! I thought, 'Oh no!' When it was time to shoot it and I had all these burning candles around me, I chose to pass out! I thought, 'Whatever happens, I'm not gonna be here for it!' and just willed myself to sleep...Happily, The Hulk picked me up over the candles, I didn't catch fire — which was a plus, and then he carried me up and right through a breakaway wall!

"After he put me down, I was completely covered in green. I couldn't believe it, because nobody could explain how he was gonna do it, but he did it and I was relieved. I found it incredibly funny after it was all over!

"I don't remember a lot about Bill Bixby, except that he was a good actor and very nice to work with. He did a series a friend of mine worked on and she was very impressed with him as a director. The creator of the show, Kenny Johnson, was a nice guy who really committed to The Incredible Hulk *and* Cliffhangers, *his other series. I co-starred as a vampire in* Cliffhangers' *'Curse of Dracula' segments, which took place in San Francisco. On* Hulk, *I was a doctor in New Orleans, but, of course, we didn't really go to New Orleans. We shot it on the Universal backlot, just like we did with 'Curse of Dracula'!"*

KENNETH JOHNSON: "Louise was a great actress on the show."

HULK FACTS

There's a funny outtake of Bill Bixby getting tongue-tied over the word "Babalao".

Emmy-winning actress Louise Sorel guest-starred on cool fantasy shows like *Night Gallery*. In "Pickman's Model," she romances fellow *Hulk* guest Bradford Dillman. On *Star Trek*, she's a robot who breaks Captain Kirk's heart in "Requiem For Methuselah"!

Michael Swan was obviously a Johnson favorite, as he did episodes of *Hulk*, the "Stop Susan Williams" segment of *Cliffhangers* and played a cop in *V*.

Babalao lives in the Norman Bates House from *Psycho* on the Universal backlot.

"CAPTIVE NIGHT"

Season 3, Episode 44
Airdate: December 21, 1979
Directed By Frank Orsatti
Written By Sam Egan
Banner's alias: "David Bowman"

Cast

Dr. David Banner . . . . Bill Bixby
The Incredible Hulk. . . . . .Lou Ferrigno
Jim. . . . . .Paul Picerni
Gary . . . . .Stanley Kamel
Raymond. . . . . Parley Baer
Mr. Edwards . . . . Dennis Holahan
Karen Mitchell . . . . Anne Lockhart
Mr. Slater. . . . . .Mark Lenard

While working the nightshift at Slater's Department Store, David finds himself in a bind. Store manager Mr. Edwards suspects Banner is going to try to rob the store because he turned down a commendation and promotion. Raymond, the elderly security guard, and assistant manager Karen, who nurses a crush on Banner, refuse to believe it, but Raymond is under orders to keep a watchful eye on him overnight.

When brothers Gary and Jim decide to rob the place that same night, Gary thinks it's a simple hold-up, but Jim plans to make sure there are no witnesses. To protect his fellow hostages, David pretends to throw in with the robbers and go after the money in the safe. David is tossed under a malfunctioning elevator and is crushed until he Hulks Out. What could have been a routine *Hulk* episode is enlivened by several impressive vignettes. Orsatti stages one of the best Hulk sequences in the series, as the green goliath wanders through the department store. The Hulk cheerfully stomps around, registering surprise and delight at the different wonders he finds inside the store. Ferrigno's Hulk is especially transfixed by the toy department, where clown heads, robots and clanging monkeys lead him through a gamut of emotions from wonder, anger, apprehension to awed amusement. Ferrigno gives Hulk a lot of expressiveness. To his credit, despite Hulk's mute status, we can understand exactly what he's thinking. A nice bit has him walk through a china shop without breaking anything — even when he smashes out of the store.

There's a humorous homage to the '60s *Hulk* cartoon (which depicted a giant Hulk foot squash a tank in its opening credits) where Ferrigno stomps a toy tank that hits him with a suction cup. Mr. Machine, the robot in the top hat that hits his foot, was a popular '60s and '70s toy, although the second half of his name is covered up on this show.

Bixby gets to show what a cool bad guy he could be, too. Good practice for the next episode, "Broken Image," where he plays his own evil twin. In a nice bit, Karen nuzzles against him, relieved he wasn't killed by the elevator. Rebuffing her, David coldly says, "I have enough friends right now, thank you." He's posing as a crook to save his friends of the week.

"Captive Night" features some weird stuff, too. Most intriguing is when Hulk confronts a green female mannequin. Noticing their shared skin color, we can see Hulk express curiosity and even amorousness toward it. Even weirder is Hulk's final encounter with Jim. Hulk confronts the three-time loser by flexing his left nipple at him! Is that supposed to scare him? When Hulk smashes out of the store, watch his pants change from white to black, as they use the same 'running down the alley' shot from "The Final Round" one more time!

Frank Orsatti also has a clever bit where Raymond the security guard comes face to face with The Hulk. In a pitch-black store, Raymond lights a match and we're suddenly face to face with Hulk. It's a good jump and is humorously paid off when Hulk calmly leans forward and blows it out!

PAUL PICERNI (Jim): *"I remember there was a big safe and I had a fight in the department store. We shot it at Macy's or Bullock's and I was gonna rob the safe. June Lockhart's daughter Annie is in it with me. Frank Orsatti directed it. Frank was a big stunt guy and I had a little fight scene with Bill Bixby. They usually give stuntmen a little adjustment [more money] for doing a fight. They don't do it for actors, but Frank gave it to me for doing my own fight! Frank was great and it's a shame that he died so young. Frank was a good friend of my brother Charlie, who is also a director."*

JILL SHERMAN DONNER: "We were scouting department stores to shoot this episode at. when we went with Bullock's on Wilshire Boulevard. Karen Harris dressed up and I didn't; I'm not a dresser. The female manager was a very chic woman, so she ignored me and talked only to Karen. After the show wrapped there, we got a call from the store saying that the woman manager's family could not find her. When they finally found her, it turned out that she ran off with Manny Perry, Lou's stuntman!"

HULK FACTS

Mark Lenard was Spock's father on *Star Trek*.

Anne Lockhart was Sheba, Apollo's sister, on the original *Battlestar Galactica*.

The name "Karen" appears to be another nod to *Hulk*'s Karen Harris.

Parley Baer was a hard-working character actor who appeared in so many shows from the 1950s to the '80s, TV Land once did "Parley Baer Week," showing nothing but his guest appearances on their various shows.

Paul Picerni specialized in playing thugs…He's also a goon in the first season's "The Hulk Breaks Las Vegas."

"BROKEN IMAGE"

Season 3, Episode 45
Airdate: January 4, 1980
Directed By John McPherson
Written By Karen Harris & Jill Sherman
Banner's alias: "David Bowman"

Cast

Dr. David Banner/Mike Cassidy . . . . Bill Bixby
Jack McGee . . . . Jack Colvin
The Incredible Hulk . . . . Lou Ferrigno
Lorraine . . . . Karen Carlson
Steve . . . . John Reilly
Teddy . . . . Jed Mills
Pete . . . . George Caldwell
Danny . . . . Chris Wallace
Police Sgt. . . . . Al White
Woman with Dog . . . . Erica Yohn

David wakes up next to a beautiful woman. He sits up and goes to the bathroom. We see he has a mustache. He wakes the woman he just slept with and tells her, "Get up. Beat it. I'm sick of looking at your face."

It isn't David, but a ruthless criminal named Mike Cassidy. One of Mike's henchmen sees David working at a fleabag motel and tells Cassidy that his double is "a drifter, a bum. He couldn't come up with a week's rent, so they are making him work it off." Cassidy sees great potential in having a lookalike. The girl next to him is Lorraine, Cassidy's moll. She sees David and thinks it's Mike.

When innocent David is repeatedly mistaken for gangster Mike Cassidy, the wily Cassidy decides to make full use of the resemblance. Jack McGee arrives and knocks on the door of David's room, wanting to ask if he saw The Hulk. Opening the door, McGee meets David face to face for the first time since the pilot.

"My God, Banner — you're alive," McGee exclaims in the episode's finest moment. He then asks every question he's wanted to ask since the series began. "You're alive. Banner. Doctor Banner, I'm Jack McGee. I think I understand why you're hiding out. It's about The Hulk, isn't it?" To extricate himself, David pretends to be Cassidy. His ruse is backed up by his henchman. "This guy bothering you, Mike?"

As "The Snare" did "The Most Dangerous Game" earlier in the season, "Broken Image" tackles another classic storyline, "The Prince and the Pauper." Another clever episode from the writing team of Harris and Sherman, who have fun with the whole "evil twin" concept. Ironically, Hulk wouldn't meet his own evil twin until the fourth season.

With the gangsters, bums and a skid row setting, it plays more like one of Nicholas Corea's episodes than Harris and Sherman, whose episodes are usually a bit more upbeat. The female writers usually throw in at least one positive female role model per episode, so it's stunning when there's a scene where David's twin, the cruel Cassidy, casually verbally dissects his moll, Lorraine (Karen Carlson).

When Lorraine says she knows that Mike Cassidy is truly good inside, he cuts her off and mocks her. "You're with me because I am mean," he tells her. "Because I don't care. It is true and I am *not* going to change. You don't want me to. You're a born victim. Goodnight." Karen Carlson, who starred in *The Candidate* with Robert Redford, registers the pain and truth in what he says — a very subtle performance. Bill Bixby is great as Cassidy. The actor seems to relish playing the nasty villain after a career of affable nice guys like David Banner and Eddie's Father. He gives cruel eyes to Cassidy.

There's a nice bit when Bixby meets his twin, but it's a surprise that they don't ever have Banner encounter The Hulk to see the creature's reaction. One funny scene has Bixby's Cassidy looking at Hulk and asking his henchman, "What the hell is *that*?!" Apparently aware of how downbeat the settings and story are, Harris and Sherman throw in some welcome comic relief. There's a funny beat where Hulk terrifies a woman and her pet, Chumly the bulldog. Chumly's eccentric owner (Erica Yohn as "Woman with dog") is a drunken, soap opera-watching apartment dweller who is hot for McGee.

Most of the people David meets on the show are principled, Salt of the Earth types who refuse to cooperate with the tabloid reporter. Instead, here, when she realizes McGee writes for the *Register*, she's a fan who calls him "a hunk" and invites him in for a midday beer. She also asks, "Mr. McGee — your paper. Is it true what they said about The Six Million Dollar Man?" Which is clearly an inside joke at Kenneth Johnson, who produced both shows. McGee assures her, "If we printed it, it's true!"

At the end of the episode, Jack McGee is still reeling after coming face to face with his quarry, only to find out it wasn't him and his journey begins anew. A cop tries to console the reporter. "Mr. McGee, the man you're looking for, this Dr. Banner, is dead. Burned to death. If I were you, I would rather be fooled by an old con, than start believing in ghosts."

KAREN HARRIS: *"That story came out of The Writers' Room. Somebody, either Kenny or Nic, I can't remember which, said, 'Bill has a doppelganger. Jack McGee opens a door and comes face to face with David Banner, except it's not David, it's his double. Jill and Karen, write the script!' So we wrote that episode, which became 'Broken Image.'*

"The whole story was about that one moment where Jack McGee faces David Banner, but it's not really David Banner. Out of that one moment sprang an entire episode. That was a lot of fun; Bixby particularly loved doing that episode! He got to play good and bad, a chance for him to show new colors in the Banner character. Bixby rarely got to play bad, which is a shame, because he was a great bad guy! It takes place in a tenement, which meant it was all shot on New York Street on the Universal backlot!"

AL WHITE (Police Sgt): *"Being on that show was a real thrill. I came down from San Francisco, where I was a member of ACT (The American Conservatory Theater), and came to Los Angeles, where I booked the first nine roles I auditioned for — including the cop on* The Incredible Hulk! *It was exciting for me, because I loved the show, never missed an episode, and everybody I knew watched it, too. So I was really happy to be on it at the beginning of my career! Jack Colvin was a wonderful guy...He played the reporter who was always chasing The Hulk and my scene was with him. Thats's where I give him that speech about being fooled by an old con, than start believing in ghosts. I never saw Bill Bixby or The Hulk when I did it. I finally met Lou Ferrigno years later on a film we did together and I liked him very much. We shot my police station scene on a set at Universal Studios. I played a lot of cops and cons, judges and junkies. It was an amazing experience to hang with that show and that's no jive!"*

HULK FACTS
Director John McPherson was *The Incredible Hulk*'s director of photography.

Erica Yohn is the Corleone governess in *The Godfather Part II* and Madame Ruby in *Pee Wee's Big Adventure*. She tells Pee Wee that his missing bike is in the basement of The Alamo!

Jed Mills returns in *Hulk*'s fourth season as a hunter in "Bring Me the Head of the Hulk."

Al White is one of the jive-talking dudes in the comedy classic *Airplane!*

"PROOF POSITIVE"

Season 3, Episode 46
Airdate: January 11, 1980
Directed By Dick Harwood
Written By Karen Harris & Jill Sherman

Cast

Dr. David Banner . . . . Bill Bixby
Jack McGee. . . . . Jack Colvin
The Incredible Hulk. . . . . .Lou Ferrigno
Mark Roberts . . . . .Walter Brooke
Muriel . . . . .Isabel Cooley
Garland. . . . . .Charles Thomas Murphy
Patricia Steinhauer . . . . Caroline Smith

Patricia Steinhauer, the publisher's daughter, takes over *The National Register* and wants to make changes, the main one comes when she takes Jack McGee off *The National Register's* Hulk beat! "There is no more Hulk assignment, Mr. McGee," Patricia tartly informs him, "*because there is no Hulk!*"

Poor Jack finds it impossible to go cold turkey on Hulk. He sees the creature everywhere. He seeks to find proof, so Patricia will put him back on his beloved Hulk beat and Mark Roberts will continue his expense account. "He's monstrous, yet I'm terrified that, sooner or later, someone's going to kill him and that we'll never know the truth," Jack finally admits. We see Hulk IS his life, that Jack's whole existence is predicated on The Hulk story, as he reflects, "I gave up everything in my life outside this story! There was a girl, and — and when she left me, I just barely noticed!" A disgusted Patricia Steinhauer tells him, 'Listen to you! You're like an alcoholic when it comes to The Hulk and the only way you're gonna be cured is to give him up entirely."

"Proof Positive" is an inspired episode that Bill Bixby does *not* appear in! Brief glimpses of him are seem in clips from previous episodes, but Banner is not missed because McGee is so compelling. We see Bill Bixby's stand-in, whose face is never seen, run away from Jack, as McGee tries to unravel the mystery of The Hulk. As with "Stop the Presses," Sherman and Donner have fun with the inner workings of *The National Register* and the quirky, acerbic personality of Jack McGee. What is it about McGee and his tabloid that inspires the writers to do such great stories? Colvin clearly appreciated it, because he does a great job. Once again, pairing Colvin's character off with a woman gives the episode a witty *His Girl Friday* vibe. Caroline Smith makes Patricia interesting. Another revelation is the "meta" quality to the episode; Jack seems to be questioning his very existence. As a supporting character on this show, his only purpose is as a plot device to chase Banner and The Hulk; the Jack McGee character only exists to hunt Banner and Hulk for suspense. If not for The Hulk, there is no reason for McGee to exist at all. Having the character realize this is both funny and gives him a touch of pathos.

KAREN HARRIS: *"If we wrote one without Bix, it was probably to give him a break, allow him time to prep for directing an episode, or he may have been on the tail end of losing Christopher. It was always a challenge to write around an actor, but it was also freeing as well. I don't remember who came up with calling the publisher of the* National Register *'Steinhauer' after* Incredible Hulk *producer Robert Steinhauer. We would all sit around a room and spitball, someone would throw it out just to have a name to give a character while we were breaking a story. Someone else would fall in love with that name and then it was set in stone, as long as it made it through legal clearance."*

HULK FACTS

As noted, *National Register* publisher Steinhauer is named after *Incredible Hulk* producer Robert Bennett Steinhauer.

Jack's editor, Mark Roberts, is also in episodes "Interview with The Hulk" and "Bring Me the Head of the Hulk."

Another flashback of Elaina Marks from the *Hulk* pilot.

Guest Caroline Smith co-starred in the cult film, *Tromeo & Juliet.*

Hulk director Dick Harwood also helmed Johnson's *Cliffhangers.*

"SIDESHOW"

Season 3, Episode 47
Airdate: October 19, 1979
Directed By Nicholas Corea
Written By Len Jenkin
Banner's alias: "David Burns"

Cast

Dr. David Banner . . . . Bill Bixby
The Incredible Hulk. . . . . .Lou Ferrigno
Nancy . . . . Judith Chapman
Mr. Benedict . . . . Robert Donner
Mr. Mason. . . . . .Allan Rich
Jimmy . . . . Bruce Wright
Belle Starr . . . . Marie Windsor
Beth. . . . . .Louisa Moritz

David befriends Nancy, a carnival psychic. She is being stalked by a deranged man who blames her for the death of his son. "Sideshow" has some interesting ideas and a strong performance by Robert Donner, as a backwoods psycho, but the concept is explored deeper in the superior *Hulk* episode "The Psychic."

LOUISA MORITZ (Beth): *"I was one of the showgirls at the carnival. I remember that particular day because it was my first job at Universal Studios and I couldn't find the place! When I finally got there, they threw me in the costume and we did all the dancing outside. I got to meet The Hulk and a lot of kind people on the show! The Hulk was nice, he worked hard. I think I might have gotten carried by The Hulk at one point, but I was ten pounds lighter than I am now! Bill Bixby was very attentive and nice to everyone working on the show. We shot it in three or four days."*

HULK HIGHLIGHT

While a fairly routine *Hulk* outing onscreen, behind the scenes, "Sideshow" changed the life of story editor Jill Sherman. She married guest Robert Donner, a frequent Clint Eastwood co-star, after a humorous misunderstanding on this episode.

JILL SHERMAN DONNER: *"I met my husband on* The Incredible Hulk! *We started dating after one episode, then we married during the series. My husband was also Exidor on* Mork & Mindy. *He was playing a sweaty, deranged person on* Hulk, *which is how we met. We were shooting nights on 'Sideshow' because the episode took place at night, so we would have dinner at midnight. Robert got up in this dirty outfit and said, 'If anyone doesn't finish their steaks, I'm taking 'em home for my dog!' I didn't know who he was, so I said, 'Ohhh, that poor man is eating used meat!' I didn't know he was a successful actor, it was the first time I had ever met him. I literally agreed to date him, looking like he did on that show, because I felt so bad for him! When we had the date, I saw the dog and the dog was clean, so it was true — Robert wasn't eating used meat!"*

ROBERT DONNER (Mr. Benedict): *"We laughed about that for years after we married; poor Jillie thinking I was eating used meat! She met the dog I got it for — he was a great dog, he deserved steak."*

HULK FACTS
Marie Windsor starred in the B-movie classics *The Narrow Margin* and *Cat-Women of the Moon.*

Louisa Moritz played Sylvester Stallone's navigator in *Death Race 2000.*

"LONG RUN HOME"
Season 3, Episode 48
Airdate: February 1, 1980
Directed By Frank Orsatti
Written By Allan Cole & Chris Bunch

Cast

Dr. David Banner . . . . Bill Bixby
The Incredible Hulk. . . . . .Lou Ferrigno
Carl Rivers. . . . . .Paul Koslo
Johnny. . . . . Robert Tessier
Doc . . . . .Mickey Jones
Agent Fitzgerald . . . . .Stephen Keep Mills
Ann . . . . .Pamela Bryant

Hitchhiking just outside of Forrest, California, a nervous David accepts a ride from Carl, a member of The Barbarians biker gang. Cut off by a truck, the two crash and Carl's arm is broken. David has to learn how to ride and steer the cycle for both of them. Mistaken for a biker,

Banner sees the prejudice Carl faces from judgmental doctors, sneering frat boys and panicky cops.

"Doctors are taught *not* to assume anything," David snaps at the ER doctor, shaming him into treating Carl's broken arm. Later when punks attack them, Carl is thrilled to be saved by The Hulk. "This guy lifts up the whole bar — he's kelly green, bigger than a semi," he says excitedly.

"The Long Run Home" biker gang having a break. PHOTO BY PHYLLIS JONES

Unbeknownst to David and Carl, the rest of The Barbarians' California chapter is chasing Carl because the gang wrongly thinks he ratted them out to federal agents. David goes with the tough but good-natured Carl to try to keep him out of further trouble.

An exciting adventure episode with a great concept: Hulk vs. bikers! It's an action-packed hour by the show's resident action specialist, Frank Orsatti. The director stages an impressive brawl between Carl, Hulk and frat boys. There are some great Hulk/cycle-smashing thrills, as The Hulk uses a tree trunk and brute strength against the murderous bikers.

"Long Run Home" neatly demonstrates the show's versatility as a one-man anthology. This week, *The Incredible Hulk* seamlessly transforms into a '60s American International Pictures motorcycle gang movie. Paul Koslo, who usually plays bad guys, gets a rare sympathetic character turn here, as a biker who just wants to go his own way. Mickey Jones, so moving as the retarded lead character in "Ricky," is wonderfully sinister as Doc. He's hidden in an aviator cap, scraggly Manson beard and shades in this episode, an apparent attempt to make sure no one recognizes him as the young innocent from "Ricky."

There's a nice bit where David Banner teaches Carl that when traveling the road, you order tea instead of coffee because "You order tea and a cup of hot water and you can use the bag twice!"

PAUL KOSLO (Carl Rivers): *"Of the few thousand or more actors that I've worked with over the last 41 years there's only a handful that you'd give your life for and Bill Bixby was one of them. He was a really great guy. I spent little time with Lou Ferrigno other than the fight scenes. He mostly kept to himself, although he did have a sense of humor. I think he was shy! Nic Corea and Kenneth Johnson were topnotch good guy producers and storytellers. They had it down; they were sincere, talented and dedicated. After the biker episode that I did on Hulk aired, a lot of bikers come through my hotel and still do. An outlaw gang was in there and they actually tried to take my head off 'cause I burned my colors at the end of the show. Things were getting dicey when one of their guys with authority and a few more brains had to explain to the others that it was the plot and that I was playing a part and it wasn't personal! Wow, thank God for the good guys!"*

MICKEY JONES (Doc): *"Doing 'The Long Run Home' was amazing. I made so many lifetime friends on that one episode. Robert Tessier and Paul Koslo became dear friends. Bob and I stayed in close contact until he died. That is also the show where I met Mic Rodgers. Mic was one of the biker stuntmen who later doubled Mel Gibson and became Mel's stunt coordinator. I am still very good friends with him."*

CARL CIARFALIO (Stuntman): *"On the show, I got to work with and learn from Tom Huff, Billy Burton Sr., Charlie Picerni and Frank Orsatti. All great personalities. I was also able to watch Bill Bixby act. To see him be completely true to his character and his commitment to the show was yet another 'on the job' learning experience that has become etched in my mind on How To Be A Pro. He showed me how to commit."*

HULK FACTS
Mickey Jones in the second of his three *Incredible Hulk* appearances.

Playboy Playmate Pamela Bryant starred in the cult slasher movie *Don't Answer the Phone.*

Paul Koslo played an evil biker on the "Hog Wild" episode of rival superhero show *The Greatest American Hero.* Koslo plays a biker with a broken arm in both shows, even using the term "busted wing" in each.

"FALLING ANGELS"
Season 3, Episode 49
Airdate: February 8, 1980
Directed By Barry Crane
Written by Eric Kaldor & DK Krzemien & James Sanford Parker
Banner's alias: "David Bannister"

Cast

Dr. David Banner . . . . Bill Bixby
Jack McGee. . . . . Jack Colvin
The Hulk . . . . .Lou Ferrigno
Rita . . . . Annette Charles
Peter Grant . . . . .Anthony Herrera
Jody . . . . Debbi Morgan
Mickey. . . . . Cindy Fisher

Working at The Chesley Heights Home for Girls, David learns that the young students are taught unusual careers: they're being trained as safecrackers, shoplifters and pickpockets.

With its utterly preposterous plot — done for laughs on the 1960s *Batman* TV show a decade earlier ("The Londinium Larcenies"/"The Foggiest Notion"/"The Bloody Tower" — the exact same storyline!), *The Incredible Hulk* comes perilously close to "jumping the shark" in this episode. What else can you say about a show where David Banner is beaten up by garbage men and locked in a dumpster at the start and then beaten up by exterminators and locked in a house full of bug bombs at the finish?! Annette Charles is beautiful as Rita, a former student criminal who realizes that she's being manipulated into helping corrupt a new generation of girls.

ANNETTE CHARLES (Rita): *"I had a lot of fun on* The Incredible Hulk! *I never even dreamed I would ever be on that show, so to end up in a guest-starring role as a bad girl was a real thrill! Everybody was so nice. Bill Bixby was very handsome and we kind of flirted with each other during film- ing, but that was as far as it went. I mean, who doesn't think Bill Bixby was a cute guy? I enjoyed working with him; I just remember him being very nice and very much the gentleman. Don't forget, my character was a bad girl, so I was with the bad guy in the episode. That villain, Anthony Herrera, was also handsome — he was in a lot of soaps. I didn't have any scenes with Hulk until Lou Ferrigno smashed in at the end of the show at the big party scene. I was glad to be in that, because who would want to do* The Incredible Hulk *and not have a scene with* The Incredible Hulk*?!?"*

HULK FACTS

Debbi Morgan went on to play The Seer in multiple episodes of *Charmed*.

Anthony Herrera starred in a TV movie as *Mandrake the Magician*.

Annette Charles was sexy vixen Cha Cha in the classic musical *Grease*.

"THE LOTTERY"
Season 3, Episode 50
Airdate: February 15, 1979
Directed By John McPherson
Written By Allan Cole, Chris Bunch & Daniel B. Ulman
Banner's alias: "David Becker"

Cast

Dr. David Banner	Bill Bixby
Jack McGee	Jack Colvin
The Hulk	Lou Ferrigno
Harry Henderson	Robert Hogan
General	Luis Avalos
Hull	Peter Breck
Announcer	Russell Arms
Lover	Peter Bruni
Mugger	Chris Corso
Man	Jack Denbo
Guard	Jimmy Hayes
Clark	David McKnight

When David saves newsstand dealer/reformed con man Harry from a mugger, they become fast friends. To thank him, Harry gives David a lottery ticket, which turns out to be worth $250,000. Complications ensue when David realizes that, as a fugitive, he cannot go on television to collect it. He has Harry do it for him, offering to give him 50% of the winning ticket. He figures he can use his half to cure himself of The Hulk. Unfortunately, greedy Harry steals all the money for one last scam. He plans to fleece a general from San Remo, a violent banana republic. In the climax, to save Harry, Hulk is able to pull a full-size helicopter to the ground, something he needed Thor's help to do in the later TV movie *The Incredible Hulk Returns*!

One of *Hulk's* "funny" episodes, "The Lottery" is breezy and enjoyable. Naturally, poor David will not get to keep one red cent of his winnings.

HULK FACTS

The mythical country Harry cons the general of, San Remo, is the name of the racetrack in "Rainbow's End."

The line "Papers? I don't need no stinkin' papers!" is a jokey homage to the classic *Treasure of Sierra Madre*.

Guest star Robert Hogan was purportedly the namesake for TV sitcom *Hogan's Heroes*.

Hogan played Reverend Winter on TV's *Peyton Place*, which is why a copy of the novel *Return To Peyton Place* is prominently displayed on his newsstand.

Guest Luis Avalos appeared on *The Electric Company* with Marvel's other big hero, Spider-Man.

"THE PSYCHIC"

Season 3, Episode 51
Airdate: February 22, 1980
Directed By Barry Crane
Written By Karen Harris & Jill Sherman

Cast

Dr. David Banner . . . . Bill Bixby
McGee . . . . Jack Colvin
The Incredible Hulk. . . . . .Lou Ferrigno
Annie Caplan. . . . . .Brenda Benet
Robbie Donner . . . . David Anthony

The Hulk is implicated in the death of Robbie Donner, a teenage boy, after an altercation with the young gang member. As The Hulk runs away, a cop kneels over the kid's body and calls in his description of the green suspect. "Male, race indeterminate, over seven feet tall!"

The media goes into a frenzy over this, while Annie, a lonely telephone operator with psychic powers, brushes against David. In a precognitive vision, Annie realizes he's The Hulk and "sees" everything that he has gone through. Annie even sees the deaths of Laura Banner, Elaina Marks and Carolyn Fields. Because of this, Annie cryptically tells David, "I know who you are and what you become." Thinking that he murdered the teenage boy while he was The Hulk, Banner plans to kill himself.

"The curse may not be the creature I turn into, but the man I have become," the grief-stricken scientist tells Annie. She also sees other accidents about to occur, and sets out to stop them. Annie is haunted by the memory of a child she failed to save despite her abilities. Meanwhile, Jack McGee is unconvinced that The Hulk actually killed the teenager. Having tracked Hulk for so long, Jack knows the creature's habits and doesn't believe he did it. He sweats the only witness, another teenage gangbanger, until he confesses.

"It's funny," McGee tells the punk. "When you spend a few years as a reporter, you get to be a human polygraph." Realizing that the reporter will expose him as the killer, the gang member becomes enraged. Annie "sees" this and realizes the murderer will kill McGee to cover up his crime.

Guest star Brenda Benet, Bill Bixby's real-life ex-wife, does an impressive job as Annie. She projects an emotional vulnerability that may have been real. As Annie, Benet has the power to see things that she can't always stop. She wears gloves in an effort to avoid the contact that gives her the visions — something M. Night Shamalan later has the young protagonist do in his film *The Sixth Sense*. "The Psychic" is one of the best episodes of the entire series, and it's given an added depth by its tragic backstory with the suicide of Benet. David Banner is terrified by what he might have done as The Hulk, just as he was in "Of Guilt, Models and Murder." Having the hero of a TV show watched in part by kids contemplate suicide is both amazing and amazingly irresponsible!

JILL SHERMAN DONNER: *"'The Psychic' is my favorite episode of* The Incredible Hulk. *It was the first one I worked on alone [without Karen Harris, her writing partner who is still co-credited]. Brenda Benet, Bill Bixby's ex-wife, appeared in the show as a psychic. Bill wanted her on to show his young son Christopher that, even though they were getting divorced, they could still get along and work together. In the episode, Brenda gives a monologue that I am very proud of. Oddly enough, she talks about a little kid that she couldn't save. Shortly after that, everything fell apart for them — their child and Brenda both passed away. It was stupidly prophetic. When their son died, Brenda committed suicide."*

HULK FACTS

The climax is again shot at the Olympic Boxing Arena, last seen in *Hulk* 's first ongoing episode, "The Final Round."

Banner himself gets psychic powers in the later episode "Deep Shock."

Teenage gang member Robbie Donner is named after frequent *Hulk* guest Robert Donner, who Jill Sherman was dating and later married. "We were running out of names for characters, so I used his name for the murder victim and it was really upsetting to his elderly mother," the writer laughs. "Who knew she would be watching *The Incredible Hulk*?!"

"A ROCK AND A HARD PLACE"

Season 3, Episode 52
Airdate: Feb. 29, 1980
Directed By Chuck Bowman
Written By Andrew Schneider
Banner's alias: "David Braynard"

Cast

Dr. David Banner . . . . Bill Bixby
The Incredible Hulk. . . . . Lou Ferrigno
Preston DeKalb . . . . John McIntire
Lucy Cash . . . . Jeanette Nolan
Randy . . . . Eric Server
Garnett . . . . J. Jay Saunders
Russky . . . . Robert Gray

David runs errands for Lucy Cash, a sweet little old lady he's board-ing with in Atlantic City. When David is arrested by about-to-retire FBI agent Preston DeKalb, he realizes that she's been having him transport dynamite in her latest criminal scheme. To make matters worse, DeKalb's partner tosses a file on the table and says, "We just set a legal precedent. We arrested a dead man, Doctor David Banner!" DeKalb tells David, "I don't give a rat's derriere, Doc, who you are or why you want to be dead. All I care about is collaring Lucy Cash. If you help me do that, I'll burn this [file]. I'll forget I ever saw you!" David reluctantly agrees, but when he Hulks Out to save Lucy from danger, she watches him change. She black-mails David to hoodwink DeKalb. If he refuses, she tells him, "I'm going straight to *The National Register*" to tell them who the Hulk is. David must find a way to please both sides and keep them from exposing his secrets.

A wacky, smarmy episode with nice character moments, "A Rock and a Hard Place" sums up a schizophrenic season. Season Three has jumped between funny and dark. On one hand, you have amusing outings like this, "My Favorite Magician" and "The Lottery," while on the other, there's the grim "Psychic," with murder and suicide, "Sideshow" and the darkest of the season, the next episode, "Deathmask." To *The Incredible Hulk*'s credit, it easily adapts to either tone.

HULK FACTS
Guests John McIntire and Jeanette Nolan were real-life husband and wife.

If Nolan sounds familiar, it's because she's the raspy voice of Norman Bates' mother in Alfred Hitchcock's *Psycho*.

Always good to see actor Eric Server, who has played cops or crooks on *Hulk* since the pilot.

That's downtown Los Angeles landmark Hotel Rosslyn, used for movies and TV shows set in New York. Most Spidey scenes in the 1977 *Amazing Spider-Man* TV series were shot on the roof with the hotel sign clearly visible.

"DEATHMASK"

Season 3, Episode 53
Airdate: March 14, 1980
Directed By John McPherson
Written By Nicholas Corea
Banner's alias: "David Brent"

Cast

Dr. David Banner . . . . Bill Bixby
McGee . . . . Jack Colvin
The Incredible Hulk. . . . . .Lou Ferrigno
Chief Frank Rhodes . . . . .Gerald McRaney
Joan . . . . Melendy Britt
Mayor Tom Fowler . . . . Frank Marth
Miriam Charles. . . . . .Marla Pennington
Man. . . . . Don Marshall

When a serial killer starts leaving corpses of blonde co-eds on the college campus of a small town, suspicion falls on new school librarian David. The police detain him and find fake IDs from previous episodes. David looks guilty, so an impromptu lynch mob forms in front of the jail.

A scary episode, "Deathmask" was made during the height of the slasher movie craze, when films like *Friday the 13th* and *Prom Night* were being churned out in the wake of John Carpenter's *Halloween*. Pushing the boundaries like it does makes "Deathmask" very suspenseful, with a nifty twist ending. It's the darkest episode ever written by frequent contributor Nicholas Corea, who gave *The Incredible Hulk* its grittiest outings.

"Deathmask" also marks Gerald McRaney's strongest appearance on the show, as a tough by-the-book cop with a secret.

The episode also contains several great sequences. After David saves a woman from the killer, she repeatedly screams, "David! David!" in horror, which leads the lynch mob to the logical conclusion that he attacked her. There's also the climax where McRaney is interrogating David until Banner realizes the detective is psychotic and is actually confessing to him. Another scene of a woman getting into her car, only to have the heavy-breathing masked killer rise up in her backseat, is the most unnerving moment of the entire series. Happily, David intervenes, as the maniac tries to drive away with his would-be victim. This sequence, where David hangs on by a car door as he Hulks Out, is genuinely suspenseful. If he lets go, the psycho will kill the woman he's just carjacked. On the show, most of Hulk's opponents are routine thugs, crooks or opportunists. Here, he's up against pure evil, a serial killer who targets women, so Hulk's rage seems entirely justified. Ironically, Hulk seems to go gentler with him than previous foes, probably because he's crazy with a depressing backstory. McRaney's character was abused by his blonde mother, so he now targets blonde women. When the killer tries to escape into a sorority house, The Hulk simply dumps the scaffold he is climbing on, knocking him out. Surely, a spree killer deserves rougher treatment.

HULK HIGHLIGHT
When the lynch mob attacks David, Hulk single-handedly takes them all on!

DON MARSHALL (Man): *"That was the one where I'm in an angry mob, about to kill Banner! We think he's a serial killer! I show up in the lynch mob because Bill [Bixby] asked me to do that! I was at the studio, Universal, and came by the set just to say hello. Bill said, 'Hey, come on in and do it, Don!' I liked Bill Bixby very much. He was one of the good guys in show business, a really nice guy who was very good and kind to me, as you can see — he hired me to do three different episodes of The Incredible Hulk. Bill was also one of the best directors that I have ever worked with. He would come to you, the actor, and tell you what he was trying to accomplish with whatever scene or shot he was about to do. In all the other shows that I have been in, no other director ever explained what they were trying to accomplish — and that's a lot of shows! I found that incredible, as it's what the director and actor are supposed to discuss, if needed."*

KAREN HARRIS: *"Nic Corea wrote 'Deathmask' and like most of Nic's scripts, it had a really dark tone. Nic was a dear friend, one of my closest, and an interesting person to know. He was my husband's mentor and Best Man at my wedding. Nic was a former Marine who did two tours of duty in Vietnam and then came back and became a cop. Nic had a lot of problems. He was a very depressed guy, openly troubled, when he wasn't absolutely delightful! You could never tell which Nic you were going to get; he was a rollercoaster ride who could also be hysterically funny."*

HULK FACTS

If actress Melendy Britt sounds familiar, that's because she's the voice of cartoon superheroine, *She-Ra*.

Frequent *Hulk* guest Don Marshall makes his third appearance, as a member of the lynch mob!

The plot twist of a cop in charge of the manhunt being the actual serial killer had just been used in Stephen King's 1979 bestseller, *The Dead Zone*. Corea's "Brain Child" also bore strong similarities to another King story, *Firestarter*.

Targeting blonde female victims was the M.O. of '70s New York serial killer The Son of Sam.

HULK PROFILE
MELENDY BRITT

The actress who guest-starred in the disturbing "Deathmask," Melendy Britt, was a guest on live action shows and had appeared in a number of TV movies. She also voiced cartoon characters She-Ra, Batgirl and Ming The Merciless' daughter, Princess Aura, on *Flash Gordon*. Guesting on *The Incredible Hulk*, Britt remembers "Deathmask" as "the only time I had ever worked with Bill Bixby and it was such a pleasure. He seemed like a dedicated actor and was able to be professional on the professional level and warm on the human level at the same time.

"It was so easy to work with Bill Bixby," praises Melendy. "Being a guest on many TV shows, I found you could never determine how the star was going to be with a guest actor he or she might never see again. Bill was sweet. He welcomed me with an open heart. Now whether or not that was because I was playing his love interest, I don't know. Whatever it was, it worked.

"With Gerald [McRaney], we had, as I remember, an adversarial relationship in the episode. But in-between takes, I remember us chatting, and he was also a warm and open guy. I remember having lots of conversations. Now, here's the funny part; I didn't meet Lou Ferrigno! We worked on different days, so we never ran into each other. I never met The Hulk!

"I hope this is correct. I did many guest shots on shows and sometimes the details get confused, but I think this episode of *Incredible Hulk*'s location was a studio in Burbank off Oak Street. I remember driving through a studio gate and they had a whole town! It was terrific — rows and rows of all different kinds of houses, some with manicured lawns and a city hall. I think all my exteriors shots were done there." When she thinks about her episode, Britt admits, "I mostly remember my confrontations with Gerald, and the scene with the self-defense class, for which I must receive the 'worst acting of the year award,' and my sweet scenes with Bill."

"EQUINOX"
Season 3, Episode 54
Airdate: March 21, 1980
Directed By Patrick Boyriven
Written By Nicholas Corea
Banner's alias: "David Beldon"

Cast

Dr. David Banner . . . . Bill Bixby
McGee . . . . Jack Colvin
The Incredible Hulk. . . . . .Lou Ferrigno
Diane Powell . . . . Christine DeLisle
Allan Grable . . . . .Paul Carr
Donald. . . . . .Henry Polic II

Working for a selfish socialite, David realizes one of her guests wants the heiress dead at her exclusive Equinox Party. Once again, a dark Corea premise with a lot of red herrings. McGee comes face to face with Banner at the masquerade. They finally have it out, in masks, while poor McGee manages to miss capturing The Hulk!

"Equinox" features one of the greatest McGee/Banner showdowns of the series. McGee confronts the masked Banner and tells him, "It's over, John — take off the mask!" Calling him "John" is a reference to "Mystery Man," where he knows the burned, amnesia-stricken Banner as "John

Doe." Banner responds, "Mr. McGee, mine is not a happy life. Why won't you leave me alone?" The reporter explains that he'll finally be vindicated, but Banner tells him, "You'll be destroying me. The creature saved your life more than once, you know that…"

When Jack tells him that Hulk has to answer for the deaths of David Banner and Elaina Marks, a shocked Banner replies, "No! No, no, no! Elaina died in the fire, not the creature. He tried to save her." McGee coldly responds, "You'll have every chance to prove that in a court of law." Naturally, David narrowly escapes!

HULK HIGHLIGHT
Both The Hulk and Jack McGee are hit on by the same girl, Kathie Spencer-Neff, who uses the same pick-up line on both of them: "Hey, how would you like to go out and use the hot tub?"

HENRY POLIC II (Donald): *"That was one of those jobs that kind of came out of nowhere! I played the spoiled heiress' brother. There were huge shots that were set up at the dining room table — every guest on the episode was at this dining room table for this one big scene. I remember they spent a ton of money for that scene, with so many people saying lines at the table, it was a major story point, one of those [mimes dramatic music] da-da-DA! moments.*

"I loved Bill Bixby, a very talented man. I knew him from back at Paramount when I was on the Mel Brooks show When Things Were Rotten. *He was doing something else at the studio. I never had any interaction with Lou Ferrigno, because The Hulk never appeared to me, but he did appear to the woman playing my sister, Christine DeLisle. Our motivations in the show were pretty simple: Her character was a bitch and I wanted her money! Playing Donald gay came with the package; it was how he was written in the script. I wasn't the villain in a knockdown, drag-out sense, I was just motivated by my greed, and my sister was more of a villain than I was. She was a hateful woman who treated everyone with great disdain — despised universally; she was the classic nouveau riche person. Bill Bixby exposed me as the culprit before he became 'Hulkcanized,' a word I just made up!"*

PAUL CARR (Allan Grable): *"I had nothing to do with Lou Ferrigno's Hulk. Lou came in, they painted him green and he did his thing. The first time I ever saw Lou on my episode of* The Incredible Hulk, *I thought I was gonna pee myself because it was the funniest damn thing I had ever seen in my life! Lou Ferrigno, The Hulk, a great big green guy, is arguing with the assistant director about his lunch! Lou was yelling, 'I WANT MY LUNCH!' They were supposed to get him his lunch and they didn't do it! He was right; it wasn't like he could go to the commissary for lunch, looking like that…"*

"It was an interesting episode of the show, because the director was the associate producer, actually directing his first show, Patrick Boyriven. Patrick was a nice guy, but I have to tell ya, Patrick didn't know continuity. I will modestly say I saved his ass one day. I said, 'Patrick, if you shoot it this way, how am I supposed

Left: Henry Polic II. *Right:* Paul Carr. PHOTOS BY PATRICK JANKIEWICZ

to be in that room over there? You can't do this. You've got to have something to cut away to! He did it the way I suggested and got the shot. I liked Patrick."

KAREN HARRIS: *"That episode has a party on an island that David Banner attends, and there's a line that I think Andrew Schneider wrote, where Henry Polic says, 'I'm too upset to boogie.' That line is way more dated than anything in 'Alice In Discoland'! I also can't believe we have a girl offering to take Hulk to the hot tub!"*

HULK FACTS

Co-star Mark Thomas McGee wrote the B-horror movie *Equinox*! No relation to this episode, despite the title.

Paul Carr was the first crewman to die under the command of Captain Kirk on *Star Trek*.

Henry Polic II voiced the sinister Scarecrow on *Batman: The Animated Series.*

"NINE HOURS"

Season 3, Episode 55
Airdate: April 4, 1980
Directed By Nicholas Corea
Written By Nicholas Corea
Banner's alias: "David Breck"

Cast

Dr. David Banner . . . . Bill Bixby
The Incredible Hulk. . . . . Lou Ferrigno
Joe Lo Franco . . . . Marc Alaimo
Rhonda Wilkes . . . . Sheila Larken
Sam Monte . . . . Frank De Cova
Mrs. Grasso. . . . . Doris Dowling
Fats . . . . Phil Rubenstein
Captain Deeter . . . . Hal Bokar
Timmy Wilkes . . . . David Comfort
Guard . . . . Dennis Haysbert

Working at a hospital, David is being coerced into letting hit men in to kill an ailing mob boss, because they have kidnapped his landlady's young son. David turns to Joe, a broken-down ex-cop, to help him prevent the murder.

Another grim and gritty *Hulk* from the dependable Corea! For a show that was watched by children in what was once labeled "The Family Hour," it's impressive to see how many seedy characters and overall darkness he got away with on a weekly basis. Particularly nice is a scene where Joe mocks the landlady's cherubic young son for being happy about his birthday. Joe yells at the 10-year-old, "Birthdays are just to remind you what you ain't done yet, kid. Birthdays are nothing."

Right after that, the child is kidnapped. Joe is motivated to help David save the boy by his own guilt, which is an interesting, not-quite-noble reason. In an episode filled with strong performances, Bixby and Marc Alaimo are the highlights. As Alaimo has guested several times on *Hulk* as a lowlife and on *Star Trek: Deep Space Nine* as an odious alien, it's nice to see him as a heroic lowlife this time around!

HULK FACTS
Look for future *24, Heat* and *The Unit* star Dennis Haysbert as a guard.

RON STEPHENSON (Casting Director): *"I love Dennis Haysbert! He's worked his way into being a top television actor and movie star. At the time he did* Hulk, *Dennis was just starting out and it was a lucky break that we got him before he took off. A fine actor, he did a really good job for us. He came in to read and pretty much knocked it out of the ballpark. Still, you always hold your breath, because some actors give great auditions and leave their performance in the room, while others hate the audition process and are not good at cold reading. They can still work miracles on screen if the camera loves them. That is why I have always preferred to use tapes of their work to make the final decision."*

"ON THE LINE"
Season 3, Episode 56
Airdate: April 11, 1980
Directed By LQ Jones
Written By Karen Harris and Jill Sherman
Banner's alias: "David Brown"

Cast

Dr. David Banner .... Bill Bixby
McGee .... Jack Colvin
The Incredible Hulk............................. Lou Ferrigno
Randy Phelps.................................. Kathleen Lloyd
Eric Wilson.................................... Don Reid
Weaver...................................... Bruce Fairbaim
Mackie...................................... Joseph Di Reda
Willard .... Tony Duke
Bennett .... Peter Jason

The Hulk changes back to human form, as David realizes his alter ego has walked him into the middle of a raging forest fire. David is enlisted by firefighter Wilson to help put it out. Wilson also suspects David started it. Things get worse when Jack McGee, coming to search for the ever-elusive Hulk, winds up fighting the fire side-by-side with David.

You can't blame Wilson for being suspicious of Banner. When Wilson, fighting a fire that has been raging for three days, meets the post-Hulk Out, shirtless David Banner, the fugitive scientist claims he's been camping in the forest for three days. Wilson notes that Banner has been camping "without a shirt, no equipment, no sleeping bag and no food?"

"On the Line" highlights one of the biggest threats Hulk faces on the series: fire. Like Hulk, it's wild, uncontrollable and unstoppable. Even the green giant finds he can't stop it. In the pilot, Banner takes the accidental overdose of Gamma Radiation because he can't free his wife from a flaming wreckage. At the end of the pilot, he struggles — and ultimately fails — to rescue Elaina Marks from a burning lab. In later episodes, Banner is severely burned on the face, hair and hands in "Mystery Man," and in this, he fights a brushfire that he can't stop with pure brute force.

JILL SHERMAN DONNER: *"Nothing comes to mind for me about that episode, except that it has a female firefighter. We were always ahead of the curve. LQ Jones directed it."*

HULK FACTS

Besides Bill Bixby and Jack Colvin, LQ Jones is the only other *Hulk* actor to direct the show.

Peter Jason is a familiar face in John Wayne and John Carpenter films, seen in *The Fog, Prince of Darkness, Village of the Damned* and *They Live.*

Kathleen Lloyd co-starred in two horror cult classics with fellow *Hulk* guest John Marley: *The Car* and *It Lives Again!*

SEASON FOUR

The Incredible Hulk enters its last full season, as Johnson, Bixby and the writers are so comfortable with the concept, they finally inject more fantasy elements into it. The Hulk now gets to confront the type of larger-than-life opponents and threats he routinely faced in his comic book on a monthly basis. From "Prometheus," the smash two-part opener that Johnson wrote and directed, which puts Banner and The Hulk in a vulnerable state and then has them captured by a top-secret government installation, Season Four hits the ground running.

This interesting season leads to Banner accidentally allowing himself and The Hulk to have murderous impulses ("Dark Side"), gaining psychic powers ("Deep Shock") and, finally, in two of the series' best episodes, Banner meets a Hulk with none of his mercy or compassion ("The First"). Midway through the fourth season, *Hulk* was joined on the airwaves by *The Greatest American Hero*, a rival superhero show on ABC that used a lot of the same guest stars and directors who worked on *Hulk*.

The show had also proven so popular with younger views, Fred Rogers of the popular kids' show *Mister Rogers' Neighborhood*, did a segment on *The Incredible Hulk*.

"I will never forget that," laughs Mark A. Burley, the UPM on *The Incredible Hulk*. "Mister Rogers did an episode on monsters and came to the set to talk to Lou Ferrigno. He showed Lou going through each stage of the makeup process. Rogers came to the set with the show's mailman, Mr. McFeely. They filmed them wandering around the backlot and ask me 'How do we find Lou Ferrigno?' I say, 'Right this way, Mister Rogers!' I was paid a dollar for my performance on camera and for years, my friends' kids would excitedly say to me, 'We just saw you on *Mister Rogers!*'"

"PROMETHEUS"

Season 4, Episodes 57 and 58
Airdate: November 7 and November 14, 1980
Directed By Kenneth Johnson
Written By Kenneth Johnson

Cast

Dr. David Banner .... Bill Bixby
Jack McGee..................................... Jack Colvin
The Hulk .... Lou Ferrigno
Katie Maxwell .... Laurie Prange
Captain Welsh.............................. Roger Robinson
Lieutenant................................... Jill Choder
Pilot... Chip Johnson
Colonel Harry Appling....................... John O'Connell
Demi-Hulk .... Ric Drasin (Uncredited)
Brad....................................... Monte Markham
Dr. Charlene McGowan .... Carol Baxter
Dr. John Zeiderman .... Whit Bissell
Dr. Jason Spath .... Arthur Rosenberg

While fishing near a dam that suddenly opens, David saves a blind girl named Katie from drowning. Helping her back to her cabin, David finds she used to be a classical violinist. Recently blinded and bitter, Katie is in the depths of despair. When a meteor crashes nearby, David goes to investigate. After being stung by bees, he starts to Hulk Out, but radiation from the meteor fuses him mid-transformation. This leaves him a Demi-Hulk, an angry mutation with great strength. Meanwhile, a group of scientists are being collected from their homes by soldiers and taken to a secret government think tank. The scientists all leave immediately, with their clothes on their back, no reason given to their friends, spouses and families. As The Demi-Hulk, Banner finds he's barely in control. It's hard to think in this form and easy to fly into a rage. Seeing his distorted features reflected on Katie's teapot, he angrily crushes it, and then smashes her table, terrifying the blind girl. Realizing he's becoming a danger to her, the Hulk/Banner hybrid tries to leave. Unfortunately, he's captured in a giant red containment cell, which resembles a giant teapot. The Prometheus Project, a United States Government lab that recruited all of the scientists, has the brute. Prometheus believes it has successfully captured a living extraterrestrial! Jack McGee and the blind Katie both join the altered Banner in a top-secret base deep inside a mountain. A truly cool two-parter with a lot of great scenes for all three series regulars, "Prometheus" is the series at it's best. Bill Bixby gets to express confusion over where The Hulk has taken him this time and relief as he's able to lose his Demi-Hulk status. Jack Colvin has fun as his snoopy reporter infiltrates Prometheus and gets the scoop on the top-secret base while Lou Ferrigno smashes his way out of it.

Laurie Prange, not seen on the show since the second TV movie where she played another feisty girl with a handicap, gets to come to grips with her newest condition.

"Prometheus" fully embraces the trappings of *The Incredible Hulk* comics. Elements like falling meteors, Hulk stuck mid-change and secret underground government labs are all regular staples of the *Hulk* comic and it's a great fit. Happily, the rest of the season goes in this direction.

KENNETH JOHNSON: *"It was Bix's idea to use Laurie Prange again and she was superb. It never occurred to me that we crippled her in the first show we did with her and then blinded her in this!"*

RON STEPHENSON (Casting Director): *"Laurie Prange was a real favorite of the producers and a wonderful actress. We knew that the 'Katie' role had to be an actress capable of bringing the audience back for the second*

"Prometheus" has Hulk stuck mid-change, the only time this happens on the show. Note Banner's Bill Bixby haircut on this cover.

part of the season opener 'Prometheus' and she really gave a performance that precluded any audience drop off. Aside from her obvious acting talents, she was a real professional and great to be around. Laurie is also a fine stage actress."

WHIT BISSELL (Dr. John Zeiderman): *"My second character on Hulk was another doctor. I don't think I met The Hulk in that one — TV scripts you don't remember as much as films…"*

HULK HIGHLIGHT
Banner gets caught in mid-transformation, stuck as a distorted half-human/half-Hulk!

HULK FACTS

Banner was first stuck in half-Hulk transformation in issue six of *The Incredible Hulk* comic. In that story, every part of his body changes into Hulk except Banner's head!

His strained, guttural voice as the Demi-Hulk is the closest the series ever comes to having Hulk talk.

The scientists being taken immediately from their lives by the government to see Hulk in an underground desert lab is an homage to Michael Crichton's *Andromeda Strain*.

All of the scientists who study The Hulk are *Hulk* two-timers, making their second appearance on the show. Carol Baxter from "Haunted," Whit Bissell from "Kindred Spirits" and Arthur Rosenberg of "Earthquakes Happen" all show up.

Katie is named after Kenneth Johnson's daughter, born earlier that season.

"FREE FALL"
Season 4, Episode 59
Airdate: November 21, 1980
Directed By Reza S. Badiyi
Written By Allan Cole & Chris Bunch
Banner's alias: "David Blake"

Cast

Dr. David Banner . . . . Bill Bixby
The Incredible Hulk. . . . . .Lou Ferrigno
Hank Lynch . . . . Sam Groom
Jean . . . . Kelly Harmon
Sen. Mack Stewart . . . . .Sandy Ward
Turner . . . . Michael Swan
Jack Stewart. . . . . Jared Martin

Traveling with a sky diving team, David learns that leader Hank has a mysterious connection to a senator and his son. A run-of-the-mill *Hulk* episode — is there anything more boring and less compelling than a TV show centered on skydiving? Stock footage of real sky divers, close-ups of TV stars badly faking it, trying to match the stock footage, add to a less-than-incredible hour.

HULK HIGHLIGHT

Hulk survives a fall to Earth from a plane without a parachute far higher than the one that kills him in the final TV movie, *Death of the Incredible Hulk*.

HULK FACTS

Sam Groom joined fellow *Hulk* guest Scatman Crothers in the killer rat epic *Deadly Eyes*.

Kelly Harmon is Mark (*NCIS*) Harmon's sister and famous in Detroit for her classic WRIF 101FM commercials.

Michael Swan is a *Hulk* two-timer who also appeared in Johnson's *V* and *Cliffhangers*.

"DARK SIDE"
Season 4, Episode 60
Airdate: December 5, 1980
Directed By John McPherson
Written By Nicholas Corea
Banner's alias: "David Barnard"

Cast

Dr. David Banner . . . . Bill Bixby
The Incredible Hulk. . . . . .Lou Ferrigno
Mike Schultz. . . . . Bill Lucking
Ellen . . . . Rosemary Forsyth
Laurie . . . . .Philece Sampler
Miss Farber . . . . .Taaffe O'Connell

David's latest attempt to cure himself goes terribly wrong, as he develops an evil split personality. He does this while staying with a sailor's family. Laurie, the sailor's teenage daughter, is emotionally vulnerable, angry at her absentee dad and nurses an innocent crush on David. In his psychotic state, David takes a truly unhealthy interest in her.

∴ Side" is another winner from Corea. Having Banner actively hit-
..g on the teenage daughter of the family that he's staying with that week
and encouraging her to rebel against her parents is daring and a true flip
on the show's usual M.O. Banner's darkened state blurs the line of right
and wrong, as we realize his Hulk will be a murderous monster without
David's values. Bill Lucking plays another dad losing his teenage daughter and suspicious of Banner's
interest in her, just as he was in
his previous episode...but unlike
"The Antowuk Horror," his fears
here are totally justified! In yet
another reversal of the show's
usual formula, when Lucking
attempts to muscle Banner just
as he did in "Antowuk," the
deranged David beats him sense-
less, a true surprise.

As with "Earthquakes Happen,"
the show demonstrates that an
obsessed, overreaching David
Banner is a far bigger menace
than an enraged Hulk. By tampering with his own mind, David
becomes a sexual threat to an
innocent girl's family and turns
Hulk into the monster that
McGee always believed him to be.

Rosemary Forsyth plays a Mom
whose family is menaced by David
Banner's "Dark Side." PHOTO BY
PATRICK JANKIEWICZ

One of the darkest Nic Corea
scripts of the entire series. Bixby is having a great time as the crazed
Banner. He seems to relish his character's unbalanced state and his interest
in the teenage daughter is gleefully creepy!

BILL LUCKING (Mike Shultz): *"In both my Hulk episodes, I play a father
who has troubled relationships with his daughters. I have two daughters of
my own and the only troubled part of our relationship was that I had high
expectations of them, too high, and they had to set me straight on that subject
so the 'troubled relationships' on film were merely creative constructs!"*

ROSEMARY FORSYTH (Ellen): *"I loved working on the* Hulk. *Bill Bixby
was one of the nicest men I ever worked with — he also directed me on* The

Barbary Coast *and he was great on that, too. I have done a lot of television shows in my life, but* Hulk *stands out as some of the most fun I ever had. We shot it on the Universal backlot. I played Philece Sampler's mom and she was a joy to work with. Bill Lucking played my husband and I remember him fondly; I see he is working all the time. We had a lot in common and he was a terrific guy to work with on* Hulk.

"Bill Bixby *and his wife Brenda were friends of mine. Lou was even nice as* The Hulk. *That was the episode where David Banner is hitting on my teenage kid. Oh wow, I thought that was pretty freaky! That dirty old man, David Banner! The Bixby character is after a teenage girl — I almost forgot about that part of the show! I've got to watch that episode again..."*

KAREN HARRIS: *"'Dark Side' was a good, but really strange show — That was the episode where Bill has African dancers in his head to show that he's crazy! As Banner, Bill also has the fixation on the teenage girl, so that was clearly a Nic Corea show!*

"Nic was in a dark place and this episode really reflects that. There was an actress in that episode who I'm not gonna name [it's not Rosemary Forsyth or Sampler!], she was hired for that episode and she was in spandex because she's dancing in a disco. The actress wouldn't wear a bra, so wardrobe put Band-Aids over her nipples, because Broadcast Standards & Practices wouldn't let nipples show. She kept taking the Band-Aids off! I was producing Hulk *by then, so it fell on me to talk to this actress about her nipples.*

"Suddenly, one of the well-known producers of the appropriately named B.J. and the Bear *came over to see our dailies of the actress with the nipples. They were about to do a spin-off called* B.J. And The Seven Lady Truckers, *she was up for one of the lady truckers and was showing her nipples on* Hulk *as an audition! He wanted to see if 'she's got the chops!' Oh, she had chops and more...Not naming the actress, not naming the producer!"*

HULK FACTS
David utters the line, "You wouldn't like me when I'm angry!" at a bar when in evil mode.

Taaffe O'Connell has an undying cult following because of her sex scene with a giant maggot in Roger Corman's *Galaxy of Terror*.

Philece Sampler replaced Genie Francis as the voice of Betty Ross in the 1990s *Hulk* cartoon with Lou Ferrigno.

"DEEP SHOCK"

Season 4, Episode 61
Airdate: December 12, 1980
Directed By Reza S. Badiyi
Written By Ruel Fischman
Banner's alias: "David Benton"

Cast

Dr. David Banner . . . . Bill Bixby
Jack McGee. . . . . Jack Colvin
The Hulk . . . . Lou Ferrigno
Edgar Tucker. . . . . .Tom Clancy
Frank. . . . . .Edward Power
Dr. Louise Olson. . . . . Sharon Acker

After sustaining an electrical shock as The Hulk, David gets psychic powers that allow him to see into the near future. One vision shows trouble for him and his co-workers at the Tres Lobos Power Plant. This episode isn't as interesting or involving as *Hulk's* previous take on the subject, "The Psychic." All of Banner's precognitive visions are fairly routine accidents about to happen and don't really grab the viewer.

HULK FACTS
Guest Sharon Acker played Odona, a sexy alien on the classic *Star Trek* "The Mark of Gideon."

"BRING ME THE HEAD OF THE HULK"

Season 4, Episode 62
Airdate: January 9, 1981
Directed By Bill Bixby
Written By Alan Cole & Chris Bunch
Banner's alias: "David Bedferd"

Cast

Dr. David Banner . . . . Bill Bixby
Jack McGee. . . . . Jack Colvin
The Hulk . . . . Lou Ferrigno
Alex . . . . Sandy McPeak
La Fronte. . . . . Jed Mills

Dr. Jane Cabot.................................Jane Merrow
Mark Roberts ....Walter Brooke

In France, mercenary La Fronte toasts a poster of The Hulk. Around the room, we see Hulk's specs; size, weight, etc. "To you, Sir," he declares. "An interesting project and I trust, very lucrative!" Sizing up the beast, the hunter notes that "aside from [The Hulk's] size and color, he almost seems *human*..."

Jane Merrow and Bill Bixby.

La Fronte comes to *The National Register* and offers to kill The Hulk. As 75% of *Register* readers believe Hulk is real, he tells McGee, "Wouldn't a dead Bigfoot serve you as much as a live one?" When Jack refuses on moral grounds, La Fronte is hired by *The Register's* competitor, *Limelight Magazine*. With *Limelight* providing backing, the hunter finances a DNA lab to lure Hulk's human identity in, who he correctly surmises must be a scientist. David is looking for Dr. Jane Cabot, a scientist the newspapers dub "The Werewolf Doctor" because of her work in cellular modification. He seeks her out in La Fronte's lab, where the assassin has invited every scientist he believes could be The Hulk. He quickly deduces that David must be The Hulk, because he says he's been out of the field for some time, but he's familiar with the most modern equipment. Reminiscent of earlier *Hulk* episode "The Snare" and the British horror film *The Beast Must Die*, where a hunter invites five people, one of whom he suspects of being a werewolf he wishes to hunt onto his secluded estate, "Bring Me The Head Of The Hulk" is exciting and fun. The show has a cool concept: instead of hunting Hulk, this hunter brings Hulk to him. Dr. Jane Cabot keeps pondering the positive effects of harnessing Hulk's power, while David talks about the dark side. "Damn it, why do you only see the negative possibilities?" Cabot asks, unaware of his firsthand experience with those negative possibilities.

Once again, Jack McGee is put into the strange position of saving The Hulk. In the climax, he literally prevents La Fronte from killing Hulk by blocking his shot with his body. At the episode's start, McGee tells his publisher and La Fronte, "It isn't a question of money. We want the creature captured, not killed…If you kill the creature, you also kill the man." This is the only episode of the series directed by Bill Bixby. He directed all but one of the later *Hulk* TV movies. Bixby picked one of the best scripts of the fourth season and does a great job with it. He makes a lot of allusions to Kenneth Johnson's pilot, and throws around a lot of interesting concepts about The Hulk and the world he lives in. This show could easily have been part of *Hulk*'s first season. It even develops Jack McGee a little more and shows The Hulk is beginning to respect the reporter.

HULK HIGHLIGHT

We see clips from the pilot, which is appropriate, as this episode strives for the first-season tone of *The Incredible Hulk*. Just as in the pilot, McGee watches Hulk carry a woman from an exploding lab, but this time the woman, Dr. Cabot, lives. Hulk hands her to McGee, showing the creature's trust of the man who has hounded him since the very beginning.

JANE MERROW (Dr. Jane Cabot): *"Lou Ferrigno was a sweet man, modest and kind. I liked him. I didn't really get to know Jack Colvin very well."*

RON STEPHENSON (Casting Director): *"I had little contact with Bill Bixby until he directed an episode of the show. Bill was a pro and a nice man. I know there were a few times when temperaments flew, but those were the typical studio/producer conflicts that all actors face. Bixby's disagreements with the studio were the same old, same old. Just like James Garner on* The Rockford Files, *it was all about money, money and more money. Not unusual as a seven-year contract at a certain salary increase each season rarely holds much power.*

"Each year of a hit show usually makes the leads feel they are worth more than their negotiated contracts stipulate. But Bill did his work on time and was a perfect Dr. David Banner. Bill seldom suggested anything for casting. He was a hired hand as opposed to these days when actors almost immediately become producers on their own shows."

HULK FACTS

La Fronte's Hulk poster is a shot from 'Terror In Times Square."

Sandy McPeak, the abusive father in "A Child In Need," plays a good guy here.

Jane Merrow is the Russian scientist out to stop the Death Probe on *The Six Million Dollar Man.*

David runs by The Hotel Rosslyn, last seen in "A Rock and a Hard Place."

"FAST LANE"

Season 4, Episode 63
Airdate: January 16, 1981
Directed By Frank Orsatti
Written By Reuben Leder
Banner's alias: "David Brendan"

Cast

Dr. David Banner	Bill Bixby
The Incredible Hulk	Lou Ferrigno
Joe Conti	Robert F. Lyons
Nancy	Victoria Carroll
Leo	Lee de Broux
Danny	Frank Doubleday
Callahan	Dick O'Neill
Mechanic	John Finn
Clint	Ben Jeffery
Clyde	Alex Rebar

David agrees to take a drive-away car across country, unaware that it's full of stolen mob loot. As Banner and Nancy, a beautiful but ditzy waitress, drive through Barstow, California, they have no idea they are being chased by a mob hit man and a greedy mechanic. Like himself, David finds that Nancy is running from her tortured past—and a young daughter—both of which he urges her to confront and make amends with. A "chase"/action episode, where David's driving skills are suddenly on par with *The Dukes of Hazzard*. Once again, David Banner is in a car with Victoria Carroll! As she was the ill-fated drunk driver Rose in "Mystery Man," David does the driving this time. Victoria Carroll is quite good as Nancy, who at first glance seems shallow and flighty, but then reveals a hidden depth. Of course, David convinces her to renew her relationship with her daughter and helps set up their reconciliation. Victoria Carroll gives a strong monologue on her life and not running from problems any longer. Amusingly, David Hulks Out after getting beaten up and thrown in a cactus patch!

LOU FERRIGNO (Hulk): *"I would just go into a steakhouse or Womphoppers (a gimmick restaurant, now gone) on the Universal backlot, because I couldn't take the makeup off. That meant I couldn't go to the gym or do anything. We were shooting in the woods behind Magic Mountain. One morning, I was pretty hungry and they made me a ten-egg omelet. It was so hot, I put it outside to cool down and a coyote ran off with it! That coyote hit the food jackpot."*

VICTORIA CARROLL (Nancy): *"'Fast Lane' came about when Bill called me up and said, 'I have a show for you to do' and sent me the script. When you establish that you can 'bring it,' you just get called for jobs without having to audition. Most of the episode is just him and me in a car. It was great fun, but it was very hot in that car. We were way out in Valencia, behind Magic Mountain, in 100-degree weather. I remember Bill told me his trick to stay cool. 'You take a cool can of soda, put it in your thighs and the large veins around your groin will cool you down immediately!' I did that and then found out he was putting me on! Bill goes, 'I just made it up.' 'I had a lot of big emotional scenes, so he kept trying to break me up. When he did his lines for me off camera, he was making faces at me and I thought, 'Nope, you're not gonna do it. I'm gonna play this exactly as I'm supposed to!' Afterwards, Bill said to me, 'Okay, you're good — I couldn't throw you or break you up!' You have to just do your job. Because we were together for the whole episode, I got to watch Bill actually Hulk Out! It was quite a process. Bill had contacts in his eyes and then he and Lou would go through several makeups. They had it down to a science, but it was a very involved process. The crew always joked about what happened to his clothes when he became Hulk. I imagined that when I played She-Hulk on* The Incredible Hulk *cartoon. I had to voice my transformation in that.*

"In 'Fast Lane,' I crash a car like I did in "Mystery Man', but I don't burn David Banner up this time! I had to do a stunt when the car turns over. I crawl out of the flipped car, but I learned early on that you don't *so your own stunts. Of the two characters I played on* Hulk, *Nancy the waitress was my favorite. I enjoyed both roles because they were so different. Nancy starts out kind of goofy, but my mannerisms and personality change when David Banner realizes that I am running away from my own daughter and my feelings of failure. Once I feel comfortable and safe around David Banner, I reveal my true self to him and he convinces me to go back to my family and daughter. Not a bad message."*

RON STEPHENSON (Casting Director): *"Victoria Carroll was a very pretty blonde who was also a really nice gal. She was a very capable actress, but her looks pigeonholed her a bit. Because she was a very sexy blonde, her look was not good for her playing nuns or brain surgeons!"*

HULK FACTS
Another *Hulk* two-timer, Dick O'Neill, returns in "The Phenom."

Alex Rebar (Clyde) was the title character in *The Incredible Melting Man*.

Lee de Broux played Sal, Detroit's biggest drug supplier, in the original *RoboCop*.

"GOODBYE, EDDIE CAIN"
Season 4, Episode 64
Airdate: January 23, 1981
Directed By Jack Colvin
Written By Nicholas Corea
Banner's alias: "David Benedict"

Cast
Dr. David Banner	Bill Bixby
The Incredible Hulk	Lou Ferrigno
Eddie Cain	Cameron Mitchell
Vicki Lang	Jennifer Holmes
Danny Romero	Anthony Caruso
Mac	Gordon Connell
Sheehan	Tom McGreevy
Norma Crespi Lang	Donna Marshall

Gumshoe Eddie Cain is being interrogated by the cops. As he sweats under hot lights and two uncaring detectives, he keeps having flashbacks of David, Hulk, gunshots and murder. "Big green men, mafia...Jeez, what a crock," says a hard-bitten cop listening to Eddie's confession. Frustrated, Eddie snarls, "Mac, d'ya wanna hear the truth?"

"We'll try the truth, Eddie — your version."

Eddie's ex, Norma Lang, is now married to a state senator. She calls Eddie to her estate because someone is blackmailing her. Norma's sexy daughter Vicki hits on Eddie and David Banner, who is working at the mansion. The chauffeur is also suspicious. Gangster Danny Romero is determined to find out who is blackmailing Norma, an ex-flame of his as well, and why. Killing a suspect in front of Eddie Cain, Romero plans to have Eddie murdered with a silencer. "Norma shoulda come to me in the first place. This is family now, Eddie. You're not family," Romero says coldly, before Eddie is saved by the timely intervention of The Hulk. When Eddie is winged, he wakes to find his wound being dressed by David. "Just a flesh wound, you're lucky," David tells him. The cigar-smoking gumshoe figures out that Vicki is Romero's daughter.

When he cracks the case, he finds that Vicki has been blackmailing her own mother. "I hate my mommy...I know it's awful, but it's true. And Daddy was icy cold, too. As if he knew his little girl was not his little girl," Vicki tells Eddie and David, as she casually prepares their double murder.

A fun tribute to '40s *film noir*, as gruff, hard-bitten private eye Eddie Cain comes to solve a murder, involving girls, gangsters and a mysterious gardener — David! Being a brilliant detective, Cain senses David's evasiveness and pegs him as a suspect.

Because the background of "David Benedict" comes up zero, Eddie dubs David "Mister Zero."

"Goodbye, Eddie Cain" is another great Nicholas Corea *Hulk*, beautifully directed by Jack Colvin. To his credit, Colvin keeps all the detective movie tropes; a *femme fatale*, several red herrings and lots of shadows. It even has an appropriately *noirish* piano score. Colvin shoots it like an old detective movie. In the opening, it's appropriate we see long-gone LA landmark Ship's Restaurant, because the whole episode is devoted to a Hollywood that is not there anymore. "It was like he had been through a lot of bad times and figured getting hysterical don't ever help. A real cool character," is Eddie's incredibly perceptive take on David Banner. The detective tosses Banner's room. Going through David's belongings, he thinks, "The guy was some kind of math nut or something. The books — Einstein would have trouble with 'em!" Framed like a *film noir*, it includes an impressive crane shot following Eddie down the stairs of his seedy detective agency to the crowded street below. Most of the episode is shot on a cleverly disguised Universal backlot. The only set that looks fake is a sleazy club called "The Devil's Advocate." It's a club that Eddie tells us "is full of dope and sex." Unfortunately, it's the laziest set in the series: A generic backlot building with a cheap black sign that simply reads "Devil's Advocate." The episode also has a voiceover, narrated by the hero — *not* David, but detective Eddie Cain. Following Eddie instead of Banner is not only clever, it helps the *film noir* elements come naturally.

'50s film actor Cameron Mitchell had been reduced to supporting roles in B-movie junk like *Without Warning* and *Frankenstein Island* when he landed this *Hulk* episode. You can see his sheer delight in having such a meaty, fun part. Mitchell seems to enjoy spitting out B-movie tough guy lines like "Dead as the proverbial doornail" and "We were busy doing the chokehold polka!" He gives everyone a nickname: "Boots," "Irish," and at one point, notes, "Maybe I was getting old. Old and stupid!" When he's chasing the chauffeur and running from The Hulk, Eddie thinks, "Here I was chasing a guy twice my size while a guy four times my size was chasing me!"

Jennifer Holmes, who would star in her own sci-fi show, the short-lived but notorious *Misfits of Science*, makes for a pretty, taunting *femme fatale*. Parading around in a white bikini and having an indiscreet affair with the help, she's an appropriately kittenish vixen. When Eddie shows up, she coos, "You look like a tough guy. So long, tough guy!" She's turned on when the evil chauffeur and his goons beat up Eddie and is unfazed when Hulk smashes her corvette. The ending where Eddie and Vicki talk through bars is a playful nod to *Double Indemnity*. Bushy-browed Anthony Caruso played many gangsters before in movies and on *Adventures of Superman*, *The Untouchables* and the classic *Star Trek*. He's quite effective as the sinister Romero. It's also a clever hint to viewers that he's the only one on the show who fondly and protectively refers to Vicki as "Victoria," clearly showing that he knows the girl's true parentage.

Bixby also gets some nice character moments. When David hears the chauffeur is dead after attacking him, he fearfully asks, "How — how did it happen?" worried he killed him when he Hulked Out. When Eddie turns to Banner and asks, "So you're the gardener?" David responds, "Quite often, yes" — a funny acknowledgement of how many times he's worked as a gardener on the show. David also passes through the suburban backlot on his way out of town that played New Orleans in "Babalao."

HULK HIGHLIGHT

When Eddie Cain looks into the past of the dubious gardener "David Benedict," he says, "On David Benedict, my man drew a complete blank — Zero. And when someone comes up zero, then it's dime to donuts he's got something to hide!"

KAREN HARRIS: "'Goodbye, Eddie Cain' was the first episode that Jack Colvin directed. Nic Corea helped him on that. I remember going to the set in Pasadena and seeing Nic kinda hold his hand as Jack directed."

RON STEPHENSON (Casting Director): *"I loved using great Hollywood character actors like Cameron Mitchell, but he was very hit and miss. I think he had such a big shot at movie stardom as Doris Day's gangster boyfriend in* Love Me Or Leave Me, *but when it didn't happen, he lost some of his desire. Cameron had to be pushed to get his finger out, so to speak, but when he did grasp the moment, he was fine. He didn't on* The Incredible Hulk *and I was disappointed."*

HULK FACTS

Hulk two-timer Jennifer Holmes appeared in "Metamorphosis." She was also the original maid on *Newhart*, before she was replaced by Julia Duffy playing her sister.

Cameron Mitchell stabs previous *Hulk* guest Victoria Carroll to death in the cult movie *Nightmare In Wax* — and then brings her head along for the rest of the movie!

Eddie Cain's last name is a nod to noir writer James M. Cain, who frequently had women and mothers with secrets in his work, like *Double Indemnity* (which the episode's final shot homages), *The Postman Rings Twice* and *Mildred Pierce*.

"KING OF THE BEACH"
Season 4, Episode 65
Airdate: February 6, 1981
Directed By Barry Crane
Written By Karen Harris
Banner's alias: "David Beller"

Cast

Dr. David Banner . . . . Bill Bixby
The Incredible Hulk/Carl Molino . . . . Lou Ferrigno
Mandy . . . . Leslie Ackerman
Solly Diamond . . . . Charlie Brill
Rudy . . . . George Caldwell
Lady . . . . Nora Boland
Trainer . . . . Leo DeLyon
Steve . . . . James Emery
Little Girl . . . . Angela Lee

In Venice, California, David is working as a dishwasher when he meets competitive bodybuilder Carl Molino. While Molino is a deaf, decent man saving up money to buy his own restaurant, he's willing to throw it all away to win a "King of the Beach" contest. Banner is worried for him, especially when he sees Carl being taken advantage of by a hustler, setting him up to fail.

"King of the Beach" is essentially a remake of the show's first episode, "The Final Round", with bodybuilding instead of boxing. It gives Lou Ferrigno his first real acting role outside of The Hulk. Clearly using elements of his own life, Ferrigno makes for a charismatic character. One can see the real-life rapport he and Bixby had in the scenes they share. What doesn't work is the climax where Molino meets The Hulk. Pre-CG trickery, the effect of the two Ferrignos meeting face to face is pretty cheesy. To the show's credit, they do establish that Hulk is much taller than Molino. There's also a funny bit where The Hulk meets a little girl on the beach and smashes her sandcastle.

LOU FERRIGNO (Hulk): *"My all-time favorite episode! 'King of the Beach' is the one where I played myself alongside The Hulk. I really loved that one, because I had the chance to be myself and Hulk. They put me on a box as Hulk so I would be taller than myself as the bodybuilder! I enjoyed doing my first real acting role in that show as Carl Molino so much; I just hated having to go back into Hulk makeup to do a scene with myself. I really enjoyed having a normal role!"*

KAREN HARRIS: *"I love 'King of the Beach' — it's actually my favorite episode. I thought Lou was really good in it. Just as with Jill and me, The Incredible Hulk was Lou's first job outside of playing himself in* Pumping Iron. *I remember he told me it was so frustrating when he was The Hulk on the show, because people would talk around him, not directly to him. It was like he wasn't even there and he felt like a giant prop!"*

ANGELA LEE (Little Girl): *"I'm a little girl on the beach, when The Hulk comes up to me as I build my sandcastle. I ask Hulk if he's wearing a special suntan lotion and talk to him. He gets mad and smashes my sandcastle. I start crying as my Mom pulls me away. The scene was an homage to the Boris Karloff* Frankenstein, *where the monster meets the little girl. I ran into Lou Ferrigno at a recent comic book convention and mentioned it. Lou remembered me immediately! He wanted to make sure I was introduced to him before he was green so I wasn't scared of him when he came out as Hulk. I was, and he was great to me, very sweet — he didn't scare me at all! My Dad was with me on set and he was excited to meet The Hulk."*

CARL CIARFALIO (Stuntman): *"Working with Lou Ferrigno was the start of a relationship that has lasted all these years. Louie threw me around a lot on his* Hulk *TV show, so we had a good working relationship. He's a gentle giant; a kind soul who is humble and very aware of who he is. Lou never uses that to push his way around. I like Lou. Louie had a series after* The Incredible Hulk *ended called* Trauma Center. *I was Lou's stunt double on that series. I also doubled Lou on a couple of films he did a few years later."*

HULK FACTS

This is only the second time Bixby and Ferrigno appear together on the show.

Charlie Brill starred in the classic *Star Trek* episode, "The Trouble with Tribbles." He reprised his role 27 years later in the *Star Trek: Deep Space Nine* episode, 'Trials and Tribble-ations."

Leslie Ackerman re-teamed with *Hulk* co-star Brill on that *Deep Space Nine* episode.

Angela Lee voiced Lucy Van Pelt on *The Charlie Brown and Snoopy Show.*

Charlie Brill actually followed The Beatles as the next act on *The Ed Sullivan Show.*

"WAX MUSEUM"

Season 4, Episode 66
Airdate: February 13, 1981
Directed By Dick Harwood
Written By Carol Baxter
Banner's alias: "David Beckwith"

Cast

Dr. David Banner	Bill Bixby
Jack McGee	Jack Colvin
The Hulk	Lou Ferrigno
Leigh Gamble	Christine Belford
Mr. Kelleher	Ben Hammer
Walter Gamble	Max Showalter

David goes to work at the Gamble Wax Museum, whose beautiful owner, Leigh Gamble, hopes to re-open it, after losing her father in a mysterious fire. Her Uncle Walter wants to close the museum, concerned over his niece's fragile mental state. Leigh is having delusions; she sees dummies coming to life and things that aren't there. When Hulk saves her from a mishap, she assumes he isn't real, despite him smashing through the wall.

Jack McGee hits town to investigate that Hulk sighting. David discovers Leigh is being fed LSD-tainted meds by Uncle Walter, who wants to use her unstable condition as an excuse to sell the wax museum. Once again, Hulk battles fire in the climax.

"Wax Museum" is as generic as its title. Christine Belford returns, gamely playing a woman who can't trust her own eyes. When she meets The Hulk, she assumes he's another hallucination and renders him in wax. Jack McGee is particularly excited when he sees it. She also makes a dummy of David, telling him that "thousands of people will look at it!" Not wanting to hurt her feelings by rejecting her tribute, David convinces her it's always been his fantasy to be a pirate. She adds a beard, stocking cap and eye patch to his enthusiastic approval.

This episode's writer, Carol Baxter, starred in Season Two's dull "Haunted," which explains why the plot is so similar to that episode, a woman being driven mad by illusions and past guilt that she was not truly guilty of. Uncle Walter was right when he told his niece they were better off opening a bar or diner. In 2005, Buena Park, California's long-running tourist trap, The Movieland Wax Museum, went out of business.

Look, I don't care how villainous Uncle Walter is supposed to be, having The Hulk chase a frail, pot-bellied old man around in the climax doesn't seem remotely fair — Pick on somebody your own size, Hulk!

HULK FACTS
Max Showalter is best known as Molly Ringwald's grandfather in John Hughes' Sixteen Candles.

"EAST WINDS"
Season 4, Episode 67
Airdate: February 20, 1981
Directed By Jack Colvin
Written By Jill Sherman
Banner's alias: "David Barrett"

Cast

Dr. David Banner . . . . Bill Bixby
The Hulk . . . . .Lou Ferrigno
Kam Chong. . . . . Richard Loo
Tam . . . . Irene Yah-Ling Sun
William Chimoda . . . . Richard Narita
Hun . . . . .Beulah Quo
Sgt. Jack Keeler . . . . William Windom

While staying in Chinatown, David finds his apartment is wanted by tough, boozy old police Sgt Jack Keeler and some Chinese crooks. All parties believe there is a fortune in gold hidden somewhere in David's room. When The Hulk battles Asian gangsters, one of them manages to cut him with a meat cleaver and draw blood, one of the only times on the series Hulk is wounded without using a gun. Other than this interesting sequence, "East Winds" is a routine adventure enlivened only by the presence of the great character actor William Windom.

WILLIAM WINDOM (Sgt. Jack Keeler): *"I had the funniest line of my entire career on my* Hulk *episode. Bill Bixby and I almost laughed ourselves out of the business! He and I are dining in a restaurant, surrounded by all these lovely Asian ladies, and my line is, 'Try a little Yellow Tail.' They would not change the line so we laughed ourselves sick! Bill said, 'Windom, you're doing that on purpose,' so I go, 'You try saying it, Bill.' He tried and he couldn't say it either! We could not say it — Oh, that was hilarious. Bill was a helluva guy."* (In the final show, he says "Maybe you'll like some yellow tail.")

JILL SHERMAN DONNER: *"The 'Yellow Tail' line was completely unintentional, although Bixby accused me of putting it in there on purpose!"*

HULK HIGHLIGHT
David winds up with a mail order bride!

HULK FACTS

William Windom won an Emmy for the *Night Gallery* episode "They're Tearing Down Tim Riley's Bar."

Windom is Steve Martin's indecisive boss in *Planes, Trains and Automobiles,* which also stars *Hulk* guest Edie McClurg.

The last role for Richard Loo, best known as Master Sun from *Kung Fu.*

Irene Yah-Ling Sun also appeared in the *Hulk* episode "Another Path."

"THE FIRST" PART ONE & TWO
Season 4, Episodes 68 and 69
Airdate: March 6 and March 13, 1981
Directed By Frank Orsatti
Written By Andrew Schneider
Banner's alias "David Barr"

Cast

Dr. David Banner	Bill Bixby
Jack McGee	Jack Colvin
The Hulk	Lou Ferrigno
Dell Frye	Harry Townes
Elizabeth Collins	Lola Albright
Case	Bill Beyers
Willie	Chip Frye
Brad Wheeler	Edward Walsh
Earl	Cliff Emmich
Sheriff Carl Decker	Billy Green Bush
Frye's Creature	Dick Durock
Walt	Jack Magee
Cheryl	Julie Marine
Linda	Kari Michaelson
Janitor	Hank Rolike

Some teens break into the creepy old Clive house in the small town of Vissaria, California. They quickly realize they are not alone. Something horrific races at them from off-camera. A year later, David arrives, having heard reports of a Hulk sighting in a town he's never been in before. He finds that in the early '50s, Dr. Clive created a Hulk of his own. In an old newspaper, David finds an even bigger bombshell: there is a blurry shot in the paper of this first Hulk with the caption, "Frye's Green Creature". Sadly, with Clive dead, David believes his cure died with him.

Dell Frye, Clive's former gardener and meek assistant, tells David the cure still exists. He leads David to the doctor's lover, Elizabeth. She shows Banner a hidden lab where he created a Hulk. Frye then tells David he was the man Clive turned into a '50s Hulk. Panicky kids beat up David and throw him down a well, then run in mortal terror at the sight of his Hulk. They believe he's *their* Hulk, who killed one of the kids in the opening, at the old Clive house. Taunted by locals, Dell Hulks Out, beats them up and kills their ringleader. Sheriff Decker tells Frye he can't prove it, but knows he's involved with the creature and suggests Frye leave town immediately.

David finally synthesizes a cure to The Hulk, but refuses to use it on himself until he stops Frye's Hulk first. He urges Elizabeth to call Frye over. Jack McGee confronts Dell first, surprised by his elderly, arthritic state, but firmly convinced that he's the John Doe Hulk he's been pursuing since the pilot. McGee pulls a gun on Frye, making it clear that he'll stop a homicidal Hulk by any means necessary. Frye knocks him out and heads to Elizabeth. As she distracts Dell, David injects him with a sedative and begins the process to prevent him from Hulking Out. Frye angrily transforms to kill David and Elizabeth. When Frye's Creature smashes the cure against the wall, David screams, "NO!" Weeping in rage and frustration, David Hulks Out and the two monsters grapple and shove each other in earnest, destroying the lab and the cure in the process.

Arriving with Jack McGee, Sheriff Decker guns down Frye's Creature when it menaces them. He turns to shoot The Hulk, but Elizabeth blocks his aim. She declares that "He's innocent" and she's alive only because Hulk protected her. Hulk flees. Coming closer to ridding himself of his alter ego than he's ever been at any point in the entire series, Banner sadly hitchhikes out of town. For those who love all-out action, these are the two best Hulk-centered episodes of the show. This is the only time Hulk literally goes toe-to-toe with another Gamma-spawned monster, something he does regularly in the comics, but never did on the show. Dick Durock's long and lean evil Hulk gives viewers an idea of what the Richard Kiel Hulk would have looked like. His malevolent Hulk is menacing, a snarling monster with a Lon Chaney, Jr. *Wolf Man* pompadour. His climactic fight with the Ferrigno Hulk is a lot of fun.

It bears mentioning that Ferrigno does a great job conveying emotion in this two-part story. At the climax, his Hulk seems truly happy to see another of his kind, then confused as the creature attacks him, and finally enraged. It gives us another side to The Hulk that we have never seen before.

The Bixby Hulk, like Banner, fights out of necessity. Andrew Schnei-

The Incredible Hulks (Dick Durock, Lou Ferrigno) battle to the death!

der's script makes the distinction between the two creatures clear. "Frye's Creature fights to kill. The Hulk, like David, fights only defensively." Ironically, one of the best moments of the show is not in Schneider's original draft. The Sheriff empties his revolver into Frye's Creature, so the moment where Elizabeth protects Hulk from his gun and McGee is a revision. "The First" pays tribute to Universal's *Frankenstein* movies of the '30s and '40s.

From the name of the town, Vissaria, an homage to *Frankenstein Meets the Wolf Man*'s Vasaria, to the character names in both episodes: Colin Clive played Dr, Frankenstein and Elizabeth was his fiancée in the 1931 Boris Karloff classic. Dwight Frye was Karl in *Bride of Frankenstein*. Moving a *Frankenstein* movie to the suburbs is clever. Having secret labs, monsters and scared villagers running around suburbia is ingenious, just as Tim Burton proved in his later films *Frankenweenie* and *Edward Scissorhands*. Orsatti clearly cast Harry Townes as Dell Frye because of his strong physical resemblance to Boris Karloff.

Writer Andrew Schnieder keeps all the classic Universal archetypes, a hunting party out to kill Hulk, a lyrical moment of Hulk sitting on a riverbank like Boris Karloff's Frankenstein Monster and the ending, where the monsters finally confront each other and battle in the lab as terrified townsfolk prepare to kill them both, just like in *Frankenstein Meets the Wolf Man*! Schneider contributed several great episodes to *The Incredible Hulk*, but this was his very best. It's fun, fast and has a really impressive cliffhanger.

David also battles Frye, who revels in the power he has as the creature. When he tells David, "I want to be strong again, healthy. It's worth the risk," Banner is stunned. He tells him, "You want to ruin your life? It's ruined mine!" Frye laughs, "My life is ruined already. I've had enough, I want the strength again!" Meanwhile, The Sheriff scoffs at Jack McGee. "The Hulk, huh? That like Bigfoot or Sasquatch?"

In his script, Andrew Schneider specifies the differences between the good Hulk and bad one. Dr. Clive is fearful of the Hulk that he's created, noting, "This creature could be particularly dangerous, I fear, due to the test subject's inherent personality…" During Frye's transformation into the creature, it's noted in the script that the evil Hulk's "color is more of a yellowish green. The features of its face, though similar, are more menacing. The creature has a definite touch of evil, which The Hulk does not." When he read Kenneth Johnson's *Hulk* pilot, Bill Bixby told the press that it reminded him of the Universal "creature features" of the '30s and '40s that he grew up on, "except The Hulk isn't evil!" This two-parter really embraces that.

LOU FERRIGNO (Hulk): *"This was a great story and one of my father's favorite shows of the entire series! Dick Durock played this weird evil Hulk. I love the scene where my Hulk is crying — he really doesn't want to hurt this other Hulk, but he has to because that one is killing people. I also love when my Hulk kicks his Hulk's ass!"*

CLIFF EMMICH (Earl): *"We shot that after Bill Bixby's son died, so [the two Hulks] was an attempt to give Bill some time off to deal with it. We didn't really work with Bill, all our scenes dealt with the guy playing the other Hulk. I played Earl, the owner of the hardware store. We had fun shooting the scene with the old guy Hulking Out and attacking us! I had a real good time on the show. Most of my enjoyment came with seeing an old friend of mine, Billy Green Bush, who plays the Sheriff. Billy's a great guy with some great stories!"*

MANNY PERRY (Stunt Hulk): *"We had Dick Durock play the older Hulk. Our Hulk was usually confronted by thugs with sticks or a cop with a gun. Here, he was actually facing another Hulk who was very similar to him. Dick Durock was 6'6" tall, with a more slender build than The Hulk. A very good stuntman and a really good actor. This is the first time we had Hulk face an opponent who was taller than him. When The Hulk looked at this creature, he couldn't quite figure out what it was because it looked like him. I really enjoyed that big drawn-out fight between the two Hulks."*

JULIE ORSATTI: *"Frank was so pleased with how those two episodes turned out, especially the big fight between The Hulks. Lola Albright, who played the girlfriend of the first Hulk, wrote Frank a letter thanking him for using her…I still have that letter."*

HULK FACTS

Guest Dick Durock played another green monster in the *Swamp Thing* movies and TV series.

Schneider's script specifies using a stock shot of David getting off a bus from "Homecoming," which he also wrote, for the opening shot in "The First."

Hulk's most powerful adversary in the comics is the Gamma-spawned Abomination.

When Ferrigno pulls up Durock's shirt as they grapple at the end of "First" part two, we see that his back isn't painted green. They must have really needed that shot!

With Frye's Creature and the prehistoric 'Cave Hulk' in "Kindred Spirits," David is the *third* Hulk to exist.

"THE HARDER THEY FALL"

Season 4, Episode 70
Airdate: March 17, 1981
Directed By Michael Vejar
Written By Nancy Faulkner
Banner's alias "David Blackwell"

Cast

Dr. David Banner . . . . Bill Bixby
Jack McGee. . . . . Jack Colvin
The Hulk . . . . Lou Ferrigno
Paul Corton. . . . . .Denny Miller
Dr. Hart. . . . . Peter Hobbs
Judy . . . . Diane Shalet
Mr. Melton . . . . .William Bogert
Al. . . . . .Joe Dorsey
Bernie . . . . Hugh Smith
Bartender. . . . . .Ralph Strait
Bobby . . . . Alan Toy

While waiting at a bus stop, David is struck by an inattentive driver whose car jumps the curb. Gravely injured, David realizes the car has done major spinal damage and he's paralyzed from the waist down. At a hospital's paraplegic ward, David succumbs to despair, while one patient, the optimistic Paul, tries to get him to accept his condition and move on with his life. Paul was an athlete before the accident that changed his life. Now he's about to get a loan from the bank so he can open a sporting goods store, proving that there's life after paralysis.

David learns how to maneuver his wheelchair, handle his handicap and bond with the guys in the ward. When they ask for David's backstory, he shrugs and says, "Not much to tell. I've been moving from town to town."

"Hope you got that out of your system," Paul says sardonically.

Unfortunately, some bad news means that Paul's attitude is about to take a turn for the worse.

"The Harder They Fall" is one of the series' best episodes, as David finds himself in a truly frightening situation: being paralyzed from the waist down. Bixby in bed, ruefully accepting his fate is one of his most impressive acting scenes in the entire series. While it was established in the *Hulk* pilot that David has a rapid healing factor that kicks in when he's shot or hurt, it takes much longer to kick in here, due to the extent of his injuries. Playing the former sportsman Paul, Denny Miller also shines. Miller's character tries to keep a positive outlook for the rest of the guys in the ward, even though he keeps getting doors slammed in his face. Miller's Paul is proud to the point of anger, getting into a skirmish with some toughs in a bar who think he and David are wounded veterans and

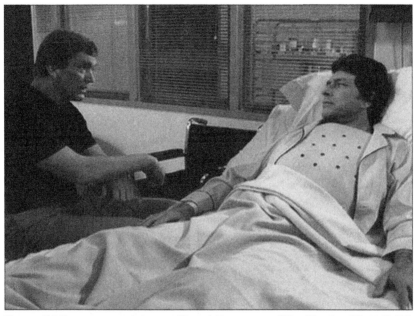

Denny Miller tries to cheer up David Banner in "The Harder They Fall."

want to buy them drinks. Paul refuses to quietly accept the drinks, even though David urges him to, and pushes them into a fight.

As great and moving as the episode is, it's a crime to find that it's the only thing screenwriter Nancy Faulkner ever wrote!

DENNY MILLER (Paul): *"I weighed 240 pounds when I played a paraplegic in a wheelchair for that episode, 'The Harder They Fall.' To prepare for it, I went to the Naval Medical Hospital in Long Beach and borrowed one of their wheelchairs for two weeks before I did the role. I lived in that chair for several days, just so I wouldn't make any mistakes. Most of the guys in the episode with me are actually from the Naval Hospital, all paraplegics and quadriplegics, except for me and Bill Bixby. Bill didn't have to learn the wheelchair, because he was playing someone who had been freshly paralyzed. It was a little horrific to see what those great guys from the hospital went through every day. All those guys playing paraplegics in the scenes with Bill and I were real paraplegics. Bill Bixby leaned over to me one day and said something really profound. He whispered, 'After this scene is over,* we're the only guys who can get up and walk out of here.' *That was true and I really respected those guys for what they went through.* "For the scene where The Hulk comes in, Hulk didn't just pick me up, he picked me up and ran with me, I couldn't believe it. Lou picked

Lou Ferrigno's Hulk carries Denny Miller in "The Harder They Fall."

me up and RAN WITH ME in his arms, like I was a doll! It made me sort of mad, because I thought I was strong! I'm over six feet tall and he made me feel like a weakling!

"*He also got green paint all over me. I had to change my shirt after every take. I just saw Lou last month and he still looks just like that, only he's not green! He's a personal trainer now and does a lot of charity work for deaf people organizations, which I appreciate, because my mother is deaf. I liked Bill Bixby very much. I used to play golf with Bill and he always beat me because he was very good. I used to watch him play.*"

LOU FERRIGNO (Hulk): "*I picked Denny Miller up and carried him in the wheelchair — and then I ran with him! Luckily, back then I was much stronger and younger, but after a couple takes, I said, 'Okay, guys, this is it!' He was a big guy. I love that shot of the wheelchair flying up the stairs and hitting the wall. That seemed like a great moment for anyone frustrated with being in a wheelchair. The doors open and you see The Hulk! The way it was done in your imagination is such a rush. Picturing David Banner so angry at what's happened to him that he hurls his own wheelchair…It's a powerful image."*

HULK HIGHLIGHT

The scene where David changes into Hulk and The Hulk is stunned to find he can't walk, even punching his own legs in frustration, is some of the best acting on the series from Ferrigno.

HULK FACTS

A real-life paraplegic and activist for the rights of the disabled, Alan Toy (Bobby) is still an actor. He can be seen alongside Tom Cruise in Oliver Stone's *Born on the Fourth Of July*, Jennifer Garner in *Alias* and Rob Lowe in *Brothers and Sisters*.

"INTERVIEW WITH THE HULK"

Season 4, Episode 71
Airdate: April 3, 1981
Directed By Patrick Boyriven
Written By Alan Cassidy
Banner's alias "David Butler"

Cast

Dr. David Banner	Bill Bixby
Jack McGee	Jack Colvin
The Hulk	Lou Ferrigno
Emerson Fletcher	Michael Conrad
Mark Roberts	Walter Brooke
Stella Verdugo	Jan Sterling
Dr. Carolyn Fields	Mariette Hartley
Laura Banner	Lara Parker
Dr. Elaina Marks	Susan Sullivan

At the *National Register*, down-on-his-luck reporter Emerson Fletcher, a Hulk skeptic, shares an office with Jack McGee while the building is being remodeled. Fletcher swipes one of Jack's Hulk leads and is shocked to meet the deceased David Banner. Amazed to find him alive, the corrupt reporter blackmails the fugitive physicist into giving him the story of a lifetime: an interview with The Incredible Hulk!

With a sick child and problems of his own, Emerson bonds with Banner and becomes sympathetic to his plight. In turn, David appreciates the chance to unburden himself. He tells Fletcher, "It's such a relief to tell someone that understands technically and still has sensitivity and compassion." McGee frets to Mark Roberts that Emerson Fletcher will break the story of The Hulk.

David Banner talking about himself to Fletcher is compelling. He explains to the reporter that The Hulk was born because "I became obsessed with finding the key to the inner strength that all people have," a nice nod to the opening credits. David also provides an impressive defense/justification of The Hulk. "From what I can gather, the creature has never wantonly destroyed anything or seriously hurt anybody. Apparently, he is motivated to deal with whatever frustrates or angers me. And I can't tell you what it's like every time when I…come back, wondering what he has done."

Being a man of integrity, Fletcher refuses to publish the story or tell McGee who the elusive Hulk really is. "Jack, sit down and relax," Roberts reassures him. "He doesn't even believe in The Hulk."

"I think that he just got converted," Jack responds.

Once again, *The National Register* leads to another great episode of *The Incredible Hulk*. "Interview with the Hulk" is anchored by character actor Michael Conrad, who would go on to Emmy-winning glory in *Hill Street Blues* later that same year. Conrad's veteran lawman would urge the cops "to be careful out there."

Patrick Boyriven only helmed two *Hulk*s, which is a shame, because this and "Equinox" are quite good. Both showcase Jack McGee. Jack Colvin does a great job, having his reporter eaten up by fear that he is going to get scooped on his Hulk story.

The episode makes a big deal over the nobility of Michael Conrad's character, Emerson Fletcher…but the only reason he lands the story is by stealing one of Jack's tips!

This episode is infamous as it was being shot when Bixby's son died.

PATRICK BOYRIVEN (Director): *"I think Michael Conrad was already sick at the time. He was a one tone guy and I had to get him to have a softness in a scene with the child playing his daughter. He's blackmailing Banner for his story so he can care for his daughter, but to me, he was just flat in this scene. As a parent, if you have a scene with a dying child, you immediately relate to it, but Michael wasn't really coming across. Conrad was a big guy playing a cop on* Hill Street Blues, *which he had just started shooting. I decided not to push it — he was just a guest star on one* Hulk *episode and Michael did the best he could. He collapsed and died two years later."*

MARK A. BURLEY (Unit Production Manager): *"Bill Bixby's son dying was devastating, Bill was a fairly private person and he did some 'self medicating' to deal with it. Drugs. I know he cleaned himself up when he quit acting to focus solely on directing. No matter what happened to him on* Hulk, *he was always nice to people and great to the crew."*

HULK FACTS
Look for flashback cameos by the dearly departed Laura Banner, Elaina Marks and Carolyn Fields!

Director Boyriven produced Johnson's *V* miniseries, and its sequel, *V: The Final Battle.*

Michael Conrad starred in *The Longest Yard* with the first Hulk Richard Kiel. He died within two years of his episode and his death was written into *Hill Street Blues.*

Actress Jan Sterling starred in Humphrey Bogart's last film, *The Harder They Fall* and Billy Wilder's dark masterpiece, *Ace In The Hole.*

"HALF NELSON"
Season 4, Episode 72
Airdate: April 17, 1981
Directed By Barry Crane
Written By Andrew Schneider
Banner's alias "David Benley"

Cast

Dr. David Banner	Bill Bixby
Jack McGee	Jack Colvin
The Hulk	Lou Ferrigno
Buster Caldwell	Tommy Madden
Gregor	H.B. Haggerty
Channing	Paul Henry Itkin

Kelly . . . . .David Himes
Promoter . . . . Joey Forman
Mitzi . . . . .Elaine Joyce

David meets Buster, a tough midget wrestler who tries to compensate for
his size by telling fibs, lies and tall tales as well as boasting of having dangerous connections. Unfortunately, these stories get him and David in trouble
with real criminals. Wow, a fourth season that has some of *The Incredible
Hulk*'s flat-out coolest episodes like "Prometheus," "The Harder They Fall"
and "The First," suddenly has David Banner trying to solve problems for
midget wrestlers! One can only conclude that poor *Hulk* has jumped the
shark. The weakest episode from usually reliable writer Andrew Schneider.

HULK FACTS
Barry Crane, who directed multiple episodes of *Hulk*, including this one,
was found bludgeoned to death in the garage of his Studio City home on
July 5, 1985. No one was ever charged and the crime remains unsolved.

Tommy Madden appeared on *The Magician* with Bill Bixby.

"DANNY"
Season 4, Episode 73
Airdate: May 15, 1981
Directed By Mark A. Burley
Written By Diane Frolov
Banner's alias: David Bentzen

Cast
Dr. David Banner . . . . Bill Bixby
The Hulk . . . . .Lou Ferrigno
Nat. . . . . .Don Stroud
Ben . . . . Bruce Wright
Red . . . . Taylor Lacher
Rachel . . . . Robin Dearden
Hugh. . . . . Art La Fleur

David befriends Rachel, a young widow with a baby, the "Danny" of
the title. Rachel is trying to get the child as far away as she can from Nat,
her volatile criminal brother-in-law. This is an action packed episode,

enlivened by The Hulk carrying a baby around! Considering that this was Mark A. Burley's directorial debut, it's surprisingly assured. What lunatic would assign the poor guy on his first time out babies, chases and stunts?

Big screen bad guy Don Stroud has a lot of fun as the angry, wild Nat. Robin Dearden is good as the determined Mom. Essentially, this is a variation on *Hulk*'s on the run episodes like "A Death In The Family", "Escape From Los Santos" and "Brain Child" (which also starred Robin Dearden), where Banner and a beautiful girl are being pursued by bad guys in an outdoor environment. "Danny" switches things up by having the girl with Banner bring a baby along. They would revisit this formula again in the fifth season's "Two Godmothers", which went even further by making the girl on the run pregnant.

MARK A. BURLEY (Director, "Danny"): *"I was 26 or 27, and that episode of* Incredible Hulk *was my directorial debut. I was young and stupid enough to think I could direct it! I started out as an assistant director and, after two or three seasons, the Unit Production Manager moved up and I became the new UPM. People like Kenneth Johnson on* The Incredible Hulk *allowed me to direct. I was a UPM on* Simon & Simon *and they didn't want me to direct, just do my UPM job.*

"Directing 'Danny' was scary, because I had to deal with a baby, car chases, fights and The Hulk for my very first time out. It was intimidating, because it was all exteriors. The show was called 'Danny' because it was named after a baby, so I had to work with a real baby. As a first time director, I was happy that Bill Bixby was very gracious to me. He was a director himself, but very nice. The shooting schedule for an episode of The Incredible Hulk *was supposed to be seven days, but they were never shot in that time…Shooting always ran over by a day or two. I did my episode in eight days because I got rained out on location. Being all exteriors, I could not shoot anything else while it rained.*

"I shot 'Danny' on the Oil Fields' land behind Magic Mountain and at Indian Dunes. Back then, everybody shot at Indian Dunes before the horrific Twilight Zone *accident. Indian Dunes is the scene where Bill and Robin Dearden have to cross the stream. When they had the helicopter crash (that killed actor Vic Morrow and two children), it was closed to filming for a long time after that. The land behind Magic Mountain had been used for a lot of* The Incredible Hulk *episodes. Robin was very sweet — she played the mother and she was great to work with. Robin was playing a woman who was trying to get her baby away from a bad guy played by Don Stroud. Bill takes Robin, the baby and a suitcase of the baby's stuff. There was one point where Bill Bixby is*

*lugging the mother's suitcase and I said to him, 'Make the suitcase look heavy.'
Bill said, 'But that doesn't match what I did before!' I thought 'Oh no, it won't
match', but it turned out okay. Don Stroud was fun as the bad guy. He did
a good job, but there was one day he turned up really late because he was…
Enjoying himself, shall we say? That kind of stuff was more prevalent on sets
in the '70s and '80s than it is today."*

*"Babies are always hard to deal with because they never do what you want
them to do. We had two babies playing Danny and each baby was only good
for about 20 minutes! I would always have a shot of Robin putting the baby
down so we could cut to a reaction shot of the baby but never had to have the
baby in the action…Of course, we had to have a shot of Lou carrying the baby
and we actually had Lou hold the real baby, who I don't think was thrilled to
be carried by a big green man! For all the action shots of Hulk with the baby,
that was always Manny Perry running with a rubber baby! I enjoyed the scene
where Hulk kicked over the windmill."*

HULK HIGHLIGHT
As noted above, The Hulk carries a baby *and* knocks over a windmill.

HULK FACTS
Director Burley was production manager on the *Hulk* TV show.

Don Stroud appears in *Frogtown II* with Lou Ferrigno and Charles Napier.

Guest Bruce Wright is a rare *Incredible Hulk* three-timer! Look for him
in "Sideshow" and "A Solitary Place."

Art La Fleur punches out Hitler in the cult movie *Zone Troopers!*

"PATTERNS"
Season 4, Episode 74
Airdate: May 22, 1981
Directed By Nick Havinga
Written By Reuben Leder

Cast

Dr. David Banner . . . . Bill Bixby
The Hulk . . . . Lou Ferrigno
Sam Brandes . . . . .Eddie Barth

Liz Brandes. . . . . Laurie Heineman
Solly . . . . .Joshua Shelley
Malamud. . . . . Paul Marin
Lesley . . . . .Quinn O'Hara

David has to protect Sam, a clothes manufacturer, from loan sharks, until his daughter Liz can launch the show introducing their new fall fashions.

An extremely dull episode, especially when this season started with such a bang from Kenneth Johnson. You've got a giant green monster who can punch through walls, so you have to ask: Are backstage problems in the fashion industry really the best use of his time?!

QUINN O'HARA (Lesley): *"I honestly don't remember doing the show at all, but I did date Bill Bixby, so it is possible…"*

HULK FACTS
Eddie Barth co-starred in the classic film *Shaft*.

Look for *Star Trek: Deep Space Nine*'s Robert O'Reilly as a bad guy.

HULK PROFILE
RIC DRASIN, THE INCREDIBLE DEMI-HULK

One of the strangest events to occur on the show came in "Prometheus." David Banner is fused mid-transformation into a brand-new life form, The Demi-Hulk. Bigger than Banner but smaller than Hulk, he's a slow-witted, quick to anger brute. The Demi-Hulk has enough of Banner's brain to know he's in deep trouble and enough of Hulk's rage to realize there's nothing he can do about it. He desperately tries to keep his temper under control, but manages to terrify the blind girl he's staying with through his sudden outbursts.

Things quickly get worse when he's captured by the US Government, who believe him to be an alien. To play the half-man/half-monster, they cast World Wrestling Federation wrestler, bodybuilder and actor Ric Drasin. The muscular, bald and goateed Drasin is an accomplished renaissance man who has produced and directed films, as well as designed the Gold's Gym bald weightlifter logo and the World Gym gorilla. "I always drew cartoons and was good at it. I designed that for fun and it became world-famous!" Ric Drasin had been playing the half-Banner/

half-Hulk glimpsed during transformation scenes since the series began. Here, an entire episode was set around that incarnation. "Ric's an old friend and he did a great job," praises Lou Ferrigno. "He was able to do those episodes while I was shooting another one. He really did look like a combination of Bill and me!" Drasin feels that "Prometheus" "was a cool two-part episode and I'm very proud of being The Demi-Hulk.

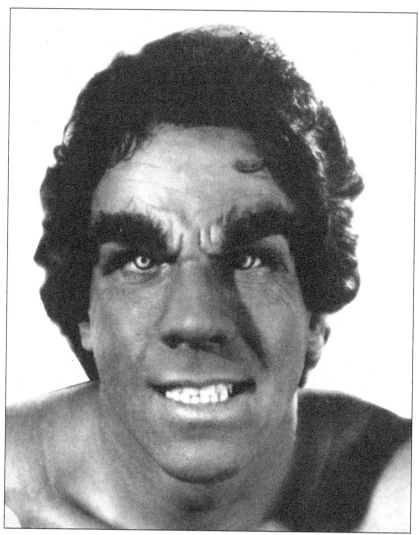

Ric Drasin is The Demi-Hulk!

Because Bill was stuck in mid-transformation for two episodes, they needed someone who was bigger than Bill and smaller than Lou. Bill was a small guy, Lou's a big guy and I was right in the middle, so I got it. I had the muscularity that Bill didn't have. Lou Ferrigno asked me to do it. Lou and I have been friends forever and he was the one who called me in on the *Hulk* gig.

Ric Drasin in human form.

"Lou said to me, 'They're looking for a middle guy for when Bill Bixby becomes Hulk. You look enough like Bill and me that it would probably work.' I went in to meet the producer, Kenneth Johnson, and he said, 'Oh, my God — It looks like Bill and Lou had a baby and you were it! You've got the part.'"

The final touch for him to resemble a Hulking David Banner came when "Bill Bixby made sure I got my hair cut at Little Joe's on Sunset to look just like his," Drasin laughs. "Little Joe was Bill's stylist. It cost $150 to make my hair look like his. I told Bill, 'I should have cut it myself and kept the money!' I thought that they spent a lot of money on something that really wasn't necessary. Bill was a wonderful guy and genuinely nice." Once he got the role, "They immediately did makeup tests on me, because they really weren't sure what color I should be. They couldn't decide if I should be brown or green. They painted me green and took me to see Kenny on the set at Universal. The Studio Tour tram suddenly goes rolling by and all of these tourists start screaming 'It's The Hulk! It's Hulk, it's Huuulllkkk!' When Ken [Johnson] saw me, he thought I should be brown like an acorn, because he felt at that stage of the transformation, it was right before I turned green. I wore a forehead appliance with a nose attached."

The makeup "was my favorite part of it. Turning me into the Demi-Hulk was a two-hour application process. It was a protruding forehead with a big nose made of foam rubber and they added eyebrows to it. The rest was just makeup.

"Every time they ripped my Hulk forehead off, I would take it home to show my kids. I tried to keep them, but they deteriorated to the point where they just crumbled into powder!"

To get the proper motivation for his Demi-Hulk, "Kenny told me that I was moody and frustrated because I was caught in the middle of the transformation. I can't go back, I can't go forward. Kenny said, 'You're stuck and you *know* you're stuck! You wanna either become Lou or go back to being Bill, but you can't.'

"Laurie Prange played the blind girl who gets trapped with me and she was sweet," he says fondly. "She was even cool when we got to the set at four or five in the morning. In the scene where I take my frustrations out on her table, I crushed the teapot out of rage and cut my thumb. Bill Bixby said, 'Get a tetanus shot — you don't want to get lockjaw!' So I did.

"The Hulk eyes were hard contact lenses," Drasin recalls. "Bill Bixby really hated wearing them. The opthane numbed your eyes, so I was fine with them and Lou was too, but within three seconds of having them in, Bill Bixby was screaming, 'Get them out! Get them out, they're driving me nuts! It feels like a thumb in my eye.' Nowadays, everything is soft lenses and he wouldn't have a problem with them today. I kept 'em and wore them once for Halloween without opthane and the contact lenses hurt like hell."

For the "Prometheus" two-parter, "We shot both episodes on the backlot of Universal and a lot of it was filmed in the woods of Valencia, California, behind the Magic Mountain amusement park for a couple of weeks. We would eat by this little creek we were filming at. Lou was in training for The Olympia. He asked if I wanted to work out with him. I said, 'I don't feel like hopping in a car and driving all the way to Venice at this hour, Lou; traffic is gonna be murder,' so Lou got a chopper to pick us up on set and fly us all the way to Venice!" All through shooting "Prometheus," "Lou was upset; worrying that Arnold [Schwarzenegger] would win The Olympia. He wanted to beat Arnold, so Lou went to the gym every day. Lou invited me into his motor home to eat with him, because we were training together and he wanted to make sure I was on a high protein diet like him.

"During the whole time we were filming, all he could talk about was Arnold Schwarzenegger and how he wanted to beat him. Lou would ask me, 'What do you think Schwarzenegger is doing right now?' I would say, 'Louie, you have a hit TV series now. It's gonna run for five years! What do you care about Arnold for?' and Lou would say, 'It's The Olympia! I've got to beat him in The Olympia!' Of course, Arnold won The Olympia.

"Arnold, Lou and I were all friends; as was Manny Perry, who played The Stunt Hulk. We'd all go to the gym and lunch together. Lou and I did a Budweiser commercial together a couple years ago and they put Lou and me in these amazing barbarian/caveman costumes. Whenever Lou and I get together, we always catch up on whatever we've been up to. I love him and always enjoyed my *Hulk* experience!"

John Goodwin gets Lou Ferrigno ready for action.

JOHN GOODWIN, HULK MAKEUP MAN

Cheerful makeup artist John Goodwin has worked on many acclaimed horror movies over the years, including *John Carpenter's The Thing*, *Critters*, the giant worm epic *Tremors*, in which he also plays a doomed road worker, and the gory TV series *CSI: Crime Scene Investigation* and its spin-off, *CSI:NY*.

"I enjoy those shows," he says happily. "I have done over seven years of *CSI*, doing all sorts of corpses and bruises." Starting out as a young makeup artist on the Universal Studios backlot, Goodwin learned under talented artists like Norman Leavitt. At the time, Leavitt was turning Lou Ferrigno into The Incredible Hulk every week on the show, so Goodwin worked on that. Eventually, Goodwin did the job on the TV movies *The*

Incredible Hulk Returns with Leavitt and *Trial of the Incredible Hulk*. When *The Incredible Hulk* first appeared in a 1977 TV movie, The Hulk was a green-skinned, wild-haired savage with dilated eyes and bright yellow teeth. His look was created by Universal Studios makeup designer Werner Keppler. "The Incredible Hulk on the show was originally designed by committee," explains John Goodwin. "The *Hulk* pilot was a little before my time, but the decision was made for doing him with a forehead piece, a nose and the teeth. You don't really need the nose on Lou Ferrigno, but it does change his facial appearance. On a forehead appliance, it helps balance Hulk's face out, adding some more rubber to the face. We used a green castor-based makeup on Lou's face. If they were to do him over today, they would probably give him a squarish jaw like the comic book Hulk has. In the comics, The Hulk has a square jaw and his whole head is shaped like a box.

"It would have been nice to add a neck and jaw piece to give him that look, but under the demands of television at that time, getting that forehead piece and nose on while making him entirely green, was incredibly time consuming on a TV schedule. You had very little time to spare for anything else, even when you had your full time."

Turning Lou Ferrigno into The Hulk "really was a two-hour makeup process. With the movie *Hulk*s, they have gone to the opposite extreme. They lost the human quality of the actor playing The Hulk. Now he's more of a CG-effect. Hulk's makeup was pretty good for the time," Goodwin notes. "To have pulled it off under a television schedule is amazing. I can't think of any other television series that had a working full appliance makeup every episode at that time. Later on, when the machinery was in place, you had shows like *Beauty and the Beast,* but even they didn't have a character like The Hulk. The transformations were so important to *The Incredible Hulk*; it was the highlight of every episode of the show when Bill Bixby would change, even when he didn't want to. If he didn't change into The Hulk twice an episode, the fans would have gone nuts!" Hulk's headpiece "was there to give him a good snarly brow and that's about it. Most of the appliance was covered by the wig. You could glue the appliance to Hulk's wig without messing with Lou's hair that much. The wig was held by rubber bands in the back, so you didn't have to glue it all down in the front. You had that nice Hulk brow that would cover Lou's eyebrows and the human part of the forehead. It was a good changeover in the transformation from Bill Bixby, because you could put a forehead/brow appliance on Bill and add contact lenses, then cut to Lou, so you had some steps to go in the change. That's one of the reasons that brow piece was there, to be part of the transformation into The Hulk. With every step as David Banner changed, Bixby would look more like what Ferrigno became," Goodwin says pleasantly. "I know that when they started the original pilot for *The Incredible Hulk*, they didn't know how they were gonna do it. It was a big feature for TV with a big star like Bixby, but they thought they could do all the changes for him onscreen into the whole Hulk. That wasn't gonna be very practical in television.

"For Bixby's part of the transformation, if you were making him up as The Hulk, he wouldn't be able to play his part on the same day of shooting. They came up with the idea of cheating one actor for another (Ric Drasin would play the in-between Hulk, during te Bixby-to-Ferrigno transformation). It's been done a lot, but not so much at that time. It worked very well. People on the show like [producer/writer/director] Nic Corea stood up for it, and took the time to get some good transformations with Bixby. If the disparity between Banner and Hulk was too great, they would come back to re-shoot the transformation. They had some shots in close-up that they would use a lot, because you couldn't see the background, but they also shot a lot of new ones. They knew the transformations were very important. The forehead really helps the transformations and sets the character of The Hulk."

Goodwin missed the first *Hulk* TV movies, but wound up working on the weekly series under Norman Leavitt. "Norman is great," says the makeup artist. "Norman Leavitt did Lou's Hulk makeup for years on the television show. The facial appliances for Lou were done in the lab, but Norman did all his other makeup. I worked at the Universal Makeup Lab and would run Hulk appliances, helping Werner Keppler do Hulk teeth as the original series was going. I also made up Jake Steinfeld and Manny Perry for the Universal Studios Tour. I made Manny Perry up on location for the show as well. I felt bad when they were doing the *Hulk* TV movies in Canada, because Manny got cut out of the action." An added degree of difficulty for makeup artists doing Hulk came "because Lou had hearing aids in both ears. It was very disorienting for him if someone fooled with his hearing aids. A makeup artist who worked briefly on the series before Norman Leavitt was told not to touch the hearing aids. I wasn't there, but a director wanted a shot of The Hulk's ear, so he started to paint the hearing aids and Lou got a bit…feisty! It was an unfortunate, unhappy situation," Goodwin says quietly. "Norman Leavitt came up with the solution of putting green balloons around the hearing aids. He went to the store, got an ordinary bag of balloons and took all the green ones, which were a fairly good match for the green used on Lou.

He used the balloons and rubber bands to hide the inner ear and hearing aids. Lou was an enormously patient guy for what he went through every episode, but you have to understand: he has two hearing aids and a lot of times, the crew would talk around him like he wasn't even there. He just wanted to know what was going on. The guy painting his hearing aids did it while Lou was concentrating on something else, so he hauled off

Hulk makeup artist John Goodwin can't get enough of large green monsters. PHOTO BY PATRICK JANKIEWICZ

and punched the guy out of sheer surprise! Doing it was a difficult job for the makeup guy, but Norman Leavitt pulled it off beautifully. I don't think they realized how good Norman was. He was starting out then. Norman works hard and gets along with everybody. Getting along with anybody is an enormous skill for a makeup man, especially when you're putting appliances on somebody every day. You've got to have a good working relationship with the person you're putting the prosthetics onto; you can't just put 'em on and leave! You've got to be part of their lives and help them put the makeup appliances on every day.

"Applying his makeup was not just putting the facial appliances on Lou, because he's green all over. Norman would be stained green every day. The Hulk's green paint was that body makeup Kryolin made and it was as good as anything at the time, but it got on everything! I would be stained green every day while doing it. I have a box of Hulk makeup at home and it's still stained with the stuff!" Working with The Hulk could be a challenge. "When I started doing *The Incredible Hulk*, Norman told me, 'John, it's a two-hour makeup and the first time you do it, Lou will roll with it, but you've got to be able to have it done in 40 minutes!' Lou put up with me, but Norman had it down to a science. I got faster as the days went by. If it took too long, Lou got grumpy," Goodwin grins. "And you wouldn't like him when he's grumpy! He had a right to be grumpy; he wanted to get it done fast. Lou was good about it. They would bring Lou in extra early and not work him 'til four hours after the makeup went on. He hated that, because it would cut into his life. The makeup artist had to talk to the ADs [assistant directors] and let them know when they should schedule Lou for makeup.

"I remember many times, Lou and I just sat for hours in his trailer watching monster movies because they had no idea what time to bring us in! He'd get very cynical about it. *'What's taking them so long?'* I would say, 'Well, Lou, they brought us in too early again.' It happened all the time. Lou Ferrigno would be brought in, made up and sit there all day without ever being used. When they really needed Lou for the first shot of the day, you would have to get him all prepped up fast." Doing *The Incredible Hulk Returns* presented some new challenges. "When they did the later TV movies, Universal's Makeup Lab was closed. They contacted Norman to do the TV movies, but he couldn't do one of them, so I did one and then for the second one, *Trial of the Incredible Hulk*, we shot in Canada. Norman and I took turns doing it because we were both doing *Moonlighting* at the time. We covered each other on the show and Lou didn't work that many days on that movie. That was on *Trial*, which was mostly about Daredevil. I made the appliances for Lou on that." To re-create Hulk for the TV movies, "There were no molds to be found for Hulk, so I re-sculpted Lou's headpieces. I knew The Hulk's shape pretty well and Norman had one foam latex appliance that he gave me. It was beginning to deteriorate, but I could still see the sculpture on it.

"I worked with Bill Bixby, but never put the appliances on him. I thought Bixby was a very good actor/director. He did 67 set-ups in one day on *Trial of the Incredible Hulk*. For the time and money spent on that, he got the most out of it and he knew exactly where and what to shoot."

One problem on *Trial* is that Bill Bixby has a big bushy beard that disappears when he Hulks Out. "We didn't deal with Bill's look on that, because I don't think a beard would have looked very good on The Hulk. I think they wanted to do that movie without using any American makeup

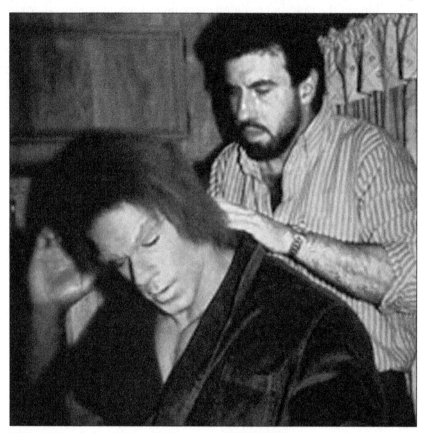

Hulk makeup artist John Goodwin fixes Hulk's hair.

artists and it showed. *Trial of the Incredible Hulk* was great for me because Stan Lee was there! Because I was doing makeup, I was on set all day, so Stan Lee and I got to talk for hours," Goodwin marvels. "Just hearing him talk about everything besides Marvel Comics, I was amazed and impressed. The man has truly led an incredible life; he's done everything!"

To re-create The Hulk's look for the later TV movies, "We went to Lou's home in Santa Monica so I could do the teeth impressions. It's funny, The Hulk's teeth make a big difference on the character and Lou

Ferrigno has really small teeth in real life. When Hulk's teeth are in, they help give a bit of squareness to his face. In the comics, you frequently see Hulk's teeth, but with Lou Ferrigno's Hulk, you rarely if ever saw his upper teeth. Lou would really work 'em, but with his small teeth, that made him really hard to fit for teeth," he reveals. "His teeth are perfect, but there's no undercuts for us to clink something onto them. Fortunately, Hulk didn't have a lot of dialogue, just growling. The Hulk's teeth on the original television show were a veneer that they would put on top of his own with polygrip. For the TV movies, I made two or three sets of Hulk teeth. Norman was the guy who had done The Hulk day to day on the show and he could answer any question I had about Hulk's look. Makeup had progressed by the time we did the later TV movies, but Lou didn't want to change a thing. He wanted to do it the way it always was. Lou's makeup was applied with Max Factor gum. We applied the pieces and blended them with dual adhesive. This is the technology that was used on the original *Planet of the Apes*. I said, 'Lou, if you let me use the [new] adhesive, it won't have to be stuck back together when you start sweating.' He said no, he didn't want any changes whatsoever." The color green used for The Hulk "was a dark lime green. There was a trick that people don't have to worry about so much anymore, but you did then. The castor makeup that went on Hulk's face with the rubber pieces was a slightly different color green than the green that went on his body — the body was a water-based makeup. Both were made by Kryolin out of Germany. Werner Keppler set that up when he created the look for the pilot. When the Universal Makeup Lab went down, Kryolin stopped making the huge tubs that we used to make The Hulk green. Happily, Norman had some he kept. If he hadn't, The Hulk would not have been the same color. If we were out of it, it was all over. Norman applied it on every episode, so he knew Hulk's makeup inside and out.

"After you powdered the castor makeup and it stayed on the skin for a little while, it actually changed color! If you judged the body makeup as being the exact same color as the face makeup, what would happen is Hulk's body would look kind of blue while his face would be lime green! So his makeup had to be really balanced. It noticeably showed up if you didn't. Sometimes you would put the castor makeup on his neck as well, to help it blend in.

"Usually, you would take the water-based makeup all the way to his chin line. It's funny, castor/appliance-based makeups look a little different in the jar than they do on the skin. Water evaporating from the water-based makeup is what would change Hulk from green to blue, or if there was too much water in the makeup. You have got to be afraid of it at first, thinking, 'It doesn't match!' But after awhile, it did match.

"When we did the *Hulk* movie in Canada, the Canadian producers didn't realize that The Hulk was an appliance makeup, where you would need a forehead appliance as well as teeth and nose. They just thought you made him green, so they wanted a makeup artist just to paint Lou green! We warned them about that, but they didn't realize it until a couple days before we shot. I was up for two nights straight getting Hulk's forehead and noses ready when they realized that was it! The producers didn't talk to Lou beforehand and he didn't want any changes. He liked the character and didn't want any changes to Hulk's makeup or the way they had been done. That's not too much to ask."

Canadian makeup artists started swiping Hulk's used foreheads. "There was nobody up there who did appliances like that, so Canadian makeup gals started taking the pieces out of the trash after we used them to find out how to reverse engineer them. You can't re-use them, but they wanted to learn how to do them. We were doing the production company a favor, but they brought us in too late on that.

"Bill Bixby was a wonderful guy, he knew the character so well and when he would direct, he came in prepared. He wanted to make sure everything was good with Lou. Bill had his own makeup people, while Norman and I did Hulk."

HULK PROFILE

DICK DUROCK: FRYE'S CREATURE

Frye's Creature makes quite an impression; a crazed, murderous Hulk who holds a small town in the grip of terror. A Gamma-powered monster, he's the only foe on the show who can kill Lou Ferrigno's Hulk in 'The First'. As Frye's Creature, we see a Hulk lacking David Banner's compassionate humanity. Instead, he's a brutal, perpetually raging Hulk with a long list of grievances. Under the green skin was actor/stuntman Dick Durock, who played the remorseless Hulk. "As Frye's Creature, I'm the bad Hulk, a very nasty guy — I'm a monster and killer," the folksy Dick Durock chuckles. "I really loved how I appeared on that show. I look like this skinny, crazy Hulk!"

Incredible Hulk star Lou Ferrigno explains that, "They used Dick Durock for the evil Hulk because he's a tall, well-trained stuntman. They didn't want to take a chance with another bodybuilder who might not be able to handle it. Dick knows how to fall, give and take punches and can handle himself as an actor. Dick does a great job as this evil Hulk! Ironically, only Dick and I know what it's like to be green superhero monsters, because he went on to play Swamp Thing!" Durock, who starred in two movies and a hit TV series as the heroic monster Swamp Thing, feels, "My Hulk is not heroic like Lou's Hulk — he's angry and murderous! My Hulk is loosely based on the *Frankenstein* legend. Dell Frye changes into an evil

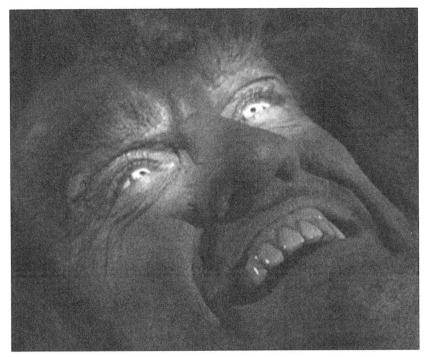

Dick Durock as Frye's Creature.

Hulk who likes to kill. In the '50s, a scientist brings this creature to life, thinking it will better mankind. Instead, it's totally berserk and the doctor has to put him down again. Cut to the modern-day Hulk, who finds the creature resurrected again. Because the Banner Hulk is essentially good and my Hulk, known as Frye's Creature, is evil, we have a confrontation, where Lou Ferrigno and I battle over the cure."

The actor/stuntman "is pleased that 'The First' are two of the most popular episodes of the show. People really love this two-parter where the Hulks fight. Basically, I was Hulk the first. I'm The Hulk who didn't really turn out right. Looking for a cure, David Banner finds a guy who worked with a scientist to improve humanity but it didn't work…Instead of improving humanity, he turned into this berserk green killer, me!

"Lou Ferrigno was fun to work with. I looked at being the evil Hulk as being a professional with something to do and you're happy when it comes out okay. I was very happy with it. There's a scene in the show that always makes me laugh. It's this sequence where I have to jump up on a windowsill and turn back to the camera and go 'RAAAARRRRGH!' with these big fake teeth," he smiles at the memory. "I would accidentally spit the teeth out of my mouth whenever I did the Hulk growl!

In oversized wax teeth, green paint and a Don King hairdo, Dick Durock's Hulk has plenty to be mad about!

"Frank Orsatti was director of both episodes and he was also a great stuntman, so he made sure the fight between the two Hulks looked really good. I fought Lou, not [stunt Hulk] Manny Perry, because we were in tight spaces in a laboratory. Manny was on hand, a good guy and an excellent stuntman. We shot onstage on the Universal backlot."

To play a Hulk, Durock notes, "they paint you green, put in the wax teeth and give you a big Don King hairdo. The hardest part was the white-out contact lenses that Lou had to wear as The Hulk. I wore them once for my episodes and that was enough for me! I never got used to 'em and I only had them in for three or four minutes! Unlike working with your own eyes, those lenses took away all your peripheral vision, you only had tunnel vision. Thank God I didn't have to wear those playing Swamp Thing!"

Dick Durock became a superhero in his own right, as misunderstood monster *Swamp Thing.*

He found being a Hulk "was a piece of cake compared to being Swamp Thing. As a Hulk, you would just wash off the green paint at the end of the day and go home, while being the Swamp Thing meant you were in a foam-rubber Swamp Thing costume that weighed 80 pounds *and* running around in a real swamp! Being Swamp Thing was no picnic. The worst part about being a Hulk — and Lou would verify this, too — were the damn contact lenses! You wear them for five or ten minutes and you want to rip your own eyes out, it hurts so bad, but they look effective. They have white lenses and if you wore them long enough, they made you want to go berserk, just like The Hulk!"

SEASON FIVE

The Incredible Hulk enters its last abbreviated season. CBS only ordered a small amount of episodes instead of a full season because network head Harvey Shepard refused to order any more. Unfortunately for CBS, every show placed in *Hulk*'s timeslot failed to attract an audience of even one-third of those watching *Hulk*. That said, the fifth season of *The Incredible Hulk* is considerably less interesting than the bold fourth one. There is no Kenneth Johnson-directed opener. Instead, the season begins with the okay "Phenom" and is hit and miss after that.

"THE PHENOM"

Season 5, Episode 75
Airdate: October 2, 1981
Directed By Bernard McEveety
Written By Reuben Leder
Banner's alias: "David Bedecker"

Cast

Dr. David Banner	Bill Bixby
Jack McGee	Jack Colvin
The Hulk	Lou Ferrigno
Joe Dumming	Brett Cullen
Audrey	Anne Lockhart
Cyrus T. McCormack	Dick O'Neill
Johnny	Ken Swofford
Bernard Devlin	Robert Donner

David accompanies Joe, a naive country hayseed from North Carolina, on his way to tryouts for major league baseball team, The Roosters. Joe is likable, but can't read or write. He's terrified that he will be found out and sent back to North Carolina to work a plow. David sticks around so

Joe's not snookered by his deceitful manager, the not-so-subtly-named Devlin. Sports reporter Cyrus warns David about Devlin, before getting drunk and passing out. When Cyrus' editor threatens to fire him, David takes the writer's notes and stays up all night writing Cyrus' story on a manual typewriter. Meanwhile, Devlin sets his pet vamp Audrey onto Joe to cut him off from David. Banner innocently goes to the pitcher's hotel room, but he's intercepted by Devlin's goons, who rough him up. The Hulk evens the score and Audrey falls for Joe after he tries to shield her from Hulk.

Considering what professional baseball players are paid, David's concern seems entirely misplaced and he would have been better off helping someone else this week! Joe and David's warm friendship feels genuine and makes the episode fresher than it should be. "The Phenom" is a loose rip-off of the classic musical *Damn Yankees*, right down to having a protagonist named "Joe." In *Yankees*, Ray Walston plays an unscrupulous manager who is really The Devil. Here, Robert Donner plays "Mr. Devlin," he's greedy and sinister, but he's not The Devil. Ironically, rival superhero show *The Greatest American Hero* did a superior episode ripping off *Damn Yankees*, "The Two Hundred Mile an Hour Fastball" within a month of *Hulk*'s. Donner gets to play a more suave villain than his usual sweaty fanatic roles while Anne Lockhart is striking as the temptress Audrey, a surprising change from her goody-goody clerk in "Captive Night". There have been some great *Hulk* episodes that revolved around sports, like "The Final Round," "Killer Instinct" and "Rainbow's End". While this isn't in their league, it is good.

MOST '80S LINE
"He's probably somewhere blow drying his hair so he'll look good on TV!"

HULK HIGHLIGHT
Hulk smacks a baseball out of the park and comes face to face with The Roosters' giant bird mascot, who promptly faints!

JILL SHERMAN DONNER: "Brett Cullen, who played the pitcher, was a really good actor. [My husband] Donner had a lot of fun doing it, which was a high compliment from him."

HULK FACTS

Sherman Field, where The Roosters play, is named after producer Jill Sherman, whose future husband stars in this episode.

Cullen went on to guest star on *Lost*.

Lockhart, O'Neill and Donner are all previous *Hulk* guests.

To show the force of Hulk hitting a baseball, it was shot out of an air-ram. Three takes were edited together to depict the ball flying out of sight. The ball was so small, the camera couldn't find it!

Bernard McEveety was a true TV genre director, doing shows like *Wild, Wild West, The Rockford Files, Airwolf, Knight Rider, Buck Rogers In The 25th Century* and *The A-Team*.

"TWO GODMOTHERS"
Season 5, Episode 76
Airdate: October 9, 1981
Directed By Michael Vejar
Written By Reuben Leder
Banner's alias: "David Barnes"

Cast

Dr. David Banner . . . . Bill Bixby
The Hulk . . . . .Lou Ferrigno
Hackett . . . . .Kathleen Nolan
Barbara Davis . . . . Suzanne Charny
Sondra. . . . . .Sandra Kerns
Grubb . . . . .Gloria Gifford
Lannie . . . . Penny Peyser

In a fun twist on the usual "convicts making a jailbreak" plot, David is grabbed by three convicts from a womens prison. Barbara, the head con, forces David to drive them when she places what he thinks is a knife to his side — it's actually a spoon! In their quest for freedom, they try to avoid re-capture by going through the mountains. They are pursued by a relentless female Warden, Hackett, obsessed with killing inmate Barbara. Hackett's assistant, Grubb, realizes her boss wants to murder the cons.

One of the escapees, Lannie, is pregnant. She's at the point of delivery and doesn't want her baby born behind bars. "I want my baby to be born in freedom," she insists. Because of his medical background, David hopes to save Lannie and her baby.

When Hackett learns Banner is a drifter using the ID of a Long Island schoolteacher, she decides "to treat him like the others, armed and extremely dangerous!" Hackett opens fire on Banner's abandoned truck, as Captain Grubb sarcastically states, "So much for due process!" Banner's hand is crushed, so he has to talk the women through delivering Lannie's baby, which turns out to be twins. Adding to their trouble, Banner has to guide them through a breach birth. One of the best episodes of the fifth season, "Two Godmothers" has three strong female leads, the pretty, hard-as-nails con Charny, sexy but unflappable tough cop Gloria Gifford and the adorable Penny Peyser. David's hand will recover because of The Hulk's fast metabolism. If the location looks familiar, that's because it's Vasquez Rocks, site of a thousand movies and TV shows but still best known for Captain Kirk's fight with The Gorn in the classic *Star Trek* episode, "Arena."

Suzanne Charny. PHOTO BY PATRICK JANKIEWICZ

SUZANNE CHARNY (Barbara Davis): "*I was a sci-fi freak, so I loved doing the series and working with The Hulk himself. I really love the scene where I break out of jail so my friend in prison, Penny Peyser, can have her baby in freedom! Of course, it's also a breach baby, to make it even more suspenseful.*

"*Bill Bixby was a great guy, very nice. Bill was a lot of fun to work with, and I had lunch with him a few times. He asked me out and I am so very glad I didn't go out with him, because I went out with Paul Brandon, his agent/manager, and it was a very good decision with a happy ending: we got married! Bill and I later became friends through Paul.*

"*Doing Hulk was great! We shot it on the backlot. I spend most of the show running from Kathleen Nolan, who is the cop trying to re-capture me. She finally arrests me at the end and I am released for good behavior and time served. Lou was sweet, but I had more of a rapport with Bill Bixby.*

"*I have a* Hulk *story, but it's off-color! We're shooting and there's a scene where The Hulk comes after me. I see him and completely freak out at this big green thing. All of the sudden, I shout 'STOP!' and I bent down, because he lost his putty nose. I look at this big green bulbous thing and say, 'He lost his foreskin!' Everybody laughed; it was an R-rated* Hulk *that week. Hulk picks me up in his arms and I felt very safe, because Lou is a big man and very strong. Hulk carries me into a cave and one of the crew said, 'Listen for when we say cut, because he can't hear.'*"

GLORIA GIFFORD (Captain Grubb): "*I did the very last year of both* Hulk *and Jack Klugman's* Quincy*. I liked Bixby and the other ladies, but I'm not a big fan of the sun or being outdoors. We shot this out at Indian Dunes; so naturally, the whole episode was shot outside! The first thing they told us when we got to Indian Dunes was 'Watch out for snakes!' I thought, 'I don't do stunts and I don't do snakes!' There's another scene where that older actor and I are going downhill in the truck. They mounted a camera on the hood and he suddenly yells, 'The brakes don't work!' The truck is going downhill and I got so nervous, I forgot to say my lines! You see him poke me with his elbow on camera to remind me to say them, but I really thought I was gonna die!*

Gloria Gifford. PHOTO BY PATRICK JANKIEWICZ

"*How I got the episode is pretty funny. I auditioned for a previous* Hulk*. In my audition, I pretended an umbrella was a gun and pulled* Hulk *casting director Ron Stephenson to the ground! I'm an acting teacher now and I always tell my students 'Never touch the casting director', but I did...And I got the gig! Then I couldn't do it. On the strength of that audition, they offered me another guest-starring role in 'Two Godmothers.' I was the tough cop, chasing all three women. I liked being this tough character. It's funny, Penny Peyser just friended me on Facebook with the line, 'We did an* Incredible Hulk *together!' Director Michael*

Vejar was very handsome and so kind to me. He was a stuntman turned director and he turned out to be a very good director."

PENNY PEYSER (Lannie): *"Bill Bixby was such a gentleman and a fine actor. You don't always see that combination. Very generous to his co-stars and fun. I also worked with him on* Rich Man, Poor Man II *prior to my stint on* Hulk. *I was new in Hollywood and he handled my naiveté with much kindness."*

HULK HIGHLIGHT

Both dog moments: Banner and The Hulk have their hand crushed by a boulder. A friendly dog licking his wound calms Hulk enough to change back to Banner. When the cops set german shepherds on The Hulk, he growls so loud, they stop, flatten their ears, put tails between their legs and slip meekly away.

HULK FACTS

Hulk guests Suzanne Charny and Kathleen Nolan also appeared on the cult TV show *Kolchak: The Night Stalker* together. Charny was a vampire hooker, Nolan a real estate agent.

Plot loosely resembles *Swamp Women*, a '50s Roger Corman movie co-starring *Hulk* guest Marie Windsor.

Gloria Gifford appeared in *Halloween II* with fellow *Hulk* guests Cliff Emmich, Jeffrey Kramer and Pamela Susan Shoop.

"VETERAN"
Season 5, Episode 77
Airdate: October 16, 1981
Directed By Michael Vejar
Story by Nicholas Corea
Written By Nicholas Corea and Reuben Leder
Banner's alias: "David Barnes"

Cast

Dr. David Banner	Bill Bixby
The Hulk	Lou Ferrigno
Doug Hewitt	Paul Koslo
Harrison Cole	Bruce Gray

David helps Jack Hewitt thwart a mugger, then tries to stop Hewitt from his obsession with war hero-turned-politician Harrison Cole, currently campaigning for office. Deranged Hewitt claims he and Cole have a shared and troubling past in Vietnam. Banner sees Hewitt has a gun and plans to assassinate Cole. Jack goes to a dance studio overlooking the stage for a Cole rally. He holds dance teacher Lisa hostage as he prepares to shoot Cole from her window.

David warns Cole, but is stunned to learn Jack Hewitt supposedly died in Vietnam. A Cole operative tortures David to learn who really hired him, when he Hulks Out and escapes. David talks to Jack's father and learns Jack died in Nam and his insane brother Doug took Jack's identity — but never actually went to Vietnam! He read all the letters from Jack and internalized them. Doug flees the asylum to kill Cole for an atrocity Jack told him about in a letter. In the end, Lisa escapes unharmed, Doug goes back to the mental hospital while Jack's old letters derail Cole's campaign. Another smart, dark story from the always-intriguing Corea, "Veteran" is an interesting morality tale about what happens when the sins of the past come back to haunt you. Having the "Veteran" of the title not be a veteran at all is a clever twist. Another surprising turn by Paul Koslo, who, like his character in "Long Run Home," looks like a villain but turns out to be misunderstood. The scenes of Koslo wandering downtown L.A. having Vietnam flashbacks and images of a killer in a silver helmet and Michael Myers *Halloween* mask are disturbing. Paul Koslo's Jack is a drifter, like Banner. After being mugged, he asks David, "Has it ever happened to you, they jump you and stuff?" "I usually run first," David replies.

The "deranged Vietnam vet" was a cliché bad guy by the time this episode aired in the early '80s — they had been used numerous times on shows like *Starsky & Hutch*, *SWAT* and *Baretta*. To Corea's credit, he was an actual Vietnam veteran and we find out that Koslo really isn't the bad guy or even a real veteran. Most of the episode is shot on the Universal backlot, at the *Back To The Future* clocktower town hall.

Having the nut sniper be the hero was unique, as the episode ran months after gunmen made attempts on the lives of Pope John Paul II and United States President Ronald Reagan, and almost a year after the murder of ex Beatle John Lennon.

PAUL KOSLO (Doug Hewitt): *"With the 'Veteran' episode, I really got to know Bill better as it was my second go-around with him and I had the guest lead in both shows. That's why I feel so strong about the man and his character. He was a beauty!"*

WENDY GIRARD (Lisa Morgan): *"I saw my character as a dancer who had spent her whole life working to be the best she could be, an intelligent, creative, cutting edge, inventive teacher who still works to make her mark in the world of dance. At that time, dance was changing radically because it was the beginning of the the Punk Rock era, which radically affected not only dance and music, but all of culture in America. A healthy. and ambitious young artist who suddenly find herself hostage by a 'Nam Vet. (As backstory), I thought her boyfriend/fiancé had gone to Nam and not come back."*

RICHARD YNIGUEZ (Detective Harnell): *"Working on* The Incredible Hulk *was very cool and very easy! All the players were down to earth people. Bill Bixby was very nice and kept to himself, he had lost his (child) at the time if you recall, and his wife not long after, so it wasn't easy for him. Paul, hard working actor that he is, made things easy…I didn't do much with Lou but he was just as easy to work with. My stuff was much more with the stunt guy whose name I don't remember (Manny Perry) but he too was just a pro and easy to work with too! I had a blast, as I have on most projects I've worked on."*

RON STEPHENSON (Casting Director): *"We did use some actors more than once, like Paul Koslo, Christine Belford, Victoria Carroll, Charles Napier and Gerald McRaney, because they always delivered and they were definite strong types. No one messed around with Napier, who was a believable screen villain. Paul Koslo was also a really wonderful actor, especially in roles like damaged war vets or bikers."*

HULK HIGHLIGHT

The green goliath encounters a little boy who challenges him to a (toy) gunfight!

HULK FACTS
Reuben Leder is the brother of *Deep Impact* director Mimi Leder.

"Detective Harnell" is an homage to *Hulk* composer Joe Harnell.

Wendy Girard introduces the lead characters in Woody Allen's *Annie Hall*.

With a gunman out to assassinate a politician as the hero, this episode shares some similarities to the Stephen King bestseller *The Dead Zone*. The same book seemed to inspire elements of the episode "Deathmask", also by Corea.

Koslo's father in the show, an embittered mechanic, is David White — good ol' Larry Tate from *Bewitched!*

Barret Oliver (Jimmy The Kid) starred in *Frankenweenie*, Tim Burton's first film.

"SANCTUARY"
Season 5, Episode 78
Airdate: November 6, 1981
Directed By Chuck Bowman
Written By Deborah Dean Davis
Banner's alias: "Father Costa"

Cast

Dr. David Banner	Bill Bixby
The Hulk	Lou Ferrigno
Sister Anita	Diana Muldaur
Rudy	Fausto Barajas
Roberto	Guillermo San Juan
Sheriff Dean	Jerry Hardin
Sister Mary Catherine	Edie McClurg
Patrero	Henry Darrow
Father Costa	Michael Santiago
Shlomo Jonas	Adam S. Bristol

At the San Miguel Mission, David works as a handyman for an order of Roman Catholic nuns. To protect Roberto, a young illegal alien teen, the nuns coerce David into posing as a priest. Roberto has been shot by Patrero, a villain who rules the town of San Miguel. The wounded boy turns to the church for sanctuary. It's fun to see Banner as a man of the cloth (something Kenneth Johnson also explored on *Bionic Woman*, in the episode "Sister Jamie"), and, of course, trying to remain at peace to stave off The Hulk. When thugs attack David at The Mission, he Hulks Out

Edie McClurg has a Heavenly time with Bill Bixby on "Sanctuary."
PHOTO COURTESY OF EDIE MCCLURG

and incapacitates one with a statue of St. Michael. The thug undergoes a religious conversion and declares it a Miracle. As crowds show up to pray, David gives a stirring sermon on the loaves and the fishes and sharing. He suggests, as several Catholic theologians have, that the miracle wasn't caused by Jesus' physically multiplying the food after the Sermon on the Mount, but by Him convincing the crowd to trust each other enough to share their food. "Sanctuary" is a nice episode, marred only by the casting of Diana Muldaur. A fine actress, Muldaur is fine as the nun helping David protect the boy. The problem is that she was so effective as David's sister in "Homecoming," it's annoying to see her back so soon as a different character. Someone in casting has a sense of humor, though, because in a nun's habit, David still calls her "Sister." Edie McClurg is flat-out charming as Sister Mary Catherine, adding some much-needed levity to the serious episode. Chuck Bowman's direction is also subtle. "Sometimes faith is all that keeps us going," David observes to Sister Anita in "Sanctuary." It's a profoundly religious take on the series itself, where David can be seen as a Gamma-powered Job, doomed to walk the Earth alone, helping strangers after his loved ones all die. And like Job, Banner's exclamation after his first transformation in the 1977 pilot? "Oh My God, My God…" Seeing David change in the second TV movie *The Incredible Hulk: Death In The Family,* a character even notes "we all have our cross to bear."

RON STEPHENSON (Casting Director): *"Bill Bixby liked Diana Muldaur and Christine Belford very much and loved working opposite them."*

HULK FACTS
Guest Jerry Hardin is best known as doomed informant "Deep Throat" on *The X-Files.*

Henry Darrow played Zorro several times, in live action and animation.

Michael Santiago gets to be on camera as a priest in this one.

"TRIANGLE"
Season 5, Episode 79
Airdate: November 13, 1981
Directed By Michael Vejar
Written By Andrew Schneider
Banner's alias: "David Beller"

Cast

Dr. David Banner	Bill Bixby
Jack McGee	Jack Colvin
The Hulk	Lou Ferrigno
Ellis Jordan	Peter Mark Richman
Bert	Charles Napier
George	Mickey Jones
Gale Webber	Andrea Marcovicci

While working as a lumberjack in the Pacific Coast hamlet of Jordan-town, David finds himself the target of ruthless millionaire Ellis Jordan, who the town is named for, because he is dating Gale. It turns out that Gale is a pretty, cheerful local girl Ellis desires, and, in a creepy twist, helped raise!

The best episode of the fifth season, "Triangle" works because writer Andrew Schneider sets up an interesting situation for our hero: David is in love with a beautiful girl, only to have a powerful man try to take her away from him. In previous episodes, David is ready to flee at a moment's notice when he's threatened with exposure or violence, only here he defies all expectations when he doesn't go. He's so smitten with Gale Webber (and as played by the impressive Andrea Marcovicci, who can blame him?), he stands up to the tycoon and his thugs, refusing to leave. In the climax, David and Gale learn that she's actually Ellis Jordan's illegitimate daughter! As The Hulk trashes Jordan's house, Ellis says protectively of Gale, "please don't hurt my daughter — my child!"

A great David Banner-centered episode where he tries to stay in one place and defend his temporary situation, "Triangle" has a haunting moment when Marcovicci's Gale takes Banner on a picnic. Because they seem to be growing serious, Gale asks David about his previous romantic entanglements and inquires if he has children. Banner says "No." and Bixby looks so sad, one can only surmise this was shot after the death of his son. If it was, considering what he had just gone through in his personal life, one wonders why they didn't cut the line to spare the actor unnecessary pain. When he's asked about his wife, he responds, "She passed away." Peter Mark Richman is great as Ellis Jordan, injecting a twisted father/daughter pathos into what could have been a stock bad guy role in lesser hands. Past *Hulk* guests Napier and Jones are first rate as his goons. Making Gale the daughter of Jordan is a nifty twist slightly reminiscent of "Goodbye, Eddie Cain". It is also like the works of William Faulkner, whose writing is mentioned here. His stories are full of fallen Southern aristocrats lording over small towns.

ANDREA MARCOVICCI (Gale Webber): *"I remember looking forward to the scene where Hulk would sweep me off my feet, but Lou Ferrigno would not pick me up! They would only place me into his arms instead, because he was a competitive bodybuilder and worried about the strain of picking me up. I weighed 115 pounds soaking wet and thought, 'Aw Shucks — I wanted to be picked up by The Incredible Hulk!' He carried me, but it wasn't the same. Tom Selleck picked me up and carried me on every single* Magnum P.I. *that I did. Peter Mark Richman is one of the great gentlemen in our business; he did a fine job as the bad guy. His thugs, Mickey and Charles, were also fun; big character actors. Casting director Ron Stephenson had all these actors on the show, actors who I had seen so many times in so many movies and TV shows, they were like old friends when I met them for the first time on* Hulk.*"*

KAREN HARRIS: *"That scene where Bill Bixby says 'No kids' may have been Bill's way of emphasizing the tragedy that he went through."*

RON STEPHENSON (Casting Director): *"Andrea Marcovicci was a perennial guest-cast lady who never really had a big movie career, only to become the world's top cabaret artist for many years! What a talent she is, stage, film, TV, singing, she really does it all!"*

MICKEY JONES (George): *"On the 'Triangle' show, it was set in the woods of the Pacific Northwest. I was shocked that the north woods where we shot was right by Lake Hollywood! I think I spent more time with Bill Bixby on that show than any of the others. He was truly a great guy."*

HULK HIGHLIGHT
Listen to the scene where Charles Napier invades David Banner's apartment and calls Bill Bixby by his real name! As he comes in, David says, "There must be some mistake —" Napier sneers, "No mistake, *BILLY!*"

HULK FACTS
The first time David imitates a pirate since "Wax Museum."

Jack McGee's last appearance on the show.

Peter Mark Richman voiced The Phantom on the Marvel cartoon *Defenders of the Earth* and an aged Peter Parker on the '90s animated *Spider-Man* series. He starred in the very last episode of Rod Serling's *Twilight Zone*.

Lake Hollywood is also where they shot parts of Charlton Heston's movie *Earthquake.*

The last episode from frequent *Hulk* contributors Michael Vejar and Andrew Schneider.

Andrea Marcovicci starred in the man-eating yogurt horror-comedy *The Stuff.*

"SLAVES"

Season 5, Episode 80
Airdate: May 5, 1982
Directed By John Liberti
Written By Jeri Taylor
Banner's alias: "David Becker"

Cast

Dr. David Banner . . . . Bill Bixby
The Hulk . . . . .Lou Ferrigno
Isaac Whittier Ross . . . . .John Hancock
Roy . . . . Charles Tyner
Marty. . . . . .Jeffrey Kramer
Christy. . . . . Faye Grant

When Southern girl Christy crashes her car, she joins David hitchhiking. Picked up by friendly African American Isaac, the two are driven to an old ghost town. Once there, they are forced to work as slaves by Isaac, an ex-convict and a descendant of slaves. Isaac forces them and a guy named Marty to dig for gold in an old mine. Isaac killed Marty's brother and Marty is now a shell of a man.

David and fellow "slave" Christy plot their escape, while the overseer makes David and Marty fight. The bad guys sit around listening to a player piano and nothing much happens.. A silly episode attempting (and failing) to say something profound about race relations, "Slaves" is redeemed only by the presence of the beautiful Faye Grant. This is *Hulk* at its most ridiculous and one of the worst of the series.

JEFFREY KRAMER (Marty): *"My favorite part of Hulk was Kenny Johnson, what a nice guy! I did* Alien Nation *with Kenny, after I became an executive [at Fox]. Kenny was the show runner and just a great guy. I liked doing the* Hulk *show because Bill Bixby was a pro. That was awhile ago, but I think he and I were both slaves in an old mine and I may have had a fight scene with him! They force us to fight. When you're a guest actor, you don't have much time to bond with the lead, but Bixby was always prepared and ready to go. It was fun to see Lou Ferrigno in action as The Hulk!"*

HULK FACTS

Faye Grant co-starred in *Hulk*'s rival superhero series *The Greatest American Hero* and Johnson's *V*.

Jeffrey Kramer was in *Jaws* before he went on to produce the hit TV shows *Ally McBeal*, *The Practice* and *Chicago Hope*.

Writer Jeri Taylor was a major contributor to *Star Trek: The Next Generation*.

This is the directorial debut of *Hulk*'s first assistant director John Liberti.

"A MINOR PROBLEM"
Season 5, Episode 81
Airdate: May 12, 1982
Directed By Michael Preece
Written By Diane Frolov
Banner's alias: "David Bradshaw"

Cast

Dr. David Banner . . . . Bill Bixby
The Hulk . . . . .Lou Ferrigno
Patty Knowlton . . . . Nancy Grahn
Cunningham . . . . .Linden Chiles
Rita . . . . Lisa Jane Persky
Sperling . . . . Gary Vinson
Tom . . . . Xander Berkeley
Mark . . . . .John Walter Davis
Jordan . . . . Brad Harris

David enters the town of Rock Springs, only to find it completely abandoned. He plays with a stray dog named Buddy. Evacuated due to a chlorine gas leak, the town is targeted by several looters, young opportunists who believe it's a hoax. It's actually an e. coli outbreak. They are quickly overcome by the effects. When Banner tries to help Patty, a female scientist, find a cure, he's set upon by Buddy again. The dog is now infected as are the greedy looters, who become sick and crazed. Banner has to find a way to save them all from themselves. "You can all be dead within an hour," Banner warns to no avail, "We've got to get you to a hospital."

Three evil lab scientists in HazMat suits begin picking up dead birds and "anything that can be biopsied" to cover their e. coli spill. The chlorine is used to hide the bacteria outbreak.. Banner and Patty discover the looters' crashed truck and see two of them are dead but the third, Tom, is very sick. David attempts to synthesize a cure for him, the dog and Patty, who is now showing e. coli symptoms. The scientists are hunting for Tom, who they know is there from his blood trail in the truck. As he's confronted by the murderous scientists, David feels the e. coli taking effect and Hulks Out. Xander Berkeley and Lisa Jane Persky stand out as the hedonistic looters in an interesting episode. As the series unintended finale, one is sorry Jack McGee is not there. Exposing an e.coli coverup would have been a perfect send-off for *The National Register's* star reporter. The silent opening, where we hear only David's clicking boot heels and Joe Harnell's score, as he wanders into an abandoned laboratory and then an equally abandoned suburb, is eerie and effective. It's experimental and daring, an atmospheric exercise the show did for it's final episode. At the very end, Patty recovers and says to Banner, "Told ya I'd make it!" Driving her, Tom and Buddy the dog to safety, David Banner utters the last line of the series, "We're all gonna make it!"

LISA JANE PERSKY (Rita): *"I loved* The Incredible Hulk *as a viewer, so I was thrilled to be on it, especially when it turned out to be the very last episode. I was excited because I knew I would see Bill Bixby and get to watch him Hulk Out! I came to the set in a two banger with another actor in the episode, Xander Berkeley. On the last season of a show, they always spend less money. Xander and I showed up for work, but there was no Bill Bixby. It turned out, the studio got cheap and fired Bill's driver because the show was wrapping up, so Bill refused to come to work. Since Bill wasn't there, Xander and I were just sittin' there day after day and became good friends while waiting for him. It was loyal of Bill, who was a stand-up guy for his driver. Day two, Bill still wasn't there, so Xander and I shot all the scenes we had without Banner. He didn't show up until day four, when the studio re-hired his driver. I respected Bill for that because you don't just fire the star's driver, especially after everything Bill had gone through."*

(One of the highlights of "A Minor Problem" is Persky's catfight with Nancy Grahn. The two roll around for about five minutes of a pure audience enjoyment that can only come from two cute girls having a catfight.)

"That was *a hot girl-on-girl wrestling match between me and Nancy Grahn," Persky laughs. "And it goes on for a ridiculously long time. It was completely gratuitous, like a women-in-prison movie! Our fight goes on so long, that seeing the episode on DVD, I was surprised at how long it is. Nancy and I fight and wrestle; it's just ridiculous. I'm sure Nancy and I made jokes. It was hot, like 90 degrees in the Valley, when we shot it.*

"I broke out the leather for our fight scene and we were very careful not to actually hurt one another. It reminded me of a song I knew by a CBGB's band, The Miamis, 'Dancin' Together.' None of the girls would dance with the boys 'cause they were dancin' together.' Nancy and I were busy earning our paycheck!

None of the guys complained about watching us girls wrestling. We filmed the whole episode on the backlot. The crew was mad at Lou Ferrigno; they thought he was crabby, so they were mean to him. All this picnic food was lying around because in the story the food was infected by chlorine, so nobody would touch it. The food wasn't real, it was rubber — so whenever Lou had to run as The Hulk, the crew would throw rubber grapes at him! You don't want to piss off your crew because the crew always works twice as hard as you do!"

MARK A. BURLEY (Unit Production Manager): *"Lisa Persky is exactly right — Bill Bixby had two close friends on the show — Frank Orsatti and his motor home driver. When they were doing the last episode, they fired Bill's driver. Bill got a 'sore throat' and would not come to work until they brought the guy back — that's how good an actor Bill was! It cleared up as soon as his driver was re-hired."*

RON STEPHENSON (Casting Director): *"I found Xander Berkeley, the wonderful character actor who was so great on 24, in an acting class, doing scenes for an invited audience. He blew me away and is one of my favorites. Xander is a funny, crazy guy to boot!"*

HULK HIGHLIGHT

The Hulk cradling the sick dog in his arms as he changes back to Banner is touching.

HULK FACTS

Writer Diane Frolov became an Emmy winner, scripting shows like *Northern Exposure* and *The Sopranos*.

Lisa Jane Persky is a friend of *Hulk* comic writer Len Wein and got him an autographed picture of actor Hugh Jackman, who played Wein's creation, *X-Men*'s Wolverine.

Blondie bass player Gary Valentine wrote the hit song "(I'm Always Touched By Your) Presence Dear" about Persky.

Xander Berkeley would deal with Marvel superheroes again, in the movie *Kick Ass.*

The scientist offering David a job interview is named "Leder," after *Hulk* Story Editor Ruben Leder.

HULK PROFILE
EDIE MCCLURG, SISTER MARY CATHERINE

One of four female guests to go onto great things after *The Incredible Hulk* along with Kim Cattrall, Susan Sullivan and Loni Anderson, busy character actress Edie McClurg is easily the most prolific. McClurg

Left: Edie McClurg as a Nun in "Sanctuary." PHOTO COURTESY OF EDIE McCLURG
Right: Edie McClurg. PHOTO BY PATRICK JANKIEWICZ

appeared in John Hughes' films, including Principal Rooney's wacky secretary in *Ferris Bueller's Day Off* and her ineffectual car rental agent in *Planes, Trains and Automobiles*. She can also be heard in Pixar's *Cars*, voiced characters on *Scooby-Doo* and has appeared in over 160 movies and TV shows. At the beginning of her career, McClurg played sweet, helpful Sister Mary Catherine, a plucky nun on *The Incredible Hulk*.

"We shot the 'Sanctuary' episode at the San Fernando Mission, North of Los Angeles," says Edie McClurg. "It was a fun show to do. Bill Bixby was starring, of course, with Chuck Bowman directing. What I liked about playing the nun is walking around in a nun's outfit, the full habit, while the real nuns who worked at the Mission wore polyester pants, sneakers and no headgear at all! One nun came over and explained to Wardrobe, 'That should be tied tighter in the back.' The irony is that she didn't look anything like a nun!

"Playing a nun was interesting. In [Catholic] school in Kansas City, Missouri, I was a good student on the college track, so we were taken to the convent to see a college that the nuns ran. We spent the weekend with the Sisters, so I brought my radio and turned it on. A nun came in and said, 'This is a Benedictine weekend, and you will spend it as though you are nuns. Nuns *do not* have radios next to their beds and I will give it back to you when you go.' We ate in silence, and the schedule said, 'Benedictine labors,' which means *work*! We had to dust a huge cathedral chapel...I decided then and there that there would be no nunnery for me! On *Hulk*, I really enjoyed the part where I try to stop the bad guys from getting away, so I jump in the window to grab the keys, but they roar off without me. It was very hot at The Mission, because we shot it in the summertime. With all of that gear on me, I was extremely hot...I do love my pictures in the habit with the St. Francis statue, standing over him and pretending to read his book.

"I felt so bad that Bill Bixby got ill. I met him on *Hulk* and he directed another show I was on and he was just getting ill at the time. You could tell when the pain would come across him; he would have to lean against a stool, not sit, because if he sat down, he couldn't get back up. Poor Bill would put his head down, the pain was so bad. It was so sad, because he was such a sweet guy and a great director," the actress laments. "Bill never yelled at anybody, he would just persuade you with a suggestion." McClurg was fond of her Mother Superior. "Diana Muldaur was a nice woman. They would make us up at Universal, then put us in a car and drive us to the set. Diana and I traveled together since we were both nuns in the show and she needed to run some errands. I was worried, 'We gotta get to the set!' and Diana said, 'I need to go to the bank first.' We were running around L.A. in our nun outfits. I kept saying to her, 'We're gonna be late to the set — ' Diana turned to me and said, 'Ever since my husband died suddenly, I realized there is no reason to rush to do anything. Time takes care of itself!' and she knew they weren't going to be ready for us. She was right — when we got there, they still weren't ready. We were fine."

McClurg also met The Hulk. "Lou Ferrigno was in a scene and he didn't like getting his makeup put on. They always had to go to Lou's room and coax him out to the makeup trailer to get his makeup and touch-ups done. It made for a very long day for everybody, because he really resisted putting on the makeup. After awhile, when you come home every day with green paint in your ears and nostrils, it could probably get to be a little bad, so I felt for him — but I was just roasting in that nun habit!"

PETER MARK RICHMAN

As the evil — but not unsympathetic — Ellis Jordan, Peter Mark Richman made an interesting heavy in the best episode of the fifth season. He's vying with David Banner for the affections of the enchanting Andrea Marcovicci.

Peter Mark Richman. PHOTO BY PATRICK JANKIEWICZ

"It was easy to play my character smitten with this girl, because I adored Andrea Marcovicci, who is a really good singer. Andrea played the object of my affection. She was very foolish in that episode…I think I was a better choice for her," Peter Mark Richman smiles. "Come on, I'm the richest man in town, the place is even named after me, and the other guy was a drifter who would turn into The Hulk! That was no competition.

"I remember sitting in a cab with my henchmen and pointing at Bill Bixby, then saying, 'Get that guy!' I remember shooting that and really liking my henchmen. I did a lot of powerful bad guys like that in my years of doing episodic television and I just love playing creeps! When I play a bad guy like Ellis Jordan, I always look for the humanity inside them. To be a cliché bad guy is really quite boring, so I always try to give them the colors that I'm just like anybody else, except I'm bad. I had put Marcovicci's character through school and felt betrayed when she took up with Banner. I like Ellis Jordan; I don't think he was a bad guy at all!

"Before doing the show, I knew Bill Bixby from when he was doing *My Favorite Martian*, because I was working at the same studio. Bill was a nice guy who died very young. Lou Ferrigno was big. As The Hulk, he showed me the error of my ways and threw me around! Lou was very powerful. He's still powerful, in fact…I ran into him recently and we had a nice reunion. I think *Hulk* took about six or seven days to shoot. If we were done shooting by 6 p.m., the producers were happy."

HULK PROFILE
WENDY GIRARD

Wendy Girard played an emotionally fragile dance teacher taken hostage on the show. "Here is what I remember about doing my show 'Veteran', one of the last episodes of *The Incredible Hulk*, March 1981 at Universal Studios: Supervising Producer: Nicholas Corea," says actress Girard. "I had met Nic Corea thanks to a friend of mine Michael Stewart, who knew Nic from their hometown, St. Louis. Michael told Nic he should see me, and somehow I got a meeting with Nic at Universal during one of my sojourns in LA from New York.

"As soon as I walked into his large office on the first floor — which looked across the commons to the cafeteria and sound stages — I was wary, but liked the guy. I liked his no bullshit directness. Nicholas was like a New Yorker. We sat down and had a long talk. He took me to lunch. We had a couple of meetings talking about our lives, and I went back to New York City.

"Soon after, he called me and told me he had written an episode of *The Incredible Hulk* especially for me. It was the part of a dancer/dance teacher, who was very talented but having a hard time making a breakthrough in to the big leagues. He flew me out to LA to shoot the episode."

Doing 'Veteran' "was a very tough decision for me to make since I had just been cast by Elia Kazan in his *Agamemnon Trilogy*, his first stage work in decades and Kazan was my idol and inspiration for getting into the business," Girard remembers. "Here I had a chance to actually work with Kazan in the play he planned for Lincoln Center of which he was originally going to be the Artistic Director, but rehearsing without pay. I had worked under him in sessions as a Life Member of the Actors Studio, but only a few times.

"Here I was being offered the leading role in one of the most popular TV series on at that time that was written especially for me, and it paid good money. The only other TV I had done was a contract role as a nurse on *As The World Turns* and I was *not* a fan of soap operas. Anyway, I bit the bullet and told my hero, Elia Kazan, I had been offered money in Hollywood and left. That was the hardest decision I ever made in my career.

"I got to LA and liked the script. For episodic television in those days, it seemed to be *about* something, and about something important, which was that a lot of Vietnam vets were coming back and suffering terribly from the psychological effects of America's first guerilla war. It seemed to speak to some real issues of Vets, and as far as I know, was perhaps the first TV show to deal with Post Traumatic Stress Disorder (PTSD). I was honored Nic had written the lead female for me and also, about my struggle as an actress (dancer) to make a living in Hollywood. We shot all my scenes on the Universal backlot."

Unfortunately, she came onto *The Incredible Hulk* at a very dark time. "When I got to the set, there was a very strange atmosphere. I had only been on one major set before, and that was when I introduced Diane Keaton to Woody Allen in the tennis scene in *Annie Hall*, my film debut. But the vibes were weird — everyone had a strange silence. Everyone was treating me strangely on the first day. People seemed distracted. Don't forget, I was just the Guest Star in for a week or ten days. Everyone else had been working together on one of the most popular series in television for years — *together as a 'family'* and knew each other well. I was a total stranger coming in. I called Nic because I was taking it all personally at the time, since it was my "first" and asked him, 'What's going on?'

"Nic told me Bill's wife Brenda had gone skiing up in Mammoth the weekend before, and their son suddenly fell ill. She took him to the clinic in Mammoth and their six year old son, Christopher, was gravely ill in the clinic. Their only child, their beloved six year old son, died. Just before we were shooting the episode. So Nic had to rewrite the show day by day, not knowing when Bill would emerge from his trailer."

Because of the leading man's grief, "Paul Koslo's part enlarged. I asked Nic if Bill was going to take time off from the show. Nic said, 'No'. He was coming back to work, though a few days late. I believe it was a Saturday or Sunday night his son died. And Bill came back to work on that Tuesday or Wednesday. To me, that was insane. I couldn't see how he could come back to work on a TV series after what had just happened. And I told Nic as much.

"We never knew what was happening from moment to moment in terms of the script. Nic told me Bill was in his trailer on the lot, but couldn't make it out. I offered to go and talk with him even though I didn't know him but obviously, that was not an option. As far as I know, he never came out and shot a scene for that show. If he did, it must have been very brief.

"The whole ten days was very surreal, which in a way only added to the surrealism of the episode. In 'Veteran', this deranged vet, as Paul played him, has gone out of his mind, wanting to kill a candidate. So it was clear that it was up to the rest of us, as guest stars. to do the show. I never actually shot a scene with Lou Ferrigno because I asked Nic, 'Whatever you do, please don't write a scene where The Incredible Hulk carries me off in his arms, saving my life'. So Nic didn't."

And why wouldn't she want to be carried by The Hulk, like almost every other guest actress in the series? "I grew up in Latin America without TV or comic books, so it seemed hokey, contrived, corny and melodramatic for me to be picked up by Hulk. I was a serious actress and a very serious student of the art of acting! When I told Nic, 'don't have him pick me up and carry me away, he might have thought all New York theatre actresses would be as chagrined by that as I. Besides," she jokes, "I didn't want that green slimy stuff all over me. I found the idea of being 'saved' by a giant green Hulk a bit condescending and offensive. I was an athlete my whole life and I wanted to save myself. So Nic wrote the script and my scenes the way he did partially because of that. I was on *Magnum P.I.* three times and I saved Magnum's life in all three shows!"

"I just kept trying to focus on my role, and do my job. I thought that was the best way I could help the circumstances, to come through for everybody by being the best I could be. At least that way, if Bill never showed up, we'd still have some story to work with. Though I had been a dancer in my youth, I hadn't kept up in dance classes and wasn't up on the latest styles and trends in contemporary dance, so I had a trainer. I hired Joanne Venora, Chick Venora's wife who was a choreographer, to coach me in contemporary dance. She gave me some tips in rhythm and movement that helped me make it contemporary.

"I remember working with Paul was very painful. I think he must have been incorporating what Bill and his wife were going through. The whole shoot was very painful, belabored, with a very heavy atmosphere of everyone holding their breath, though I don't know if Nic told me Bill's son had died until after we had finished shooting."

Girard was fond of producer Nicholas Corea. "We were friends and we were more than friends. He grew up in an Italian family on the rough side of St. Louis. His father was fresh off the boat. Nic joined the Marines and was shipped to Vietnam. He became a sergeant with 20 or so men in his unit and they all called him 'Padre' because he was the oldest man in the unit at the age of 20. Nic was just a kid himself. Maybe a few months older than some of his unit, but he held this huge position of knowledge, wisdom and authority. They all looked up to him, relied on his counsel, and turned their lives over to his authority. And he lost them all. He told me he was the only one to survive his unit in Vietnam. He lived with that every day of his life. And that was obvious. The responsibility and 'survivors guilt' he felt. He was very hard on himself and he didn't suffer fools gladly. He didn't have much patience for people who didn't apply themselves with everything they had to give, and he didn't deal in bullshit.

"I always felt safe in his office during our many hours long conversations, because I felt no one was going to disturb us. People on the lot respected him and his history, so they knew not to bother him with bullshit. I know he was a maverick at Universal. I guess Don Bellasario liked him. When I did the 'Veteran' episode of *The Incredible Hulk*, Nic was the Supervising Producer and writer. He directed a number of episodes and may have had titles above.

"He had a dark side — whether it was from being a cop in St Louis, or being in 'Nam and being 'in charge' at the age of 20, or coming from a working class Italian immigrant family from the other side of the tracks in St Louis, I can't say. But he was also a painter, artist, and novelist. He was a deep thinker, a realist, and obviously very hurt and shaken by his experiences. Not obvious to most, perhaps, but he had a hard exterior that could be quite cynical. He gave me one of his large framed drawings that is quite 'dark': a naked couple turned away from each other in charcoal on white paper.

"Yet another side of him was very sensitive to the human condition, an artist in temperament, and a collector of fine art. He collected masks, and on my travels around the world, I always brought him back a mask from some indigenous culture wherever I had traveled. In looking back, I think he was compelled to tell his stories. To share his viewpoint of the human circumstances he had experienced in his life — and he knew how important that was. He knew that was what made literature, theatre, TV or film.

"Nic cared about things. He cared about the state of affairs, yet at the same time, he looked at everything with a jaundiced eye. I think part of him had given up before he left Vietnam. I felt as though a part of him died there. That he had given up a part of himself when he left there, and that he was just surviving back here stateside, in Hollywood. I was very saddened to learn of his premature death in 1990 from pancreatic cancer. But he had been a fairly heavy drinker during the ten or so years I knew him.

"His brother, Johnny, was a sweetheart–and gay. Nic was this incredibly macho guy — all hulk and brawn, a marine, a St Louis cop, with the physique and attitude all that required. Yet his younger brother was this very sensitive, gentle and caring creature — almost as if they were two sides of the same person. Johnny was suffering discrimination in

St Louis because he was gay. Nic invited Johnny to come to LA and live with him without blinking an eye. He didn't care what anyone thought and he fiercely loved his little brother–not giving a shit whether or not he was gay."

Sadly, the actress and Corea lost touch. "A few years after *Hulk*, we worked on another project called *The Outlaws*. He talked to me a long time about dong the female lead in it but Universal decided to go with someone who had more TVQ. I was very disheartened, and I think it affected our friendship. But he gave me a wonderful part in it. I was sick of the 'good girl' roles where the dialogue was always basically the same...He wrote a part for me of a sassy bad girl, a gun moll type, which I enjoyed immensely. And getting to work with Richard Roundtree and Rod Taylor was a true honor."

HULK PROFILE
XANDER BERKELEY, "TOM"

Character actor Xander Berkeley has made an impression in big movies like *Terminator 2: Judgment Day* and *Air Force One*, as well as George, the doomed boss of CTU, on *24*. At the beginning of his career, he starred in "A Minor Problem," the very last episode of *The Incredible Hulk*. Tom, Berkeley's character, starts out as a looter, before e. coli, chlorine and David Banner help him develop a conscience. "I had just made the movie *Mommie Dearest* with Faye Dunaway and *Hulk* was one of my first — if not my very first — television episode. I played a 'punk with a conscience,' which is why I live and not die like the others," Berkeley laughs. "Every *Hulk* episode was a morality tale, which is why the show was so interesting. Because I don't want us to loot, the infected dog and I get to live. You truly can't kill a dog or the guy saying, 'We shouldn't be doing this!'

"My sister Pernel and I grew up watching *My Favorite Martian*, so I can't tell you the massive thrill I got out of being carried away by Bill Bixby! Because I have been sickened by the chlorine, I cry out to Bill, 'Help me...' Banner loads me into a Volkswagen to drive me to the hospital. Bill teased me because I'm supposed to be dying as he drives me. I gave myself a tremor in the back of the car. I wanted to keep it real, and show that I was sick. I remember Bill Bixby gave me a hard time about that in a sweet way. Bill says, 'Oh, look at the kid in the backseat doing The Method!' I thought, 'Give me some time, Bill — I haven't sold out yet!' But I would never have said that to him; it was one of my first jobs...I didn't want to get fired! My sickness in that anticipated the airborne

Plutonium that kills me on *24*. On *Hulk*, I'm sweaty and covered with lesions, so I mailed one of my skin lesions to Pernel, who got a big kick out of it! We both loved Bill Bixby, but when I did the show, he seemed like he was already 'Out of there.' He was on TV non-stop for many years, and this was the end of his long run on *The Incredible Hulk*. I didn't talk to Bixby much because I didn't want to be disillusioned. I mean, he was teasing me, a kid, for getting into character, but God knows I was thrilled to meet him and be around him! Lisa Jane Persky and I became very close friends and we still are, 30 years later! Lisa had worked with the director before, Michael Preece, and he was a cool, nice guy. I believe we shot the show on the backlot, by the *Back to the Future* clock tower. Except it was so far back in the past that they hadn't gone back to the future yet, so needless to say, I didn't recognize it as such at the time. It was Universal's small-town Americana set that must have been used for so many towns in so many shows over the years.

"Lou Ferrigno impressed me. When it was time for me to get thrown around by The Hulk, I watched him slam my stunt double repeatedly onto a picnic table! Because there is a chlorine leak, there's untouched food lying around. They had plastic fruit on the tables, because everyone fled town except for us looters. When Lou Ferrigno is running around as The Hulk, he was painted green and almost blind in his contact lenses. One of the Grips had the Teamsters chucking rubber grapes at poor Lou. Finally, he turned around and said, 'The next guy who throws a grape at me is really gonna get it!' He sounded so hurt — you could see him from when he was the little boy with the speech impediment on the playground," the actor notes. "Seeing that happen, I suddenly knew how Lou was that kid when he decided to start working out. Now, as the star of his own TV show, he has to deal with this garbage again. That really moved me. Lou was as big as a house; if he saw who did it, he *would* have destroyed them!"

CANCELLATION!

The Incredible Hulk ended with "A Minor Problem," cancelled by Harvey Shepard, the new head of CBS. David Banner would now hitch-hike into syndication. The cast and crew were still stunned to see the hit show come to an end.

Mark A. Burley remembers, "We only found out that the show was cancelled after hearing it on the radio. Nobody told Bill (Bixby) or the rest of us! That was terribly embarrassing. Once the show was cancelled, we had several episodes left to shoot and Universal slashed our budget. The studio also held us tightly to our seven day shooting schedule per episode of *The Incredible Hulk*. They had been gracious about it before. We had been a hit show, but once we were cancelled, they forgot all about that."

Lou Ferrigno says, "I was in Washington, about to meet President Reagan, when I heard the news. We were supposed to go another season, but they pulled the plug. I heard the news of our cancellation over the radio. I called the set and they confirmed it, so I was devastated. We worked really hard for five years and I truly believe we could have gone longer. They should have at least let us finish the fifth season." He wasn't alone in his feelings of sadness. "At the wrap party, I went in a T-shirt and blue jeans because I just couldn't deal with the show ending," admits story editor/ producer Jill Sherman Donner. "Robert Bennett Steinhauer yelled at me for not dressing up. He said it was disrespectful and he was right, I should have, but I just felt so bad! The end of *The Incredible Hulk* was the saddest day of my life, with all these mixed emotions of love and hate. Everyone was going through so much, no one more than Bill [Bixby]."

"Cancelling us was a huge mistake," Ferrigno adds. "We were still getting good ratings." After *Hulk*, the cast and crew remained busy. Bixby plunged into another CBS show, the sitcom *Goodnight, Beantown*, where he would act, produce and direct. The show was a reunion with his *Hulk* wife, Mariette Hartley. They played feuding newscasters. When the show was quickly cancelled, Bixby focused on directing. Outside of the green skin, Lou Ferrigno played larger-than-life characters like gladiators and Sinbad, as well as a paramedic on the TV series *Trauma Center*. Starring in Cannon Films' *Hercules*, Ferrigno did a funny publicity stunt where he wore his Hercules toga and drove a horse-drawn chariot down Hollywood Boulevard! The actor wound up getting a traffic ticket from a less-than-amused cop. The event was heavily covered by *The Los Angeles Times*, *The Herald-Examiner*, *Variety* and *Entertainment Tonight*.

"I made sure Cannon Films paid that ticket," he smiles. Ferrigno played Hulk again, in a 1985 episode of *Amazing Stories*, where TV characters like Hulk, Mrs. Cleaver from *Leave It To Beaver*, Face from *The A-Team* and Arnold from *Diff'rent Strokes* start coming out of the TV.

Kenneth Johnson had amazing success with his miniseries *V*, which spawned a sequel, a weekly TV series, toy and book lines and eventually a remake.

Of course, it was hard to keep a character as exciting as The Incredible Hulk down. In the late 1980s, B-movie company New World Pictures acquired Marvel Comics. This is long before the modern era of hit Marvel movies like *Spider-Man, Iron Man* and *X-Men*. At the time, Marvel was known for two things: the hit Bill Bixby *Hulk* television series and George Lucas' notorious mega flop adaptation of *Howard the Duck*. New World decided to revive The Hulk.

David Banner and his alter ego are back in action in *The Incredible Hulk Returns!*

THE INCREDIBLE HULK RETURNS

Directed By Nicholas Corea
Written By Nicholas Corea

Cast

Dr. David Banner . . . . Bill Bixby
The Hulk . . . . Lou Ferrigno
Jack McGee. . . . . Jack Colvin
Maggie Shaw. . . . . Lee Purcell
Mike Fouche . . . . Charles Napier
Joshua Lambert . . . . John Gabriel
Zack Lambert . . . . Jay Baker
Jack LaBeau. . . . . Tim Thomerson
Thor . . . . Eric Kramer
Donald Blake. . . . . Steve Levitt

David Banner is having a nightmare. Between flashbacks of the lab explosion from the pilot and The Hulk, we see brief glimpses of a beautiful woman. He awakens still human. David has successfully avoided transforming into The Hulk for two whole years. The beautiful woman is his girlfriend, biogeneticist Maggie Shaw. David and Maggie work at The Joshua Lambert Institute. Lambert, a millionaire philanthropist, knows David — now working under the psuedonym 'David Banyon' has something to hide. Because of the quality of David's work, the millionaire respects his wishes to stay out of the limelight and let the world believe him to be dead. Lambert's younger brother Zack is suspicious of David.

To hold back the change, David uses Maggie as his touchstone, focusing on her face to get past his rage. "I use you — your image — to maintain control," he tells her. "It's sort of like AA." David refuses to live with Maggie "for her own safety." She tells David that while she knows he feels he has a "monster in you", Maggie assumed he meant it as a metaphor of self-destructive behavior. When she urges Banner to let loose, he cautions "Some things you *can't* let loose!"

Now, David has finally reached the end of his quest — with Lambert's funding, he's built a Gamma Transponder that will permanently cure him of being The Hulk. He refuses to be identified as the creator of the device, preferring free lab time instead, to work on his cure. David is being spied on by a young guy who shadows him everywhere. The spy turns out to be Dr. Donald Blake, a former student with a unique problem. On a trip to Norway, Blake found "the sarcophagus of a grim warrior king named Thor." He finds the skeleton clutching an ancient hammer that summons the Viking warrior Thor! Blake is now pestered by the swaggering, pushy Thor, who he conjures by shouting "Odin."

Blake summons Thor into Banner's lab. In his helmet and battle armor, the boastful Viking loves to drink and fight. When Thor meets David Banner, he excitedly blurts out "This must be Banner the warlock" and tries to force him to become Hulk. Thor roughs up the good-natured sci-

Hulk is back to bending steel and thrashing villains in *The Incredible Hulk Returns!*

entist and scoffs when he's warned, "Don't make me angry." Thor soon finds himself face to face with a snarling Hulk. Knocked across the lab, an impressed Thor notes, "Odin's Beard, for a big troll you're a fighter!" The two heroes begin pushing and throwing each other into Banner's machines. The two brawl on, damaging the Transponder before the fight spills into the street below, attracting unwanted police attention. Oblivious to the havoc he has just wreaked on the scientist's life, Thor proudly tells David, "A fine battle we had, Banner, me and your troll!"

Although Banner is amazed by Thor, calling him "The wrath of God in a bottle", he feels Blake uses him irresponsibly. Angry at breaking his two year Hulk-free existence, he blasts Blake for bringing Thor into his lab to begin with. "I have stayed away from people like you," Banner snaps at Blake, "people who start trouble and run away!" When reports of The Hulk/Thor skirmish make the national news, Jack McGee, still reporting for *The National Register*, is sent to hunt for the elusive Hulk again. He demands his boss, Mark Roberts, give him back his expense account. Zack Lambert hires Cajun criminals Mike and Jack to steal the Transponder. Finding they can't get hold of it, they abduct Maggie instead, to get Banner to turn it over. When Zack objects to the kidnapping, they kill him for trying to back out of their deal..

Worried for her life and about putting his device in the wrong hands, Banner tells Blake he needs help. After a helicopter attack, Hulk and Thor meet again. They briefly battle to a stalemate, and just as in the comics, Hulk and Thor realize they are basically on the same side and team up to save Maggie! They storm an auto yard in Ontario, California, rescue the beautiful scientist and make short work of the Cajun killers. In the end, David kisses Maggie goodbye and once again takes to the road. Don Blake and Thor leave together, inspired by the way David Banner and The Hulk handle their dual existence.

Bill Bixby, Lou Ferrigno and Jack Colvin all return in a *Hulk* TV movie that was a ratings blockbuster. It's also nice that clever *Hulk* writer/director Nicholas Corea was able to do the honors on this. The TV movie came out in 1988, the 10th anniversary of the weekly TV series. Lou Ferrigno is in great shape as The Hulk; Bixby looks the same as Banner and seemed happy to talk about his character in this budding *Hulk* movie franchise.

Bixby told *Comics Scene* Magazine, "There's a loyal following of people who want to know what happened after Banner hit the road that last time. Now we're going to let them know...When the idea of the reunion film came up, I sat down and ran the original pilot, just to re-acquaint myself with The Hulk. It was pure dynamite even 11 years after the fact. I'm not playing him that much different. Banner is a little bit more mature and he has settled down to the point where he can have a satisfying relationship with a woman. Basically, he's still the same sensitive, compassionate individual, but he is now finally on the verge of getting away from this alter ego who has made his life a living hell."

The Incredible Hulk Returns is an enjoyable romp filled with a lot of action. Frankly, it's just plain fun to watch Bill Bixby's pupils dilate again as he transforms, as well as seeing Lou Ferrigno ripping up bulldozers and bending steel. As on the show, Bixby refers to Hulk as a disease and his "condition". Marvel Comics fans finally get to see a live-action Hulk battle a live-action Thor. Unfortunately, so many liberties are taken with

The Mighty Thor; he's almost unrecognizable from his comic-book counterpart. Instead of having Donald Blake strike his wooden stick upon the ground and transform into the thunder god Thor, he summons Thor by using that discredited '80s New Age fad, Channeling.

Besides Frye's Creature in "The First," Thor is the only other person in *The Incredible Hulk* TV series who can match Ferrigno's man-brute blow for blow. Unfortunately, once they team up, all suspense ends, as their crooked Cajun opponents don't stand a chance.

No longer the son of Odin, this Thor is an arrogant, boastful and brawling 11th-century Viking. Denied passage to Valhalla by Odin, he must first perform selfless acts for Mankind to redeem himself and become worthy to enter. Thor and Blake co-exist uneasily, sharing an apartment where they "hang out." There is a funny bit where Donald Blake attempts to bond with Thor, so the two go drinking and see Dave Alvin, lead singer of legendary rockabilly band The Blasters at a biker bar.

Eric Kramer puts a lot of gusto into Thor, you like his take on the character, a carefree Norse hellraiser. Kramer's Thor is playful and funny, especially in the fight scenes, where he calls Hulk "a troll." To Kramer's credit, he almost overcomes the ridiculous costume. Instead of his impressive Jack Kirby-designed warrior outfit from the comics with the stylized chest plate, winged and spiked helmet, cape and hammer, TV's Mighty Thor looks like he was dressed out of clothes found at Mardi Gras.

LOU FERRIGNO (Hulk): *"Getting to fight The Mighty Thor was a lot of fun! That's always been the big question in Marvel Comics: who is stronger, Hulk or Thor? It gave me the chance, as Hulk, to finally meet another superhero. It was a big change and I thought Eric Kramer had a great look as Thor. Eric was a stage-trained actor who played Thor well! Everybody wanted to see The Hulk fight Thor. Because Eric Kramer was from theater, he convinced me he was Thor — I really believed him! It made my job easier, because I kept thinking 'He's Thor!' In a Thor/Hulk fight, I think Hulk would win. Thor may be a Norse god, but he doesn't have The Hulk's inner rage. He is unstoppable; Thor would not be able to handle it.*

"I was ecstatic about New World doing The Incredible Hulk *reunion movie, because Bill was back, Jack Colvin was there as McGee and Nic Corea, one of the best* Hulk *writers, wrote and directed it. I remember me, Bill and Nic had a meeting in 1987 to set it up and I was so excited, I said to myself, 'We are finally bringing The Hulk back.' When we realized we were really gonna do it, I trained hard to get myself in the best shape of my life for The Hulk! Bill said we were gonna shoot in L.A., but because of New World producing, we*

weren't going to be under network pressure and I thought it was one of the best Hulks *that I have ever done.*

"*Coming back to play The Hulk was strange, since I had kids now…My son Louie came into my motor home, but he was so little, he didn't put together that his dad was this Hulk character. My young son knocked on the door, I opened it and said, 'Hi, Louie,' but I was all green, with the hair, eyes and teeth in. My son looked at me, slammed the door and ran! When my wife finally caught up to him, he said to her, 'MOMMY — KEEP DADDY IN THE MOTOR HOME AND KEEP THE DOOR LOCKED FOREVER!'"*

CHARLES NAPIER (Mike Fouche): "*I had a good time on that; I really enjoyed seeing Nic, Bixby and Ferrigno again! Tim Thomerson and I were the bad guys and I even did the voice of The Hulk again!*"

JOHN GOODWIN (Hulk Make-Up artist): "*Nic Corea was very unhappy with Thor. We all thought Eric Kramer did a great job, but we felt he should have gotten a body cast so they could have built armor for him. Problem was, there was no money for a body cast. The crew was paid nothing, so they just threw something together. Thor's hammer looked like it came from Home Depot! The armor was pathetic — they either couldn't get it done or didn't have the money. I could have made Thor's armor, but they kept peeling the budget on us. Nic really wanted Thor to work and the Hulk/Thor fight to be a grand battle. I could tell that he was really sad about it, he didn't really get what he wanted out of the movie.*"

MANNY PERRY (Stunt Hulk): "*I did the reunion movie, too. I really enjoyed seeing Lou, Bill, Jack and Nic Corea again.*"

CARL CIARFALIO (Stuntman): "*Doing* The Incredible Hulk Returns *TV movie meant a lot to me, because the* Hulk *TV series was pretty much my introduction to the world of entertainment. I was lucky enough to meet one of the finest stuntmen, stunt coordinators and all-around gentlemen in the industry, the late Frank Orsatti.*

"*Frank took a liking to me and gave me numerous opportunities to learn about stunts and hone my skills as a stuntman while I was surrounded by some of the best in the business. I also got to know and work with Nic Corea, one of the main writer/directors of the series as well as the following TV movies. Another wonderfully talented man who was full of life. He was taken from us far too soon.*"

LOU FERRIGNO (Hulk): *"Charlie Picerni was a wonderful stuntman; I trust my life to Charlie and did on several episodes. At the climax, when Thor and I pull down the helicopter? That's Charlie flying it! Charlie could fly a helicopter with the blades two feet above my head and I wouldn't worry at all. Eric Kramer, who played Thor, was a little nervous, but I told him, 'It's okay, Charlie Picerni is flying it!'"*

HULK FACTS

Lou Ferrigno bulked up by 40 pounds to play Hulk again.

Steve Levitt (Donald Blake) starred in *Hunk,* a *Hulk* parody, a year before he got *The Incredible Hulk Returns.*

Writer/director Corea wanted Hulk paired with Daredevil and Dr. Strange in future TV movies, but felt he should not team up with The X-Men or The Silver Surfer "because it would not work."

Tim Thomerson played the hero's brother in *The Flash* TV movie, as well as the sci-fi movie superheroes Jack Deth and Doll Man.

HULK PROFILE
ERIC ALLAN KRAMER: THE MIGHTY THOR!

In a dressing room on the set of his Disney Channel show *Good Luck Charlie*, Eric Allan Kramer sits behind a door labeled "Gene Simmons." "They wanted to know what our pseudonyms should be and he was the first name I thought of, as I play The Bat Demon in Ssik, my Kiss tribute band."

The tall, cheerful character actor "is a typical Disney Dad" on the family sitcom, but he actually has many offbeat characters under his belt. He was Little John in Mel Brooks' *Men In Tights*, Bear the flamboyant dancer in *American Wedding: American Pie 3*, a no-nonsense bodyguard in *True Romance* and The Skipper in the hit TV film *Surviving Gilligan's Island: The Incredibly True Story Of The Longest Three Hour Tour In History.*

Before all that, however, the Michigan native was The Mighty Thor, a brash, immortal Viking who tries to take on the green-skinned giant in *The Incredible Hulk Returns.* Seeing the error of his ways, he instead joins Banner and The Hulk on an epic adventure.

"I saw Thor as a fun-loving guy," Eric Allan Kramer explains. "Playing him was sort of like re-living my university parties! The character is a huge kid; Thor just wants to have fun and play, drink and knock guys around. That was an easy approach for the character. Even though he does battle with The Hulk, Thor was *not* a villain — he was actually as good as it gets."

The performer had to pinch himself, "because I loved the original *Hulk* TV show, it was a thrill to get a part in their reunion movie. I was such a huge fan of the *Hulk* television series when I went in, I remember thinking,

The Incredible Hulk and The Mighty Thor, Marvel's two strongest heroes, battle and bond!

'They will never hire me for this in a million years!' But one audition led to another and here I was. *Hulk* was a very lucky experience for me. I was in my twenties, and really didn't know L.A. then."

Doing battle with The Incredible Hulk "was very strange…There are some things that you just cannot believe you are doing, indelible moments you will never forget, and that was truly one of them! I think I had two

For Asgard: Eric Kramer carries The Hammer of Thor!

'Hollywood moments' on *Hulk*, where it became very apparent where you are. One of those moments was being in a full suit of Viking armor, standing across from Lou Ferrigno, all done up in green makeup, as I was waiting to get knocked around by The Hulk.

"It's one of those days where you get halfway through the shooting day and say, 'I can't believe I'm doing this!' It was great fun and Lou was a sweet guy. I first met Lou at the photo shoot to promote the show. Actually, I don't even remember Lou's face, all I recall are those huge arms walking in the door, because he bulked up for the role.

"When we shot it, Nic Corea told me that he was as big as he had ever been. Lou really looked phenomenal; huge arms and this giant set of shoulders. I said, 'Well, I guess you would have to be Lou Ferrigno!' I saw him at a recent audition and Lou still looked incredible. My body has certainly gone to pot a little bit, but Lou still looks phenomenal."

During the show's Thor/Hulk brawl, "Thor himself is excited as hell to fight Hulk, because he feels he has finally found a worthy opponent who can give him a good fight," Kramer proclaims. In the movie, Thor repeatedly shoves and attacks Hulk, repeatedly calling him a "troll."

"I call Hulk a troll because that was our throwback to Viking lore and that's what they believed. Thor knows nothing about Gamma Radiation, so to him, this big green guy must be a troll! That kind of thing was cool; if *Thor* had gone to series as they planned, you would have seen a lot more of that stuff. We would have brought in a lot more Norse mythology.

"They actually let me do some of my own moves during the Hulk/Thor fight. Lou Ferrigno is a very big guy — again, it's phenomenal to see a build like that up close and then feel a hand like that wrapped around the back of your neck," he says in wonder. "It's, um, very convincing when you get into the fight scenes and he's standing there, screaming in your face! He's throwing you onto transducers and into electrical panels, so it's a good day of getting knocked around."

His first day on the *Hulk* set "was so amazing, I will never forget it. I was staying on a friend's couch, when I headed for the set and could not be more nervous. I'm driving scared, because I didn't know where I was going, and I was using a Thomas Guide [an old-fashioned, pre-MapQuest map of L.A. freeways] to find it. We were shooting at Zuma Beach, so I took Topanga Canyon over to Pacific Coast Highway. It's 3:30 in the morning and I have a 4:30 call time.

"I start to drive as the fog rolls in. I'm driving up Topanga Canyon and I cannot see two feet in front of me! I feel like I'm in an episode of *The Twilight Zone*. The drive is going on forever; I'm in this thick, soupy fog all the way down to the beach, as I think, 'Where am I? What have I gotten myself into?' I finally hit Pacific Coast Highway, the fog breaks off and I can see the ocean. I find the set, get my make-up started and I have my leather Thor pants on, no shirt, walking on the beach just as the sun is coming up. I have my coffee and I see something break the water, crest and land with a huge splash. It was the whales migrating to

Eric Kramer is Thor!

Mexico! My very first morning in L.A. is this incredibly beautiful scene right out of a movie. The whales are really close to shore with their tails coming up as I stand there watching shirtless in Viking pants! It was like a Bob Seger song."

He was able to familiarize himself with Southern California through working on *Hulk*. "It was perfect because we shot all over the place.

Eric Allan Kramer. PHOTO BY PATRICK
JANKIEWICZ

David Banner's home was out at Zuma Beach, the lab was in a studio in Culver City, we shot in downtown L.A. alleyways…At the time, I remember thinking it was a great way to see Los Angeles, because I had to go to all of these locations. That allowed me to learn my way around the city very fast.

"Everybody on the show had a blast. You walk on the set and here are all of these faces that you had grown up with, like Bill Bixby, Tim Thomerson and Charles Napier. These guys had done it all, so it was a kick to sit down and talk to them. To be on the same set and the same TV screen as them was an honor. What was most amazing about that set was that everybody was approachable. We all got along, so for the first big 'Movie of the Week' of my life, it was a great experience. Every time you turned around, here was another familiar face that you knew from watching television yourself. There were times when I just looked around and said to myself, 'I am one lucky son of a gun, to get to come here and play with these guys.'"

Kramer found Bill Bixby to be "one of the warmest, funniest people that I had ever met. Bill was just the nicest, greatest guy. Incredibly smart, creative and very soft-spoken. There are certain people you meet that are so bright, you just shut up and listen to them — Bill was one of 'em! To just listen to Bill talk about his career, what he had done and what his life was like was an amazing learning experience. It also gave me great insight into who he was. This gave me a chance to learn from someone who had been there and had a heckuva resume! Bixby was not chatty but very approachable; he had a very comfortable presence about him. Bill was not at my auditions. I remember meeting Bill only after I first got cast.

"As a fan of the show, I liked that Jack Colvin, who played the reporter McGee, and I would share rides back to base camp in the van. We got along, but didn't have any really deep conversations," Kramer says. "Jack told me at that point, he had kind of been out of it for awhile, so he told me about his downtime and a home he was setting up. Colvin and I have that one scene together, which is an embarrassing story.

"I was in a towel, holding a beer in my hand for this scene where Jack McGee shows up looking for a story and I push him out into the hallway. We shoot that and then the director, Nic Corea, comes up to me. He says, 'Eric, I know you guys like to play around and get into character, but I have to tell you: you could use a little deodorant!' He thought it was a Method thing that I was a little ripe…I had to confess, "I'm so sorry, Nic — It was one of those mornings where I got up a little late and just charged out of the house!'

"Nic Corea also wrote it. He was a fabulous guy, fun to work with. The last time I saw Nic, I was playing racquetball. I looked back and in the little window on the door, I see Nicholas Corea's face — it had been several years after the show, so that was a surprise. We caught up a little bit."

Actress Lee Purcell says that in all her scenes, Bixby directed, not Corea. "Oh, really? That wasn't the case in my scenes. In all our time filming, it was clear that Nic was the director. They were obviously good friends on set, so maybe he let Bill do those scenes with her."

Thor "literally landed in my lap," he says of the role. "I came out to California in pilot season, and literally, my first audition was for *The Incredible Hulk Returns*! I remember going through the process, but they kind of told me at the audition that I had the gig. I told my agent, 'I think I got it' and there was a huge silence and then my agent said, 'You're kidding!' I got very lucky with Thor. I think I was as amazed as my agent was. I was a big comic-book buff and knew who Thor was — although I was a bigger Batman/Spider-Man comics fan."

Another kick was meeting Hulk and Thor creator, Stan Lee. "Stan was one of the guys who got me through my childhood; so it was great to associate the name I had seen on all of those comics that I had boxes of. It was really a great moment to finally meet the guy who had such an effect on me growing up. He was The Man! Stan got me interested in superheroes, which eventually led me to Thor."

Unlike the comic-book Thor, "I did not fly. When you're 6'3", 250 pounds like I am, they usually don't stick you up on wires. The only other superhero thing I did was a couple episodes of *Lois & Clark: The New Adventures of Superman* as an evil Kryptonian. I actually got to fly in that! On *Lois & Clark*, I got to be in a flying harness."

Thor's outfit looks thrown together. "They didn't even do a body cast of me," laughs Kramer. "There was a fellow named Clark Acton, whose company Wonder Works did all of Thor's armor. It *was* a little thrown

The Mighty Thor roughs up David Banner.

together, but it also looked cool. It was all beat up, so you could imagine Thor wearing it as he went through numerous wars.

"Clark and his company were all members of the SCA, a group called The Society of Creative Anachronisms. When *The Incredible Hulk Returns* aired, we had a big party at one of their houses. When they said my name, '*The Incredible Hulk Returns* with Bill Bixby, Lou Ferrigno and Eric Kramer,' everybody cheered. I realized that I wasn't going back home."

Thor was especially proud of his Uru Hammer. "It was great," Kramer praises. "We actually had two hammers. One was a rubber hammer, which was a little easier to swing around and then we had a heavier one that could do a little bit of damage, which I carried around. For the most part, it was the rubber hammer that you see me smiting people with. That was the one I used to knock Hulk around — it was all Wonder Works, they put that stuff together, including my hammer and my armor.

"The guy who I really felt bad for was my stuntman, Rex…My poor stunt guy kept getting hurt all through filming! The first thing we did was a scene down on the beach, when he was hanging onto the helicopter. The Thor outfit had a couple of edges on it, so when he came down, he had cut his chin open on the breastplate! You feel bad, because it's just some poor guy trying to make you look good.

"When he had to go through a window, they wanted him to go through the breakaway. He jumped up and hit the window headfirst. It stopped him cold, like in a cartoon, and then the window popped out as one solid piece, hung in midair so you could see that it wasn't broken, and crashed to the ground. They put a charge in it for the second time he jumped through, but he came out of it all cut up. A tremendous guy — he didn't deserve all that abuse," the actor sympathizes.

As for his favorite scene, "I actually have two favorites in *The Incredible Hulk Returns* for two different reasons," Kramer states. "The one scene that I really loved was the bar scene, Thor's first night out on the town. It's this one scene where Don Blake and I go to a bar. I'm able to go crazy, fight, throw people around and drink beer. Just for the sheer energy and physicality of that scene, I had a blast. My other favorite scene is a speech I give as Thor that I had on my demo reel for ages.

"In this speech, I try to explain to Steve Levitt, who played Thor's sidekick, Dr. Donald Blake, what it was like to be in Limbo for all those years. Now, to finally have this opportunity to live again and finally feel this body, to breathe and take in air and experience life again means a lot to Thor. The first time we did that scene, I had the helmet on and they didn't like that, so we actually went back and re-shot it. They wanted to see me in the shot, not have my face covered by the helmet.

"I remember I was sick as a dog the first time we shot it, so I was incredibly grateful to have a second shot at doing it. On the second time through, I was a lot more comfortable on set and with the character of Thor. For me, it was a very successful, memorable scene that made me feel like I truly belonged in Hollywood."

As *The Incredible Hulk Returns* was a ratings blockbuster, did Kramer's career get a bounce from it? "Did I get a bounce from *Hulk*," he muses. "Yes and no. It certainly gave my agent some ammunition and opened up some doors audition-wise. But you're playing a superhero named Thor, so it took a bit to convince people you could do other stuff. New World Pictures told me it was gonna be a backdoor pilot for a *Thor* TV series and they tried to sell it as one the year we did it. In the beginning, there was quite a bit of interest, but I do know that the Writers Strike hurt it.

There was a six-month Writers Guild Strike and by the time it ended, interest had passed. They were looking at it as a *Perfect Strangers*-type buddy show."

This Thor lost track of his alter ego. "I haven't seen Steve Levitt in ages. Steve was great as Don Blake. I used to bump into him in the oddest places. He would turn up in some sandwich place off the coast. It was always fun to see him. Kenneth Branagh directed a big-budget *Thor* movie and it would have been fun to do a cameo, just to acknowledge being a part of his past history. Being the first guy to be Thor is a great thing to tell the kids," Eric Allan Kramer shrugs. "To say to them, 'That was me, throwing the hammer at Hulk!' My kids have seen my *Hulk* movie. I think it surprised them to see their father minus 20 years!"

HULK PROFILE
LEE PURCELL

As sexy scientist Dr. Maggie Shaw, actress Lee Purcell plays a charming love interest in *The Incredible Hulk Returns*. She looks more like a model than a Gamma specialist, but the hardworking Purcell has been seen in dozens of movies and TV shows, including the cult classic *Valley Girl*.

Being a girlfriend to The Incredible Hulk was a new experience for the actress, who has been seen onscreen with Michael Douglas, Tommy Lee Jones, Charles Bronson and Orson Welles. "Hulk was probably my biggest leading man," Purcell jokes.

She also has a pivotal role in the film, as Banner focuses on her in his mind to hold back his Hulk Outs.

"I didn't have any interest in doing the original *Incredible Hulk* TV show because I was doing movies at that time," Lee Purcell admits. "I was happy to do the TV movie, because it got huge ratings — I felt really good about that. I loved Charlie Napier and Tim Thomerson, who kidnapped me. Great guys, just wonderful — if you're gonna get kidnapped I highly recommend getting kidnapped by them!

"Being rescued by two big, good-looking guys like Hulk and Thor also makes a girl feel special! Getting saved by them was fun," she says proudly. "Eric Kramer was sweet as Thor, and Lou Ferrigno is a big, big guy with hearing loss. I really liked him. He and his wife Carla are very nice people. Being carried by The Hulk was certainly a different experience! You're not used to being carried by a big green guy — an incredibly good-natured big green guy."

As it was an '80s TV movie, she has wild hair, crazy jewelry and, of course, big *Dynasty*-era shoulder pads. "I laugh thinking about my '80s wardrobe in that. It was the '80s, so I was dressed like every other woman in the '80s: big curly hair, gigantic shoulder pads and geometric jewelry, even though I was playing a scientist!

"When I auditioned, [writer/director] Nicholas Corea told me I got the part when I walked in the room. I remember that I cried on the audition, because my character had a scene where she's sad about something involving David Banner. Bill Bixby was a wonderful man, very brave. I was very impressed with him as an artist and a director. Although Nic was credited, Bill really directed it. I don't know why Nic got the credit, because Bill made every single decision. Bill decided everything, even how my hair and wardrobe looked. Bill even decided how short my skirts would be — he wanted to show my legs because I was a dancer. I fondly remember doing a scene with him and a dog on the beach. He had a thing for my legs, but it was not sexual," Purcell shrugs. "Bill said, 'You have dancer's calves; I love your legs!' Bill was handsome, smart and charming. If I had been single, I would have gone out with him in a second! I would also have gone out with Nic Corea — Nic was a rebel! A Vietnam vet, Nic was quite sexy with his long hair, tattoos and he even rode a motorcycle! A quintessential bad boy who was really a good boy underneath it all.

"I knew Bill was sick, but he looked good. You look at his life and the enormous tragedies he had, and it breaks your heart. I had a five-year-old son at the time and Bill talked about him and his own son. He showed me pictures of him in his wallet and only later told me that he had died," Lee Purcell says sadly. "He talked about his late [ex] wife Brenda, too. He only spoke of Brenda with deference and love."

HULK PROFILE
TIM THOMERSON

With his square jaw, steely eyes and mop of salt and pepper hair, Tim Thomerson looks like a hero. He has shared the screen with Robert Downey, Jr., Gene Hackman, Mel Gibson and other stars in big studio films, but the stand-up comedian-turned-actor really excelled in low-budget cinema, battling robots, zombies and aliens. He is so famous for his work in the fantasy genre, *The L.A. Weekly* declared him, "The Harrison Ford of B-Movies."

Thomerson played Jack LaBeau, a bad guy out to hijack Banner's Gamma Transponder by any means necessary.

"*The Incredible Hulk Returns* was a fun show. I like the fact that it took both The Hulk and Thor to stop me! I have a funny fight scene with The Hulk, where I try to take him down! The Hulk wraps a big metal bar around me and lifts me up off the ground as I wiggle around like a worm on a hook! I did that with Charlie Napier, who is a great, bitchin' guy. We were Cajuns in it, but that wasn't in the script, it was just Charlie's idea! He goes, 'Hey, Tim, let's be Cajuns!' I said 'Charlie, why are we Cajun?' and he said, 'Why not?'

Tim Thomerson. PHOTO BY PATRICK JANKIEWICZ

"I just did a Southern accent, because I couldn't quite get the Cajun patois. Charlie was more Cajun than me, because he's from Kentucky and knows how to talk that way. I was in the Army with a bunch of Cajuns and never knew what the hell they were talking about! 'Aye you fam O?' What was that about??

"The greatest part for me about doing *The Incredible Hulk* TV movie is that Bill Bixby gave me my very first job. It was *Mannix* and Anthony Zerbe got me the interview with Bill Bixby, who was directing the episode. Bill said, 'Yeah, fine, hire him!' I will never forget Bill for that. Doing this show gave me a chance to finally thank him for that and to tell him how much I appreciated it. Bill Bixby was classy. He came up to me on *Hulk* and said, 'How ya doing, man? I remember you!' I said, 'Bill, you gave me my career and my first job!' He wasn't sick then, but he didn't look as good as he usually did. Maybe he was just getting sick? I was sad about that — he was a great guy.

"It was a fun gig, because it was *Hulk*, man — that thing still plays worldwide! They run it in England all the time. The stunt coordinator, Frank Orsatti, was nice and Nic Corea, who directed, did the original TV series. Frank was a helluva nice guy. I still see Lou Ferrigno at the gym and we always bullshit about Hollywood."

Disorder in the court, as The Hulk objects, in *Trial of The Incredible Hulk!*

TRIAL OF THE INCREDIBLE HULK

Directed By Bill Bixby
Written By Gerald DiPego

Cast

Dr. David Banner . . . . Bill Bixby
The Hulk . . . . Lou Ferrigno
Ellie Mendez. . . . . .Marta DuBois
Christa Klein. . . . . Nancy Everhard
Edgar. . . . . Nicholas Hormann
Al Pettiman . . . . .Richard Cummings, Jr.
Albert G. Tendelli . . . . .Joseph Mascolo
Wilson Fisk. . . . . .John Rhys-Davies
Matt Murdock/Daredevil . . . . Rex Smith

When David tries to thwart a mugging in the subway, he ends up on trial for assault. His blind attorney, Matt Murdock, is secretly the superhero Daredevil who is trying to bring down notorious gangster/music producer Wilson Fisk. Although blind, Daredevil has a radar sense that allows him to combat crime. Fisk deduces that Daredevil is blind, which is not hard to do, since the character runs around wearing s black blindfold with no eyeholes in it as a mask, and sets a trap to finish him off once and for all.

A dull movie with a lot of talk and endless courtroom scenes, *Trial of the Incredible Hulk* is a boring disappointment from start to finish. It should have been called The *Dull Origin of Daredevil with a Brief Appearance by the Incredible Hulk.* The title was clearly chosen because of the popularity of legal shows at the time, like *LA Law.*

The TV movie takes its premise loosely from the comics. Hulk is put on trial for his life only to be defended by Matt Murdock in the classic comic-book story, "The World, My Jury," from *The Incredible Hulk* #153. From the title, one hoped it would really be the trial viewers waited for since the first TV movie, where David Banner is found alive and put on trial for the death of Elaina Marks and his involvement with The Hulk, so he can finally go face to face with Jack McGee. Instead, it's just a run-of-the-mill TV courtroom trial. Worse, it's not even The Hulk or Banner's *Trial*. It's a dragged out backdoor pilot for a *Daredevil* TV series. Nothing seen here would make you want to re-visit this take on the DD character.

A bushy, bearded Bill Bixby Hulks Out on the stand.

In the comics, Daredevil has no super powers other than his radar sense. He inhabits a gritty world of punks, creeps and lowlifes in bars and pool halls, so it's surprising that so little is done with him here. One is especially amazed that Nicholas Corea, whose *Hulk* scripts were filled with punks, creeps and lowlifes in bars and pool halls, didn't direct this movie. Very little is done with the Daredevil character. Slow-paced and turgid, things

Stan Lee appears in his first cameo in a Marvel movie (look for him over the shoulder of The Hulk) in *Trial of The Incredible Hulk!*

are only enlivened by a dream sequence where Banner Hulks Out in the courtroom. He attacks a jury box where the jury foreman is *Incredible Hulk* creator Stan Lee! This is the first Alfred Hitchcock-type cameo by Lee, who regularly makes fun appearances in the films made from his famous creations.

This great scene starts off as Matt Murdock tries to prepare David Banner's case for trial. Banner tells Murdock, "I *can't* stand trial. You don't understand, I — I can't. I have to avoid people, conflict — "

"You mean medically? You're not well?," asks a female lawyer helping Murdock. "I change...I *change*," Banner insists firmly. "I can't stand trial. You can't force me to go on the stand. I can't be held responsible...I'm telling you that its dangerous! I'm telling you that its impossible — " They jump to a dream sequence where David Banner, browbeaten and screamed at by the prosecutor, judge and even Matt Murdock, changes into The Hulk in a crowded courtroom. He beats up several bailiffs, hurls the prosecutor, shoves Murdock, smashes the jury box to bits and goes after the judge. A fun sequence that pumps up the otherwise dull movie.

As a director, Bill Bixby is energetic, with a lot of creative shots. As an actor, Bill Bixby seems to be phoning it in this time around, as he sports

Daredevil and The Hulk.

a big bushy beard as Banner that mysteriously disappears whenever he transforms into The Hulk. The wig on The Hulk looks better than the giant green mullet he sported in *The Incredible Hulk Returns*. Rex Smith is equally bland as both Daredevil and blind attorney Matt Murdock, lacking the fun that Eric Kramer brought to Thor.

This TV movie marked the first time a bad guy was taken from the comics, and it's The Kingpin, a Spider-Man/Daredevil villain. Kingpin is played here by John Rhys-Davies. Rhys-Davies, who was in such great films as *Raiders of the Lost Ark* and *The Lord of the Rings* trilogy, is at his hammiest here, a big chubby non-entity...His worst performance this side of his SyFy Channel stinkers *Sabretooth* and *Chupacabra: Dark Seas*! Rhys-Davies performance as Fisk turns the muscle-bound comics mobster into a fat, sunglasses-wearing MTV-style music impresario, with greasy hair instead of The Kingpin's bald head. His disrespect for The Kingpin even extended to interviews, where he mistakenly referred to the character as "The Lynchpin"! One far prefers Michael Clarke Duncan's take on The Kingpin in *Daredevil*. Despite not being half as enjoyable as *The Incredible Hulk Returns*, *Trial* was another ratings blockbuster. The Hulk would be back...

STAN LEE: *"When I saw Daredevil's costume in* Trial Of The Incredible Hulk, *I noticed that he didn't have any eyes on his mask. I said, 'Hey, where are his eyes?' They said, 'He's blind, right?' and I yelled, 'Yeah, but nobody's supposed to know he's blind!' I really enjoyed doing my cameo as the jury foreman — when Hulk smashes the jury box, I improvised a thumbs-down! Lou Ferrigno and Bill Bixby were really sweet guys and it was fun to see them together again."*

LOU FERRIGNO (Hulk): *"I loved having that scene with Stan Lee in the courtroom! I remember when I first met Stan; I was struck by the way he talked! I wanted to meet Stan since I was a kid and here he was, with that great New York voice!!"*

HULK FACTS
Marta DuBois starred in the gang movie *Boulevard Nights* with fellow *Hulk* guest Richard Yniguez.

DuBois had another trial, when she faced Captain Picard as The Devil, on *Star Trek: The Next Generation*.

As a Space Vampire on *Buck Rogers In The 25th Century*, Nicholas Hormann sucked out Erin Gray's life force — to the envy of teenage boys' everywhere!

In the comics, Hulk has never encountered The Kingpin.

Gerald DiPego wrote the hit fantasy films *Phenomenon* and *The Forgotten* for John Travolta and Julianne Moore.

DEATH OF THE INCREDIBLE HULK

Directed By Bill Bixby
Written By Gerald DiPego

Cast

Dr. David Banner .... Bill Bixby
The Hulk .... Lou Ferrigno
Jasmin .... Elizabeth Gracen
Dr. Ronald Pratt .... Phillip Sterling
Amy Pratt .... Barbara Tarbuck
Bella/Voshenko .... Anna Katarina
Zed .... John Novak
Kasha....................................Andreas Katsulas

Tagline: "The end of a superhero legend!"

David is at GeneCore Labs, where he poses as a mentally retarded janitor to get access to their equipment. He thinks he finally has a cure for his Hulk problem. With the help of newfound scientist friends Dr. Pratt and his wife Amy, David builds a machine that may be able to eliminate The Hulk forever. Jasmin, a beautiful spy, sabotages the experiment. Instead of being angry, Banner falls in love with her. David resolves to help rescue her sister from Kasha, her brutal spymaster from an evil, unnamed foreign power. When Jasmin is mortally injured, Banner saves her with a transfusion of his Gamma-irradiated blood.

In the process of saving Jasmin and her sister, Banner Hulks Out. After knocking out Kasha in a fight to the finish, he goes after the spies in a small plane on a rainy night. When The Hulk battles them in the cabin, villainess Voshenko fires a gun at him, causing the plane to explode. Thrown back from the blast, The Hulk flails and falls through the air. Poor Hulk slams into the concrete runway, cracking it with his body. The Pratts watch helplessly, as Jasmin runs over and holds the dying Hulk's hand — just as Hulk held Elaina Marks' hand in the original pilot.

Hulk gets weaker from his injuries, changing back to David Banner for the very last time.

"David, don't, don't die," a weeping Jasmin pleads. "We can be free — " The fatally injured Banner looks up at her with a peaceful expression, still holding her hand, and says "I am free," before succumbing to his injuries. His body is framed in a spotlight as a guitar version of "Lonely Man" plays.

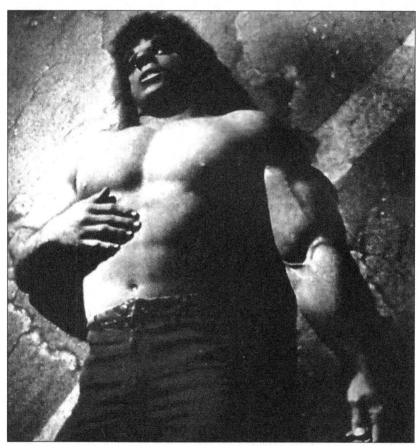

Hulk prepares to meet his maker – God, not Stan Lee!

A haunting, impressive end to a haunted, impressive character.

Bixby and DiPego make up for the dull *Trial* with this action-packed finale. Because the movie isn't saddled with superhero guest stars and origins, it feels like a really good episode of the series. This movie has everything, except Jack McGee. Jack really should have been in it. This is the death of The Hulk, as Jack McGee was there for his birth, he really should be on hand for the big finish.

As director, Bixby strives for a comic book look this time out, with the lab being lit in flashy blues and yellows. There's a great showy bit in the opening, where Hulk trashes some muggers and then smashes his way through the entire first floor of an apartment building, as shocked residents notice him passing through each of their homes. That's a regular event in the comics, but had never been attempted with such scale on the TV series.

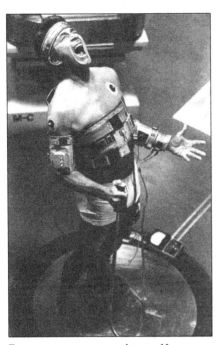

Banner tries to cure himself.

Banner also has a nifty *Day The Earth Stood Still* moment, where he fixes up one of Dr. Pratt's equations and Pratt realizes that David is actually a genius.

We see Hulk taking on terrorists and spies, two types of criminal he didn't confront on his TV show. Cool character actors abound, from a pre-*Babylon 5* Andreas Katsulas, whose sneer and bushy eyebrows made him born to play evil spies, and the interesting Anna Katarina, who makes her cliché character Voshenko somewhat more interesting than she needs to be. Because The Berlin Wall fell the year before *Death* aired, having evil spies from behind the Iron Curtain seems a little retro and dated, but it also fits, because early Stan Lee/Jack Kirby *Hulk* comics had him squaring off against evil Russians all the time, starting with his origin story.

It's easy to see that former Miss America Elizabeth Gracen was being groomed for a *She-Hulk* pilot. She gets that blood transfusion from David Banner — and at one point, mentions it "tingling" afterwards. Nothing is done with this interesting subplot. Bixby praised Gracen to Washington Post's *TV Week*, calling her "a natural" and noting that because "she was Miss America in 1982, we had a hard time selling her to the network. [They said] 'A beauty queen?'"

Gracen makes Jasmin memorable, despite the heavy '80s makeup leaving her looking like a dancer in Robert Palmer's "Addicted To Love" video. Gracen later became a superhero herself, in *Raven*, a *Highlander* TV series spin-off.

The highlight of the movie is Hulk's death scene, which is quite moving. Stopping the bad guys, The Hulk falls from the air to the ground in slow motion to sad music. Although he survived greater falls than that on the TV show, Hulk crashes to Earth. Obviously done for, he changes back to David Banner, says goodbye to Jasmin and his scientist friends, and then promptly dies.

For his final appearance, Ferrigno's Hulk replicated his look from the pilot...and still found time to break stuff!

In *TV Week*, Bill Bixby said, "It's a tragedy, which is good theater and [death is] something we all have to face. I have no doubt the last five minutes of the show will be very emotional for *Hulk* fans...It's a reality of life-death-and it can be handled well. And for David Banner, it's a way to be free."

Bixby was proud of *Death Of The Incredible Hulk*, telling *The Oregonian* newspaper that "It's certainly the best thing I've ever done as a director, and I'm very pleased with my acting in it. It's a very emotional show, as the title would imply. If the ratings are good you never can tell what might happen, but there is a sense of finality to it. While we were watching the last scene in the picture, several people in the room were crying, and no one could speak when the lights came up."

The actor/director admitted that, "I really do love [The Hulk]. I have great respect for Kenneth Johnson and once I had this finished, I put his first *Hulk* show up on the projector. [I] went from the very end of [the pilot] directly into mine. I wanted to have a flow of the style that really was established by Kenny and to bring it into the 1990s and it worked. I really could not be more pleased."

Because the story is about the end of The Hulk, the star did not want to burden it with any extraneous super-hero guest stars. "This is the whole reason for which The Hulk was born," Bixby declared, "and it doesn't involve many outside characters. It's a story in itself, a wonderful love story and a very thrilling adventure."

Lou Ferrigno was depressed to lose his alter ego. "I didn't like Hulk dying — it's one of the few shows that I would really like to forget," he admits. "The death scene itself was scary, because it was done late at night. They had the airplane going and it was raining very hard. If I went outside, my green make-up would run, so Bill told me, 'Run for the plane and, as soon as you get close to the wing, make a banana turn around and go beyond the plane.'

Banner and Hulk make the cover of *TV Week* for *Death of the Incredible Hulk*.

"With the rain and contact lenses, I could barely see anything at all in front of me. I turned and suddenly the plane's wing was right at face level — my face," the bodybuilder shudders. "I put my head down just in time! If that wing had hit my head, I would have seen Jesus! I incurred more injuries on that one show than any other *Hulk* I did. It really felt cursed to me."

As for Hulk's untimely death, Bixby praised Ferrigno's final Hulk performance, announcing that "Lou will move you emotionally in this picture. He's really improved as an actor." The director/star told *The Milwaukee Journal* that "Nothing successful on television is ever closed off. I don't want to give away the ending, but let's just say 'death' is a relative word when it comes to TV."

LOU FERRIGNO (Hulk): *"My wife Carla plays a bank teller in it. Onscreen, she's seven months pregnant with our son Brent. I was delighted to see her in a scene with Bill Bixby — it was like watching the whole family of The Hulk! We shot it in Vancouver."*

CARLA FERRIGNO (Bank teller): *"It was fun to do that little scene with Bill. I did plays and commercials, I was the 'Delta Dental' girl and guest-starred on the TV show* Super Force, *so it was fun to appear in The Hulk's final TV movie!"*

HULK FACTS

Anna Katarina menaced The Dark Knight, when she helped Penguin attack him in *Batman Returns*. She also played a Vulcan in J.J. Abrams' *Star Trek* reboot.

Andreas Katsulas murders Harrison Ford's wife in the movie version of *The Fugitive*, based on the TV series that inspired Kenneth Johnson's *Hulk*.

HULK PROFILE
BARBARA TARBUCK: SWEET SCIENTIST

A wonderful and busy actress, Detroit-born Barbara Tarbuck is as familiar as your next-door neighbor. She's the woman with 12 dogs on *ER*, Cliff's secretary on *Dallas*, Dwayne "The Rock" Johnson's mom in the remake of *Walking Tall*, and, for *Death of the Incredible Hulk*, the London Academy of Music and Dramatic Art-trained actress was Dr. Amy Pratt, Gamma scientist, who was helping her doctor husband Ronald Pratt and their friend David Banner rid Banner of his monstrous alter ego. Unfortunately, Banner and Hulk are killed by a fatal fall to the tarmac after leaping from an exploding plane. As Banner dies, Tarbuck is there.

Ironically, that wasn't her first brush with The Hulk. "The first thing I did on *The Incredible Hulk* was get cast to guest star as a nurse on the episode, 'Mystery Man,' but I never shot it. The night before I shot it, I slept at my boyfriend's place — he became my husband later. As this was before cell phones, they called my apartment to tell me they decided to shoot my scene earlier. They shot it without me, even though I get a credit. I thought my career was over — but Bill Bixby laughed and said, 'We'll work together again' and we did — he cast me in a major role in *Death Of The Incredible Hulk!*"

Death of the Incredible Hulk "was five weeks' work in Vancouver," Tarbuck says happily. "Bill Bixby was the star and the director. He was really keyed up, driven, focused on his work. In retrospect, I wonder if he knew he was sick at the time? He reminded me a lot of Michael Landon, as they were both stars in their own right who became directors. Landon and Bixby were the only directors who would hire me without making me read. Ironically, they both died of the same type of cancer. The two kindest directors I ever worked with, I remember thinking, 'How could this happen?!?'"

The actress found her part expanded during shooting. "Bill was so good to me; he even beefed up my role. I played Amy Pratt, who was supposed to be the nurturing wife of Banner's scientist friend, Ronald Pratt [Phillip Sterling], but Bill said, 'No, no, no, Barbara — you're not just 'the wife,' you are a fellow scientist and you do all the work with him!'"

The actor/director even gave her practical advice. "One day, I was ruminating about a scene, when Bill said to me, 'You've got to stop that second guessing, Barbara — you're better than that!' I wasn't second guessing my performance, but I didn't want to sound arrogant by saying to him, 'Oh, I know I'm better than that, Bill!' I did occasionally overthink things and it was a really valuable lesson. Bill made the shoot creative and fun. He had a real 'live-live-live!' attitude.

"It was a really fun shoot. The only problem I had on the shoot is my niece was getting married in the United States and I wanted to come home for the wedding," Tarbuck recalls. "I needed this extra day off, but I was slated to work. Bill came up to me and said, 'What's the problem?' He listened to my wish to go to my niece's wedding and finally said, 'Family is important.'

"Bill made it happen — he knew it was important to me. Not only did he give me that day off, he hired an extra, put her in my clothes, and had her photo double me in all of the aerial shots on the day I was supposed to work. I knew exactly what Bill meant when he said, 'Family's important.' Years earlier, my daughter's pediatrician, Dr. Landau, was also his son's doctor, Christopher Bixby. My daughter had an appointment the day Dr. Landau got word that Christopher died on that ski trip he went on with his mother. I was with her that day, when Dr. Landau came into our room just ashen and shaking. Oh, that was horrible; I never forgot that."

She was excited to see The Hulk in action. "I remember, one day on *Death Of The Incredible Hulk*, The Hulk had to bust through several walls — three in a row. Because of all the plaster and props involved, it was an expensive scene and they could only do it once. Bill was excited, on edge, but had no anger at all. I'm an actress who was trained in London — I have done Pinter plays, but I remember standing there, watching Hulk smash through walls and just having the time of my life! As loquacious and outgoing as Bill was, Lou Ferrigno was very quiet and trying to hold it together. We gave Lou his space, because he had to go through a lot of makeup for that role. I only appreciated what he went through in retrospect, when I did my first *Star Trek* role. After three hours in makeup and prosthetics for the very first time, all I could think was, 'Poor Lou Ferrigno!'"

The Hulk literally dies at her feet. "I'm standing there with the guy playing my husband, Phillip, when Hulk changes back to David Banner and dies. It was not gonna be a permanent death for The Hulk — we were supposed to revive him in the sequel! That's why our characters were there when he died."

Barbara Tarbuck remembers, "Bill Bixby was generous to a fault. He was a really remarkable man who truly touched my life. We had a wrap party in Vancouver, Canada when we completed, but Bill said, 'You know what? We deserve another wrap party — a real one!' He threw another one when we came back to Southern California. He rented out Chasen's Restaurant and threw a very expensive party. Everything was on Bill personally, which was extremely generous. I was very excited; because that was the only time I had been there before it closed!" (Chasen's opened in 1936 and finally shut its doors in 1995.)

REBIRTH OF THE INCREDIBLE HULK

(Unproduced TV Film)
Written By Robert McCullough

Despite the death of The Hulk in the previous movie, New World Pictures had no plans to let their big green cash cow rest in peace. "I knew if there was one thin dime left to be made from him, the studio would not let The Hulk go gently into that good night," jokes Kenneth Johnson, who had no involvement with the reunion films.

The lab set was left standing, as Hulk was not going to be dead long and a script was written to show how he survived his brush with doom. The TV series had already established Hulk's rapid metabolism, giving him a healing factor that helped him escape numerous jams on the show. *Rebirth* was going to pick up right where *Death of the Incredible Hulk* left off, as The Pratts, David Banner's husband-and-wife scientist friends, take his body back to the lab and find a way to revive him. The scientists were going to save Banner and The Hulk.

"We were definitely coming back to shoot this movie," Barbara Tarbuck confirms. "The sets were still up, we were gonna wear our wardrobe from the last movie and go right back to work. Bill Bixby was very excited about directing this. Bill and The Hulk were not going to be dead permanently... We were gonna revive David Banner and The Hulk in the TV movie called *Rebirth of the Incredible Hulk*!

"Bill said our goal was we would take an 8-12-week break after shooting *Death of the Incredible Hulk*, and then come back for *Rebirth*. We were so shocked when Bill got sick and then Phillip Sterling, who played my husband, died. Phil and I had stayed close because it was such a memorable shoot — we had a wonderful time making it and we both loved Bill so much after working with him."

"I was sad to see the Hulk go, but I always knew that Bill and I were going to be doing another one," Lou Ferrigno sighs. "The network thought it was a great concept to kill The Hulk and then we would come back with another TV movie that had a great storyline: The Hulk is revived with David Banner's mind controlling him. I believe it was going to be called *Revenge of the Incredible Hulk*, but unfortunately, Bill got sick."

Marvel Comics ran a blurb announcing that the title would be *Rebirth of the Incredible Hulk*. Writer Robert McCullough, who had scripted episodes of *Star Trek: The Next Generation* and *JAG*, wrote the film, alternately called *Revenge* and *Rebirth of the Incredible Hulk*.

"It was going to be action-packed," McCullough remembers. "I brought The Hulk back in a unique way and really had fun with him. There was a lot of cool Hulk action — I tried to have him do stuff he had never really done before. At one point, The Hulk was going to be underwater, pulling a dock behind him like the shark from *Jaws*, as the bad guy fires a machine gun at him. It would have been a lot of fun, but sadly, Bill Bixby became ill and the project was scrapped."

METAMORPHOSIS

The SHE-HULK TV pilot
Directed By Bradford May
Written by Jill Sherman Donner

Cast

Dr. David Banner . . . . Bill Bixby
The Hulk . . . . Lou Ferrigno
Jennifer Walters. . . . . Mitzi Kapture
She-Hulk. . . . . Gabrielle Reece

> *"Headlights converge on an Amazonian vision of a woman in a short, skin-tight black body suit and black boots, with GLOWING GREEN eyes and flaming red hair. She is over six feet tall, her long, lean muscles rippling beneath skin that seems to shimmer in the dark…it is SHE-HULK!"*
> From the "Metamorphosis" teleplay.

Jennifer Walters is an assistant district attorney haunted by the unsolved murders of her parents from when she was a child. At work, she is close to exposing Jonathan Cole, a popular businessman known for his philanthropy, who she believes is actually a criminal mastermind. When she gets too close, her boss, the D.A. — a friend of Cole's — forces her to take a vacation. Going to the Bahamas, she meets a handsome towel boy, who is actually fugitive scientist David Banner. In this tropical paradise, Banner has finally found a way to hold back The Hulk.

On the island, only Dr. Joseph Bahia knows David is The Incredible Hulk and helps him control his Hulk Outs with orchids and herbs in his tea. This cleverly references Karen Harris and Jill Sherman Donner's *Hulk* episodes "Rainbow's End" and "Kindred Spirits." After showing her around, Jennifer and Banner start getting romantic, as they are not cousins in the TV version. Jennifer finally asks David what he used to do before working at the resort.

"Lots of different things," David Banner responds enigmatically, refer-ring to all the different jobs he held on the series. "A little of this...a little of that...Nothing you'd be interested in." As things grow serious between Banner and Jennifer, the two ride on an island bus that is blown up by a hit man sent by Cole to eliminate Jennifer. David changes into The Hulk, who lifts up the bus, saving Jennifer and the other passengers. In the hospital, Jennifer is dying from her internal injuries.

Dr. Bahia urges Banner to give Jennifer a blood transfusion. David disagrees, telling him, "The metamorphosis accelerates the cell regenera-tion...I can't give her blood. You saw the creature...We don't know what the side effects might be. It's too big a risk.

When Bahai tells him, "Yes, there is a risk...But without it, she'll hemorrhage again, and this time a hundred normal transfusions won't save her. David, you're her only hope." A pressed and wary Banner reluctantly agrees and gives Jennifer his blood. As Jennifer is recovering, David tries to tell her about her new condition.

"Jennifer...Something happened...after the accident. They gave you a transfusion of my blood..." She is too groggy to understand, so David follows her back to California. Attacked again by Cole's thugs, Jennifer beats them up as The She-Hulk.

Transforming back, she wakes the next day thinking it was all a dream. "It was scary. But then all of a sudden, I wasn't afraid. I felt like I was in the middle of a tornado," Jennifer muses. "Or I was the tornado. I was powerful...I was strong...I was fearless." A California doctor checks Jennifer's Gamma irradiated blood and declares, "These results are inac-curate — in fact, they're humanly impossible." To further the TV show connection, *The National Register's* roving reporter, Jack McGee, shows up on the trail of She-Hulk, hoping it's a mistaken Hulk sighting.

Interviewing two homeless guys who saw She-Hulk in action, McGee tells them, "This creature *couldn't* have been female. Now you guys could have been mistaken. After all, it was dark." One of the bums tells him, "When it comes to women, it's never that dark!" The other bum describes She-Hulk as "A woman and a half!"

Jennifer's indignant boss refuses to listen to her theory on Cole's crimi-nal ties and leaves in his Corvette. Jennifer becomes She-Hulk, easily catches him in his prized sports car and, the script declares that "SHE-HULK pushes the car into a concrete wall, squashing it into a $50,000 accordion." She-Hulk also tears through elevator doors like cardboard.

David Banner shows up after She-Hulk reverts to Jennifer. Back in her apartment, David makes her tea and urges her to get more sleep. "I'd just have another nightmare," Jennifer replies. "The trouble is they're *not* nightmares, are they, David?" Banner is stunned that she actually remembers being She-Hulk. As he explains to Jennifer, "I have no memory once my metamorphosis begins." He then briefly tells her his origin: "A long time ago, I was exposed to a huge overdose of Gamma Radiation. It altered my body chemistry and, under certain conditions, I turn into

someone…some*thing*…not quite human."

Jennifer interrupts, "And now that happens to me." David Banner adds, "The only way to save your life was a transfusion. Somehow, the genetic mutation was carried in my blood."

"Mutation," a stunned Jennifer repeats. "My God…"

David tracked her down when he saw *The National Register* headline "She-Hulk sighted in L.A." Jennifer looks at the paper, which has an artist's conception of what her alter ego looks like.

"That's the thing I turn into…When it happens, it's like a thousand explosions going off inside my head. I feel like I'll go deaf from the noise and blind from the light. Every nerve in my body is on the outside of my skin. Oh, David, I wish I couldn't remember…" She and Banner race to the Mirage Casino in Las Vegas to find out who's trying to kill Jennifer. After they both Hulk Out in The Mirage, Hulk leads her out of the crowded casino because, as Jennifer notes, She-Hulk is blinded by bright lights. Jack McGee shows up looking for Hulk. He also takes note of the existence of The She-Hulk. McGee points out, "The witnesses said he [Hulk] did all this with a little help from 'a golden-skinned Amazon with flaming hair and emerald eyes.' You wouldn't have happened to see a female creature that matches that description?"

The Savage She-Hulk, Stan Lee's comic-book spin-off that was inspired by the Bill Bixby TV show, finally gets adapted by one of *The Incredible Hulk* TV show's best writers, Jill Sherman Donner. The script was done in 1990, exactly one decade after She-Hulk's comic book debut. A clever character full of witty comments and observations, She-Hulk seemed ideal for her own TV series. Unfortunately, outside of the cameo appearances by David Banner, Hulk and Jack McGee, the pilot is pretty dull, with a perfunctory set-up that was probably forced upon Jill Sherman Donner by New World Pictures.

Donner captures David Banner's voice so well, you wish New World would have let her dump their take on She-Hulk entirely and just do a fourth *Hulk* TV movie. She and writing partner Karen Harris did some of the best Jack McGee/*National Register* episodes of the original series, so it would have been nice to have a bit more with him in this. Instead,

Jill Sherman Donner. PHOTO BY PATRICK JANKIEWICZ

it's just Jack Colvin doing his routine, "Have you seen a big green creature?" shtick.

"At the time, New World Pictures owned Marvel Comics. I got a call from New World that they were doing The She-Hulk," Jill Sherman Donner explains. "They had gone through a number of drafts and asked me to do one. My script was the only draft that Bill Bixby approved."

Although David Banner was quite dead in the last TV movie, he shows up here very much alive with no explanation given. "The Hulk *was* dead, but we establish that he was hiding in the Caribbean," smiles Donner. "I didn't have him give any reason for being alive." Bill Bixby also returned to help usher in his series' spin-off, in what would prove to be the very last time he played Dr. David Banner. "Yes, we needed Bill in it because we couldn't launch it without some tie-in to his character.

"I really loved seeing Bill again, as he played David Banner for the final time," the writer states. "Bill had been so angry toward the end of the TV series, with Christopher and Brenda's deaths. He had really mellowed by the time we did *She-Hulk* together. Bill was there for at least a week and we shot for several days, maybe a dozen or so pages of the script. Most of what was shot included him."

In "The She-Hulk Lives," the fast 17-page story that began her comic-book series, Stan Lee nimbly introduces Jennifer Walters, her relationship to Bruce Banner, her career, enemies, her origin and The She-Hulk. Donner's TV script is five times longer than that comic and drags. The pilot feels like it's being choked by studio notes. The main note seems to have been "*Batman* it up!"

Jennifer's nightmares over her parents' unsolved death and Newman, the reporter hunting She-Hulk, are both stolen from Tim Burton's *Batman* movie, which was the highest grossing movie the year before "Metamorphosis" was written. Jennifer's father is alive in the comic. Nice reporter Newman, an obvious imitation of Robert Wuhl's Knox in *Batman*, should wear a sign reading "Jennifer's Love Interest." There are some similarities between the comic and the pilot: both Jennifers are lawyers attacked by hit men sent by a powerful man. Stan Lee has her gunned down by gangsters and both are saved by a blood transfusion from Banner, which turns them into She-Hulks. Both comic and TV She-Hulks tear a sports car apart and rip through elevator doors.

In her comic-book origin, Banner saves her in the driveway of her California home, rather than taking a pointless trip to the Bahamas, which plays like a bad John Grisham novel. After she's injured, David Banner has to be pressured by Doctor Bahai into giving Jennifer a life-saving blood transfusion, while he willingly volunteered to help Jasmin despite the risks in *Death Of The Incredible Hulk*. That movie seemed to be setting Jasmin up as a She-Hulk, but she's totally ignored here.

David Banner has an interesting role in the pilot. Besides giving her the transfusion, "he has terrible guilt over turning her into The She-Hulk," Jill Sherman Donner points out. "Banner knew that she had no chance for survival without his blood transfusion, but now she has to deal with this beast within her. In my script, Jennifer is an attorney like she is in the comics, but she isn't his cousin. After the pilot, Jennifer would no longer be an attorney — she would have been on the road, searching for her cure."

Because the TV *Hulk* is their framework, the normally verbose She-Hulk is now a mute, growling creature, which is how she was depicted in the first issue of her comic. Marvel found that making her breezy and happy-go-lucky increased her popularity and differentiated her from the morose life of Bruce Banner and The Hulk.

The She-Hulk's iconic look in the comics of a tall, sexy green woman, is also thrown out. Now she's a tall, golden woman with bright red hair and green eyes. Doing She-Hulk without green skin really makes no sense. Just like Kenneth Johnson, Sherman Donner tried to rebel against

With her beautiful green skin, *Wizard* Magazine felt *Star Trek: Enterprise* alien Bobbie Sue Luther would make a perfect She-Hulk!

the Gamma Green skin color of The Hulk. By doing so, she alienates the character from her base and loses She-Hulk's most recognizable characteristic that ties her to The Hulk: her green skin.

"I made her golden instead of green because green isn't pretty. Changing her skin color made her seem more feminine, prettier and different than just making her green," says Jill Sherman Donner unconvincingly. Of course, as any casual *Star Trek* viewer would note, a tall green woman can be pretty damn sexy, too. Whenever they do a story on the comic-book She-Hulk, comic industry bible *Wizard Magazine* usually runs a picture of *Enterprise'* green Orion slave girl Bobbi Sue Luther because of her strong resemblance to the She-Hulk character in the comic.

"There's nothing like a green woman to get everybody's attention," says actress Bobbi Sue Luther. "I learned firsthand that a beautiful green woman tends to stand out in a crowd. Having her own unique skin color fascinates you. I don't know why so many people respond so strongly to the green skin, but they really do. Being the Hulk's cousin, She-Hulk's green skin would make her stand out! I was pleased that *Wizard Magazine*

Baywatch/Silk Stalkings star Mitzi Kapture was cast as Jennifer Walters, the lawyer who turns into She-Hulk. PHOTO BY PATRICK JANKIEWICZ

thought I looked like the perfect She-Hulk. Any *She-Hulk* producer would already know that I look good in green!"

When it came time to cast a female Hulk, Lou Ferrigno made a suggestion. "I actually recommended a woman who I thought would be perfect to play She-Hulk, Nicole Bass. Nicole is a female bodybuilder and I thought she had the physique for it."

Instead of Bass for the live-action She-Hulk, Jill Sherman Donner remembers that "We cast Gabrielle Reece, who became the new Nike spokesperson after we shot the pilot. Gabrielle is gorgeous; a tall model/volleyball player and divinely classic Grecian beauty. This woman looked like a lioness and she was going to be our She-Hulk!"

As for the Gamma girl's personality, "I played She-Hulk right out of the Kenneth Johnson legacy," says Donner. "We played her absolutely straight; it was strong emotions that triggered Jennifer's transformations into She-Hulk, not just anger."

Problems for the pilot started when seeking someone to play Jennifer Walters, the She-Hulk's alter ego. "We could not find an actress," Sherman Donner groans. "We needed the female equivalent of David Banner. We looked for an actress that the network felt could carry the pilot and finally found Mitzi Kapture."

With their She-Hulk cast, Jennifer Walters, the important "female Banner" would be played by Mitzi Kapture, a striking performer who had experience as a life-saving heroine: she had been a lifeguard on *Baywatch*! Instead of being relieved that they had a beautiful, talented actress playing Jennifer, the short-sighted studio and network were greedily obsessed with finding a bigger name.

"With Mitzi, we cast an actress that we thought was very talented, but the network didn't feel she was strong enough to carry the show," says Jill Sherman Donner. "They didn't feel she was a big enough name."

Despite not having a big enough female "name," shooting began with Kapture and Bixby. "We prepped and filmed on St. John in the Virgin Islands," Sherman Donner adds. "We started doing film tests of actresses for Jennifer Walters, but She-Hulk was cast with Gabrielle. We were on our way to the Virgin Islands the next day or the day after."

Mitzi Kapture was amazed to go almost instantaneously from the audition to location. "I auditioned on a Saturday morning and they cast me by eleven o'clock," the actress shrugs. "There were a hundred girls reading for it. Everyone else had been testing for it, so they were all nervous. I was not nervous and the whole *She-Hulk* experience was quite magical for me. I just walked in from the casting session and they sent me straight to ABC. I went to ABC, the executive told me, 'We're picking it up and we want you to do it. We also want you on a plane by eight o'clock tonight [to the Virgin Islands].' That's how fast it happened.

"It was interesting, because it took three plane rides and a boat to get to the location," a still-stunned Mitzi Kapture says, shaking her head. "On the flight, I started reading the script more thoroughly. The script was called *Metamorphosis*, or *Metamorphosis: The Search*, but I got about halfway through and realized, 'Oh, my God — she's She-Hulk!'

"The highlight for me was meeting and working with Bill Bixby. He was a divine actor and human being. I met him a short time before he…," Kapture says, stopping thoughtfully. "He was just such a gentleman and scholar. He made me feel totally comfortable. Because of that, I had a really great time on this *She-Hulk* pilot. My first scene in the pilot was where I meet Bill on the beach. It was so great; Bill Bixby was a real pleasure to work with. To be quite honest, I thought *She-Hulk* was an interesting idea for a female superhero series. Playing a woman who turns into a She-Hulk was gonna be a blast."

While she and Bixby filmed, the network fretted that the Jennifer Walters character should have a bigger "name" in the role. Sherman Donner remembers, "The network said their first choice for Jennifer was Melissa Gilbert." Gilbert, a former child actress from *Little House on the Prairie*, rose to become a major star of bland made-for-TV women's dramas and miniseries. She also became a producer and Screen Actors Guild president. Ironically, she talked herself out of the pilot.

"Melissa unknowingly said something on a set I was on," Jill Sherman Donner reveals. "She had no idea who I was, when she mentioned to someone that a studio had sent her [disdainful tone] 'something called *She-Hulk*, where I would actually turn green!' There's still a little residual bitterness about that. It was good enough for Bill Bixby; if he could see all the dimensions in that series, why couldn't she? I don't think Melissa or her agent realized that she would get to play such an interesting character."

For the part of Jennifer, "We needed someone like Bill Bixby, which could have been Melissa Gilbert. It's a lesson for actresses. There are too few lead characters on TV series written for women to be dismissed out of hand, especially after Bill Bixby and Kenneth Johnson made it such a classy thing to be associated with. We needed a female name and it seemed all of the female names it was offered to just didn't get it."

As the pilot was being made, "the deal was that the network would look at what we shot and determine if they wanted it," Sherman Donner explains. "The entire crew, including Bill Bixby, was in The Caribbean, the only ones over here were the director [Bradford May] and me. At 7 a.m., [casting director] Barbara Claman called and said, 'I've got three more actresses' [to audition for Jennifer Walters]. Ironically, the night before, the director and I went out and got plotzed with our spouses and said, 'It's over, we'll call everybody back home tomorrow.'

"Because of no [big name actress for] Jennifer Walters, the project stalled. We went in to see the actresses and shortly thereafter, the plug was officially pulled. That was after four days of footage was filmed. I think we could have pulled off a good two-hour TV movie, but so much had been spent on pre-production, travel and expenses…It would have been Bill's last performance as Dr. David Banner and it would have been a direct handover from one *Hulk* series to the next. With Bill's death, there was no way to hand over the franchise."

Mitzi Kapture remembers being told that "The network was having trouble with the rights to She-Hulk; supposedly they were upset because the She-Hulk had been used in a cartoon and that somehow affected the pilot's rights. I never knew that Gabrielle Reece had been set to play She-Hulk. I was really bummed when they cancelled the pilot, because how often do you get a sci-fi project with a strong female lead? I mean, it would have been like being Linda Hamilton in *Terminator!* I wanted to be Jennifer, the woman who turned into this badass She-Hulk."

Not finishing the pilot with Mitzi Kapture starring proved to be a costly mistake for New World. Mitzi Kapture went on to star in *Silk Stalkings*, a show that lasted briefly on network TV before becoming a basic cable blockbuster, not to mention her syndicated success with *Baywatch*. By finishing the film with Kapture and not chasing the former star of *Little House on the Prairie* would have given them a TV movie with a star who had a huge syndicated audience.

Lou Ferrigno had looked forward to reprising The Hulk. "Bill Bixby had gotten involved with it, so I was happy to bring Hulk back. They didn't finish the movie, which is too bad, because it would have been fun to see my Hulk and She-Hulk in action together. She-Hulk's a great character and being around her shows another side of The Hulk, almost protective and brotherly. Hulk teamed up with She-Hulk on the animated show and She-Hulk brought a lot to it. Having her in live action would have worked really well."

Seemingly cursed, She-Hulk failed to show up as either a television pilot or as a Brigitte Nielsen film.

Being reunited with Bill Bixby was a highlight for Donner. "The very best part for me on *She-Hulk* is that Bill Bixby and I got to work together again, years after the original series. I had not seen Bill in a while and we did not leave on great terms after *Hulk*. On the pilot, I was 'all grown up' now and Bill was no longer 'Daddy.' We truly got to work together on *She-Hulk*, which was thrilling.

"After we were cancelled, Bill and I had a couple of days together to go boating and relive the good old days. I'm not sure if he knew that his illness had returned or felt he'd beat the cancer, but he was very kind, introspective and, as always, witty and endearing in his own unique way," Sherman Donner says thoughtfully. "It was wonderful to have that time with him, especially now that he's gone. In fact, he told me a secret that I gave my word I would never tell. And I haven't. Not even to my husband. It was a small one, but it's my honor to keep it. After I and the crew left, he stayed on the island for a vacation."

To this day, every attempt to make a live-action *She-Hulk* has failed. An attempt at making a *She-Hulk* movie starring Brigitte Nielsen, written by *Jaws* scribe Carl Gottlieb, also collapsed. "There are currently no plans for a *She-Hulk* movie of any kind," announces Marvel Films President Kevin Feige.

HULK FACTS

Mitzi Kapture, cast as Jennifer Walters, had appeared on *Liberty & Bash* with Lou Ferrigno.

"Metamorphosis" director Bradford May helmed the *Smallville* episode "Aqua" that introduced Aquaman.

Melissa Gilbert later played a superheroine when she voiced Batgirl on *Batman: The Animated Series*.

In the script, we learn that David Banner is Blood Type O, making him a universal donor.

THE INCREDIBLE HULK CARTOON

After Lou Ferrigno's Hulk died, the character took a long hiatus from movies and TV, until Marvel produced a 1996 *Hulk* cartoon. An ambitious attempt to do The Hulk's adventures faithfully, the show had great designs by illustrator Joel Adams, who gave the monster a distinct Jack Kirby look.

"When I came onto *The Incredible Hulk* animated series in 1996, I took over for another character designer [Kurt Conner] who had begun to establish the look," Joel Adams says. "He had not gone so far with the style that there was no flexibility with it and I was given permission to push the look where I could. The Hulk had been big and bulky, but simple in shape with bad anatomy. I was able to add character, form, and anatomy to the designs."

He also got to design Hulk's sexy green cousin. "With She-Hulk, I had more freedom and wanted to design a She-Hulk who was not just a giant of a woman but had muscle. I think we found that happy medium of muscularity and femininity. My inspiration was bodybuilder Cory Everson for the She-Hulk's physique."

Hulk fights a collection of comic-book villains who would be too expensive to use in the live-action movies, like the electrical enemy Zzyzax. Soap siren Genie Francis voiced Betty Ross, John Vernon, Major Glen Talbot in the 1966 *Hulk* cartoon, was promoted to General Thaddeus "Thunderbolt" Ross. Neal McDonough voiced Bruce Banner and *Beverly Hills 90210* star Luke Perry was Bruce Banner's loyal teenage sidekick, Rick Jones. For the voice of The Hulk, the producers chose an actor named LOU FERRIGNO!

"As a kid I was a huge fan of the TV series. There was a bit of nerd in me that thought it was really cool that Lou was going to do the voice for Hulk," Adams grins.

Finally allowed to voice his alter ego, Lou Ferrigno gave Hulk a formidable growl and an angry, guttural sound. "In the very beginning, for the first episodes of the cartoon, Hulk was very serious, but when the series went on, he has a little sense of humor," says Ferrigno. "Hulk says, 'I'm mean, I'm green and I'm gonna crash, bash and smash you!' That's the child in Hulk, just having fun.

"It's an honor to finally do the voice of The Hulk," Ferrigno continues. "I always wanted to do it on the original show. When you speak as The Hulk, you don't talk in complete sentences. I have to bring emotion to

those words and it's not an easy thing to do, but I love the challenge. When I'm in the sound booth, I really get into the character; I stand up and the whole place trembles with my growling! Still, it's not the growl that works; it's the emotion that you put behind it. Every time I did the Hulk voice, Luke Perry would move three feet away!"

The actor saw the comic-book potential to the show. "Because it's animated, there was no limit to what you could do! Hulk could battle the Army, aliens and all of his greatest villains! My favorite was The Gargoyle, played by [*Star Wars*] Mark Hamill. Gargoyle is this little bald guy with huge bulging eyes who works for The Leader. Those two made a great team and The Hulk can't stand either one of 'em! Mark gave Gargoyle this evil little voice. It's exciting to work with people like Hamill, Peter Strauss and [supermodel] Kathy Ireland."

"It's fun to be a bigger-than-life monster and fight Batman, Spider-Man or The Hulk," says Mark Hamill, a giant in the action cartoon community. "You look at a character like The Joker or The Gargoyle and determine what he sounds like."

Hulk's cousin was also added to the series. "Lisa Zane was the voice of She-Hulk," Ferrigno recalls. "She-Hulk was fun, because Lisa would do her lines with a really sexy voice. When you saw the animated character, Lisa's voice matched her perfectly."

The show also allowed Hulk to do things that had never been seen outside the comics because, unlike live action, the scale of cartoon carnage was limitless.

"Hulk really got to be Hulk," an enthusiastic Ferrigno raves. "I got to fight Iron Man on a collapsing California freeway as well as The Thing from *The Fantastic Four*, and even Thor!" Having an all-star cast to fight with impressed Ferrigno. "Matt Frewer was wonderful as The Leader, Shadoe Stevens was good as Doc Samson and Richard Moll was really formidable as The Abomination. I loved The Abomination, because he seemed like the one guy who could actually give Hulk a hard time. Sometimes you would have me growling as Hulk, Richard growling as Abomination and two or three other actors growling and you would realize that we were all just a bunch of big kids having fun!"

As Bruce Banner, "Neil McDonough was great. It's neat, when they did transformation scenes, because Neil would groan as Bruce while they go right into my growl — it was seamless!" The live-action *Incredible Hulk* TV series reared its head in the second season, when Genie Francis returned to soap operas, only to be replaced as Betty Ross by another soap actress named Philece Sampler. Sampler had co-starred on the *Hulk* episode "Dark Side," where she played a confused teenage girl who develops a crush on David Banner. "Oh, I thought that was great," laughs Ferrigno. "This little girl was now Betty Ross!"

HULK FACTS

The show marks the first appearance of satanic cyclist Ghost Rider outside the comics, voiced by *21 Jump Street*'s Richard Greico.

John Rhys Davies, who wrecked The Kingpin in *Trial of the Incredible Hulk*, voices The Mighty Thor.

Hulk/She-Hulk creator Stan Lee voiced She-Hulk's dad, Cliff Walters.

She-Hulk was voiced by both Lisa Zane and Cree Summer.

FILM

HULK

Directed By Ang Lee
Written By John Turman, Michael France and James Schamus
Based on characters created by Stan Lee & Jack Kirby

Cast

Dr. Bruce Banner.	Eric Bana
Betty Ross	Jennifer Connolly
Ross.	Sam Elliot

"You're making me angry. You wouldn't like me when I'm angry!"
Bruce Banner

Scientist Bruce Krensler works at a lab with his gorgeous ex-girlfriend, Betty Ross. His Gamma experiments have no practical application, other than making frogs explode. He accidentally alters his body chemistry, turning into a creature of monstrous appearance and strength that comes to be known as The Hulk. He finds out that his father was actually David Banner, a crazed scientist who murdered Bruce's mother and disappeared. His adopted mother, Mrs. Krensler, hid his true identity from him to spare him his destiny, even though he has vivid memories of his real mother's murder in front of him as a child. Now a janitor at the same lab that Bruce works at, David Banner has also become something more than human. David is thrilled to see his son transform into The Hulk. After running amok, The Hulk clashes with several Gamma-irradiated Hulk dogs that David created, protects Betty and as Banner, argues with her father, General Thaddeus Ross, before having a rampage through downtown Berkeley. In the big finish, Hulk battles his own mutated father in the desert.

When a Gamma bomb is dropped on both monsters, Hulk and his father are believed dead. In a rain forest off the Amazon, a bearded Banner is distributing medicine to the poor. Soldiers begin stealing the medicine. When Banner warns their leader that they're making him angry, we hear

The Hulk suddenly growl, machine gun fire and screaming soldiers. A big-budget adaptation of *The Incredible Hulk*, the movie made quite a few changes to the comic-book storyline, adding more than a few elements from the Kenneth Johnson television series. Most controversially, David Banner's name is used for the name of Bruce Banner's mother-killing sadist of a father, played by Nick Nolte. Ironically, Nolte broke into the public

eye when he did *Rich Man, Poor Man* with director/co-star Bill Bixby.

The Hulk was played by a computer-generated effect seven feet tall and full of raging fury. He grows to a sixteen-foot-tall special effect who seemed unable to maintain realistic eye contact with anyone sharing a scene with him. We hear, "You're making me angry — you wouldn't like me when I'm angry" in English and Spanish. They also continue Johnson's tradition of not calling The Hulk "Hulk." This is epitomized when the National Security Advisor, a Condoleeza Rice takeoff played by Regina McKee Redwing, gives him the codename of "Angry Man."

Scenes of The Hulk running amok in the city are impressive and a lot of fun, as are the ILM scenes of Banner changing to and from The Hulk. The FX house has a brilliant way of depicting Hulk's transformation to Bruce Banner. When Hulk's rage is spent; the extra mass boils off him as steam! Unfortunately, when Hulk grows to sixteen feet tall, he resembles the uncredited *Hulk* influence, *The Amazing Colossal Man*. By making

The Hulk that huge, he's too big for the audience to identify with, especially since he's a zombie-eyed CGI construct. In the less-than-rousing climax, he fights his father, a half-hearted take on Marvel's classic Hulk/ Thor villain, The Absorbing Man. Much of *Hulk*'s storyline concerns events that occurred long before Bruce Banner becomes The Hulk. While Bruce's father in the comics, Brian Banner, is an abusive murderer, all of

the "added elements" not from the comics or TV series feel extraneous and tacked on, like Banner being named "Bruce Krensler" for no real reason. We have a number of flashbacks that are extremely unpleasant and have nothing to do with The Hulk.

Repeated scenes of David Banner abusing his wife culminate with her being stabbed to death with a butcher knife... This is made all the more distasteful *because Banner is trying to kill their three-year-old son!* Mother Banner is viciously stabbed protecting the boy, which made the movie too intense for kids who enjoy Hulk's cartoons and comics. These segments are so dour and gloomy, they detract enjoyment from the film, even during rousing scenes where Hulk battles the military or simply wanders Berkeley, California, smashing cars and fire hydrants. It sucks all fun from the movie, so it's no wonder this *Hulk* isn't called "Incredible."

A long scene where Nolte, as David Banner, and Bana as Bruce, argue over what to do with their power is so dull, it plays like a bad theater production of *True West*. The ending battle between Hulk and his father is so confusingly written and shot, you literally do not know how the incoherent battle concludes. Bewildered audiences were left scratching their heads.

Hulk also borrows the storyline from the 1977 TV pilot, where David and Elaina search for a cure together and place Banner in a purportedly

Ang Lee shows fx man Michael Lantieri how he wants Hulk to smash!

inescapable pressure chamber. The Hulk's transformation is triggered in both with Banner unconscious as he's forced to dream of traumatic incidents. (His wife's death in the TV movie and his mother's murder here.) Just like the Ferrigno Hulk, he can only speak in growls and snarls, although he does say "Puny Human" and "Hulk Smash" in a dream sequence. As the movie's Bruce Banner, Eric Bana revealed to *Starlog* Magazine that "I hadn't read the [Hulk] comics, but I knew the [Bill Bixby] TV show. I had probably seen every episode. That was on in Australia, but I wasn't a huge comic book reader as a kid." To depict Hulk's rage in live action, "Ang wanted Hulk to be at a bigger scale than Lou Ferrigno's Hulk on the TV series," explains Oscar-winning FX man Michael Lantieri, the man who oversaw the dinosaur destruction of all three *Jurassic Park*s and *Terminator 2: Judgment Day*. Lantieri supervised the CG Hulk and the damage he causes in the film.

"On *The Incredible Hulk* TV show, they used breakaways. For the movie, we didn't build any breakaways at all. We used real force, real power and real physics to break real glass, real wood and real plaster. Everything you see smashed is real! Ang wanted me to give special movements to The Hulk. We tried very hard to give Hulk human characteristics. I didn't see The Hulk as a monster, I saw him as somebody struggling with forces that he doesn't understand. Hulk has a real personality, but he struggles to control his strength and power.

"With the Hulk, I have to bring a nonexistent creature into reality by using physics," Lantieri explains. "When The Hulk leaps, I have to calculate his weight and the power he has behind the jumps."

There's also a cameo by Lou Ferrigno as a security guard alongside STAN LEE! Although he interacts in a couple scenes with Banner, sadly, there's never a scene where he meets the Hulk.

Stan Lee was amused that "Lou Ferrigno and I are co-security guards. If you want to die laughing, watch for that scene of Lou and I. Lou is about 200 feet tall, weighs 1,000 pounds and is the strongest, greatest-looking guy you'll ever see, and there I am, next to him! I weigh about 12 pounds, with skinny little pipe-stem arms and we're supposed to protect the area!" Ang Lee told *Dreamwatch Magazine*, "I thought it would be a wonderful thing to bring Lou Ferrigno and Stan Lee back. It's an homage to the [TV] series and the comic book. Their appearances are showstop-pers." Indeed, audiences applauded at the two men in screenings around the world.

Lou Ferrigno told *Maxim* Magazine, "When I heard about Ang Lee's *Hulk*, I wanted to reprise the role (of Hulk), but they wanted to do CG [computer-generated FX]. So basically, they spent $175 million when they could have spent maybe a tenth of that. The big difference [between the CG Hulk and Ferrigno's Hulk]? No feelings. The original Hulk shows feelings. The CGI Hulk still looks rubbery, not real." At the 2002 San Diego Comic Con, *Hulk* director Ang Lee was excited to have Ferrigno in his film. "We had Lou because he was the first Hulk," Lee enthused. "Shooting that [scene] was funny—Lou Ferrigno's the nicest man I ever met in my life. I was sitting in a jeep, when Lou [mimes Ferrigno growl-ing like The Hulk] bends down to lift the jeep. It was so real that, for two seconds, I thought he could actually do it!"

Kenneth Johnson was decidedly unimpressed with Ang Lee's *Hulk*. "One of the writers on *The Hulk* feature film told me that 'Don't make me angry—you wouldn't like me when I'm angry' was the only line that ever got a rise out of the audience. Ten writers working on that movie over

12 years and the only line the audience reacted to was mine! And did the creature have to look like *Shrek?!* I have great admiration for Ang, but the film is a disaster. Someone came up to me after the premiere and said, 'Don't make me Ang Lee, you wouldn't like me when I'm Ang Lee...'"

Audiences agreed with Johnson's sentiments, as *Hulk* opened strongly, raking in $62 million in one North American weekend—smashing the previous June opening record. *It then set the biggest second week drop in Hollywood history:* The movie opened in first place and then had a horrifying -69.7% drop in its very next week! An infamous record it holds to this day, "Pulling a *Hulk*" is something no producer wants to do. Made for an estimated $137,000,000.00, the movie had a disappointing domestic gross of $132,122,995.00 and a worldwide take of $245,284,946.

Ang Lee's *Hulk* gained a cult following on basic cable, getting the highest ratings of any movie debut on USA Cable and the SyFy Channel in over a year. The DVD also sold briskly, paving the way for another cinematic adventure for The Hulk.

HULK FACTS
The US President in *Hulk*, Geoffery Scott, starred in "The Secret Empire" segments of Kenneth Johnson's *Cliffhangers.*

Banner gets transformed by a Gamma Ray machine, like in the show, eschewing the comic's mushroom cloud origin, which is used for his father.

When Banner transforms, there's a close-up of his pupils dilating white and changing color, Kenneth Johnson's first unmistakable sign of "Hulking Out."

"You wouldn't like me when I'm angry" was a major part of marketing the movie, in TV, radio and print.

As with the show, the film ends with Banner in a new place, helping people under an alias.

Sam Elliot played another Marvel character in *Ghost Rider.*

Jennifer Connolly's husband, Paul Bettany, voiced Jarvis, Tony Stark's automated house, in the hit *Iron Man* movies.

In backpack and blue jeans, Edward Norton's Banner was a tribute to Bill Bixby.

THE INCREDIBLE HULK

Directed By Louis Leterrier
Written By Zak Penn
Based on characters created by Stan Lee & Jack Kirby

Cast

Dr. Bruce Banner. . . . . .Edward Norton
Betty Ross . . . . Liv Tyler
General Ross . . . . William Hurt
Emil Blonsky. . . . . Tim Roth

"Don't make me hungry...You wouldn't like me when I'm...hungry!"
Bruce Banner, mangling a classic phrase in Portuguese

Bruce Banner is working in a bottling plant overseas, when he's chased by a jealous co-worker. Evading the man and trying to keep from getting excited, Banner loses it when General Ross storms in with the US Army. Hulking Out, Bruce flees to America and renews his romance with Ross' daughter, Betty. Hulk is relentlessly hounded by super soldier Emil Blonsky. In his quest for physical perfection and the ability to destroy Hulk, Blonsky has scientists repeatedly "improve" him until he morphs into the grotesque, reptilian Abomination. Back in New York, Bruce Banner tries to stay with Betty, avoid capture by the armed services and try to calm the raging spirit that dwells within him. The Abomination goes nuts and begins attacking Harlem, so Bruce is forced to fight him. Tranquilized, Banner is too calm to trigger his transformation, so General Ross has him hurled out of a helicopter. Fearing death, he panics and becomes Hulk. Ross also meets with Tony Stark to discuss ways to stop The Hulk. At the end of the film, scientist Samuel Sterns transforms into The Leader, another of Hulk's greatest enemies.

Although The Incredible Hulk is second only to Spider-Man in Marvel character recognition worldwide, a sequel to *Hulk* seemed like a gamble, even five years later. Universal and Marvel went for it, re-casting every character, starting with *Fight Club's* Edward Norton stepping in as the troubled Banner and *Lord of the Rings'* Liv Tyler as the beautiful, concerned Betty. William Hurt is her father, General Thaddeus "Thunderbolt" Ross.

Norton does a great job, deftly throwing in little tributes to Bill Bixby

along the way. He makes Bruce Banner a sympathetic, likeable character with a warmth that Eric Bana could not generate in the first film. Bana was a distant, aloof Banner. The Hulk's origin, which took most of the overlong Ang Lee film to tell, is dispensed with in the opening credits. The new origin is shot just like the opening of the *Hulk* TV series.

A successful rebooting of the Hulk franchise, this *Hulk* wisely blends elements of the comics with Kenneth Johnson's TV show. In fact, the show is used for major plot points. Banner now gains his powers in a Gamma Chair just like the one Bill Bixby used. He's a fugitive with a knapsack, just like in the show. We even hear Joe Harnell's haunting "Lonely Man" in a crucial scene, and it was also used in the trailer. The film embraces Hulk's TV show connection further by introducing a younger version of Jack McGee and Lou Ferrigno reprises his role as "Security Guard" from the previous film... He even provides the voice of The Hulk, just as he did in the 1990s cartoon. Ferrigno even gets to bellow The Hulk's popular battle cry, "HULK SMASH!" William Hurt does a great job as the bullish General Ross. Sam Elliot looked more like the character and truly seemed concerned about Betty's well-being in the first film, while Hurt's Ross is more interested in getting Hulk's blood to create an army of super-soldiers. Banner does battle with government agent Emil Blonsky, who alters and upgrades his body to keep up with The Hulk, before finally using Gamma Rays to turn himself into The

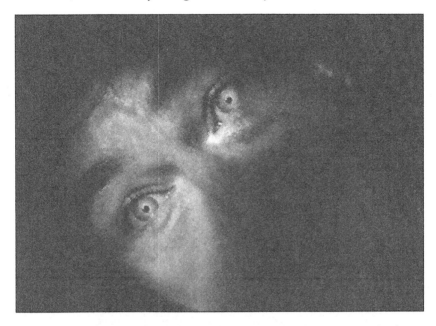

Abomination. Unfortunately, this causes him to run amok in the heart of Manhattan, where he and Hulk have a satisfying slugfest in front of Harlem's Apollo Theater.

After defeating the monster, Hulk changes back to Banner, who slips away to an isolated cabin, as Banner frequently did in the show and the comic. The movie is much more fun than Ang Lee's ponderous, solemn one, and Norton injects a lot of pathos into his performance. This *Hulk* has a lot of cool ideas, like when a hitchhiking Banner suddenly realizes that Hulk has taken him into a different country! Having the amount of days between transformations appear on screen like an industrial accident sign is clever, as is Banner trying meditation, hypnosis and other calming techniques.

There's also a funny running gag where he wears a blood pressure monitor that sounds an alarm when his BP starts going up — even when he tries to make love to Betty! Besides a surprise cameo by Robert Downey, Jr. as Tony Stark, Iron Man's alter ego at the end of the movie, the DVD extras also have a blink-and-you-missed-it glimpse of a frozen Captain America! Although Norton was listed as co-writer on early posters and formally announced that he was writing the film at Comic Con, he gets no such credit on the final film.

Although Ferrigno actually voices Hulk in the movie, voice actor Fred Tatasciore, who does the animated Hulk in the films *Hulk vs.* and

Ultimate Avengers #1 & #2, also contributed. Tatasciore can be heard in the Norton *Hulk* movie, when Hulk occasionally screams and growls. "I was actually directed by Edward Norton, who was also in [dubbing] Bruce Banner," Tatasciore reveals. "Edward was cool and easy to work with. He had a say on what happened in the film, especially early on. I did some of The Hulk screaming in a couple scenes, and people shouting for him. Three different people did Hulk's voice, but you don't always get credit. Lou Ferrigno deserved the credit, because he's The Hulk as far as I'm concerned!

"When I got the job as The Hulk in a Marvel cartoon, I remembered I had a shot with Lou Ferrigno from when I was a kid! Lou *is* Hulk and a childhood hero of mine. I met Lou Ferrigno when I was 9 years old and he guested on *The Dinah Shore Show*, which my dad produced. Meeting

The Hulk as a kid was a big deal for me — I was a huge *Incredible Hulk* fan. To meet him as a child, was such a thrill! I vividly remember Lou shaking my hand gently, like he was the strongest man in the world and didn't wanna crush me. What a terrific guy! I showed him that picture years later at the San Diego Comic Con and he signed it, and then asked me for $25.00," chuckles Fred Tatasciore. "Next time I see him, we'll have to have a Hulk-Off!"

Made for an estimated $150,000,000, this *Hulk* opened to $55,000,000 on its way to a domestic gross of $134,000,000.00. Worldwide, *Hulk* brought in $263,427,551.00. Incredibly, this was a virtual tie with the original film's gross.

LOU FERRIGNO (Hulk): "*I was really pleased to do the voice of The Hulk! I loved doing it in the animated series and I really enjoyed doing it here! If I had it my way, I would have done my voice on the TV series. That was something I lobbied very hard to do—to voice The Hulk in the movie! I just had to do it.*

"*I really liked [director] Louis Leterrier! I had met him at the San Diego Comic Con two years earlier and I told him that I would love to be part of his film. Louis agreed and said he was a big fan of my Hulk and believed I should be part of it, too, which I felt really honored by.*

"*I had a lot of fun with Edward Norton, because we shot that scene 7 or 8 times and he tried it differently every time. While we were doing it, I kept saying to myself, 'This is EDWARD NORTON!' I love him and felt a little intimidated, because he's such a fine actor. We're doing this scene together, Edward and I, alone in a room, at 10:00 at night, and they were rushing this scene. It gave me a chance to work with him and be in a* Hulk *movie! To me, doing the second* Hulk *was more exciting than the first film. I feel that way because it was a real acting role, not a campy cameo. Louis Leterrier made sure the scene was* not *campy.*"

KENNETH JOHNSON: "*While I haven't seen the film, I was pleased to hear that they used both Lou and 'Lonely Man.' I was also happy to see the poster showing Norton wearing the same kind of knapsack that Bix had on the TV series. There are lots of memories in that knapsack! I saw from the commercials that he still looks like* Shrek.*"

JILL SHERMAN DONNER: "*People like to make fun of Lou in that green paint and wig, but I think the movies, with their computer-generated Hulks, are a disaster!*"

JENNIFER CONNOLLY: *"I thought it sounded interesting to re-cast it and re-start it like that, but I still haven't seen it."*

One of the biggest laughs in The Incredible Hulk *movie is a surprise appearance by Bill Bixby, on a TV set showing* The Courtship of Eddie's Father, *with his young co-star, Brandon Cruz.*

BRANDON CRUZ: *"I knew it was gonna happen, because they had called me for clearance of an* Eddie's Father *clip. They wanted to pay tribute to Bill, so I said, 'Of course — use anything, it's for Bill!' When I went to the premiere, Lou Ferrigno said, 'That clip of you two is great; it's in the first minute of the movie because it's so fun.' I took my son, we watched the movie and it was the back of my head! I wish they showed my face, but it was a tribute to Bill and when it appeared, the audience applauded! My son was truly impressed; he didn't know that I knew The Hulk!"*

HULK FACTS

Bruce Banner having to stress out and transform after falling from a helicopter came from Marvel's *Ultimates* comic, as did the plot point of him becoming Hulk by trying to replicate Captain America's super soldier formula.

Paul Soles, who plays Stanley, the kindly pizza-maker in the film, was the voice of both Bruce Banner and Rick Jones in the very first 1966 *Hulk* cartoon!

Louis Leterrier had a worldwide hit with his fun, exciting remake of *Clash Of The Titans*.

Hasbro released The Smashin,' Stompin' Electronic Hulk, an action figure based on the movie Hulk. Pressing the toy's abdomen, its eyes flash as it screams, "You're making me angry — you wouldn't like me when I'm angry."

I LOVE YOU, MAN

One of the greatest tributes to *The Incredible Hulk* TV series and its star came in the 2009 Dreamworks comedy hit, *I Love You, Man*. Paul Rudd plays a driven, friendless real estate agent who is trying to sell Lou Ferrigno's mansion so he can get married. Troubled that he has no best friend, his fiancée (Rashida Jones) insists that he find one to be his best man before she will marry him. He finally makes a friend, the eccentric Sydney Fife (Jason Segel), and Fife wants to prove his loyalty to Rudd.

Throughout the film, Lou Ferrigno frequently calls Rudd to scold him for not selling his mansion. Running into Ferrigno at The Grove outdoor mall, Rudd is berated by Ferrigno for not selling "The Ferrigno Estate." Angry to see his friend treated in such a

Lou Ferrigno chokes out Jason Segel in *I Love You, Man*.

demeaning manner, Fife deliberately provokes a fight with Ferrigno by repeatedly calling him "Hulk"!

"Please don't call me that, I am a human being," Ferrigno says pleasantly. When Sydney persists and then takes a sucker punch at the TV star, an incensed Ferrigno places him in a chokehold and knocks him out. Humorously, the movie version of Lou Ferrigno is hot-tempered, egotistical and narcissistic; his home is covered with statues and pictures of himself. When we see him on a set in the film, he wears a bathrobe with his name in giant letters monogrammed on it, but he is ultimately shown to be a decent guy. The big-hearted Ferrigno even serves as one of the groomsmen at Rudd's wedding in the end. Ferrigno's sequences became the highlight of the film, winding up prominently in the trailers and dvd case. "I was very excited to do *I Love You, Man* because the director, John Hamburg, made me a real character in this funny romantic comedy," Lou Ferrigno enthuses. "John's a very talented guy who had also done *Meet the Parents*. I laughed at what happened in the script and John gave me a lot of stuff to do! John Hamburg wrote me a letter mentioning that he was a fan of mine and wanted me in his film playing myself. He also said that his father was hard of hearing. I met with him, then I read the script and just loved it. My wife read it and she loved it, too. We liked how I became part of the fun; they incorporated my playful side into it. It feels like a dream… Here I am in this great comedy with Jason Segel and Paul Rudd!

"I can play myself as a bad guy in a funny A-list feature film. Because it's a romance and 'bro-mance,' I have more people who want to talk me about that than even being The Hulk! It's a touch-ing movie and people relate to that. The end of the movie is about embracing, forgiving and making

I Love You, Man writer/director/ Ferrigno Fan John Hamburg. PHOTO BY PATRICK JANKIEWICZ

up—it's a great positive message. At the end, we're all friends and I'm even in the wedding party! I own the largest collection of Hulk memorabilia in the world, so John Hamburg used a lot of it in the movie."

I Love You, Man co-writer/director John Hamburg says, "Lou Ferrigno was a sweetheart; a great guy and a lot of fun. I was really happy he did it. I figured if we made Paul Rudd's character a real estate agent, he could be trying to sell Lou Ferrigno's estate. And when he doesn't sell it, Lou could be getting angry. The idea of using Lou Ferrigno as him-self just popped in my head one day and that seemed a great idea with great potential. We figured we could have a lot of fun if he's trying to sell Lou's house, so that gave us a lot of funny possibilities. We had a bronze statue of Lou in the yard, torn pants that he wore as The Hulk framed on the wall and pictures of himself everywhere! "I didn't keep the statue of Lou after we shot the movie because I live in New York and just had no room for it," Hamburg grins. "But if I had the room, I definitely would have kept it!"

I Love You, Man was a surprise hit, earning great reviews and grossing $91 million dollars.

AFTERSMASH!

Today, *The Incredible Hulk* TV series' impact is still felt. It runs on the Retro Channel, discovering a brand-new generation of kids who prefer strong stories to computer-generated mayhem. The show and The Hulk character have always been popular in the rap community. Dr. Dre, Ludacris and Jermaine Dupri all have songs namechecking *Hulk*. Rapper David Banner took his name from the show and the hit series is frequently referenced in TV, movies and comics.

Both *Family Guy* and *Robot Chicken* pay homage to the show. One episode of *Family Guy* actually recreates the opening of *The Incredible Hulk* shot for shot, even using Joe Harnell's theme. In 2008, Bill Bixby's David Banner posthumously won as "The TV Land Award for Character You REALLY Don't Want to Make Angry." The 2009 Spike TV Scream Awards ran the opening credits of the *Hulk* show as one of fantasy TV's highlights. Butterfinger candy did a funny Internet viral, "I Love You, Lou Ferrigno," where the former Hulk played himself.

Lou Ferrigno found himself in the news again in 2009 when pop star Michael Jackson died. Personal trainer Ferrigno had been getting the King of Pop in shape for his comeback tour, which Jackson did not live to embark on.

"Michael Jackson was a huge fan of The Hulk," the actor reveals. "I stayed at The Neverland Ranch for a couple days and Michael had every single episode of *The Incredible Hulk*! It was like walking into a Block-buster; he had everything. Michael told me he felt like The Hulk, too. Michael and I had similar treatment by our fathers growing up. He said that he really identified with The Hulk. Michael also told me he liked having me around because he felt protected by The Hulk. I liked him."

Mark Ruffalo plays the tormented Bruce Banner in *The Avengers* movie, which is written and directed by *Buffy The Vampire Slayer* creator Joss Whedon. Ruffalo also acts physically for the digital Hulk—Marvel announced that Lou Ferrigno will reprise The Hulk's voice. Ruffalo told *Entertainment Weekly* that his decision to play the part was influenced by the TV series. Ruffalo liked the character because "He's a guy struggling with two sides of himself — the dark and the light — and everything he does in his life is filtered through issues of control. I grew up on the Bill Bixby TV series, which I thought was a really nuanced and real human way to look at The Hulk. I like that the part has those qualities."

Marvel's television division, headed by former *Incredible Hulk* comic-book writer Jeph Loeb, announced The Hulk would be coming back to TV in a live-action series. Hulk can also be seen in animated form in both *Avengers: Earth's Mightiest Heroes* cartoon and in a less angry, younger, kid-friendly way on *Marvel Superhero Squad*.

One of the fringe benefits to the big-budget *Hulk* movies is that they finally prompted Universal Home Entertainment to release all five seasons of the show on DVD, prompting a moving reaction from the man behind the show. The TV movies, made by New World, were all released earlier.

"Seeing *The Incredible Hulk* finally go on DVD was very bittersweet," says Kenneth Johnson. "It's still strange that I can't pick up the phone and call Bix. We were very close right up until his death. Many of the episodes are still very moving and quite good. I was blessed to work with such a great group of actors, writers, producers, and crew."

All episodes of *The Incredible Hulk* are out on DVD. They can be ordered from Universal Studios at *www.incrediblehulkdvd.com*. Episodes not to be missed: The pilot, "Of Guilt, Models and Murder," "Killer Instinct," "Married," "The Snare," "Prometheus," "Bring Me the Head of the Hulk," "Ricky," "The Harder They Fall" and "The First."

EPILOGUE

Stan Lee: The Walt Disney of comics, Stan Lee revolutionized the industry with his smart, literate stories about his flawed heroes and equally misunderstood, nuanced villains. With a battery of artists, he created The Incredible Hulk, The Amazing Spider-Man, The Fantastic Four, The Invincible Iron Man, The Uncanny X-Men, The Mighty Thor and literally hundreds of other classic characters. Ignored by producers adapting his work in the '70s and '80s, most of which flopped, with Sam Raimi's *Spider-Man* and Bryan Singer's *X-Men*, the film adaptations became faithful to the source material and reaped billions. Stan also makes Alfred Hitchcock-like cameos in all of them, a practice he started in *The Trial of the Incredible Hulk*. Marvel Comics was bought by The Walt Disney Corporation, which means Spidey and The Hulk are now siblings to Mickey Mouse and Donald Duck. On January 4th, 2011, Stan Lee received the 2,428th Star on The Hollywood Walk of Fame for creating all his colorful characters, who now grace the movie and TV screen. For the occasion, Hollywood declared it "Stan Lee Day." The great man joked, "Some Stan Lee Day — the schools are still open and mail is still being delivered!"

Kenneth Johnson: The busy writer/producer/director had the biggest international hit of his career with the landmark, *V*. After turning down the TV series *Beauty and the Beast* and directorial reigns on the original *RoboCop*, Johnson attempted to return to superheroes with the film *Steel*. Giving 7'1" Shaquille O'Neal a peppy girl sidekick in a wheelchair meant he had to keep bending over for them to chat. Attempts to revive (and unfortunately re-think) his hits *The Bionic Woman* and *V* by other producers were underwhelming. Both shows were cancelled. The new *Bionic Woman*, which had the heroine being told what to do by a bunch of men — something Johnson never did — was a giant flop. Johnson wrote his own *V* sequel, the novel *V: The Next Generation*, and teaches college classes. Interviewing over 70 of his former employees for this book, not a single one of them had a cross word or complaint about him, on or off the record.

Bill Bixby: Although married several times, Bixby never had another child after the death of Christopher. He made TV movie sequels to *The Incredible Hulk*, directing most of them. No other series he did afterwards matched that show's popularity. The intensely private Bixby did not even tell his closest friends when he developed prostate cancer. His condition was outed by *The National Enquirer* and other tabloids. Bixby soldiered on, directing episodes of the sitcom *Blossom*, in which he also guest-starred as a cop. He was in so much pain from his condition, he directed the show hunched over. Bixby died November 21, 1993. He was cremated, as were his ex-wife Brenda Benet and son Christopher. In April 2010, Oscar-winning actor Nicolas Cage told MTV that he would remake and star in *The Courtship of Eddie's Father* because "I really enjoyed Bill Bixby in the TV series." Reportedly, actor Hugh Jackman, who resembles Bixby and also plays a Marvel hero (*X-Men's* Wolverine), wants to star in a biopic about his life.

Lou Ferrigno A popular guest at comic-book conventions, he had a 200-person line at the Emerald City Comic Con. Ferrigno is beloved by fans of all ages for his work on *The Incredible Hulk*. Besides his TV Land reality show, *The Incredible Ferrignos*, he was sworn in as a Los Angeles County Sheriffs Office reserve officer in 2006. He also does charity work, seeking to help children coping with the same hearing and speech impediments that he did. He was the youngest winner of the bodybuilding title "Mr. Universe," which he won twice. He also won the bodybuilding title "Mr. America" and "Teenage Mr. America." Ferrigno drew new fans for his very funny turn as himself in both *I Love You, Man* and on the popular CBS sitcom *King of Queens*. Ferrigno also has two dogs — one of which, his pug Bandit, seems bound and determined to train Lou! "He thinks he owns me, not the other way around," laughs Lou.

Jack Kirby: The comic-book artist played a sketch artist on the TV series *The Incredible Hulk*. Besides co-creating Hulk, he also had a hand in dozens of other characters, including Captain America, Fantastic Four, The New Gods and The Silver Surfer. Although he did not design Spider-Man, he drew the cover of the character's first appearance in *Amazing Fantasy* #15. Several of his co-creations wound up as feature films and on postage stamps. Kirby died in 1994. So famous for his comics work, his passing prompted a joke on *Saturday Night Live*. Announcing his death on Weekend Update, viewers were assured he would return in a double-sized issue later in the year. When Disney purchased Marvel late 2010,

Kirby's estate sued for rights to the characters he drew for the company. That lawsuit was not yet resolved as this book went to press.

Alan J. Levi and actress wife, *Sondra Currie*, remain busy. Levi is directing *CSI: LA*, while Currie reprised her hot Mom character in *The Hangover* sequel. She is the daughter of actress Marie Currie. When Currie's sister Cherie was the subject of a movie, *The Runaways*, Sondra's sister and mom were played by Dakota Fanning and Tatum O'Neal.

Martin Kove: After playing Rocky, the punch-drunk boxer in the *Hulk*'s first episode, Kove hit a career wave. Besides playing the evil John Kreese in the *Karate Kid* movies (where he menaces the pupil of *Hulk* guest Pat Morita!), he and fellow *Hulk* guest Charles Napier betray Vietnam POWs in *Rambo: First Blood Part II*. Kove also had a long run as a detective on *Cagney & Lacey* and appeared in the cult movies *Last House On The Left* and *Death Race 2000*. The actor remains a popular supporting lead in sci-fi, horror and other genre films.

Paul Koslo: Played bikers, henchmen and evil Russians in numerous films and TV shows. He went against type in both his *Hulk* episodes, as a biker and a Vietnam veteran, both of whom were unexpectedly sympathetic. He also appeared in Charlton Heston's *The Omega Man* as one of the last people on Earth, was so good as a noble Soviet bad guy in Stuart Gordon's *Robot Jox*, Gordon changed the script so Koslo would live at the end. He's also in the cult classic *Vanishing Point*.

Laurie Prange: Pale, freckled actress Prange specialized in playing frail women, weak — either by willpower or physical infirmity — and preyed upon by others. Acted with Diane Keaton and Bette Davis. Her husband, film composer Richard Lyons, did the music for Lou Ferrigno's *Cage II*. Prange broke an 18-year acting hiatus to appear in *The Intervention*, directed by a woman she babysat as a girl.

Xander Berkeley: Since his appearance in the final episode of *Hulk*, Berkeley has become one of Hollywood's busiest character actors. Besides appearing in Ron Howard's *Apollo 13*, Wolfgang Peterson's *Air Force One*, James Cameron's *Terminator 2: Judgment Day* (where his robot wife spears him through the head!), Michael Mann's *Heat*, Steven Spielberg's *Amistad*, he's also done TV. After playing Jack Bauer's ill-fated boss on *24*, Berkeley married the show's *femme fatale*, Sarah Clarke, and they have a daughter. He returned to superheroes by voicing Captain Atom, Sinestro and Spidey villain Mysterio in cartoons and then played a corrupt cop out to catch the hero in *Kick-Ass*.

Julie Cobb: Before *Hulk*, Julie was the first female "red shirt" to die on classic *Star Trek*, and is personally mourned by Captain James T. Kirk himself! She co-starred in acclaimed miniseries *Salem's Lot* and *Brave New World*. Daughter of *Exorcist* actor Lee J. Cobb — who she appeared with on *Gunsmoke* — Cobb also works as a life coach.

Rosemary Forsyth: After playing Charlton Heston's love interest in *The War Lord* and James Stewart's in *Shenandoah*, she became a busy character actress. Working a long run on the soaps *Days of Our Lives*, *General Hospital* and *Santa Barbara*, she appeared on *Monk*, *NYPD Blue*, *Star Trek Voyager* (as an alien doctor eager to dissect living humans!) and *Without a Trace*.

Linda Pawlik: Co-starred in the cool TV chiller *Desire the Vampire* as a hooker and had a recurring role on the *Starsky & Hutch* TV series. Pawlik married actor Robert Picardo and raised two daughters.

Lara Parker: Best known as Angelique the witch on the long-running *Dark Shadows*, Parker guest-starred on numerous shows like *Kolchak: The Night Stalker* (another witch!) and is in the cult horror chiller *Race With The Devil*, where, in a refreshing change of pace, she's only killed by witches! She is still stunned to have not received credit as Banner's ill-fated wife in *The Incredible Hulk* pilot. Both *Dark* and *Race* are about to be remade.

Ernie Hudson: has had an amazing career, with brilliant turns in *The Hand That Rocks The Cradle*, *Congo* (where he saves an otherwise crappy film by playing his character as Clark Gable) and the series *Oz*. He is still best known as Winston Zeddmore in *Ghostbusters*. The Michigan native was pleased to guest on *The Incredible Hulk*, but still marvels, "That my kids would root for The Hulk over their own dad...I like The Hulk, but I would *not* have rooted for The Hulk over *my* dad!"

Austin Stoker: Played the heroic cop Bishop in John Carpenter's fantastic *Assault On Precinct 13*, as well as another cop in the cult horror classic *Twisted Brain*. He was a heroic human in the last original sequel to *Planet of the Apes*. Stoker also shared the screen with Pam Grier, William Marshall and Carol Speed. Offered a cameo in the big-budget *Precinct 13* remake, he agreed to do it but Canada denied Stoker entry to shoot a role "that could be played by a Canadian actor" — showing how exclusionary the country had become since *Trial of the Incredible Hulk*. Stoker is now an acting teacher and proud grandfather.

Tony Burton: A popular guest actor on many TV shows, he starred in *Assault On Precinct 13* with Stoker and made the first *Rocky* the same year, as Apollo Creed's trainer, Duke. He's the only one in Creed's camp who realizes that Rocky Balboa is a threat to the champ. When Russian killing machine Ivan Drago slays Apollo in *Rocky IV*, Tony Burton was happy, not sad. "With Apollo dead, I got to be Rocky's trainer. This was a great break, as Sly's always fun to be around!" Burton was turned into an action figure for Duke. "I didn't expect that."

Ric "Demi-Hulk" Drasin: An actor who does a lot of commercials, a wrestling star, a designer, screenwriter, producer, director and family man, the impressively versatile Ric Drasin also designed the Gold's Gym logo and starred as the missing link in the cult movie *Mistress of the Apes*. He and Lou Ferrigno reunited as barbarians on a beer commercial.

Mitzi Kapture: Survived the crash of the unfinished *Metamorphosis/She-Hulk* pilot to star in her own hit TV series, *Silk Stalkings*. Both *Stalkings* and *Baywatch*, which she also recurred on, became the first series to leave network TV and become syndicated blockbusters. She even directed several episodes of *Silk Stalkings* and had two kids. The brainy actress was a contestant on *The $10,000 Pyramid*, where she won $1,100 and a 7-day Caribbean Cruise. Kapture recently co-directed *The Process*, a documentary about famed acting teacher Larry Moss.

Sally Kirkland: Cool, funny actress who played a battered wife on *The Incredible Hulk*'s second season. Has been everything from hookers to detectives. Appeared in Roger Corman's *Big Bad Mama, Candy Stripe Nurses* and as a sexy rock star opposite Kevin Costner in Tony Scott's grim *Revenge*. She was Oscar nominated for a down-on-her-luck Polish actress in *Anna*.

Eric Kramer: After playing The Mighty Thor in *The Incredible Hulk Returns*, he earned rave reviews for his role as Bear, the gay dancer/dress designer in *American Pie 3: American Wedding*. Kramer is now the easily befuddled bug exterminator dad on the Disney series *Good Luck Charlie*.

He still performs with his Kiss tribute band, Ssik. Thor had his own feature film in 2011. There is still no consensus on who would win in a fight between Hulk and Thor!

Lee Purcell: David Banner's girlfriend in *The Incredible Hulk Returns*, Purcell is best known as the mom who sleeps with her daughter's boyfriend in the '80s classic *Valley Girl!* She also did movies with Hollywood legends and another one with their sons. You can see movies with her and Kirk Douglas, as well as with Michael Douglas. She also worked with Lloyd Bridges and son Beau Bridges. She appeared in the movie *Clawed: The Legend of the Sasquatch* with her son, Dylan. It runs once a month on The SyFy Channel.

Manny Perry: Manny is now a member of the Directors Guild and a stunt coordinator on films like *Eagle Eye* (in which he also acts), *True Lies, Daddy Day Care* and *First Daughter.* As an actor, he's the bartender in the original *Rush Hour* and a cop who tries to help Al Pacino in Michael Mann's *Heat.* Ironically, Manny is best known for a commercial he starred in that ran in movie theaters. He explains that as a stuntman, when his movie is pirated onto the Internet, he's risking his life for nothing. The commercial was widely joked about and *Boondocks'* Aaron Magruder did a strip of Manny, parodying it. "I was flattered by that," laughs Perry. "Everybody called me when it ran and Magruder gave it to me."

Julie Adams and her son *Mitchell Danton*, remember husband/father/ *Hulk* director *Ray Danton* fondly. Julie guest-starred on *Lost* and is a popular guest at horror conventions. She also did a memorable episode of *Kolchak: The Night Stalker.* Mitchell won an Emmy for his work on *The Path To 9/11.* He was also nominated for editing the first season of *Survivor.* He edits *Greek, Trauma* and *In Plain Sight.*

Simone Griffeth: is the female lead in *Death Race 2000*, with David Carradine and Sylvester Stallone. The late Carradine told me in his last interview that not hitting on Simone was "one of the biggest regrets of my life!" Griffeth guested on numerous shows besides *Hulk,* including *Silk Stalkings, Magnum, P.I., Rip Tide, T.J. Hooker* and *The Greatest American Hero* — where she played the superhero's ex-wife! Simone Griffeth now resides in her home state of South Carolina, teaching acting and working with her husband Wayne as a real estate agent in Hilton Head Island, South Carolina.

Richard Kiel: After being replaced as The Hulk, he instead played unstoppable James Bond villain Jaws in *The Spy Who Loved Me* and *Moonraker*. Kiel made the character a sympathetic underdog and became the only Bond villain besides Blofeld who was allowed to live on to another film. In *Moonraker*, he even got his own love interest! He battled Clint Eastwood in *Pale Rider*, co-wrote *Kentucky Lion: The Cassius Marcellus Clay Story*, a biography on Cassius Clay, the man Muhammad Ali was named after. He got a new cult following with his role in the Adam Sandler movie *Happy Gilmore*.

Louisa Moritz: As Myra, Sylvester Stallone's ditzy navigator/girlfriend, in *Death Race 2000*, she has several impressive nude scenes before he tells her, "You know Myra, some people might think you're cute. But me, I think you're one very large baked potato!" She appears in that classic film with fellow *Hulk* guests Kove and Griffeth, before working with Sean Connery on *Cuba* and going on to a cheerfully eclectic B movie career. Her work included teen sex comedies (*Last American Virgin, Hot Chili, Lunch Wagon*), Women in Prison (*Chained Heat*), slasher (*New Year's Evil*) and sci-fi (*Galaxis*). Moritz then switched careers, passed the bar and became a lawyer.

Edie McClurg: Since playing a snotty high-school tormenter of Sissy Spacek in *Carrie*, Edie McClurg has had a spectacular career, with over 160 movie and TV appearances. She's the put-upon secretary in John Hughes' *Ferris Bueller's Day Off*, the uncaring car rental clerk in *Planes, Trains and Automobiles* (she gets to tell Steve Martin "You're fucked!") and Minny the MiniCooper in *Cars*. McClurg is also a founding member of The Groundlings, and she had scenes with her fellow members Elvira and Pee Wee Herman in their retrospective films. McClurg is an in-demand cartoon voiceover actress and a very nice lady.

Andrea Marcovicci: Besides starring in the killer yogurt comedy *The Stuff*, she was the guest ingénue on multiple episodes of *Magnum P.I.*, *Trapper John M.D.* and *Hill Street Blues*. Marcovicci is also a popular nightclub singer. Her music was heard on the TV show *Roswell*.

Don Marshall: Besides being one of the few *Incredible Hulk* guests to do three episodes, Don Marshall co-starred on *Land of the Giants* with fellow *Hulk* guest Deanna Lund. Marshall was one of the rare crewmen to go to a planet full of savage monsters with Mr. Spock on the "Gallileo 7" episode of *Star Trek*…and survive!

Jill Sherman Donner: She went from scrubbing toilets to story editor and producer on the Universal Studios backlot. Jill Sherman produced *Hulk, Voyagers!, Magnum P.I.* and *Baywatch.* She also began dating *Hulk* guest *Robert Donner,* whom she married. Tragically, he passed away in 2006. She remains best friends with writing partner Karen Harris.

Karen Harris: Besides producing and writing *The Incredible Hulk* with Jill Sherman Donner, Karen Harris also produced *Knight Rider, Street Hawk, Highlander: The Raven, Adventure, Inc.,* and *Life In General. Hulk* writer/ producer/director Nic Corea was Best Man at her wedding. She currently writes for soap opera *General Hospital* and has won two Daytime Emmy Awards. She ran for a seat on the WGA Board of Directors.

Rick Rosenthal: Directed many films and TV shows, including two of the *Halloween* franchise and episodes of *Buffy the Vampire Slayer.* He directed one of Sean Penn's first starring roles, *Bad Boys.*

Gloria Gifford: An impressive acting coach, the lively, charming Gifford remains busy as an actress in numerous feature films, having worked with everyone from Eddie Murphy and Mr. T to Dylan McDermott.

Lisa Jane Persky: Although best known for her role as Dirty Dee in the immortal *KISS Meets The Phantom of the Park,* Lisa Jane Persky had a Blondie song written about her and put in an impressive amount of work in big-screen comedies like *Coneheads* and small-screen work on *The X-Files.* She gave Quentin Tarantino his first screen kiss in *Destiny Turns on the Radio* and is married to Andy Zax of *Beat the Geeks.*

Penny Peyser: Appeared on numerous shows, including *Hulk, Knight Rider, MacGyver, Tour of Duty, Knot's Landing* and *Walker, Texas Ranger.* Played the feisty daughter-in-law on *Crazy Like A Fox* before marrying radio talk show host Doug McIntyre. The two wrote, co-directed and produced the acclaimed documentary *Trying To Get Good: The Jazz Odyssey of Jack Sheldon.*

Paul and Charlie Picerni: The Picerni Brothers are interesting guys. Paul starred in *House of Wax,* taking on Vincent Price *and* Charles Bronson! He was a regular on *The Untouchables* and wrote his autobiography, *Steps to Stardom.* Charlie became a stuntman, stunt coordinator, actor and directed the recent vampire/monster truck epic, *The Bleeding* with Kat Von D and Vinnie Jones. Sadly, Paul passed away January, 2011.

Patrick Boyriven and *Mariette Hartley* divorced after 16 years and two children together. Both kids work in the industry, their daughter is an actress. Boyriven associate produced Kenneth Johnson's *V* and co-produced the sequel, *V: The Final Battle*. Hartley appeared on the second-to-last episode of the original *Star Trek* where Spock falls in love with her, an episode of the original *Twilight Zone* and several acclaimed sci-fi TV movies. She co-wrote her autobiography, *Breaking The Silence*, and spoke honestly about her father's suicide. Hartley formed a suicide prevention group and bravely revealed having a bipolar disorder. Her one-woman show, *If You Get To Bethlehem, You've Gone Too Far*, was an acclaimed adaptation of her book. She guest-starred on *Grey's Anatomy*.

Jeffrey Hayden: Director who helmed five episodes of *The Incredible Hulk*, including the ambitious "A Solitary Place," "Blind Rage" and "Stop the Presses," Hayden also did such TV classics like *The Andy Griffith Show*, *Mannix*, *Quincy, M.E.*, *The Donna Reed Show*, *Ironside*, *Magnum P.I.* and *That Girl*. Showed he had a flair for fantasy shows, which he put to good use on *Knight Rider*, *Misfits of Science* and the Adam West *Batman*. He is married to Hitchcock actress Eva Marie Saint.

John Hamburg: Besides co-writing and directing the hit *I Love You, Man*, Hamburg wrote *Meet the Parents*. He wrote and produced the third installment of the Ben Stiller/Robert De Niro comedy franchise, *Little Fockers*.

Nicholas Corea: The prolific writer/producer of shows like *Hulk*, *Renegade*, *Outlaws* and *Gavilan* was also a police officer and a Marine Sergeant who earned a Purple Heart in Vietnam. Wrote the darkest, most morally complex episodes of *The Incredible Hulk*. His last script was for *Walker: Texas Ranger*, an uncredited remake of *Hulk* episode "Rainbow's End," which was also titled "Rainbow's End." Died in 1999.

Mickey Jones: Besides his autobiography, Jones is prepping for a reunion with Kenny Rogers and the First Edition, known for their hits like "Ruby (Don't Take Your Love To Town)." Just did a pilot called *Wish Riders*, a reality show done with the Make-A-Wish Foundation, where Mickey and several bikers ride around granting wishes for critically-ill children. "I do a lot of charity stuff anyway, but this would be great — getting to ride a 'cycle and help sick kids." His wife Phyllis, mother of Jones' five children, was a waitress in Vegas who was kissed by Elvis "for luck" every night before he would go on in the late '70s. "He would line up the waitresses and kiss us all on his way to the stage…You just had to know where to stand," she giggles.

RC Matheson: Co-wrote three above-average episodes of *The Incredible Hulk* before becoming story editor on *The A-Team, Hunter* and *Quincy*. Wrote the cult movie *Three O'Clock High* with writing partner Thomas E. Szollosi. Matheson has worked as a prolific novelist and short story writer, also adapted Stephen King's "Battleground" for the acclaimed cable series *Nightmares & Dreamscapes: From The Stories Of Stephen King*.

Cliff Emmich: Beloved character actor who frequently plays cowboys, coroners and creeps. He runs afoul of Frye's Creature, the evil Hulk, in "The First." He's also in *Barracuda, Invasion of the Bee Girls, Halloween II* (Michael Myers dispatches him with a hammer) and he's The Mayor in Dreamworks' very first film, *Mousehunt*.

Deanna Lund: The beautiful redhead starred in the cult series *Land of the Giants*, was one of Vincent Price's hot Fembots in *Dr. Goldfoot and the Bikini Machines*, guest-starred on *Batman*, appeared in movies with Elvis Presley and was even on hand for the birth of NASCAR. A wonderful lady with amazing stories, she also makes a killer egg salad.

Susan Sullivan: Worked as a Playboy Bunny and appeared on Broadway with Dustin Hoffman. Has never stopped working since playing David Banner's unrequited love interest in the *Incredible Hulk* pilot. She had a long run as ingénues, in *Another World, Falcon Crest* and Charlton Heston's girlfriend in *Midway*. Played the wacky mother on *Dharma and Greg* and can now be seen every week on *Castle*, as — you guessed it — the hero's wacky mom.

Barbara Leigh: Besides her *Hulk*, she appeared in *Pretty Maids All In A Row, Terminal Island, Smile Jenny, You're Dead, Junior Bonner* and memorably posed for *Playboy* and several famous magazine covers as Vampirella. She was the lover of Elvis Presley, Steve McQueen and studio head James "The Smiling Cobra" Aubrey, all of which she covered in her autobiography, *The King, McQueen and the Love Machine*. She's terrified that people will recognize her from *Mistress of the Apes!*

Ang Lee: Endured the blowback to his *Hulk* movie — which included Lee being mercilessly parodied as a puppet on *Robot Chicken*! Ang Lee went on to win the Best Director Oscar for *Brokeback Mountain*.

Bill Lucking: Played two vastly different dads on *The Incredible Hulk*. Lucking is a classic character actor who has done every type of genre. He co-starred in George Pal's last movie, *Doc Savage: Man Of Bronze*, was a green slave trader on *Star Trek: Enterprise* and took on Dwayne "The Rock" Johnson in Peter Berg's *The Rundown*. Starting out in biker movies like *Hell's Belles*, it's only appropriate that he's come full circle to play a savage biker on the acclaimed series *Sons of Anarchy*. He's played aliens, Babe Ruth, gangsters, soldiers & cowboys.

John Goodwin: The busy makeup artist has come a long way since turning Lou Ferrigno into The Hulk. He's worked on *Men in Black*, *John Carpenter's The Thing* and *Legend*. Goodwin has provided mutilated bodies, blood lividity, bruises and general carnage to over 100 episodes of *CSI: Crime Scene Investigation* and *CSI: NY*, even appearing on the show as an actor. He's also Howard, a short-lived road worker eaten by a giant worm, in *Tremors*!

Frank Orsatti: Hulk's stunt coordinator began his long career doing stunts on the original *Planet of the Apes*. He doubled Bill Bixby in fight scenes on the show and for Arnold Schwarzenegger on *The Terminator*. He was the son of legendary stuntman Ernie Orsatti and brother to another impressive stuntman, Ernie F. Orsatti. Frank Orsatti became an accomplished director on *The Incredible Hulk* with the "Ricky" episode and dated the show's AD trainee, Venita Ozols. Had a falling out with James Cameron on *Terminator 2: Judgment Day*. The amazing Orsatti is the only stuntman to work as a male model and star in his own shaving commercial. Once saved the family cat with mouth-to-mouth CPR. Survived by several children and his widow, Julie Orsatti.

Loni Anderson: Put herself into the zeitgeist playing Jennifer the sexy secretary on *WKRP In Cincinatti* after starring as a kung-fu killer on *The Incredible Hulk*. Became so famous, she was even spoofed on *Saturday Night Live*. Had a tumultous marriage to Burt Reynolds. After decades of light, comedic roles and dramatic women in TV movies, Loni Anderson became the go-to girl for sexy Milfy Moms. She's Will Ferrell and Chris Katan's Mother in *A Night At The Roxbury* and Tori Spelling's super-rich but clueless Mom on *NoTORIous*.

Henry Polic II: Although he's recognized as Jerry from *Webster*, he also The Sheriff of Nottingham on Mel Brooks' underrated *When Things Were Rotten* and Dracula on the Saturday morning TV show *The Monster Squad*. He voiced The Scarecrow on *Batman: The Animated Series*.

Peter Mark Richman: With his rich, textured voice and wonderfully intimidating eyes, Richman has carved a long career from soaps like *Santa Barbara* to guesting on shows like *Hulk*, *Vega$* and *Fantasy Island*, playing cops or powerful bad guys. He was Suzanne Somers' disapproving father Reverend Snow on the hit *Three's Company* and starred as a police officer in the very last original episode of Rod Serling's *The Twilight Zone*. Richman has also used his stentorian voice in cartoons, playing The Phantom on *Defenders of the Earth*, a Guardian of Oa on *Superman* and even an elderly Peter Parker on *Spider-Man*!

Melendy Britt: Although she's a guest actress who appeared on everything from *Kojak* to *Starsky and Hutch*, *The Love Boat*, *The Rockford Files* and *Cheers*, she's best known for her voice. Britt was the voice of Princess Adora and her alter ego, She-Ra, on the popular cartoon. She's voiced such iconic cartoon characters as Batgirl, Princess Aura (daughter of Ming the Merciless) and Plastic Man's girlfriend. Mother of two daughters, she coaches acting and voiceovers.

Denny Miller: UCLA basketball star who wore the loincloth in a remake of *Tarzan the Ape Man*, played opposite Peter Sellers in Blake Edwards' subversive comedy *The Party* and went on to do the TV series *Wagon Train*. Did two memorable episodes of *The Incredible Hulk* and appeared on *Wonder Woman*. "I actually preferred being rescued by Hulk over Wonder Woman," he reveals. "When Lynda Carter saved you and hugged you, that metal eagle at the top of her costume's bustier would really tear your chest up...It hurt!"

Carl Ciarfalio: Besides being a stuntman on numerous episodes of the original *Hulk* show and the reunion movies, Carl has appeared in everything from *24* to the feature film *The Green Hornet*. He played Lou's gun-toting bodyguard who is stunned and sickened to be covered by Brad Pitt's blood in *Fight Club*. He was the very first actor to play The Thing in Roger Corman's unreleasable adaptation of *Fantastic Four*.

Annette Charles: Although best known as bad girl Cha Cha in the John Travolta/Olivia Newton-John smash *Grease*, she's been rescued by everybody from The Hulk to Magnum, P.I. Charles is now a teacher at Cal State Northridge. On the 30th anniversary of *Grease*, her character was finally honored with a doll.

William Windom: Charming, wonderful character actor who is also cheerfully and caustically blunt about his work, as witnessed by his stories on his *Hulk* episode. He is confused by his popularity from appearing on the *Star Trek* episode "The Doomsday Machine," "because it was so crappy!" He appeared on the original *Twilight Zone, To Kill a Mockingbird, The Greatest American Hero* and several John Hughes' classics. Very pleased with his Emmy-winning turn in the *Night Gallery* episode "They're Tearing Down Tim Riley's Bay," he adds, "I only got that Emmy because of Bill Bixby! He told me later, 'Windom, I was on the committee and told 'em to give it to you!'"

Wendy Girard: Starred in the West Coast premiere of the controversial play *Extremities*, the actress has appeared in many TV shows and films, including Woody Allen's *Annie Hall*. Besides appearing on *The Incredible Hulk*, she was friends with producer/writer Nicholas Corea. Now teaches acting.

Olivia Barash: Actress best known for her turn in Alex Cox's cult classic *Repo Man*, as well as beloved B-classics *Tuff Turf* (with future *Iron Man* Robert Downey, Jr.) and *Dr. Alien*. She appeared in the *Repo Man* sequel, *Repo Chick*, and is now a film producer, currently working on *The Bride of El Charro*.

Suzanne Charny and *Paul Brandon* — guest actress and Bill Bixby's agent who presciently urged the star to do *Hulk*, are happily married and reside in Southern California.

Richard Yniguez: A cool character actor who specializes in cops. Has been on *The Shield, C.S.I, Miami, Pacific Blue, Murder She Wrote, The A-Team, Hunter, The Flash, Simon & Simon, Airwolf, Hill Street Blues* and *Dynasty*. Starred in the amiable made for TV *Jaws* rip-off *Shark Kill*, where he took on a cute man-eating shark that looked like a pool toy.

Fred Tatasciore: Voices Hulk in Marvel cartoons and videogames. Played The Beast on *Wolverine of the X-Men,* frequently guests on *Family Guy* and flawlessly impersonates Mr. T and Darth Vader on *Robot Chicken.* He can be heard in the *Left 4 Dead, Call of Duty* and *God of War* videogame series. Currently does The Hulk on *Avengers: Earth's Mightiest Heroes.*

Dorothy Tristan: As an actress, she was in *Bang the Drum Slowly* with Robert De Niro, *Scarecrow* with Al Pacino and Gene Hackman, the hit comedy *Down and Out In Beverly Hills, Rollercoaster* and *California Dreaming.* Married to director John Hancock, the two were briefly involved with *Jaws 2.* Her script was better than the film that was made. Dorothy co-wrote Hancock's acclaimed Nick Nolte film *Weeds* (co-starring *Hulk* guest Ernie Hudson), as well as the thriller *Suspended Animation.*

Rick Springfield: After his *Hulk* spin-off didn't happen, Rick Springfield went on to a starring role as improbably handsome, blow-dried Dr. Noah Drake on the soap *General Hospital* and recorded "Jessie's Girl," one of the biggest pop hits of the 1980s. It's still frequently used on soundtracks for films like *13 Going On 30* and *Hot Tub Time Machine.* Springfield died in the pilot for the original *Battlestar Galactica,* as The Cylons' first casualty. Starred in the pilot for *Nick Knight* as a pre-*Angel* vampire detective but did not do the hit syndicated series that sprang from it. Played Christopher Chance, *The Human Target,* in the first series adapted from the obscure DC Comics character and spoofed his own image to great acclaim as a coke-snorting, stripper-boffing Rick Springfield on David Duchovny's *Californication.* Wrote his autobiography, *Late, Late at Night.*

Venita Ozols: Now one of Hollywood's busiest First Assistant Directors, Venita Ozols has worked on everything from *Veronica Mars, X-Files, The Shield, C. S. I., Space: Above And Beyond, The Dukes Of Hazzard, On Golden Pond* (where she befriended Katharine Hepburn) and *Xanadu.* The proud mother of two, Ozols also associate produced Kenneth Johnson's *Steel* and two *Alien Nation* TV movies. Ozols is prepping her directorial debut.

Yvonne Craig: Even though she costarred in several films with Elvis Presley and James Coburn, played *femme fatales* on *Wild, Wild West, Six Million Dollar Man, Man from U.N.C.L.E.* and *Star Trek* (as a striking green Orion schizophrenic who tries to seduce and destroy Captain Kirk, before being subdued by a Vulcan neck pinch), Yvonne Craig will always be known as the plucky and beautiful Batgirl on the Adam West *Batman*

TV series. She and her sister, Meridel Carson, are an amazing duo at comic conventions.

Mark A. Burley: A young Englishman when he started on *Hulk* as an assistant director, the ambitious Burley worked his way up to Unit Production Manager and even made his directorial debut on the show's fourth season episode, "Danny". Burley became a producer and writer on many hit shows, including *Murder, She Wrote, Simon & Simon, Freakylinks* and *Hidden Hills.* He is now the Emmy nominated producer of the hit Showtime series, *Weeds.* "I do it on the Universal backlot — my alma mater from *Hulk*," laughs Burley.

Tim Thomerson: Although he's been in big-budget movies opposite Gene Hackman and Mel Gibson, the effortlessly hip Thomerson is best known as "The King of the Bs" — the cool hero who gets the girl and slugs it out with aliens, robots and monsters in numerous low-budget outings. Plays retro-futuristic detective Jack Deth in the *Trancers* movies, opposite Oscar-winning actress Helen Hunt.

Victoria Carroll: Helped found The Groundlings and been in numerous films and TV shows. She's done many cartoon voices as well. Besides three appearances on *The Incredible Hulk*, she was the first person to play The She-Hulk in an '80s *Hulk* cartoon. She is married to Michael Bell and their daughter, Ashley Bell, starred as the demonic victim in horror hit, *The Last Exorcism.*

Jeffrey Kramer: Besides appearing in *Hulk, Jaws & Jaws 2*, Jeffrey Kramer became an Emmy-winning producer on *Ally McBeal.* He worked with Johnson again, this time as an executive, when the *Alien Nation* TV series was launched.

Jane Merrow: A Royal Academy of Dramatic Arts-trained actress, Merrow began with a splash in a string of British films and TV shows like *The Prisoner, The Avengers* (she was seriously considered as a replacement for Diana Rigg), *My Partner the Ghost, Secret Agent, The Saint, The Island of the Burning Damned* and *The Lion In Winter.* Merrow guested on numerous American shows, including *Hulk, The Magician, Hart To Hart, Airwolf, Greatest American Hero* and *Magnum, P.I.* She later moved back to England to run the family business.

Charles Napier: Cinematic tough guy and voice of Hulk, Charles Napier started out in Russ Meyer movies and as a singing space hippie who runs afoul of Captain Kirk in the infamous *Star Trek* episode "The Way To Eden." Since then, he has created a slew of memorable movie characters, like the leader of The Good Ol Boys in *The Blues Brothers,* a paper pusher who betrays Stallone in *Rambo: First Blood Part II,* The Judge in Jonathan Demme's Oscar-winning *Philadelphia* and a guard on Dr. Lecter's bad side in Demme's Oscar-winning *Silence of the Lambs.* Demme frequently casts Napier in his films and the actor's snarling voice can also be heard in many cartoons and commercials.

Brandon Cruz: A classic example of a child star who turned out great, the affable Cruz starred in *The Courtship of Eddie's Father* and movies like the original *Bad News Bears* before becoming a singer in the Southern California punk band Dr. Know. He replaced Jello Biafra in The Dead Kennedys for a period. Cruz also worked for *South Park* creators Trey Parker and Matt Stone. An avid surfer, the father of two is covered in tattoos and credits Bill Bixby as one of the biggest influences in his life... Although he still believes he should have ignored his mentor's advice and done *Porky's!*

Ronald Stephenson: Hulk/Simon and Simon casting director Ronald Stephenson now lives in England. "It's an ancient market town called Amersham," he says happily. Stephenson finds that the town meets his three main Qs: "Quaint, quiet and quality."

Herb Trimpe: After Kirby, there is no artist more closely identified with The Hulk. Trimpe, nicknamed "Happy Herb" by Stan Lee and "Trimpe-Dog" by inner-city students in the high-school art class that he taught in the '90s, is also a pilot and Vietnam vet. Had a long run on Hulk's book and drew the very first comic starring Wolverine, the first American *Godzilla* comic, and drew hundreds of characters, including Spider-Man and the Fantastic Four. His Hulk was famous for vivid facial expressions which was accomplished by Herb Trimpe drawing an exaggerated version of his own face for The Hulk!

Barbara Tarbuck: Has had an impressive 14-year run on *General Hospital,* and appeared on almost 100 different TV shows. She graduated from Michigan's Wayne State University, whose distinguished alumni include Casey Kasem, Ernie Hudson and Anthony Jankiewicz.

Robert McCullough: As producer/writer, he worked on *Falcon Crest, Star Trek: The Next Generation, Zorro* and Jerry Bruckheimer's *Soldier of Fortune*, besides scripting the unproduced *Rebirth of the Incredible Hulk*. As a writer, he and Kenneth Johnson co-wrote the highest-rated episode of Johnson's *Bionic Woman*, "In This Corner, Jamie Sommers," which was liberally borrowed and re-tooled for the first episode of *The Incredible Hulk*, "The Final Round." "I didn't know they did that," he laughs, "but imitation is the sincerest form of television!"

Joel Adams: The son of classic Batman artist Neal Adams, Joel Adams has made a living behind the drawing board since age 17, with his work appearing in comics, posters and animation character design, such as his work on The Hulk. He also does licensing & pinup art. Creator of the popular Lilz.net, Joel Adams is creative consultant, artist and web designer at Carrie Leigh's NUDE Magazine, art studio manager at Continuity Studios, studio manager at Neal Ad. He also did licensing art at Warner Bros. consumer products, licensing art at FOX Family Consumer Products, as well as character designer at Saban/Fox Family.

Bobbi Sue Luther: Her appearance as a green Orion slave girl spiked up ratings on the flagging *Star Trek: Enterprise*. She brought sexy green women back to the *Star Trek* universe after an almost 40-year absence. Luther played a Terminator on *The Sarah Connor Chronicles*, became a St. Pauli Girl, hosted *Junkyard Wars* and starred in a remake of '80s horror thriller *Night of the Demons*, where she gets her breast ripped off! Now a film producer.

Len Wein: A comic-book writer who imbues his stories with a lot of emotion, Wein introduced Wolverine in an issue of *The Incredible Hulk* and created many other members of the new X-Men, including Storm, Nightcrawler & Colossus. He also created Swamp Thing and Christopher Chance, The Human Target, now the star of his own Fox TV series. Wein also created the popular Punisher villain, Jigsaw. To *Hulk* readers, Len Wein is best known as the man who killed Hulk/Bruce Banner's girlfriend Jarella. In 2009, a freak electrical fire broke out, raging through Len Wein's Southern California home. While Wein managed to save Michael, his wife's son, Len's beloved dog Sheba ran outside with them, then panicked and raced back into the home, where she died. He lost irreplaceable original artwork from his career and his entire comic collection. That same year, *Wolverine: Origins*, with Hugh Jackman playing Wein's creation for the fourth time, opened to over $100 million dollars.

Paul Carr: Has the distinction of being the first "red shirt" to die under Captain Kirk on *Star Trek*. Carr, who passed away in 2006, had a wonderfully self-deprecating sense of humor. He specialized in playing shifty doctors and lawyers "usually in movies starring Shannon Tweed," Carr joked. He also appeared in such beloved B-movies as *Truck Stop Women*, *The Severed Arm* and *Bat People*. "It's truly not fair," he added with a laugh. "I have done Pirandello and been on Broadway, but all you want to know about is *The Incredible Hulk*, *The Severed Arm* and *Bat People!*" Carr's wife Meryl and teenage son Michael lovingly spoke of the actor's amazing life at his funeral.

Whit Bissell: One of Hollywood's greatest character actors and a founder of the Screen Actors Guild. Whit played doctors, bartenders, FBI agents and generals in scores of movies and TV shows. He's memorably mauled by *The Creature From the Black Lagoon*, believes Kevin McCarthy when he warns him of *The Invasion of the Body Snatchers* and plays a senator in Rod Serling's scary *Seven Days In May*. Karl Malden gave the eulogy at his funeral.

Pat Morita: Guested on the show after playing Arnold on *Happy Days*. Morita faced off against fellow *Hulk* guest Martin Kove in the *Karate Kid* film series. With the first, he became the first American-born Asian nominated for an Oscar for Mr. Miyagi. Starred in a final *Karate Kid* film where he trains Hillary Swank, before she won two Oscars. He passed away in 2005. In 2010, a *Karate Kid* remake was released, with martial arts superstar Jackie Chan as the Miyagi-type mentor.

Robert Donner: As nice off-screen as he was villainous on, Donner excelled at killers, thugs and cowards in classic films like *Cool Hand Luke*, *Vanishing Point* and the sleazy preacher in *High Plains Drifter*. He became an actor when Clint Eastwood urged him to. He played Exidor, the lovable, robed fanatic on Robin Williams' *Mork & Mindy*. After a meet-cute on the set of *Hulk*, he married producer/story editor Jill Sherman, until his death in 2006.

Dick Durock: An impressive Hollywood stuntman, you can see Dick box Clint Eastwood in *Any Which Way But Loose*, get killed by Dirty Harry in *The Enforcer*, break a crewman's neck on *Star Trek* and play Imperious Leader on the original *Battlestar Galactica*. Durock is best known as Swamp Thing in the Wes Craven film of the same name. Originally intended to only double Ray Wise, the actor set to play the character, he wound up playing the character himself. Durock's halting, poignant delivery and overall portrayal of the reluctant monster turned it into a cult movie. He came back in Jim Wynorski's *Return of the Swamp Thing* (where he has a bizarre, on-camera plant sex scene with Heather Locklear!) and starred in 71 episodes of his own TV series. *Swamp Thing* writer/producer Steven Sears says, "Dick was a sweet guy — we had to give him an episode off to fix his makeup when we found it was eating away at his face, but Dick never complained or gave us any grief — a wonderful guy." Durock also played Frye's Creature, the only villain who could really knock Lou Ferrigno around on *The Incredible Hulk*! A popular fixture at San Diego Comic Con and Sci-Fi conventions, Durock passed away in 2009.

WEBSITES

Can't get enough of *The Incredible Hulk* TV series? By all means, check out these sites:

Kenneth Johnson: *www.kennethjohnson.us*

Lou Ferrigno, The Hulk: *www.louferrigno.com*

Ric Drasin, the "Demi-Hulk": *www.ricdrasin.com*

Dick Durock, the Evil Hulk: *www.myspace.com/dickdurock*

Lara Parker, "Laura Banner": *www.laraparker.com*

Sondra Currie ("747"): *www.sondracurrie.com*

Barbara Leigh: *www.barbaraleigh.com*

Mickey Jones ("Ricky"): *www.mickeyjones.com*

Melendy Britt ("Deathmask"): *www.melendybrittfansite.net*

Excellent Hulk TV show Fan sites:
www.bryanshulkpage.com
www.incrediblehulktvseries.com

Tell 'em all Pat Jankiewicz sent ya!

ACKNOWLEDGEMENTS

Special thanks to *Hulk* creator Smilin' Stan Lee and his wife Joan, Lou Ferrigno, The Hulk himself, his wife Carla as well as Kenneth Johnson and his wife Susie. If you told me at age 10 that I would be hangin' with The Hulk, Stan the Man and Kenny Johnson, my head would have exploded! Kenny, Lou and Stan were all great with their time, stories and advice. Lou doing the foreword is a massive honor. Mega Props to my peerless publisher, Ben Ohmart, at BearManor and Brian Pearce, who did a beautiful job designing this and my previous book, *Just When You Thought It Was Safe: A JAWS Companion.*

I am grateful to everybody connected to The Incredible Hulk who made time to talk to me...Especially Mickey Jones and Venita Ozols — who both provided many of the stunning behind-the-scenes photos in this book. When Venita asked "Will these help?" and dropped an amazing photo album of never before seen images she took of Hulk's first season into my lap at the Vineland Starbucks, my howls of joy could be heard all the way to Tarzana.

Alan J. Levi and his charming wife, Sondra Currie, Paul Koslo, lovable Laurie Prange, Xander Berkeley, Julie Cobb, Rosemary Forsyth, Linda Pawlik, Austin Stoker, Ric "Demi-Hulk" Drasin, one of the most gregarious, amazingly well-connected guys you will ever meet; Ric knows everydamnbody! Mitzi Kapture, Eric "The Mighty Thor" Kramer — who gave me an interview on the set of his Disney series, Good Luck Charlie, Lee Purcell, Manny Perry, Andrew Robinson, Julie Adams and her son Mitch Danton, Simone Griffeth, Richard Kiel who talked about his brief time as The Hulk, Louisa Moritz, awesome Edie McClurg, who got me amazing onset photos the day the book was going in, Andrea Marcovicci, Don Marshall, Jill Sherman Donner (who even went that extra mile and found her "She-Hulk" pilot script for me), Karen Harris, Lisa Jane Persky, Penny Peyser, Paul and Charlie Picerni, Richard Yniguez, Quinn O'Hara, Patrick Boyriven, Mariette Hartley, John Hamburg, RC Matheson, Cliff Emmich and the dynamic, delightful Deanna Lund, who makes an amazing egg salad!

Also appreciated: Loni Anderson, Al White, Michael Lantieri, Barbara Leigh, Sally Kirkland, Mark A. Burley, Wendy Girard, Ang Lee, Lance & Mary LeGault, John Goodwin, Bobbi Sue Luther, Yvonne Craig, Julie Orsatti, Henry Polic II, Peter Mark Richman, Melendy Britt, Denny Miller, Carl Ciarfalio, Annette Charles, Cliff Emmich, William Windom, Olivia Barash, the sweet Suzanne Charny and her husband Paul Brandon — Bill Bixby's agent who presciently urged him to do Hulk, Mark Hamill, Rick Springfield, Joel Adams, Fred Tatasciore, Dorothy Tristan, Barbara Tarbuck, Ernie Hudson and the living legend known as Tim Thomerson. Actress Victoria Carroll, a very close friend of Bixby, shared some very personal, intimate stories. Hulk runs in her family — besides doing the series three times, she was also the first actress to play She-Hulk and married voiceover king Michael Bell, who voiced Bruce Banner in that same cartoon. Their daughter, Ashley Bell, is also a talented performer.

I first met Bill Lucking when my brother & I played his goons in Peter Berg's The Rundown. Everyday, I cajoled Bill to talk about his impressive career (He starred in George Pal's last film, was an alien on Star Trek and played everything from bikers to Babe Ruth!). When I asked about "The Antowuk Horror" Hulk episode, a smiling Pete Berg & Dwayne "The Rock" Johnson immediately joined us, saying "Bill was on Hulk? We loved The Incredible Hulk!" Other Hulk people include Martin "Sweep the Leg" Kove, Tony Burton, Jeffrey Kramer, Jane Merrow, charming Charles Napier who truly impressed me by doing his "Hulk growl" into my tape recorder, Brandon Cruz, Ron Stephenson, Herb Trimpe, Gloria Gifford, Denise Galick-Furey, Christina Hart, Jennifer Connolly, Pamela Shoop, the late Paul Carr, Whit Bissell, Pat Morita and Robert Donner. I was especially moved by the great Dick Durock, who tragically passed away after granting me a spontaneous interview at our friend Dan Roebuck's house. Mark Banning, Mike Joffe, Al "The Pal" Callaci (great friend, better proofreader), Lisa LeiAnn, Lisa and Jen Orris, Mark Phillips, Dave Konow, Brian P. Hunt, Dave McDonnell, Stephen Payne, Mickey Sinardi, Len Wein, Brad Lohan, Dennis Madalone, Jeff McLaughlin (my favorite Canadian), Buddy Delgadillo, Tara M. Meisner, Becky Lizama, Jarrad Arbuckle, Allie Nelson, Conan Jankiewicz and Matt Almanzar all rank high in my cool book. Welcome nephew Ajax Jankiewicz, born at the tail end of writing. Also fond of Tommie & The Bartender, Diane Baron, James Zahn, Justin Humphreys, Claire Herting, Sheena Metal and singer Tim Polecat. Tim wrote one of my favorite songs "Make A Circuit With Me" — on my ipod while writing this — and told me, "I would really fancy reading your Hulk book!" Now you can, Mate.

A very sincere bow and "Domo Arigato" to Marla Newborn (who conducted my very first radio interview. Thanks, Marla!), Heather Fenech, Elliot & Suri Brodsky, Dawn Leonard, Francine ("The Teenage Dream") Selkirk, Yvo Morales, Lotti Knowles, Bob Almanzar, SR and the awesome Eric Caidin of Hollywood Book & Poster. The idea for the book came to me when I saw a copy of Herbie Pilato's entertaining Bionic Book. "Jeez," I groaned to my brother Don Jankiewicz, "why can't somebody do one of these for the Hulk TV show? I would read it…" Don encouraged me with brotherly advice, "Why don't you quit whining and write one, dummy?" So I did, although I still think the "dummy" was gratuitous and unnecessary. Brother Tom Jankiewicz adds, "I'll be glad when you're done with this book; we haven't discussed Hulk this much since you were 10!"

AUTHOR PHOTO BY DON JANKIEWICZ.

ABOUT THE AUTHOR

Patrick Andrew Jankiewicz has written over 400 magazine articles. A CSUSB grad *(Go, Coyotes!)*, he has interviewed everyone from Francis Ford Coppola and James Cameron to Natalie Portman, Anne Hathaway and Nic Cage. His work has appeared in Marvel Comics, *Fangoria, Wizard, Shivers, Femme Fatales, Film Review, Star Trek* and *Starlog*.

Born in Michigan to a litter of five, Jankiewicz has worked as a reporter, copywriter, journalist, publicist, teacher and actor. He has starred in commercials for Burger King, Carl's Jr., Coca Cola, Liberty Mutual Insurance, Turner Classic Movies and conducted on-camera interviews for The SyFy Channel.

When he's not writing, Patrick Jankiewicz can be found in a backpack, workshirt and blue jeans, hitchhiking from town to town as sad piano music plays every week after helping strangers resolve their problems. He's a helluva guy! Like The Hulk, he frequently battles the US Army in nothing but torn purple pants.

NOTES AND SOURCES

Birth Of The Incredible Hulk
    In Person interview with Stan Lee
    Kirby quotes from *Starlog: 100 Years Of Comics* Magazine by Will Murray
    Incredible Hulk #1, "The Coming Of The Hulk," by Stan Lee & Jack Kirby
    In Person interview with Bert I. Gordon
    Origins Of Marvel Comics By Stan Lee, Simon & Shuster, 1974

Friends And Foes
    In person interview with Len Wein
    In Person interview with Herb Trimpe
    The Savage She-Hulk #1, by Stan Lee & John Buscema, 1980

The Coming Of The TV Hulk
    In Person interview with Kenneth Johnson

Name Game
    Stan Lee's Soapbox, April 1977

Paging Dr. Banner
    Bill Bixby interview, *The Kansas City Star,* 1978
    In Person interview with Paul Brandon
    Bill Bixby interview, *The Chicago Tribune,* 1978
    "Hulk Smash TV," *Comics Scene,* by Marc Shapiro, 1988

The Incredible Hulk
    "An Interview With Bill Bixby," *The Hulk Magazine,* 1978

Hunting A Hulk
    In Person interview with Richard Kiel
    In Person interview with Julie Orsatti

Being The Hulk
    In Person interview with Alan Levi
    In Person interview with Lou Ferrigno

Designing The Hulk
    "The Incredible Hulk" pilot screenplay by Kenneth Johnson, 1977
    US Magazine, 1978
    In Person interview with Brandon Cruz

514   YOU WOULDN'T LIKE ME WHEN I'M ANGRY: A **HULK** COMPANION

Hulking Out
> "An interview With Bill Bixby," *The Hulk Magazine,* 1978
> Bill Bixby interview, *The Kansas City Star,* 1978
> In Person interview with Ric Drasin

Sound Of The Hulk
> In Person interview with Charles Napier

Hulk Talk
> *Pizzaz Magazine,* Stan Lee's Soapbox, 1978

"Don't Make Me Angry. You Wouldn't Like Me When I'm Angry."
> "The Hulk On The Rampage" Marvel Treasury Edition, 1975

The Incredible Hulk: Death In The Family
> Interview with Dorothy Tristan

Laura Banner
> In Person interview with Lara Parker

Olivia Barash: Hulk's First Rescue!
> In Person interview with Oliva Barash

Laurie Prange, Damsel In Distress!
> In Person interview with Laurie Prange

Hulk Goes weekly
> In Person interview with RC Matheson

Bill Bixby: Lonely Man
> In Person interview with Lee Meriwether
> In Person interview with Yvonne Craig
> *From Ballet To The Batcave And Beyond* by Yvonne Craig
> *TV Guide,* "The 50 Greatest TV Dads Of All Time," 2004
> In Person interview with Jane Merrow
> "TV's Hulk It's not a Comic Book Show," by Merrill Shindler, *US Magazine,* 1978
> In Person interview with Jill Sherman Donner
> In Person interview with Sondra Currie
> Interview with Jeffrey Hayden
> Interview with Patrick Boyriven
> In Person interview with Deanna Lund
> In Person interview with Victoria Carroll

A Death In His Family
> In Person interview with Karen Harris
> In Person interview with Mariette Hartley
> In Person interview with Gloria Gifford
> Interview with Andrea Marcovicci
> In Person interview with Denny Miller
> In Person interview with C. Courtney Joyner
> "TV's Hulk It's not a Comic Book Show," by Merrill Shindler, *US Magazine,* 1978
> "Hulk-Out" By Mark Phillips, *Starlog,* 2003

Manny Perry, The Incredible Stunt Hulk!
    In Person interview with Manny Perry
    In Person interview with John Goodwin

Danger Dennis Madalone, Fall Guy
    In Person interview with Danger Dennis Madalone
    In Person interview with Stephen J. Cannell

Jack Colvin, Roving Reporter
    "Incredible Hulk" TV review by Kevin Thomas, *Los Angeles Times,* 1978
    In Person interview with Don Marshall
    Jack Colvin obituary, by Myrna Oliver, *Los Angeles Times,* 2005

Season One
    In Person interview with Martin Kove
    In Person interview with Loni Anderson
    In Person interview with Pamela Susan Shoop
    "Hulk Has Competitors Turning Green With Envy," *St, Petersburg Times,* 1978
    Interview with Denise Galick-Furey
    Interview with Simone Griffeth
    In Person interview with Paul Picerni
    In Person interview with Jennifer Darling
    In Person interview with Julie Adams
    In Person interview with Andrew Robinson
    In Person interview with Sherry Jackson

Hulkamania!
    Outside The Ring by Hulk Hogan
    Marvel Two In One, "Battle In Burbank," by Paul Kupperburg, 1978

Season Two

> In Person interview with Lance LeGault
> Interview with Bill Lucking
> "New Sci-Fi TV Season," *Starlog Magazine,* 1979
> In Person interview with Mickey Jones
> Jaron Summers interview, *Starlog Magazine,* 1997
> Interview with Sally Kirkland
> Interview with Ron Stephenson
> James D. Parriott interview, *Starlog Magazine,* 2003
> In Person interview with Mitchell Danton
> In Person interview with Barbara Leigh
> In Person interview with Julie Cobb
> In Person interview with Pat Morita
> Interview with Mark A. Burley
> In Person interview with Kathryn Leigh Scott
> In Person interview with Tony Burton
> In Person interview with Ernie Hudson
> In Person interview with Austin Stoker
> In Person interview with Rick Springfield
> In Person interview with Whit Bissell
> In Person interview with Christina Hart

Venita Ozols

> In Person interview with Venita Ozols

Season Three

> In Person interview with Gary Graham
> In Person interview with Charles Picerni
> Interview with Linda Pawlik
> In Person interview with Rick Rosenthal
> In Person interview with Louise Sorel
> In Person interview with Al White
> In Person interview with Louisa Moritz
> In Person interview with Robert Donner
> Interview with Paul Koslo
> In Person interview with Carl Ciarfalio
> In Person interview with Annette Charles
> Interview with Melendy Britt
> In Person interview with Henry Polic II
> In Person interview with Paul Carr

Season Four

> In Person interview with Rosemary Forsyth
> In Person interview with Angela Lee
> In Person interview with William Windom
> In Person interview with Cliff Emmich
> In Person interview with Quinn O'Hara

Dick Durock, Frye's Creature
    In Person interview with Dick Durock

Season Five
    In Person interview with Suzanne Charny
    Interview with Penny Peyser
    Interview with Wendy Girard
    Interview with Richard Yniguez
    In Person interview with Edie McClurg
    In Person interview with Jeffrey Kramer
    In Person interview with Peter Mark Richman
    In Person interview with Lisa Jane Persky
    In Person interview with Xander Berkeley

The Incredible Hulk Returns
    In Person interview with Lee Purcell
    In Person interview with Tim Thomerson
    In Person interview with Eric Allan Kramer

Death Of The Incredible Hulk
    "Hulk's Big Finish," TV Week 1990
    Interview with Barbara Tarbuck
    In Person interview with Carla Ferrigno

Rebirth Of The Incredible Hulk
    Interview with Robert McCullough

Metamorphosis: The She-Hulk Pilot
    "Metamorphosis" screenplay by Jill Sherman Donner, 1990
    In Person interview with Mitzi Kapture
    In Person interview with Bobbi Sue Luther

The Incredible Hulk Cartoon
    In Person interview with Mark Hamill

Hulk
    In Person interview with Ang Lee
    In Person interview with Michael Lantieri
    "Confessions Of A Geek God," *Maxim,* 2008

The Incredible Hulk
    In Person interview with Fred Tatasciore
    In Person interview with Jennifer Connolly.

I Love You, Man
    In Person interview with John Hamburg

AfterSmash
    Mark Ruffalo interview, *Entertainment Weekly,* 2011

INDEX

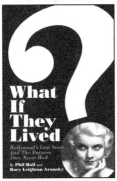

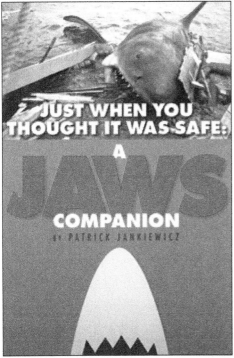

CPSIA information can be obtained
at www.ICGtesting.com
Printed in the USA
BVOW06*1415210517
484651BV00004B/16/P